Acclaim for *The Imprisoned Guest*

"Learned and sensitive . . . Gitter's primary interest is in Bridgman as an artifact of Victorian morality and psychology. . . . Gitter provides a sophisticated bit of speculation on the causes of [Howe's] disenchantment [with Bridgman]."
                                                                    —*The New York Times*

"Gitter provides nuanced portraits of Laura Bridgman and Samuel Howe, and the relationship between them as well as between Laura and the teachers who did the actual work of teaching and rearing her."
                                                                    —*The Washington Post*

"Compelling . . . an important contribution to historical understanding as well as a paean to human triumph over adversity."   —*Choice*

"A compelling biography, remarkable for both is breadth and detail, its complexity and accessibility . . . Gitter succeeds in a difficult task. She manages to engage the reader with two complex, and not always attractive, personalities. . . . A beautifully written and carefully researched biography offering a wealth of scholarly detail in clear, elegant prose."
                                                                    —*The Roanoke Times*

"Debates in intellectual history . . . inform Gitter's book, but she provides other, useful (and sometimes more personal) contexts for understanding Bridgman's significance."   — *The Boston Globe*

"Brings the two major players to life on the nineteenth-century New England stage. . . . Gitter is to be commended for reintroducing Laura Bridgman and her benefactor to the attention of the twenty-first-century reader."   —*The Women's Review of Books*

"Stimulating . . . Gitter excels at describing the fluid and dynamic intellectual currents of the Victorian era. . . . A challenging mix of American history and unique biography that at times can wring the heart."
                                                                    —*Kirkus Reviews*

"Elisabeth Gitter's *The Imprisoned Guest* is powerful and important. Vivid and dramatic, it is a brilliant biography of Laura Bridgman. Evocative and timeless, her struggle reminds us of the possibilities for excellence even under the meanest emotional, physical, and political circumstances."

—Blanche Wiesen Cook, author of *Eleanor Roosevelt*, vols. I and II

"This is an exciting, profound, highly readable narrative of the lives of a once-famous disabled child and her physician-mentor. Gitter's account illuminates the drama and tragedy of their relationship while brilliantly mirroring the social history of their times—and providing cautionary insights for our own."

—Albert J. Solnit, Sterling Professor Emeritus of Pediatrics and
Psychiatry, Yale School of Medicine, and former director
of the Yale Child Study Center

"This compelling study of the relationship between Samuel Howe, founder of the first American school for the blind, and Laura Bridgman, his star pupil, provides a fascinating tour of reform-minded New England before and after the Civil War. An important book for readers interested in that era or in the history of disability generally."

—Kathryn Kish Sklar, author of *Catharine Beecher:
A Study in American Domesticity*

The Imprisoned Guest

SAMUEL HOWE *and* LAURA BRIDGMAN,

the Original Deaf-Blind Girl

ELISABETH GITTER

PICADOR USA

FARRAR, STRAUS AND GIROUX

NEW YORK

www.picadorusa.com

Picador® is a U.S. registered trademark and is used by Farrar, Straus and Giroux under license from Pan Books Limited.

For information on Picador USA Reading Group Guides, as well as ordering, please contact the Trade Marketing department at St. Martin's Press.
Phone: 1-800-221-7945 extension 763
Fax: 212-677-7456
E-mail: trademarketing@stmartins.com

Permission to quote from Donald Davie's poem "To Helen Keller," from *Collected Poems*, 1950–1970, courtesy of Carcanet Press Limited.

Library of Congress Cataloging-in-Publication Data

Gitter, Elisabeth.
The imprisoned guest : Samuel Howe and Laura Bridgman, the original deaf-blind girl/ Elisabeth Gitter.—1st Picador USA ed.
p. cm.
Originally published: New York : Farrar, Straus and Giroux, 2001.
Includes bibliographical references and index.
ISBN 0-312-42029-3
1. Bridgman, Laura Dewey, 1829–1889. 2. Howe, S. G. (Samuel Gridley), 1801–1876. 3. Blind-deaf women—United States—Biography. 4. Teachers of the blind-deaf—United States—Biography. I. Title.

HV1624.B7 G57 2002
362.4'1'092—dc21   2002025155
[B]

First published in the United States by Farrar, Straus and Giroux

First Picador USA Edition: August 2002

10 9 8 7 6 5 4 3 2 1

FOR MAX

Be thine the task, O! Generous Howe, to guide
  The imprisoned guest, through Nature's ample fields
To draw the curtain of her wealth aside,
  And show the pleasure that true science yields;
To tread the path by learning seldom trod,
  That leads "from nature up to nature's God."

W. HOLMES, "To Laura Bridgman," c. 1850

I am not who you think I am.
Rather, from wherever you are,
You have written me another being
And breathed another's spirit with your lips . . .

The image of your own conceiving
Is the woman that you praise,
And being yours, she well deserves
Your very own applause.

"En Reconocimiento a las Inimitables Plumas
de la Europa," SOR JUANA INÉS DE LA CRUZ (1648–1695)

CONTENTS

PROLOGUE ❖ Laura   3

CHAPTER ONE ❖ The Chevalier   11

CHAPTER TWO ❖ Institutions   23

CHAPTER THREE ❖ Mind   45

CHAPTER FOUR ❖ Found   66

CHAPTER FIVE ❖ Awakening   78

CHAPTER SIX ❖ The Angel   102

CHAPTER SEVEN ❖ Second Acts   125

CHAPTER EIGHT ❖ Sea Changes   148

CHAPTER NINE ❖ Teachers and Teaching   176

CHAPTER TEN ❖ Attachments   199

CHAPTER ELEVEN ❖ Lamentations   221

CHAPTER TWELVE ✦ Legacies   246

CHAPTER THIRTEEN ✦ Revisions   272

EPILOGUE ✦ Passing   289

NOTES ✦   295

ACKNOWLEDGMENTS ✦   327

INDEX ✦   331

The Imprisoned Guest

Laura

IMAGINE LAURA BRIDGMAN, deaf, dumb, and blind. Picture her in 1837, just before Samuel Gridley Howe, the director of the Perkins Institution for the Blind, found her in a New Hampshire farmhouse and brought her to Boston to be educated. She is seven years old, a pretty, delicate, sprightly child, appealing in looks and manner. Five years have passed since scarlet fever raged through her family, killing her two older sisters and leaving her without sight, hearing, or speech, and with only a faint sense of smell or taste. Only touch remains to her now.

At seven, Laura can no longer recall her mother's face or voice, and if she ever saw the image of herself in a mirror, she has forgotten it. Deprived of stimulating sights, sounds, and odors, she inhabits a world of deadening monotony. All conscious memory of verbal language is gone. She lives in exile not only from sounds and words, but from the human community of exchanged smiles and glances, the mirroring of face-to-face communion. Her parents pat her head to show approval and tap her back to reprimand her, but there is no other way to let her know that she is a being—a person—to whom others respond.

Because she had two developmentally normal years before her devastating illness, Laura has perhaps maintained an awareness of a core self that silently experiences and records the muffled impact of external events. No doubt she experiences her own body as something that feels pain, hunger, thirst, or satisfaction and that moves at her bidding. She can make a few rudimentary signs to communicate her needs. But cut off from the sights and sounds of the outside world, deficient in language, and lacking an image of her own face, she can have little sense of an active, conscious self, a self that can share in the world of other people, a self that can tell its own tale. She does not know her name.

FIVE YEARS LATER, this pitiful little girl had become the most celebrated child in America. Although today she is virtually unknown, in her own time it was said that, with the exception only of Queen Victoria, Laura Bridgman was the most famous female in the entire world.[1] The first deaf-blind person ever to be educated, she became not only the subject of scientific and pedagogical research, but a universal darling. Before Laura Bridgman proved otherwise, deaf-blind people had been classified with idiots; according to the influential British jurist William Blackstone, they were "incapable of any understanding, as wanting all those senses which furnish the human mind with ideas."[2] By learning to read raised print, to write intelligibly, and to "talk" using the finger alphabet, Laura established that even the most sensorially deprived person could gain access to language and, through language, to the world of human culture.

Because she had been almost completely isolated from sense data, Laura was the ideal subject for investigation of the nature and origin of language and ideas. Scientists of the period imagined her as a living laboratory for experiments into the nature of the human mind, a psychological blank slate, John Locke's *tabula rasa* come to life. But Laura was more than an ideal subject for research and investigation; she was also the perfect Victorian victim-heroine: small, pleasing to look at, innocent, and frail, a paragon of cheerful suffering. Scores of articles and poems in religious tracts and women's magazines glorified her as a redemptive angel whose plight would touch the most hardened hearts, whose instinctive innocence and purity were exemplary, and whose rescue from spiritual imprisonment movingly reenacted the Christian drama. Born and educated fifty years before Helen Keller, Laura was the valiant little victim of her own day. And like Keller, she was an intellectual phenomenon, a kind of genius.

At the peak of Laura's popularity, in the 1840s and early '50s, thousands of sightseers flocked to see her on exhibition days at the Perkins Institution for the Blind in Boston, and local guidebooks listed her as a major tourist attraction. She numbered among her many admirers almost every intellectual and philanthropic luminary of the day: psychologists, phrenologists, reformers, ministers, writers, and philosophers. Lydia Sigourney, Edward Rowland Sill, and numerous other minor poets celebrated her in verse. She dined with Louis Kossuth, the Hungarian revolutionary hero; even Charles Darwin wrote about her.[3] Most important for her fame, Charles Dickens devoted almost an entire chapter of *American Notes* to the "sightless, earless, voiceless child" who had moved him so profoundly in 1842 when he visited Laura in Boston.

The public Laura Bridgman who attracted such intense interest and sympathy was the creation of the director of the Perkins Institution, Dr. Samuel Gridley Howe, who supervised and wrote about her education. He publicized his work with Laura and made her into a popular heroine through a series of widely circulated annual reports to the trustees of the Perkins Institution. Couched in the language of religious conversion, her story, as he shaped it, demonstrated that even the most hopelessly imprisoned soul could be brought into the warmth of human community and into the light of moral knowledge.

Howe framed this inspirational narrative with scientific passages that explicitly connected his pioneering education work to a tradition of post-Enlightenment inquiry into the nature of man. The Laura of his reports was at once a walking religious metaphor and the embodied answer to the most urgent philosophical questions of the time: how language is acquired, whether ideas are innate, how mental and moral development can best be fostered. His experiments in teaching her had not simply saved her soul; they had also revealed the workings of the human mind.

In his celebrated reports, Howe skillfully combined and exploited the religious passions and the intellectual preoccupations of his day in order to promote Laura—and through her, to advertise himself. If she symbolized the power of the human spirit to triumph over darkness, he exemplified intellectual daring, scientific imagination, and humanitarian zeal. At a period when reformers in many parts of the United States were establishing schools and other institutions for the disabled, Howe's tales of Laura ennobled the work of the asylum: after reading his reports, Horace Mann could say in all seriousness, "I should rather have built up the Blind Asylum than have written Hamlet."[4]

LAURA'S FAME WAS intense, but brief. As she outgrew her appealing girlishness, visitors gradually stopped coming to see her and poets lost interest in singing her praises. By the time she died in 1889, she had been almost totally forgotten, eclipsed by the nine-year-old prodigy Helen Keller. Stories about Keller usually include a mention of Laura as the odd, aging woman who taught the finger alphabet to a Perkins student named Anne Sullivan. Otherwise Laura has disappeared from public memory.

Yet her life bears telling. Laura was the creation of a particular time—the 1830s and '40s—and a particular place—Unitarian Boston. At that time and in that place, a new confidence in the perfectibility of humankind and the redemptive power of education made her rescue possible. Laura received an education because reformers like Howe believed that they could find scientific solutions to social problems, and she became famous because her success confirmed that optimism.

In some ways, there was no one like her. She was the first: the pioneering experiment and the living proof that a deaf-blind child could learn verbal language. Aware of her importance, her friends, teachers, and relatives preserved the letters and journals that might otherwise have been lost. At the same time, she was typical. Like the hundreds of other blind, deaf, or "feeble-minded" children institutionalized in the period, she was the beneficiary—and also the victim—of America's early efforts to help the disabled. Her accounts of her dreams, letters of bitter complaint, and pleas for companionship provide a window into the mind of an institutionalized person. No other figure of her time offers a more complete and compelling picture of the daily life of a mid-nineteenth-century asylum inmate.

In both women's history and the history of the disabled, Laura is a significant character. Her sex, as much as her blindness or deafness, determined the course of her life. Howe chose her because she was an endearing little girl; the public flocked to gaze at her (as they would later at Helen Keller) because the spectacle of a pretty deaf-blind girl drew them; people read and wrote about her because she reminded them of the helpless, suffering little heroines of sentimental literature; and she fell out of favor because she changed from an adorable girl into a strange, plain-looking woman. No deaf-blind boy could have evoked such an intense public response.

Laura's story still matters. The record of her successes and sorrows adds historical depth to current debates about the disabled: their legal and moral entitlements, the costs and benefits of "mainstreaming," the role of sign language in the education of the deaf, the purpose of special schools. Her fall from youthful popularity into adult obscurity challenges us to analyze our own fears and fantasies about the disabled. Although schools for the deaf and blind no longer hold public exhibitions of their students, as they did in Laura's day, charities continue to raise money by displaying adorable disabled children; we rarely see images of disabled older people. Perhaps, as the popularity of "blind girl" movies—*City Lights, A Patch of Blue, Magnificent Obsession, Dark Victory, Wait Until Dark, Jennifer 8, Blind Terror, Blink, Blind Witness*—suggests, even in our own enlightened age, audiences find pleasure in the spectacle of sightless young women.

There are moral, historical, and political lessons to be drawn from Laura's life, but her story is also a romance. Before Howe found her, she was, he said, like a maiden locked up in a tower in some chivalric tale. By bringing her to Perkins and teaching her language, he saved her from a numbing, terrifying isolation. But she rescued him, too. When they first met, he had long been searching for a way to achieve intellectual and social distinction, to be "of use to the country and known to its best and

most powerful citizens."[5] Because, against all odds, Laura had the tenacity and intelligence to learn language, Howe fulfilled his knightly ambitions. Hers was an extraordinary mind: its unfolding made him a hero.
She created his life, just as he created hers. Together, they earned a place
in history.

IN 1886, HELEN KELLER'S MOTHER learned that there was hope for her afflicted daughter by reading Dickens's account of Laura in *American
Notes*. A century later, researching a talk on Victorian travel writing, I
too discovered Laura through Dickens.

When I read his touching description of Laura in the Boston chapter
of *American Notes*, I began to wonder what had become of the deaf-blind
girl who had captured his imagination. If Dickens had been more impressed by her than by any other person he met in Boston, why had I, a
specialist in Victorian studies, never heard of her? The next year, on a
visit home to Boston, I stopped in at the library of the Perkins School to
see if any traces of this mysterious figure remained.

To my astonishment, I found the buried story of Laura's life fully
documented in bundles and boxes of uncataloged, unpublished manuscripts that have been stored, along with her teachers' journals and
Howe's voluminous correspondence, in the Perkins basement. These
documents—some penciled in Laura's distinctive square lettering, others
written by eminent reformers, members of her family, ministers, and
teachers—record her poignant struggle to create a life for herself and to
preserve her singular identity.

That first quick visit to Perkins stretched into an entire summer. The
more I read, perched day after day on a rickety chair among the piled-up
boxes in the basement archive, the more I was drawn into Laura's world.
Fascinating people surrounded her: Howe, noble, arrogant, and infuriating; his wife, the redoubtable Julia Ward Howe; his best friends, Charles
Sumner and Horace Mann; Laura's earnest female teachers; and the
ornery Bridgmans of New Hampshire. Above all, Laura herself stirred
me. She was such an odd, intriguing person: finicky, impatient with fools,

ardent in her affections, and voracious for knowledge. I never intended to become a biographer, but I began to imagine rescuing her.

In the twelve years since I first encountered Laura's writing, I have not been able to get her plaintive voice out of my head. I tell her story now so that Laura, silenced in life and forgotten by history, can at last have her say.

CHAPTER ONE

The Chevalier

LIFE STORIES USUALLY begin with mothers and fathers. From the dynamics of the family—the parents' ancestry, marriage, and economic and social fortunes—biographers trace the origins of their adult subject's character. In Laura Bridgman's case, her biological parents matter less. After her second year, she could not see or hear Daniel and Harmony Bridgman; they had neither the time nor the skills to communicate with her; and once she had moved from the family farm in Hanover, New Hampshire, to the Perkins Institution in Boston, they appeared in her life only intermittently.

The biographies published by Howe's daughters—Maud Elliott and Florence Hall in 1903, and Laura Richards in 1928—paint a Currier and Ives picture of the Bridgman home. The Howe daughters depict Daniel and Harmony Bridgman as hardy, independent farmers of "good old New England stock."[1] Certainly the Bridgmans were hardworking: through trying years of fluctuating agricultural prices and poor crops, they persevered, raising Laura's five surviving siblings and even managing to send their two sons to college.

The youngest of nine children, Laura's mother, Harmony Downer Bridgman, was born in 1804 on a farm just a few miles north of Hanover, in Thetford, Vermont, a tiny town that her Downer grandparents had helped settle forty years earlier. Her parents or an older brother may have taught her to read and write at home, but Harmony Downer more likely attended a one-room town school for a few years, as almost all rural New England children of the period did. Despite her rudimentary education, Harmony Bridgman had a way with words. Her thoughtful, often touching letters to Howe not only record her family's financial struggles, but also reveal her concern for her stricken daughter. Although Mrs. Bridgman never learned to communicate effectively with Laura when they were together, she worried about her daughter's well-being, wrote to her from time to time, and remained a distinct, if often distant, presence in her life.

Laura's father is more of a cipher. The Bridgmans were an old, if not especially distinguished or prosperous, Hanover family. Daniel Bridgman's fellow townsmen thought enough of him to elect him twice to public office: he served as a selectman in 1836 and as a representative to the New Hampshire Legislature from 1856 to 1857, but does not otherwise figure in Hanover history.[2] If he ever wrote any letters to Howe or Laura, none has survived. In any case, neither Howe nor Laura had much use for Daniel Bridgman, who suffered, Howe believed, from the effects of a nervous temper and a small brain.[3] In her letters home from Perkins, Laura neither inquired after her father nor ever sent him her regards. After a rare visit from her parents in 1843, she wrote—tellingly—in her journal: "My mother and my father . . . came at ten o'clock i was very much pleased to see my mother."[4]

The father who mattered for Laura was not Daniel Bridgman, but her psychological and spiritual father, Howe. He brought her back into the world, gave her language, arranged for her material support, organized her time, and provided her a home. In his will he left her a small legacy; Daniel Bridgman bequeathed her nothing. Howe's past, far more than her parents', formed Laura's identity; his vision, far more than theirs, shaped the course of her life.

LAURA'S RESCUER WAS a complex and contradictory figure, vain, pugnacious, rigid, and arrogant, yet passionately committed to doing good.

Until he died, Howe devoted himself to educating the ignorant, liberating the enslaved, raising up the downtrodden, and empowering the weak. Practical and resourceful, he had a knack for solving problems. He disdained wealth and luxury, worked tirelessly, and genuinely loved children. Still, Howe was sometimes a hard man to like. An abiding sense of intellectual and social inferiority made him susceptible to flattery and greedy for public acclaim. Compromise seemed to him a sign of weakness. Despite his well-deserved reputation as one of the century's great humanitarians, he had trouble getting along with individual people, including those closest to him. An enthusiastic quarreler, he could be vindictive toward anyone who opposed or criticized him.

Howe began life on the margins of Boston society. Although his mother and father both came from old Boston families, neither the Howes nor the Gridleys could boast of intellectual distinction, significant wealth, or acceptance in Boston's rising Brahmin class. For the first years of Samuel Howe's life, from 1801, when he was born, until after the War of 1812, his father, Joseph Howe, prospered manufacturing rope and cordage, an important business in that time of sailing vessels. After the war, however, the business foundered, apparently because the federal government defaulted on payments for wartime materials. The servants and luxuries of Samuel Howe's early childhood vanished, and the family had to adjust to greatly reduced circumstances. Young Samuel never experienced real poverty, but the Howes always had to worry about money.

During Howe's youth, his family remained both financially embarrassed and, at a time when partisan passions ran high, politically out of step. Like most of the Boston elite, the Howes practiced Unitarianism, the "Boston religion," but they did not subscribe to the conservative politics of their Unitarian neighbors. In a militantly Federalist city, the Howes were among a small minority of Jeffersonian Democratic Republicans. At the Boston Latin School, where Howe was an indifferent student, the other boys tormented him for his political noncomformity. To avoid neighboring Harvard, a bastion of Boston Federalism, Howe in 1817 enrolled instead at Brown, in those days a small, tolerant, but nominally Baptist college that offered the additional advantage of charging considerably less. Since tuition, room, and board rarely exceeded $100 a year, Brown attracted young men whose families were in straitened circumstances—young men like Samuel Howe and Horace Mann, a farmer's son who graduated two years ahead of Howe.[5]

Howe, restless and without direction, did not make a success of his college years. The monotonous, highly regimented routine of life at Brown in those days tried his limited patience: he performed poorly academically, was suspended several times for pranks and rowdy behavior, and graduated without distinction in 1821. Eulogizing Howe after his death in 1876, Alexis Caswell, a former president of Brown, recalled (rather tactlessly, under the funereal circumstances) that Howe's college life "was not altogether a happy one, and was not as productive in the line of good learning as it might have been." Howe had not been "deficient in logical power," Caswell assured the assembled mourners, "but the severer studies did not seem congenial to him."[6]

From Brown, Howe went on to Harvard Medical School, from which he took a degree in 1824, notwithstanding his distaste for the practice of medicine. His lackluster performance at both Brown and Harvard left him with an uncomfortable feeling of directionlessness and intellectual inadequacy. Not only had his education been "imperfect," but, he complained, he had never had a mentor, a "direct personal influence" leading him "to the best use of his powers."[7] In an undated letter to Mann, who had done brilliantly at Brown, Howe confided, "My schooling was very poor: very. My father an uneducated man, only wished, without knowing how to make me a scholar."[8] To the phrenologist George Combe, whom he admired greatly, Howe explained that he had always had "high aspirations for extensive usefulness, and a desire for intellectual attainments of a high order." These aspirations were undermined, however, by "a sad conviction" that his intellectual capacity would never allow him to rise above "mediocrity."[9] He knew that he did not want to drag out his days "in the dull, monotonous round of a professional life," but he did not have the money, social status, or intellectual distinction to achieve the fame and stature that he craved.

For a restless, unmoneyed, adventurous young man in Howe's position, the Greek revolution of the 1820s was a godsend. Here was an outlet for both ambition and idealism. Here was a chance to be heroic; to liberate an ancient and noble race—the descendants of Homer and Socrates—from tyranny; to escape the mundane, moneygrubbing life of Boston. The philhellenes, partisans of Greek independence, had waged an extraordinarily effective propaganda campaign in Christian Europe and America, whipping up an international campaign against Turkish oppression. Lord Byron, Howe's favorite poet, had set a gallant example, sailing for Missolonghi in 1823 to join the fight. In Boston philhellenism became the cause *du jour* in 1823, when the charismatic Edward Everett, at the time the Eliot Professor of Greek at Harvard, exhorted readers of *The North American Review* to aid the Greek revolutionaries, in "a war of the crescent against the cross."[10]

Answering Everett's call to arms, Howe sailed for Greece in 1824, not long after Byron died there of fever. For Howe, war against the "unspeakable Turk" promised not only adventure and fame, but also an opportunity to aid the weak against the strong: Howe always saw himself as a defender of the underdog. In Greece, as a guerrilla fighter and a military surgeon, he found the excitement, power, and praise that he had sought. In 1825, he wrote enthusiastically to his father:

> It astonishes me much that young men of fortune do not come to Greece; that they do not enlist heart and soul in this most sacred of all causes and gain for themselves the gratitude of a nation and a place in history; more particularly, too, when they have such a scene before their eyes as is presented by the treatment of Lafayette in our happy and flourishing country.[11]

Like most other philhellenes who fought in Greece, including Byron, Howe soon became disillusioned with his unglamorous comrades-in-arms, who failed to resemble the heroes he had read about in Homer. The righteous campaign against foreign oppression repeatedly deteriorated into civil war among competing factions, and Howe, never slow to pass judgment, complained that the modern Greeks were deceitful, corrupt, ignorant, and selfish.[12] Nonetheless, he relished the drama of the war, the opportunity to command, the variety and scope of his work, the constant travel, and the gratification of serving a noble cause.

Howe devoted the next six years to Greek independence, immersing himself in the kind of frenetic activity that he would always thrive on. In addition to battling the Turks and treating wounded Greek soldiers, between 1824 and 1827 he was also busy organizing a hospital at Nauplia and, on behalf of the American-Greek relief committees, traveling around the countryside to distribute emergency supplies of food and clothing to the suffering Greek women and children. In February 1828, at the behest of the Greek government, he returned for several months to the United States, where he embarked on a speaking tour to raise money for the Greek cause and published his hastily written but moderately successful *Historical Sketch of the Greek Revolution,* a florid and melodramatic work, even by the standards of the day.

With the American-Greek relief committees paying his passage and expenses, he returned to Greece in November to begin a series of ambitious relief projects. His work on these projects demonstrated the administrative efficiency, organizational skill, and ingenuity that would later serve him well as founding director of an asylum for the blind. Acting on his lifelong conviction that doling out charity promoted idleness, he employed hundreds of destitute refugees in hauling and setting stones to build a harbor wall to restore the port at Aegina. When that task was completed, he persuaded the Greek government to grant him land at Hexamilia to establish an agricultural colony, which he named "Washingtonia." Supported by the American relief committees, Howe chose twenty-six refugee families to be his colonists, provided them with seed and cattle, and established a school based on the innovative system of the English educator of the poor Joseph Lancaster.

During most of 1829—the year Laura Bridgman was born—Howe reigned over his very own utopian colony, a benevolent Mr. Kurtz. Not until he ran his own asylum in Boston would he again enjoy such a satisfying combination of power and social usefulness. Thirty years later, he recalled his days as ruler of Washingtonia as among the happiest of his life:

> I was alone among my colonists, who were all Greeks. They knew I wanted to help them, and they let me have my own way. . . . I labored here day and night, in season and out, and was governor, legislator, clerk, constable, and everything but *patriarch*.[13]

This idyll, of course, could not last. Inevitably, Howe had a bitter falling-out with the president of Greece, who after years of Turkish domination may have objected to ceding a portion of Corinth to an American. Resentful that his well-intentioned efforts to bring good government to a chaotic nation had not been appreciated by its leaders, Howe left the country in January 1830, carrying with him Byron's helmet, which he had picked up at auction.

Howe spent the next year touring Europe, and then set sail for home. He was almost thirty years old, a seasoned veteran of bloody combat and a world traveler, but he remained essentially the same man he had been when he first set out for Greece. The boyish characteristics of his adolescent letters—expressions of longing for "reputation" and heroic distinction; boasting masked by self-denigration—persisted in the letters he wrote to friends long after his return. As idealistic and vaguely ambitious as ever, he continued to dream of following "a path as yet untrodden in this country by the multitude, and . . . to do something in it."[14] Neither his exposure to terrible human suffering in Greece nor the many personal hardships he had undergone had altered him: he was, as John Jay Chapman observed, "one of those singular men in whom we can trace no course of development."[15]

Howe returned to Boston at an opportune moment. In 1831, an intellectual, spiritual, and literary awakening—"the New England Renaissance"—was dawning. A new, idealistic generation of "men of letters" had just begun to announce itself: Howe's contemporaries, George Ticknor, George Bancroft, William H. Prescott, Theodore Parker, Ralph

Waldo Emerson, Henry Wadsworth Longfellow, John Greenleaf Whittier, Oliver Wendell Holmes, and Nathaniel Hawthorne, among others, were joining together in the "community of aspiration" that would soon take shape in antebellum Boston, Cambridge, and Concord.[16]

In this period of rapid, sometimes alarming, social and economic change, an intense humanitarianism was in the New England air, and reform movements abounded. Seeing their city as a center of progress, Bostonians of diverse religious and political opinions organized to do battle against ignorance, intemperance, corruption, heathenism, libertinism, and slavery. While conservative evangelicals, fired by the preachings of Lyman Beecher and the revival meetings of Charles Finney, established Bible, tract, and missionary societies, and called for a revival of personal piety and morality, liberal Bostonians looked for ways to eliminate social evils by fostering individual perfection.[17]

For Boston's progressive Unitarians in this period, rejecting the Calvinism of their forebears increasingly meant opposing the old idea that suffering was inevitable, irremediable, and providential. Along with an Enlightenment belief in scientific progress and human perfectibility came optimism that social problems could be solved through reason and love. The high priest of this liberal humanitarianism, the great Unitarian Awakener, William Ellery Channing, inspired and shaped Boston's social reform movement. Throughout the 1830s, Channing exhorted his Federal Street Church congregants to confront the scourges of poverty, illness, ignorance, and slavery. Aging but still impassioned, Channing had come to believe that it was no longer enough for individuals to eschew materialism and cultivate inner goodness. While little Laura Bridgman was learning to grope her way around her New Hampshire farmhouse, Channing urgently called upon the Unitarians of Boston to recognize the essential beauty and perfectibility of every human being, however degraded or deprived, and, in emulation of a loving, impartial God, to lift up the poor, the disabled, and the suffering.

IN AN 1832 ORATION, Josiah Quincy, the president of Harvard, attributed the proliferation of the city's charitable institutions—hospitals, asylums, public libraries, almshouses, and benevolent associations—to the "silent and secret outswellings of grateful hearts, desirous unostentatiously to acknowledge the bounty of Heaven in their prosperity and abundance."[18] But altruism, even in Boston, is seldom unalloyed. The grateful, swelling hearts of midcentury Bostonians also felt the flutterings of ambition and the pangs of fear.

By the late '20s, the upper class had good, earthly reasons for supporting Boston's charitable institutions. The old merchant families, newly enriched and invigorated by intermarriage and business partnership with self-made textile manufacturers, had consolidated their economic, cultural, and political power. Despite changes in the city's commercial structure, Brahmins still firmly controlled industry, trade, and finance. (In midcentury Massachusetts, the top one percent of the adult population, mostly Bostonians, owned approximately half the state's total wealth.)[19] Scions of Brahmin families occupied most of the faculty chairs at Harvard, preached from many Unitarian pulpits, and ruled the statehouse and city hall.[20] Nevertheless, the Whig patricians felt uneasy. Andrew Jackson's election to the presidency in 1828 seemed to them to threaten the coming of mob rule—and the end of political propriety, social order, and the sanctity of property. At the same time, their once tranquil Yankee town was changing before their eyes, transformed by urbanization and industrialization into a chaotic city, plagued with social problems and populated by strangers.

Revolution and anarchy in Europe had taught Boston's patriciate a moral lesson: neglecting the poor, helpless, and ignorant can have bloody consequences.[21] Spurred by anxiety about civil disorder—riots, crime, and drunkenness—and also inspired by noblesse oblige and a religious ethic of benevolence, Boston's richest families enthusiastically supported progressive legislation and subscribed to private philanthropies.[22] For the Brahmins, enlightened reform—relieving the poor, healing the sick, educating the ignorant, rehabilitating the criminal, and employing the idle—was at once the safest way to avoid class conflict and the highest moral duty.

Philanthropy was also, not insignificantly, a pleasure. Membership on an exclusive charitable board—like membership in an exclusive club—affirmed patrician identity. Participating in philanthropic activities in the company of friends, business associates, and relatives induced a sense of upper-class solidarity; it defined Boston's elite families, brought them together on charitable projects, and justified their wealth and power.[23]

By 1840, Bostonians could boast supporting thirty charitable institutions through private contributions and public funds. (Of the estimated $2,938,020 donated to Boston charities between 1830 and 1845, more than half went to organizations controlled by upper-class boards: the Lowell Institute, the American Board of Foreign Missions, Massachusetts General Hospital, the Bunker Hill Monument, Harvard, and the Perkins Institution for the Blind.)[24] The state legislature, responding both to the philanthropic mood of the electorate and to underlying anxieties about public order, also played an increasingly active role in the charitable and reform activities of the period. In the socially fluid and (until the crash of 1837) economically expansive 1830s, the legislature frequently appropriated public money to investigate social problems, forestall dependency, and ameliorate human suffering.[25] For Channing, this period of philanthopic flowering proved that human progress was not an illusion. In 1841, near the end of his life, he rejoiced that "benevolence now gathers together her armies. . . . There is hardly a form of evil which has not awakened some antagonist effort."[26]

Visitors agreed, praising Boston as America's City on a Hill, an example to all the world of civic enlightenment and benevolence. Even Harriet Martineau, an English writer who despised most of what she saw in the United States, admitted that she knew of no other large city in the world "where there is so much mutual helpfulness, so little neglect and ignorance of the concerns of other classes."[27] When Charles Dickens first visited in 1842, he was even more effusive:

> I sincerely believe that the public institutions and charities of this capital of Massachusetts are as nearly perfect as the most considerate wisdom, benevolence, and humanity, can make

them. I never in my life was more affected by the contemplation of happiness, under circumstances of privation and bereavement, than in my visits to these establishments.[28]

Coming home after six years, Howe discovered not only that his city was changing, but also that his own position was considerably stronger than it had been before. The publication of his philhellenic speeches, his letters from Greece, and his *Historical Sketch of the Greek Revolution* had made him known in intellectual and philanthropic circles. In the course of his Greek relief efforts, he had corresponded with many important humanitarians and had established a valuable relationship with Edward Everett, who was rapidly becoming one of the most powerful men in Massachusetts politics. Howe himself was now politically in the mainstream, having joined most of elite Boston in despising the Democratic president, Andrew Jackson.

As a returning war hero, Howe suddenly cut a glamorous figure. In her biography of her father, Laura Howe Richards claimed that "his presence was like the flash of a sword. There was a power in his look, an aspect of unresting, untiring energy, which impressed all who looked upon him; they turned to look again."[29] As evidence for this adoring depiction, Richards quoted "a lady of his own age," who testified that in the 1830s Howe was the handsomest man she ever saw: "When he rode down Beacon Street on his black horse, with the embroidered crimson saddle-cloth, all the girls ran to their windows to look after him."[30] Portraits confirm that Howe was indeed a tall, imposing-looking man, and that his daughter was not altogether fanciful in describing him as "slender, erect, with the soldierly bearing which marked him through life; with regular features, jet black hair, clear color glowing through the tan, and eyes of piercing blue."[31] At the peak of the classic revival, when churches and banks on every Main Street were built to evoke Athens, even the more staid Bostonians confessed that they were dazzled by this veteran of the Greek revolution, this Byronic figure galloping through town on his black stallion, this embodiment of the Ciceronian ideal of the active, virtuous man. He seemed, as Whittier would later rhapsodize in "The Hero," his poem about Howe's Grecian exploits, "a knight like Bayard."[32]

Despite his improved social and political status and heroic reputation, Howe floundered during his first months home. Impecunious and directionless, he knew that he could never settle into the conventional life of a practicing physician, that money did not matter to him, and that he wanted to do something extraordinary. He thought about managing a new daily newspaper in Philadelphia or of taking charge of the "Negro colony" of Liberia, but neither prospect materialized.

It was only a matter of time, however, until a man of Howe's reputation, energy, and idealism found his vocation. In a city stirring with philanthropic projects, there were opportunities for someone like him—someone who hoped to do socially useful work and to avoid the humdrum business of plying a trade. Such a person could now hope to earn a modest, middle-class living as a salaried, full-time humanitarian.

The days of ignorant, venal wardens like Mr. Bumble, the unscrupulous parish beadle in *Oliver Twist*, were over. Wealthy Bostonians wanted educated, professional managers to run their philanthropic institutions according to the most up-to-date scientific principles. By the summer of 1831, Howe seemed perfect for this new role. With his presentable Boston Latin and Brown education, medical training, travel abroad, past success as a fund-raiser, organizational abilities, and heroic credentials, he was the very model of a modern asylum manager. When the trustees sought an energetic director to launch the New England Asylum for the Education of the Blind (later to become famous as the Perkins Institution and the home of Laura Bridgman), Howe was a natural choice.

CHAPTER TWO

Institutions

THE IDEA OF establishing a school for the blind in Boston originated
with John Dix Fisher, a doctor who had been a year ahead of Howe at
both Brown and Harvard Medical School. After finishing his schooling,
Fisher, like many ambitious American physicians of the period, set off
for Europe to study the latest scientific developments and broaden his
horizons. In Paris he visited the world-famous Institution des Jeunes
Aveugles, founded in 1784 as the first systematically organized school for
blind children. Inspired by Enlightenment goals of remedying injustices,
reducing differences, and ending social, economic, and political exclusion, the Paris institution aimed not only to make the blind literate, but
also to teach them the manual skills necessary to become independent of
charity.[1]

Fisher was astonished and moved to see the school's blind students
reading embossed letters (the Braille system, invented in 1829, was not
widely used until much later in the century), writing, manufacturing useful and decorative objects of various kinds, singing, and playing musical
instruments. The curriculum and teaching apparatus impressed him as
innovative, practical, and humane. When he returned to Boston in 1826,
he resolved to start a similarly progressive institution for the blind in
New England.

Recent critics of the nineteenth-century asylum movement have looked at the Institution des Jeunes Aveugles and other such ostensibly benevolent institutions with a more skeptical eye than Fisher's. They have noticed, for example, that despite a declared purpose of mitigating difference and ending exclusion, asylums and schools for the disabled inevitably have the effect of defining and rationalizing their difference from "normal" people and, accordingly, of justifying their segregation. As one scholar, William Paulson, has put it, special schools, for all their lofty intentions, "replace one kind of social isolation, that of the blind beggar, with another, that of the blind pupil or ward."[2] Influenced by the French historical theorist Michel Foucault, more radical critics have identified the need of modern societies to exclude and regulate "marginalized" people as the real force behind the establishment of benevolent institutions in the nineteenth century. Foucauldians see in the mid-nineteenth-century asylum movement another aspect of the period's empire-building and its accompanying tendency to classify certain groups as abnormal, inferior, or pathological. At a time when the colonizing of "savage" peoples was usually justified as a benevolent attempt to rescue them from spiritual and cultural darkness, the disabled were also segregated, infantilized, and subjected to "civilizing" experiments.[3]

Of course, Fisher simply meant to be helpful when he began his campaign to establish a school for the blind in Massachusetts. Later in his life, he would pioneer the use of ether in childbirth. For him, the two endeavors were not very different: the uneducated blind and unanesthetized women were suffering people in need of scientific succor. Shaped by the beliefs and ideologies—and, to a great extent, the realities—of their time, he and his humanitarian friends saw the blind not as "differently abled" individuals, but as a population in distress, illiterate, isolated, dependent, and sometimes reduced to humiliating and grotesque forms of beggary. As problematic as the new asylums and segregated schools proved to be, they almost certainly improved the lives of the many blind children whose families could not support them. No doubt the legislators and philanthropists who cooperated with Fisher in establishing his school were motivated by the uncomfortable mixture of emotions that most people feel toward the disabled: pity, dread, anxiety, curiosity, and a sentimental and paternalistic solicitude. At the same time, the early supporters of the Perkins Institution were neither insincere nor completely unjustified in congratulating themselves on their progressive humanitarianism.

Fisher set his plan in motion in early 1829, the year of Laura Bridgman's birth. At a meeting that he had organized to enlist the support of influential philanthropists and legislators, he told of the educational wonders that he had observed at the school for the blind in Paris and exhibited the French books in embossed letters that he had brought back with him. Fisher's audience received his report with enthusiasm: a committee was formed, and after hearing its report, both houses of the Massachusetts legislature voted unanimously, without debate, to incorporate "The New England Asylum for the Blind, for the purpose of educating blind persons." The Act of Incorporation authorized the trustees to receive grants, bequests, donations, and subscriptions, and reserved the right of the legislature to send as many as thirty blind persons at public expense. The final paragraph of the trustees' first report captures the exuberant spirit of patriotic optimism with which this quasi-public institution was founded:

> We conjure the philanthropist and the patriot to assist in adding an Asylum for the Blind to the many charitable and humane establishments that ennoble and beautify our land. . . . Let our Hospitals, our Asylums, and our Infirmaries be cherished and venerated by us in place of mouldering ruins and relics of ancient art. Let these be the monuments by which our age and country shall be distinguished. They are the infallible evidence of an enlightened, refined and Christian community.[4]

The legislature supported Fisher's plan without knowing much about the numbers, ages, or geographical distribution of the blind. From the 1820 census and surveys sent to Massachusetts town ministers (many of whom failed to respond), the trustees guessed that the blind population of New England numbered about 1,650, of whom 320 might be young enough to benefit from an education.[5] But that may have been a very low estimate: as Howe later observed, the census probably failed to count many of the blind, who

> from their very misfortune, are hidden from the world; they sit sad and secluded by the firesides of their relatives; the dawn of day does not call them into the haunts of men, and they vegetate through life and sink into the grave, unknown even to their neighbors.[6]

Regardless of their exact numbers, however, the blind unquestionably needed help: they were more likely than the sighted to begin life poor and to end up living in poverty, as wards of the parish, residents of almshouses, or vagrant beggars.[7]

Despite the enthusiasm with which the trustees endorsed the establishment of the new asylum, for the next two years the project went nowhere. Fisher, who had a busy medical practice as well as other philanthropic interests, wanted to promote the school, but not to run it, and he began to look around for an energetic man to organize the institution and get it started. His first choice was someone with experience: Thomas Hopkins Gallaudet, the founding director of the renowned American Asylum for the Deaf and Dumb at Hartford, Connecticut.

Gallaudet, an evangelical minister, had become interested in educating the deaf out of sympathy for Alice Cogswell, the pretty little daughter of a friend. In 1807, at the age of two, she had lost her hearing to a fever, just as Laura would almost a quarter of a century later. Fearing that Alice would fail to develop mentally, her influential father rallied support for a school for the deaf in Hartford and in 1815 persuaded Gallaudet to lead it. To prepare for the task, Gallaudet traveled to Europe to study the latest methods of instructing the deaf. He went first to England and Scotland to learn the speech-based "oralist" method favored there, but because the British schools kept their techniques secret, he adopted the French system of communicating with deaf students in sign language.[8]

The Hartford school flourished under Gallaudet's leadership, and it is not surprising that Fisher wanted to hire him, but Gallaudet rejected the offer. Life at a school for the blind would most likely not have appealed to his wife, a signing deaf woman. Besides, he had just retired from the Hartford school in exhaustion and was not interested in starting over.

At a loss, Fisher discussed the problem of finding a director with Howe, his old college acquaintance, while they were out riding together on a summer day in 1831. Howe recognized a good opportunity when he saw it and immediately volunteered himself for the job. With his credentials, connections, and experience, he was an ideal candidate, and Fisher easily got the approval of the other trustees to hire him.[9]

In later years, Howe's family and friends liked to tell the story of his appointment to direct the asylum as providential, a meeting with destiny. In this romanticized version—a version that his wife and daughters may have conjured up—Howe, returned from his Greek adventures, was in quest of a noble mission. One day Dr. Fisher was walking along Boylston Street with two other trustees of the Asylum for the Blind, earnestly discussing the necessity of finding just the right man to launch their stalled project, when he looked up and saw Howe approaching. As the story goes, Fisher stopped and exclaimed: " 'Here is Howe! . . . The very man we have been looking for all this time.' " It was, in Laura Howe Richards's effusive telling, "the meeting of flint and steel; the spark was struck instantly." At once Howe "kindled like a torch; doubt and hesitation vanished; here was his work, ready to hand."[10]

In this version, Howe was not a man looking for a social work job, but a knight-errant answering a call for help, a wandering hero who had found his mission. With its emphasis on the drama of a chance meeting and of Fisher's instant recognition—"Ecce homo!"—this story insists on the glamour and manliness of Howe's new vocation. Although he is to be the teacher of blind children, his will not be mundane women's work. The Howe of this story is no humble schoolmaster—and certainly no motherly schoolmarm—but a virile combatant enlisted in the glorious Good Fight.

The masculine rhetoric that Howe customarily used about himself—and that his admirers used about him—explicitly distinguished him from the women who were at that very moment transforming education into a female profession. Although town schools did not employ significant numbers of women as teachers until the 1820s, by 1834, more than half the teachers in Massachusetts were female; by 1860, the percentage rose to almost eighty.[11] At the same time, women were beginning to assume positions of educational leadership. When Howe accepted Fisher's offer, Emma Willard, the pioneering founder of the Troy Female Seminary, was already well known. Catharine Beecher had opened her first school—the Hartford Female Seminary—and written her first book: *The Elements of Mental and Moral Philosophy, Founded Upon Experience.* Dorothea Dix, too, had earned a reputation as an educational reformer, both as a teacher and an author of didactic children's books. And more radical than any of them, Elizabeth Palmer Peabody, by 1831, had read widely in European educational theory, run a school with her sister Mary, published *First Lessons in Grammar on the Plan of Pestalozzi*, and translated Joseph-Marie Degérando's *Self-Education; or, the Means and Art of Moral Progress.*[12]

Perhaps as a reaction to the feminization of teaching, Howe always represented himself—and was always represented by others—as the manliest of heroes. To a remarkable extent, the theme of chivalric romance infuses not only his daughters' writings, but almost every nineteenth-century account of Howe's work with the blind in general and Laura Bridgman in particular. In the encomia that his friends and family regularly churned out, he is a "Bayard," "the Lafayette of Boston," a "New England Paladin," "one of the most romantic characters of our century," a "red-cross knight," "the Cadmus of the Blind," "the best specimen extant of all that was noble and valiant in the old chevaliers . . . as terrible and as generous a warrior as Godfrey or Amadis de Gaul."[13] When, in the early 1830s, the Greek government somewhat belatedly conferred upon Howe the title of Chevalier of the Greek Legion of Honor, the romantic aura that already clung to him became in a sense official. For the rest of his life, Howe's friends and family, without a trace of irony, called him by the nickname "Chev."

Howe's motives, appearance, and manner may have been heroic, but the job ahead of him was both difficult and in many ways pedestrian. The new director would be required to engage in continual private fundraising and public lobbying. He would have to oversee every aspect of a total institution: hiring and supervising personnel, purchasing equipment and supplies, enforcing discipline, maintaining sanitary conditions, managing a budget. Since the families of blind children had not asked to have them educated, the director would also have to recruit students by persuading parents—many of whom were uneducated themselves—that their blind children should be sent away to the school. Most important, the director would have to figure out the best method for teaching the blind to read and write at a time when no one in America had the slightest notion of how this could be done. Although New York and Philadelphia were beginning to organize schools for the blind, there was still no institution in the United States that Howe could visit to get information, no experienced teachers of the blind, and almost no books for the blind in embossed letters available in English.

The nineteenth-century American remedy for problems of ignorance was almost always a trip abroad to study—and ultimately improve upon—European models. On his tour, the fact-finding American customarily stopped in Paris, London, Edinburgh, and, by the 1830s, Berlin and Vienna, too. The backers of the Hartford school had funded Gallaudet's European tour in 1815, and sixteen years later, the trustees of the New England Asylum understood that they would have to underwrite a similar trip for Howe. As patriotic Boston rationalists, however, they expected him to turn a skeptical Yankee eye to his examination of European practices. With the nationalistic self-confidence characteristic of their time, they assumed that by observing the numerous schools for the blind that had sprung up in Europe—along with schools for the deaf—in the first quarter of the nineteenth century, he would return to Boston having reshaped and improved European pedagogical methods, materials, and philosophies for American use.

Howe remained abroad from September 1831 until July 1832, but his investigative mission was not completely successful. Although he was traveling at the trustees' expense, once he found himself back, as he put it, in "this vile old Babylon of Europe," knightly opportunities beckoned, and he could not focus on doing his pedagogical homework.[14] Almost immediately after his arrival in Paris in the fall, Howe got in touch with the venerable Marquis de Lafayette, who enlisted him in a romantic new revolutionary crusade: Polish independence. Before long, Howe was chairman of a committee of Americans in Paris formed to support the Polish cause and provide relief to refugees of the abortive Polish uprising against Russia of the summer of 1831.

Once again, Howe flourished in his heroic element: the committee met weekly in the home of the famous James Fenimore Cooper; Lafayette himself was often present; and best of all, the others deferred to Howe, who, as a veteran of the Greek revolution, was experienced in aiding insurgents. Caught up in this new adventure, Howe also maintained open house for refugee Polish nationalists and coordinated the efforts of the American Polish relief committees at home and in Paris.[15] In January 1832, after inspecting a school for the blind in Berlin, he journeyed east to administer relief and encouragement to the suffering Polish refugees who had fled across the border into an unwelcoming East Prussia; in his possession were 20,000 francs donated by sympathetic Americans, as well as certain politically embarrassing documents. Although he later insisted that his sole intention had been to dispense humanitarian aid and moral support to the desperate Poles stranded in refugee camps along the border, the Prussians—no friends of revolutionaries—did not welcome the intrusion of the New England Paladin. The authorities summarily ordered Howe back to Berlin; he had time to hide his incriminating papers, but was nevertheless held incommunicado in a Prussian prison for a month, and then driven under guard in "a miserable cart" over "rough roads" to be dumped unceremoniously across the French border.[16]

Back on French soil, humiliated and a little guilty about neglecting his mission for the blind, Howe wrote an outraged letter to the American minister at Paris, demanding "redress" for the "wrongs" he had suffered at the hands of the Prussians: "I have been kicked out of the country as it were like a criminal . . . cruelty has been added to injustice, and insult to cruelty."[17] Neither his noisy indignation, however, nor the protestations of the America Polish Committee in Paris could altogether conceal that the entire episode had been deeply embarrassing for all concerned. In a letter published in American newspapers, Cooper, on behalf of the committee, did his best to respond to awkward questions about how the Polish relief money sent by Americans had been spent. Howe also owed an accounting to the trustees who were paying his salary and funding his trip: his Prussian escapade, undertaken without their knowledge or permission, had cost him valuable time and made it impossible for him (given the close alliance between Prussia and Austria) to visit Vienna, which reputedly had the most enlightened and successful school for the blind in Europe.[18]

In his explanatory letter to John Fisher, written while he was still imprisoned in Berlin, Howe characteristically refused to admit any fault. While "it might be supposed," he wrote, that he had neglected his duties to the trustees by engaging "in some political intrigue," he had in fact been acting "in the spirit" of his original mission when he went "in the name of thousands" of his fellow citizens "to clothe those who were naked, and to say to all that they had the sympathies and the hearty good wishes of America." Despite the failure of his mission and the misery of his imprisonment, he did not regret his chivalric "digression":

> I keep good heart, and recollect when I was shut up in a little castle in Candia, with no food but biscuit, and the Moslem dogs whetting their sabres to dissect us when we should have eaten all our bread and been forced to come out. Even as I escaped then, shall I be again delivered from the Philistines who persecute me.

If he were not tormented by "the distracting thought that it may be supposed at home" that he had neglected his duty to the blind, he could hold his imprisonment, he said, "as a mere trifle." Even in the darkness of his damp dungeon cell, however, he would carry on with his work and, if he could get paper and pen, translate "some good things" from the German works on educating the blind that he had gathered before his arrest.[19]

Perhaps in response to the rumble of American disapproval over the handling of the Polish relief effort, Lafayette published a commendation of Howe in July 1832, just after Howe's return to the United States. This endorsement from the beloved French hero of the American Revolution undoubtedly helped silence American questions and criticism, and, in the absence of any public reproach from the trustees, the tale of Howe's courage in the face of cruel imprisonment soon became part of the larger heroic Howeian legend. But the episode illuminates important and unchanging aspects of Howe's personality that would eventually have implications for his various philanthropic and reformist activities, including his work with Laura Bridgman.

In his Prussian adventure, Howe had been, as usual, certain that he was in the right. Accordingly, those who had opposed or questioned him were wicked or foolish. A situation that to others might have seemed dauntingly complex presented no problem to him: he never doubted that he knew what had to be done for the Poles and, without much study or consultation, he set out to do it. Restless and eager, always, for action, he was unfazed by obstacles and unburdened by self-questioning. At the same time, he needed—and cultivated—the esteem of important people: thus, with a little flattery, Lafayette had been able to persuade him to neglect his work for the blind to embark on what turned out to be a dangerous fool's errand. Finally, as much as Howe sought and enjoyed praise, he hated criticism. Any public disapproval elicited from him an outraged and occasionally less than truthful self-defense. As Howe's future wife, Julia Ward Howe, would later privately observe, Howe was not only "much led by flattery," but also "incapable of enduring criticism or of profiting by it."[20]

HOWE'S FRIGHTENING AND humiliating month in a Prussian dungeon brought to an end the chapter of his life that his worshipful younger friend and first biographer, Franklin B. Sanborn, entitled "Youthful Daring." When Howe returned to Boston, he was thirty-one years old and, in Sanborn's admiring estimation, "had guarded his arms, won his spurs, and proved his knighthood by deeds as valorous and patient as those of any chevalier of the Middle Ages." Having battled fierce Turks and Russians in contests that "repeated the barbarism, the superstition, the ferocity and the simplicity" of the Age of Chivalry, Howe was now ready in earnest to take up arms for humanitarian causes at home.[21]

Although his investigations had been interrupted and eventually curtailed by his Polish relief activities, Howe nonetheless felt sure that he had seen enough to surpass the accomplishments of any of the European schools for the blind. The Europeans may have been ahead of Americans in establishing their schools, but, as Howe explained in a lengthy essay published in *The North American Review* in 1833, the Old World, with its undemocratic traditions, economic inequalities, and resistance to change, could not possibly develop the kinds of benevolent institutions that would be acceptable to progressive Americans. In educating the blind, the true aim of the philanthropist, Howe emphasized, should be *"to enable them to pass their lives pleasantly and usefully in some constant occupation, which shall ensure to them a competent livelihood."* Achieving this aim in Europe was impossible. "Strange as it may seem in this age," Europeans—unlike egalitarian Americans—harbored "stubborn and cruel prejudices" against the blind and were unable to imagine them as other than ignorant and degraded. Even if the Europeans could overcome their prejudices, the blind would not be able to compete under an oppressive economic system: where able-bodied laborers could barely subsist on their wages, there was little hope that even the best-educated European blind man could earn his own keep.[22]

Under these circumstances, Howe maintained, an innovative American educator had little to learn from foreign schools for the blind, except to avoid the "dangerous error" of copying them: complacent and ineffectual, these schools were more useful as "beacons to warn rather than lights to guide." The most famous of them, the Paris institution, was in many ways the worst. At first glance, Howe wrote, he had agreed with

Dr. Fisher that the school presented a "delightful spectacle" of "smiling faces" gleaming with "awakened intellect." Deeper investigation revealed to him, however, that "a spirit of illiberality, of mysticism, amounting almost to charlatanism" pervaded the establishment. The students were trained for mere intellectual display: their showy accomplishments bore no practical fruit, and few of them graduated with any prospects of earning their own livelihood. More common sense could be expected from the Scots, and indeed the Edinburgh institution, because it concentrated on teaching useful trades such as mattress making and rug weaving, was to Howe's mind the best of an unimpressive lot of European schools.

Howe also scorned the devices for teaching the blind that he had seen used abroad. In Paris he had studied the apparatus that Abbé Valentin Haüy, the revered founder of the school, had developed in the last decades of the eighteenth century. Working from the inventions of self-taught blind people, Haüy had created pasteboard relief maps and mathematical slates, and had originated an embossing method for printing raised, enlarged letters that the blind could read by touch. Like so much that old Europe had produced, these devices seemed to Howe absurdly clumsy, expensive, and impractical. "It is obvious to anyone," he said of Haüy's maps, "that common ingenuity could devise material improvement." Haüy's mathematical slates were no better. Far too large for the hands of the blind and needlessly confusing, the French slates were made "in defiance of common sense." Although Haüy had correctly understood the importance of providing books for the blind, the volumes he had produced were impossibly bulky and prohibitively expensive. Howe estimated that the New Testament, printed in its entirety by the French method, would extend to at least ten volumes of folio size.[23]

For Howe, the failure of the Europeans to develop a practical method of embossed printing epitomized their stagnation. At a time when missionary societies were busily shipping copies of the Scriptures to "the benighted heathen" in the remotest corners of the world, the blind in Christendom still lacked Bibles of their own in raised letters.

"Surely," Howe protested, "it is as much an object and a duty to print the Scriptures for these unfortunate beings, to whom any book would be a treasure, as to print them for the heathen." Since the French and English had been unable to provide the blind even with the New Testament, "let it be then for America to effect this; let her bestow this inestimable blessing upon the blind, and their prayers will be her rich reward." The time had come for inventive Yankees to tackle the problem of producing practical, affordable books in raised letters, for "there is nothing on which the man of science and ingenuity can turn his thoughts with more hope of accomplishing a desirable end, and bestowing an immense benefit on an unfortunate class of persons."[24]

Although Howe found little to emulate in the European schools, their inadequacies did help him define—in reaction—some fundamental principles for the education of the blind. These principles not only shaped his innovative efforts in his own school and his teaching of Laura Bridgman, but also profoundly and enduringly influenced the educational programs for the disabled throughout America.

His premise was that the blind must be encouraged and taught "to exert their own faculties, to develope [*sic*] their own powers, and to do something to break the listless inactivity, which constitutes for them the *taedium vitae*."[25] Asylums and charities that coddled and infantilized them only added to their miserable sense of inferiority and helplessness. The progressive philanthropist's main objective, Howe argued, should be to train the blind to take their place in the social and economic life of their home communities. To achieve this integration, a school's program should aim to

> overcome, as far as possible, the obstacles which want of sight presents to the full developement [*sic*] of the physical powers; to develope and strengthen the religious sentiment; to elevate and give tone to the moral character, by inspiring proper self-confidence, and holding out the prospect of useful and honourable employment; to store the mind with useful knowledge; to accustom the body to useful toil.[26]

Educated according to these principles, most blind students would be saved from "despondency, and the alms-house" and made into productive, happy citizens.

In Paris Howe had seen the futility of giving all children an academic education; in Edinburgh he had recognized the folly of training all children for manual labor, at which they would inevitably be less successful than sighted workers. Warned by these European errors, Howe argued that American blind children should be seen as individuals and taught according to their dispositions, talents, and station in life. He proposed that the individual potential of each child should be recognized and fostered: some children would excel at mathematics, others at weaving, music, the mechanical arts, languages, or handicrafts.[27] At the same time, the curriculum for all the children should be well rounded, so that they could not only learn to live independently and support themselves in later life, but also have "opened to them . . . a new world of intellectual enjoyment."[28] Mental training should not, however, come at the expense of physical education. Because blind children naturally feared running about and playing with their comrades, they were liable, Howe believed, to become physically inert, weak, and listless. If they were to develop the self-confidence and competitiveness necessary for independence, they would need to follow a vigorous program of healthful exercise.[29]

To Howe's mind, the European schools also neglected "the personal demeanor" of their blind students, who were liable to contract "disagreeable habits" at home and in public institutions. "They swing their hands, or work their heads or reel their bodies; and seem in this way to occupy those moments of void," Howe complained. These "blindisms," as they are called, contributed to the public's prejudice, as did the social backwardness of the blind children he observed in his travels. "They are apt . . . to be exceedingly awkward and embarrassed in company, and are often very bashful while very vain." Yet these problems were easily cured. Like any other children, the blind needed to be exposed to social situations, to grow accustomed to conversing with others, and to be corrected when their appearance or deportment fell short. They would not be accepted socially unless they were taught to look and behave "normally."[30]

Howe could—and frequently did—produce treacly inspirational prose about blind children for political or fund-raising purposes, but as an educator he avoided sentimentality. He believed that only by being thrown on their own resources would blind children learn the essential lesson that deprivation of one sense need not cut them off from "the human family." Trained to excel at pursuits that did not require vision, blind students would come to see themselves as American citizens, fully capable of competing economically with the sighted. They would neither feel nor be pitiable: their strenuous, practical education would have taught them that any disadvantage caused by their blindness could be "counterbalanced by superior industry and ingenuity."[31]

Like the Greek refugees whom Howe had put to work in Corinth, the blind should be the objects of rational benevolence, not handouts. Their educational salvation was both humane and useful: training otherwise dependent people to earn their own keep removed from society "so many dead weights." With the "sun of science in the ascendant" and "the broad blaze of education pouring upon every class of men," the time had arrived, Howe argued, to transform the helpless blind into happy and productive workers. The investment of capital in educating them should not be considered simply as charity, but "as a provision for preventing the blind from becoming taxes to the community."[32]

With its emphasis on economic utility, Howe's philosophy departed significantly from Gallaudet's. Deeply religious, Gallaudet held that his ultimate purpose was "training up the deaf and dumb for heaven."[33] Like the evangelical reformers who ministered to captive or benighted groups—slaves, criminals, the insane, alcoholics, and "savages"—he saw himself as a missionary to the excluded. Disability cut people off from Christian community and kept them ignorant of the gospel; the most urgent job of the educator, then, was neither to teach vocational skills nor to impart academic knowledge, but to open hearts and save souls.[34]

Howe, on the other hand, cared most about citizenship. He was happy for his students to read the Bible, go to church, and develop morally, but his primary goal was to reduce the natural inequalities between the blind and the sighted.[35] If schools could teach the disabled to be as "normal" as possible—if education could, as it were, correct nature's mistakes—then even the most disadvantaged would be able to participate fully in community life.

Like most nineteenth-century Unitarian activists, Howe was an eclectic thinker. He tended to combine appeals to natural rights and republican virtues with utilitarian arguments, occasionally sweetening the mixture with the kind of liberal piety he heard in Channing's sermons. Enlarging on Jeffersonian principles, Howe proposed that productive, gainful employment should be included in the list of inalienable human rights: "Indeed, the blind may claim such labors as a *right;* for surely no right is more sacred than that of exercising one's talents in a useful and profitable manner." At the same time, he pointed out that by any Benthamite calculus, enabling the disabled to work was useful—morally, economically, and politically. "Society belongs to us as well as we to it," he argued; "by promoting the interests of all its members we promote our own."[36]

Howe's philosophy of teaching the blind was suffused with Unitarian optimism and a quintessentially American confidence in the equalizing power of effort, ingenuity, and education. Science, he said, "may be more useful to the world than charity."[37] His motto, "Obstacles are things to be overcome," defined—but also limited—his vision. In many ways, this motto represented a pedagogy that was astonishingly enlightened and progressive, that promised to remove the stigma from disability. Rejecting the separatism and paternalism that he believed marred Gallaudet's approach, Howe insisted that the blind should not be regarded as a special class of beings: they were no different from other people, except that their eyes did not function. Like "normal" people, he said, they "have faculties, and they want to have them employed;—they have moral and intellectual natures which require to be developed and cultivated."[38] The job of the educator was simply to figure out how best to eliminate or circumvent the practical problems created by sightlessness. Once these problems had been addressed, education would allow the blind to make unlimited progress.

The conviction that ingenuity and determination could solve all problems led Howe to experiment until he developed better embossed printing methods and more effective teaching apparatus. By using thinner paper; modifying the typeface to create compact "Boston type," and raising the *g, p,* and *y* to shorten interlinear spaces, he succeeded in producing smaller, cheaper volumes. Determined to establish his own press, he raised money from private donors and Bible societies to print, in addition to an entire New Testament, a variety of essential classroom books, many of which he prepared himself: history outlines, a grammar, an atlas, a speller, a series of readers, and a Latin textbook. In an attempt to avoid duplication of efforts and to make as many embossed volumes as possible available, he set up a free exchange of books with the Philadelphia and New York schools for the blind; lobbied Congress to establish a national library of embossed books; and, when that effort failed, tried—again unsuccessfully—to organize a consortium of the New England states to provide the blind with copies of every book printed. Although he did not succeed in establishing libraries or in getting any appropriations of public money for printing, he managed to raise enough private money to print more books for the blind than any other school in the world. Thanks to his tenacity, embossed volumes were distributed not only throughout the United States, but also in England, Ireland, Holland, and even India.[39]

His can-do motto energized Howe and inspired his many innovations, but as a philosophy it was both overly optimistic and, in practice, a little heartless. His insistence that the blind were not different from others and could therefore be taught to make their own way in the world required that he ignore an unpleasant but pervasive psychological and social reality: the sighted often feel profoundly uneasy in the presence of the sightless. For many sighted people, the enucleated or unfocused eyes of the blind represent a terrifying exile from human community.[40] Because the blind cannot participate in the social code of affiliative facial signals, in the ritual exchange of nods, smiles, and glances, they deprive the sighted of the sense of a seen—and therefore secure—self.[41] Not finding themselves mirrored in the eyes and expressions of the blind, the sighted may experience a sense of dread mixed with guilty anger and revulsion, a feeling of uncanniness that Howe's mid-nineteenth-century contemporary, Charles Baudelaire, captured in a brutally honest poem, "The Blind" ("Les Aveugles"):

> *Contemplate them, my soul: how horrible!*
> *Like dummies; vaguely ridiculous;*
> *Terrifying, eerie as sleepwalkers;*
> *Darting their darkened eyes who knows where.*[42]

Howe apparently felt little of this squeamishness around blind people. He had recognized "stubborn and cruel prejudice" in Europe, but, immune to it himself, simply denied that it would or could be a problem in America. Needless to say, he was wrong. Progressive, humanitarian nineteenth-century Boston could offer the educated blind neither full social acceptance nor, in an industrializing economy, enough suitable work. These were obstacles that Howe had difficulty acknowledging and that his students could not, by their own efforts, overcome. Although he reluctantly opened a workshop in 1840 to employ Perkins graduates who had been unable to find other jobs, he never revised the basic principle that the educated blind, if they only tried hard enough, could be self-sufficient. (No doubt he would have been disappointed to know that even in the year 2000, seventy percent of the disabled in the United States are unemployed, and that the deaf and the blind have an especially hard time finding work, despite the invention of technologically sophisticated aids.)[43]

Howe's philosophy was not only unrealistic about the situation of the blind, but also inappropriate for the complex needs of the deaf. In his habitual certainty that he knew best, he assumed that the requirements of the blind and the deaf were virtually the same: both populations should be taught to function as "normal" people in the larger society. Without ever consulting Gallaudet, Howe became an ardent advocate of teaching the deaf to speak. Although he knew nothing about Sign (which he confused with pantomime) and had no appreciation of the difficulty of teaching speech to the deaf, Howe unhesitatingly condemned the teaching of Sign as "quackery that has been imposed upon the world."[44] If the deaf were to take their place in society along with the blind, they must be forced to abandon Sign and learn to speak; problems in articulation were only obstacles to overcome.

While Howe remains a hero in most histories of the blind, his fierce opposition to sign language has earned him, along with Horace Mann and Alexander Graham Bell, a prominent place in the deaf community's catalog of historical villains: Oliver Sacks calls Howe's campaign against signing schools an "egregious" example of extremism, while Harlan Lane, the preeminent historian of the deaf, condemns him as an arrogant, contentious man who found in reform both an excuse and an outlet for his aggression.[45] Howe's contempt for Sign not only contributed to the breaking up of successful signing schools and communities later in the century, but also prevented him from experimenting with sign language in educating Laura Bridgman. Whether such an experiment would have been useful to science or beneficial to Laura we can never know; the principle that the disabled should be taught to conform to the ways of the world was, for Howe, always paramount, and so Laura learned to communicate with others only in English.

FOR ALL ITS limitations, Howe's optimistic, pragmatic approach to educating the blind produced rapid results and garnered enthusiastic public favor. In August 1832, only a month after his return from his European tour, he opened the New England Asylum for the Blind in his father's house, on Pleasant Street in Boston. Two male teachers, one of whom he had brought back to Boston from the Paris school to teach literature, and the other from the Edinburgh school to teach crafts, assisted Howe in the instruction of six hastily recruited indigent blind students, ranging in age from six to twenty. Within a few weeks he had managed to devise teaching materials, develop a curriculum, and establish a rigorous daily regimen of work, study, and outdoor exercise lasting from the wakeup call at

5:30 A.M. to prayers at 8:00 P.M. and bedtime at 10 P.M.[46] Years later, Elizabeth Palmer Peabody provided a touching description of Howe at work in the first months of the "infant institution":

> In the simplest surroundings, we found Dr. Howe, with the half-dozen first pupils he had picked up in the highways and byways. He had then been about six months at work, and had invented and laboriously executed some books with raised letters, to teach them to read, some geographical maps, and the geometrical diagrams necessary for instruction in mathematics. . . . I shall not, in all time, forget the impression made upon me by seeing the hero of the Greek Revolution, who had narrowly missed being that of the Polish Revolution also; to see this hero, I say, wholly absorbed, and applying all the energies of his genius to this apparently humble work, and doing it as Christ did, without money and without price.[47]

Carried away by enthusiasm, Peabody may have imagined Howe as a Christlike volunteer, but in fact he was a salaried professional who appreciated the importance of cultivating financial backers. After six months, he realized that his students had progressed so dramatically that he could raise more money by exhibiting them to the Massachusetts Legislature. The precedent for such public exhibitions had been established in the 1780s by Haüy, who built support for his Paris school by displaying the accomplishments of his students at popular demonstrations and concerts. In the United States, Gallaudet had already successfully used exhibitions to gain recognition for his school for the deaf. (Although putting the disabled through their paces in public may strike us today as bizarre, in fact exhibitions remained a common fund-raising practice for institutions in the United States until the middle of the twentieth century.)

Howe disliked exhibitions, fearing that they stirred up an unhealthy love of display in his students, and that the "sensitive minds" of the younger ones—especially the girls—would "recoil from the very thought" of appearing in public. At the same time, however, he understood the need for impressing legislators and satisfying the "reasonable curiosity" of taxpayers.[48]

As he had hoped, his first exhibition "proved so incontrovertibly the capacity of the Blind for receiving instruction" that the legislature immediately appropriated $6,000 a year to maintain twenty poor blind students in Howe's school. More exhibitions quickly followed, and the cause of blind education suddenly became fashionable. In 1833, Colonel Thomas H. Perkins, a shipping tycoon who had never before evinced much interest in the blind, donated a mansion on Pearl Street as the institution's home, on the condition that $50,000 be donated to maintain it. Boston and Salem "seemed to contend with each other in the race of benevolence" to raise the money, and donations poured in. By the end of the year, the institution, which had started out $2,000 in debt, had received $61,279.43.[49]

Under Howe's energetic leadership, the school—officially renamed the Perkins Institution and Massachusetts Asylum for the Blind in 1839—grew and thrived: at the end of 1834, forty students were in residence; by 1838, there were more than sixty, and the institution moved from what had become cramped quarters in Pearl Street to a more spacious location, a hotel building in South Boston. Throughout the 1830s Howe, always restless, maintained his favorite kind of hectic schedule. Besides overseeing every aspect of the expanding institution, he lectured and traveled to promote education for the blind; during the first decade of his directorship, he was on the road for weeks at a time, exhibiting his best students to legislatures and the general public in seventeen states.

All this successful—and visible—philanthropic activity won Howe entree into Boston's most exalted intellectual and social circles. Before the end of the decade, he was well on his way to becoming a person of consequence. The prestigious *North American Review* had published his essays. Distinguished men of letters, many of them with patrician connections, now knew him or knew of him; his acquaintances included rising stars such as William Prescott, the historian; Rufus Choate, a lawyer and later a renowned orator; Samuel Eliot, cousin of the president of

Harvard; and Longfellow and Cornelius Conway Felton, both at the time professors at Harvard. Horace Mann, as his own prominence and influence grew, continued to be a valuable ally and tireless promoter of Howe's reputation. Most important, Howe had begun an affectionate friendship with Charles Sumner, a younger Harvard graduate who, even when he later gained fame in the United States Senate, would prove a devoted and useful friend.

Yet, despite access to Boston's intellectual and patrician circles, Howe had not fully arrived. The exhibitions of his students, the legislative lobbying, the public lectures on his work, the fulsome praise of his friends, could not conceal the reality that he had done only what the equally competent directors of the new asylums springing up everywhere were also doing. He had been useful, energetic, and clever, but he had not demonstrated any particular genius. To achieve satisfying and lasting distinction, he would have to prove both to the world and to himself that he could accomplish something brilliant.

The education of Laura Bridgman proved to be that brilliant, impossible accomplishment. As Howe's admirers remarked, she had been like someone buried alive until he lifted the cover of the sarcophagus and set her free. That feat, John Jay Chapman later marveled, was "almost like the discovery of America or communication with Mars."[50]

CHAPTER THREE

Mind

ALTHOUGH THE MEMORY was shadowy and distant, in her twenties Laura believed that she could still recall the scarlet fever that had nearly killed her in early February 1832, a month after her second birthday. In the three fragmentary memoirs she composed in the 1850s, she described the intense sensations of that devastating illness: the feeling of being "so choked up" that she could barely swallow; the painful sores that covered her face and body; the soothing rocking of her "nice old cradle"; the peppermint-flavored sugar that she enjoyed taking "for a sort of medicine."[1] After the crisis had passed, her inflamed eyes could not tolerate bright light. The sunshine streaming in the kitchen window, she said, "made the tears flow from my eyes like a heavy shower. I dropped down my head into my little hands as the ray of the light stung my eye lids like a sharpest needle or a wasp." As she lay, weak with fever, in her cozy cradle "nest," she was often overcome by a strange fancy: the "sensation of a veil drawn along my poor head."[2]

To Harmony Bridgman, of course, the memory of her daughter's illness remained clear and indelible. In an 1841 letter to Howe she recalled:

It was thursday morning about nine oclock the 28th of january (her Father was then gone for the Doctor for Mary who was

taken sick Tuesday eve previous) she went to her Aunt Phebe as
she was sweeping and said Pebe by by (meaning to have her take
and rock her) she sais again Pebe by by, I told her I thought she
was not well she took her and in a few moments she was a distressed little creature as you ever saw.

By the seventh of February, Laura's sisters, Mary, six years old, and
Frances Collina, four, had both succumbed to the fever. At first, her parents thought that Laura, too, would die, but after a difficult week she rallied. Against all odds, the crisis seemed to have passed.

Suddenly the infection moved into her head. Her eyes swelled shut
and pus oozed from her eyes and ears. When the doctor returned ten
days later, he gave the Bridgmans the terrible news: "He says to me,"
Mrs. Bridgman wrote, "your Childs eyes are spoilt she was the only one
of the three Children which remained and in that situation, my feelings
would be more easily conceived than expressed."[3] It was another five
weeks before the Bridgmans realized that Laura's hearing, too, had been
destroyed. Months later they began to suspect that the fever had damaged even her sense of smell.

According to her mother, Laura's eyes had been bright blue until,
ravaged by inflammation, they shriveled and disappeared behind closed
lids. Before her illness she had had "a verry pleasant and smiling countenance . . . and a most sweet disposition," as well as a "sound quick per-
ceptible mind."[4] A bright and active child, she had begun speaking at
eighteen months; by the time she took sick she could "talk quite plain"
and put short sentences together. Indeed, her mother remembered, she
was "rather more forward in talking than the generality of children at
that age."[5] With her hearing gone, however, Laura could not hold on to
her small store of words. At first, after her recovery, she would repeat
"dark dark," as if confused by her new blindness, but by the end of the
year language had faded entirely from her conscious memory. "Book"
was the last word that Mrs. Bridgman ever heard her daughter speak dis-
tinctly.[6]

Laura's convalescence lasted two years. She lay in her bed in a darkened room for five months; it was a year before she could walk unsupported and another year before her strength fully returned. Still mourning the loss of Mary and Frances Collina, Mrs. Bridgman struggled to nurse Laura through her long and difficult recovery. "I was so very restless and unwell," Laura recalled, "that it gave her very great anxiety and trouble continually . . . in tending to me." During the months that Laura remained too weak to walk, her mother, pregnant with another child, was obliged to drag her from room to room in a chair, to prepare special foods that she could swallow, and to get up in the middle of the night to bathe her eyes with oil.

With some help from a hired girl and, occasionally, from Daniel Bridgman's sister Phoebe, Mrs. Bridgman somehow managed to nurse Laura and at the same time carry out the domestic responsibilities of a typical early-nineteenth-century New England farmer's wife. Laura later proudly enumerated her mother's regular chores: cooking and baking for her family and the hired hands; melting tallow to make candles and soap; churning butter and making cheese; boiling potatoes for the pigs; caring for the chickens; drawing water from the well; carding wool; spinning and winding yarn; weaving on a large loom; sewing and mending; wadding and quilting comforters; pounding the clothes with a wooden shovel to wash them; spreading the clothes on the ground, winter and summer, to dry (her mother, Laura noted, never had a clothesline); ironing; mopping the floor with a rag mop; knitting mittens; making maple syrup.[7] In addition, in the years following Laura's illness, Mrs. Bridgman attended church every Sunday and cared for her two new babies, Addison Daniel, born in August 1832, and John Downer, born in July 1834.

Once she had nursed Laura back to physical health, her mother did what little she could to help her function. It was almost unheard of for a child to lose both sight and hearing to infection, even in those days of devastating epidemics, and Mrs. Bridgman must have felt bewildered and overwhelmed.[8] Staggering under the burden of her household work, she nevertheless managed not only to keep Laura neatly groomed, safe, and well fed, but also, astonishingly, to teach her to perform some simple tasks—setting the table, churning butter, sewing, knitting, and braiding.

Yet, as Laura came to understand, immersed "most monotonously" in her domestic affairs, Mrs. Bridgman had neither the time nor the skill to satisfy the extraordinary emotional and cognitive needs of a deaf-blind child. "My dear Mama could not dream of how to encourage or comfort me much . . . only by way of patting my back or face or also by giving me some kind of food or article." The notion that it might be a good idea to provide amusement or stimulation for Laura simply never crossed Mrs. Bridgman's mind. Afterward, in explaining why her only childhood plaything had been an old boot, Laura pointed out that her mother "never obtained a doll nor any play toys for her little children because she had not the knowledge of dolls."[9]

Nothing in Harmony Bridgman's background or experience could have equipped her to do more for Laura. Her own early years had been bleak and bruising. The ninth and youngest child of hardscrabble Vermont farmers, at ten years old she had lost her own mother in an outbreak of fever that also killed three of her brothers. Soon afterward her family broke up and her three surviving brothers scattered to towns in upstate New York. Her widowed father—a veteran, at fifty-two, of both the Revolutionary War and the War of 1812—moved with her and her two sisters across the state line into Hanover, New Hampshire, where she met and in 1824, at the age of twenty, married Daniel Bridgman.[10]

All that Mrs. Bridgman did for Laura she accomplished with little help from the members of the Bridgman household. Neither Daniel Bridgman nor his ill-tempered younger brother, who at that time still lived with the family, assisted much with Laura's care, except occasionally to frighten her into obedience by stamping hard on the floor so that she would be startled by the vibrations. According to Laura, the hired girl, "Miss Hall," was equally unhelpful: "She could not bear to have me standing in silence near her side." Once, when Laura lingered too near when Miss Hall was washing dishes, the hired girl "was much vexed and nervous . . . she drew her wet hand out of the water and repulsed me so violently down on the kitchen floor. . . . She caused me to sob so bitterly." With considerable relish, Laura remembered that her mother, whose temper could be explosive, came in "like a tempest" and scolded Miss Hall for this "wicked and unjust" behavior.[11]

Emotionally isolated from everyone in her household except her mother, and unable to communicate except by a few mimetic signs for eating and sleeping, Laura was sometimes seized by loneliness, panic, confusion, and anger. The family farm itself could be a frightening place for a deaf-blind child. The animals—"huge beasts"—with their strange smells and sudden movements terrified her; she found the pigs disgusting and could not bring herself even to go near the cows. The carcass of an animal her father had butchered felt horrible to her touch: "As I perceived it, it made me shudder with terror because I did not know what the matter was."[12] When her mother, her essential link to the world, was away or too busy to attend to her, Laura complained that she felt forlon: "I murmured so sadly when she made escape from me for hours. I did not like to be deserted at home by her." At times a kind of frenzy of neediness and rage toward her mother would overwhelm her:

> I would cling to my Mother so wildly and peevishly many times.
> I took hold of her legs or arms as she strode across the room.
> She acted . . . as if it irritated her very much indeed. . . . I could
> not help feeling so cross and uneasy against her.[13]

In these moods of wild frustration, Laura would occasionally become unmanageable. At such times, Howe later observed, her mother's system of tapping Laura's back or rubbing her hand to signal displeasure proved inadequate; the "willful" child would yield only "to the sign made by the heavier hand of her father." That stern paternal hand, said Howe, "was not lightened, as was that of the mother, by woman's timidity. It said plainly, 'I am mightier than thou,' and she yielded."[14]

Much as Laura suffered from moments of terror, rage, and desolation—her "very sad & painful days"—she also insisted that as a young deaf-blind child she had enjoyed "many very delightful merry days." In memory, at any rate, her dark, silent New Hampshire world had an intense and sensuous particularity. Years later she could still describe in eerie detail her early pleasures: feeling the fallen apples under her feet in the orchard as she reached for "sour & sweet apples suspending on the branches of the trees"; "rocking backward and forward constantly" in her little chair before the fire while her mother prepared breakfast; enjoying bowls of berries with "very rich milk & maple molasses" in the summer; dipping into the maple syrup, still hot from boiling, "which was so delicious & pure to my mouth." She remembered the delight of running barefoot in the warm weather: "Some times the green grass used to irritate my sensitive feet very badly. It amused me so much to ramble about on a carpet of the grass." Her mother had "some very tiny books," which, Laura wrote, "I loved to hold in my own little hands"; she also remembered pretending that the old boot she played with was a "little baby," although, as she noted ruefully, "I never knew how to kiss my boot or my folks."[15]

Laura owed most of her happy childhood memories to her "fine and good Benefactor . . . a most excellent & odd gentleman named Mr. Asa Tenney." Her strange and intimate relationship with Tenney, a mentally impaired hired man who sometimes lived with the Bridgmans, helped her to stay connected to the external world and to resist the alienation and psychic disintegration that can overwhelm deaf-blind children. With the birth of Addison and John, her mother had less and less time for her, but Tenney filled the void, becoming her tenderly devoted companion and teacher. A Quaker in a town dominated by Congregationalists and Baptists, he was destitute, shabby, strange in his manner, and incoherent in his speech, but he understood how to reach Laura. "I do not think," Laura wrote, "that I should have been so happy as a bird, if Mr. T. was not my best acquaintance."[16]

Together, she and Tenney explored the Bridgman farm, picking berries, playing on the swing in the barn, lying on the warm grass. Holding Laura gently by the hand, Tenney led her on long rambles through the meadows: sometimes, she recalled, "he influenced me with something like geography" by showing her how to put a stick in the brook so that she could feel the flowing of the water, or by making a game of throwing sand, gravel, stones, and branches into the water "for my amusement and also a lesson."[17] Using signs to communicate, he taught her how to collect eggs in the barn. "I liked so much to grope in hollowed nests with my little hands, seeking for a single egg. . . . Mr. T. commanded me not to rob the poor hen of her very last egg by a gesture which I understood so clearly."[18]

With Tenney, Laura experienced a warmth and physical intimacy that she certainly never had with her parents and that she would never find again. Although in later years she would not allow most men to touch her, she fondly remembered snuggling beside Tenney on his "comfortable bed" while he relaxed after his chores, reading the newspaper. She loved how he would greet her "most ardently" by stroking her cheeks. "He used to lift me up in his arms and transport me from one place to an other. I liked to be carried as a little Babe in his great arms." Affectionate, patient, indulgent, and always available ("Mr. Tenney would never abandon me," Laura said; "he never had a mind to scold or punish me"), Tenney was Laura's emotional anchor. "I loved him as a Father . . . he was so very tender hearted and affectionate. . . . I was so very happy to stay with him constantly and forever."[19] Even after she had come to understand Tenney's outcast status in Hanover, Laura maintained that he had saved her life. "He was an Angel and a messenger to me from the hands of God."[20]

Although she never wavered in her loyalty to Tenney, Laura knew that her teachers at Perkins regarded him as a figure of fun. "They could not help laughing so heartily at his writing. They could not understand by all his meant words, nor could puzzle out in any way. . . . He made the people laugh by his remarks."[21] In the account of Laura's life that Howe published in 1857, ten years after Tenney's death, he ridiculed the illegible, ungrammatical, "endless epistles" that Tenney had faithfully sent to her after she left home. Tenney, as Howe portrayed him, was a quaint New England eccentric, a "sort of philosopher with a crack in his skull," too ignorant to appreciate the benefits of a scientific Perkins education.

At the same time, however, Howe admitted that Laura had benefited from the "stream of love and kindness" that had flowed toward her from Tenney's warm heart. "The bare presence of one whose love she could feel by his gentle attentions, would have been enough to make the child happy; but, beside this, the simple man contrived to teach her much in various ways."[22]

Contemporary descriptions of Tenney do not reveal the cause of his oddity and social isolation. How the oldest son of Major Silas Tenney— veteran of the Revolutionary War, five-term Hanover selectman, incorporator of the first town library, pillar of the Congregational church— wound up a penniless, semiliterate Quaker remains a mystery. He was not retarded: he could read the newspaper, kept his tattered clothes scrupulously clean, and, according to Laura, her mother had a "glowing respect" for him.[23] Howe's daughters speculated that Tenney suffered from a speech impediment, but his writing, too, was somewhat incoherent.[24] With its inkblots and misspellings, his only surviving letter suggests mental disorder rather than deficiency. Laura had been told that "he was much confused in his poor mind," and that "his mind was not in the natural state since a Boy." But even if his thinking tended to be irrational, his mood was unvaryingly calm and good-humored. Laura attested that even when in a fit of temper she seized the spectacles from his "poor eyes" and "crushed them with great fury," he remained unperturbed.[25]

In the absence of a reliable diagnosis of his condition, it is tempting to romanticize Tenney, to imagine him as a Holy Fool or one of Dickens's eccentric fairy godfathers. After Tenney's death, even Howe could not resist waxing poetical: "May the grass grow green, and the birds sing blithely over thy grave, good Tenny [sic], Laura's first and most loving teacher."[26] Yet Tenney deserves a less patronizing epitaph. Whether intuitively or as the result of thought and experimentation, he understood how to break through to a deaf-blind child. His success invites a respectful question: how did this mentally impaired hired laborer manage not only to win Laura's trust and affection, but also to engage her in explorations of an external world that she could not see, hear, or smell?

In the early 1970s, David Goode, a graduate student in sociology, spent three years as a participant-observer in a state hospital ward for deaf-blind children born with rubella syndrome. His conclusions, published in *A World Without Words: The Social Construction of Children Born Deaf and Blind,* may help shed light on Tenney's ability to reach her. After months of observing the fruitless and frustrating interactions between the children and the hospital personnel, Goode began to think that although the staff used the rhetoric of individualized, child-centered education, they were in fact driven by their own needs and their own emotional reactions to the children's disabilities. As a result, even the most well-meaning clinicians, teachers, and social workers could not recognize or take into account the individual qualities and goals of the children themselves. Goode concluded that instead of engaging in a futile attempt to rescue, repair, and "normalize" the children—an attempt motivated by unexamined feelings and assumptions about the deaf-blind—the staff should work with each child to achieve "a mutually recognized mutual understanding, or a mutually recognized interiority to a same world." To arrive at this understanding—this "intersubjectivity"—staff members should try to enter and inhabit their patients' kinesthetically experienced reality, a reality that Goode characterizes as "thin," immediate, unpredictable, and therefore dangerous.[27]

Perhaps Tenney's gift was a capacity for achieving "intersubjectivity" with Laura. His own mental disability, whatever it was, may have made it easier for him to enter her frightening and chaotic world, to share her frustrations and terrors, and to understand her needs. Maybe his reality was "thin" and unpredictable, too. Linguistically impaired himself, he might well have been skilled at nonverbal communication. As a nonconforming outsider, he had no civilizing mission, no educational agenda, no need to make Laura behave; as a Quaker, he would have disliked coercion.

According to her recollections, Tenney offered Laura intimacy, warmth, diversion, and mental stimulation, but he never attempted to train her. Indeed, convinced that signing would serve her needs better than English, he tried to convince her parents not to send her away to Perkins:

> The indain chief that I have seen in this village, when the younger indian spoke of talking by signs, said the chief held the opinnon there was one language that was universal, and he could talk that language. Laura was improving in that verry language as well as knitting work before leaveing home.[28]

Life in the city would only spoil her innocence, Tenney warned: "When she was attended at home she brought to remembrance, Adam and Eve before the aspireing mind of the tempter came to tempt them to greater improvement, promising great things and so forth." The argument that learning English would allow Laura to learn about God failed to move him. "How could I learn her better than to show a tender care and guard against deception[?]," he demanded. Most of all, however, Tenney feared that Laura would miss him painfully if she left New Hampshire.[29] Nobody else could—or would—inhabit her reality and, in the deepest sense, keep her company.

IN THE MID-1830s, while Laura and Tenney were exploring the New Hampshire countryside together, Howe was in search of a deaf-blind child for purposes his own. He had come to hope that the right child— someone like Laura—might provide him with exactly the philanthropic and scientific opportunity that he was looking for.

After just a few years of work at Perkins he had accomplished wonders with his blind students. For more than a decade, deaf children at Gallaudet's American Asylum at Hartford had been learning how to read and write. But the systematic education of the deaf-blind had never before been achieved: it was at the very frontier of scientific philanthropy, the ultimate educational feat.

Harriet Martineau, hard of hearing herself since childhood, argued that an American should undertake the experiment. As much as she disliked American manners and customs, her tour of the United States in 1834 had convinced her that only a researcher unfettered by Old World prejudices could "put away theory" and simply observe, test, and record the behavior of the deaf-blind. The "material" for this project lay close at hand, she pointed out, in the new republic's many schools and asylums for the disabled. Discovering and describing the ideas of the deaf-blind inmates might well allow an enterprising American to make "an advance in the science of Mind equal to that which medical science owes to pathology."[30]

By the time Martineau visited Boston, Howe was already thinking about this very challenge. He knew that earlier philosophers had wondered about the educability of the deaf-blind, and that the former director of the school for the deaf in Paris, the celebrated Abbé Sicard, had gone so far as to make "some rough observations" on the subject, without ever finding a promising student for the actual experiment. As Howe considered the "open question" of whether a deaf-blind child could be taught, he became increasingly intrigued; at last, he said, "I resolved to make the attempt to teach the first one I should hear of."[31]

Educating a deaf-blind child would not only be an act of extraordinary benevolence, but also, as Martineau suggested, a major contribution to philosophy and science. Because the deaf-blind were cut off from most sensory information, their minds had not been "modified" by experience. A careful observer, systematically teaching a deaf-blind child and tracking its cognitive development, could, Howe supposed, distinguish between what came into the student's mind from the outside world and what was already there, innate.[32]

Since the deaf-blind appeared to live entirely outside of language—and thus outside of culture—Howe speculated that their behavior might also establish the origins of our moral and spiritual capacities. As a believer in the essential dignity of human nature, he wanted to prove that "all the higher and nobler attributes of the soul, all that part of man which is truly in the likeness of God, is independent of sensation."[33] If he could induce a deaf-blind student to develop a strong and sensitive conscience more or less spontaneously, he could claim to have demonstrated that even the most isolated, ignorant, and deprived person is by nature perfectible.

NEITHER MARTINEAU NOR Howe invented the notion that a deaf-blind child would make a promising subject for psychological research: they got the idea from reading British and French Enlightenment philosophy. Indeed, the very concept of a psychological case study—of a "primitive" human specimen who could be observed and analyzed—came from eighteenth-century philosophers. Their fascination with "the science of mankind," with the nature and origins of the human mind, awakened Howe's interest in questions of cognition and morality, and their quest for experimental human subjects inspired his own.

"Of all the branches of human knowledge, the most useful and the least advanced seems to me to be that of man," Jean-Jacques Rousseau announced in the preface to his *Discourse on the Origin of Human Inequality* of 1754.[34] For Rousseau and his contemporaries—George Berkeley, David Hume, François-Marie Arouet (Voltaire), Étienne Bonnot de Condillac, and Denis Diderot, among others—the primary task of philosophy was to explore and explain the unknown realm of human knowledge and behavior. The proper study of man was man himself: the origin and character of ideas and judgments, language, moral beliefs, and social and political institutions.

The difficulty with this project, as these eighteenth-century philosophers realized, lies in our blindness to our own original nature. Understanding human language, judgments, religion, and morality requires that we trace them back to a primordial time before the intervention of culture. But shaped by our own individual experiences and by our civilization, by "all the changes that the succession of time and things must have produced" both in our own minds and in our society, we can neither see ourselves as nature formed us nor separate what we have learned and acquired from what we were in our "primitive state." Ironically, science and history only make the problem worse. Every "advance" made by the species takes us further from our own origins: "The more we accumulate knowledge, the more we deprive ourselves of the means of acquiring the most important knowledge of all"—knowledge of our own nature. As Rousseau lamented, "It is by dint of studying man that we have rendered ourselves incapable of knowing him."[35]

The idea that self-consciousness could itself be the subject of philosophical inquiry originated more than a hundred years before Rousseau, in the work of the French physicist, mathematician, and philosopher René Descartes. He was the first to make self-reflection the key to understanding. A metaphysician at heart, Descartes did not set out to create a philosophy of mind: he said that his real object was to lay the foundations for a proof of the immortality of the soul. But his famous assertion *Cogito ergo sum* (I think, therefore I am) placed individual human consciousness for the first time at the very center of philosophical inquiry. The Enlightenment thinkers who came after him all in one way or another took up the problem that he had defined: solving the mystery of how and where human knowledge originates, what it is, and how far it extends.

Descartes approached this problem by dividing the mind and soul from the physical body. The mind—a "thinking thing"—and the material body—"an extended thing"—consist of totally unlike substances. The body resembles a machine—a clock, say; the mind and soul are "lodged in . . . the body as a pilot in a vessel."[36] Like a workman who stamps his trademark on his product, God has imprinted on the minds of his human creations "innate ideas"—fundamental concepts such as being, number, duration, extension, form, motion, thought, and the existence of a divine Creator.[37] These clear, distinct, and God-given ideas are the foundation of all our certain knowledge; they exist alike in the blind and the sighted, the deaf and the hearing, the "savage" and the philosopher.

For all its neatness, Cartesian dualism created a problem of its own. If the mind and body, immaterial and material, are completely different substances, how do they interact? How, for example, does drinking a material martini produce disorder in the immaterial mind? By what means does mental excitement or spiritual exaltation make the heart beat faster? Descartes's answer—that the pineal gland functions as a bridge between mind and matter—failed to persuade even many of his disciples.

Fifty years later, an English philosopher, John Locke, suggested a modest alternative to Descartes's grand, metaphysically driven system: a "historical, plain method." Modeling his approach on natural science, he proposed to proceed inductively, using as evidence the operations and ideas he discovered in his own mind. By methodically retracing mental development from its highest stages back to its beginnings, he would explain human understanding; by studying the development of ideas in the mind, he would reveal the nature and scope of our knowledge.

Rejecting Cartesian mind-body dualism and what he saw as the empty notion of innate ideas, Locke maintained that our minds at birth are like blank slates—*tabulae rasae*—ready to receive information supplied by the senses. Although we have some natural capacities for organizing this information, all our knowledge ultimately comes from two kinds of experience: sensation of the external, material world and reflection on the operations of our own minds. "These two," he wrote, "are the fountains of knowledge, from whence all the ideas we have, or can naturally have, do spring."[38] Some ideas arise from one sense only, some from more than one sense, some from sense data perfected by reflection, and others from reflection alone. Simple ideas make up even our most complex conceptions, and our judgments develop only gradually, from experience.

To show how ideas received through the senses can be altered by judgments of which we are not even aware, Locke introduced into modern philosophy the figure of a hypothetical blind man. This blind man, to whom later eighteenth-century philosophers would frequently refer, was the subject of a thought experiment that had been sent to Locke in 1693 by his Irish friend William Molyneux. An astronomer and philosopher married to a blind woman, Molyneux posed to Locke this intriguing problem: Suppose a blind man who had been taught to distinguish a cube from a sphere by touch suddenly had his sight restored. Would he then be able to tell these forms apart using just his eyes?

Because Descartes believed that geometrical conceptions such as "sphericity" and "cubeness" are clear, universal ideas knowable through reason alone, he would most likely have said "yes." But Locke and Molyneux were confident that the answer was "no." Visual recognition would develop gradually, after the blind man had begun unconsciously to connect the two-dimensional images produced by his newly restored eyes with the three-dimensional forms he knew by touch. Only with time and repeated exposure to sense data would the man experience the lights and colors presented by his eyes as three-dimensional geometric forms. By remembering and reflecting upon the information supplied by his hands and his eyes, he would slowly learn how to see.[39]

Molyneux's question effectively highlighted the cognitive gap between raw sense data and judgment—between vision and seeing—because it provided a way around a fundamental difficulty in Locke's "historical, plain" method. For Locke, explaining the development of knowledge requires that we go backward, retracing the steps of understanding, rewinding the mental videotape, as it were, to the earliest stage before experience. But how can this be done? The minds of newborns are essentially unknowable. It is theoretically appealing but morally and practically impossible to perform the cruel experiment of rearing an infant in isolation from all human contact or education.[40] And self-reflection, as Locke understood and as Rousseau would reemphasize, is of limited use: because we are not even aware of many of the judgments that we habitually and unconsciously make, we cannot simply set them aside and turn back the clock on our own cognitive development. To return to the beginning, we need an experimental subject, real or imaginary.

Molyneux's brilliant problem provided that experimental subject. The model of the hypothetical blind man gives clarity and substance to the elusive notion of the *tabula rasa;* it allows us to conceptualize a mind untouched by visual experience. When we perform the thought experiment of healing the blind man's eyes, we can suddenly see past our own unconscious, habitual judgments not only about form, but also, as Berkeley would subsequently argue, about distance, motion, spatial orientation, number, and magnitude. Comparing the blind man's mental world, constructed by four senses, and the mental world of the sighted, constructed by five, we can begin to imagine how visual sense data develop over time into complex judgments. The powerful role of experience in shaping human understanding becomes apparent as soon as we reflect on what the newly cured blind man can actually see.

Molyneux's hypothetical blind man was the first experimental subject in cognitive psychology, the first in a line of experimental subjects that leads directly to Laura Bridgman. Recognizing the blind man's usefulness as a paradigm, eighteenth-century philosophers after Locke both invented and discovered sensorially deprived subjects for experiments of their own. As models of minds untouched by experience or culture, these blind and deaf subjects, along with imaginary subjects such as Rousseau's noble savage, made discussion of the origins of human knowledge, society, language, and morality possible.

Perhaps the most famous insensate subject of the time was the animated marble statue imagined by the French "sensationalist" philosopher Condillac. To show how raw sense data can turn into judgments, Condillac envisioned a statue constructed exactly like a human body, both inside and out, on which he could conduct complex—but imaginary—psychological experiments involving varying combinations of the five senses. By unlocking the insentient statue's senses one by one, beginning with smell and ending with the most important, touch, Condillac proposed to show how interactions of the senses create knowledge. As the statue's senses awakened, the statue would experience sense data as a succession of new pains and pleasures; these feelings would be transformed into memory; memory would give rise to comparison; and once the statue could compare, it could make judgments. Comparisons and judgments would eventually become habitual and, stored in the statue's memory, lead to associations of ideas. Fully awakened at last, the statue would be purely the product of sensory experience. And if the statue were "nothing but the sum of all it has acquired," might not, Condillac asked, the same be true of man?[41]

While a hypothetical blind man and an imaginary statue proved useful for thought, real subjects—living deaf and blind people on whom ac-tual cognitive tests could be performed—would of course provide more certainty. When, in 1728, an English surgeon, William Cheselden, suc-cessfully removed cataracts from the eyes of a thirteen-year-old boy who had been blind since infancy, philosophers welcomed the opportunity to verify their solutions to the Molyneux problem. As Locke and his follow-ers had predicted, Cheselden's young patient did not in fact know how to use his eyes to see. Not only could the boy not judge distance, magni-tude, or form, he could not even tell his cat from his dog.

Cheselden's blind boy confirmed the correctness of Locke's answer, but at the same time opened new avenues of speculation and experimen-tation. Would the boy ever really see? Exactly how would he learn to transform a jumble of visual impressions into ideas or to name the mean-ingless lights and colors he perceived? Condillac ended his treatise on his imaginary statue with an enthusiastic call for further experimentation on living subjects such as Cheselden's patient. Overlooking the possibility that live human subjects (unlike marble statues) might object to such ex-periments, Condillac recommended that in the future patients recovering from ocular surgery be isolated immediately inside a glass cabinet so that scientists could methodically test their responses to color, size, shape, distance, and movement.[42]

Condillac, like most Enlightenment philosophers, was primarily in-terested in the blind as models of paradigms: thinking about their sen-sory deprivations helped him conceptualize problems of perception and cognition. His countryman and contemporary Diderot went further. A profoundly influential encylopedist, novelist, satirist, dramatist, critic of art and literature, and philosopher, Diderot was fascinated by the blind and the deaf in and of themselves. In his *Letter on the Blind for the Use of Those Who See* (1749) and *Letter on the Deaf and Dumb for the Use of Those Who Hear and Speak* (1751), he set out not to solve a particular philosophical problem, but, with a sympathetic eye and imagination, simply to observe and ruminate about blind and deaf people. Watching the deaf and imagining their mental lives led him to speculate about lin-guistic theory, drama, painting, and poetry; contemplating and interviewing the blind, and even inventing stories about them, prompted him not only to address the old Lockean problems of knowledge and perception, but also to consider the relationship of perception to religion, morality, aesthetics, and language.

Diderot reasoned that if all our ideas originate in the senses, as Condillac and others argued, then a person lacking one or more senses ought to have radically different moral, aesthetic, and metaphysical ideas from someone with five senses. Indeed, a society made up of five persons, each having only one of the five senses, would be "an amusing one," for each person would have a worldview constructed by his own sensory equipment and would treat the other people as senseless. Once we recognize this, we must concede that even our most cherished ideas and beliefs are not absolute, but dependent on our perceptions. "How different," Diderot wrote, "is the morality of the blind from ours! And how different again would a deaf man's be from a blind man's; and how imperfect—to put the matter kindly—would our own system of morality appear to a being who had one more sense than we ourselves!"[43]

Diderot's speculations in *Letter on the Blind* were radical enough to earn him a hundred days' imprisonment in the Château de Vincennes. Characterizing himself as one who prefers to spend his time "creating clouds rather than dispersing them, questioning opinions rather than forming them," he posed a series of irreverent queries. What sense can the rules of physical modesty ever make to a blind man, who can see no point to covering one part of the body rather than another? Unable to recognize the beauty of the world, can the blind possibly believe in the God that sighted people worship? Given their own physical deficit, can the blind trust in a divinely ordained and perfect order of nature? And if there is for them, in their sightlessness, no difference between a man urinating and a man bleeding, can they be fully capable of human sympathy?[44]

In his approach to the deaf and blind—his curiosity about their values and perceptions, his willingness to speculate based on firsthand observations, and his conviction that studying them would provide clues to "civilized" man—Diderot had anticipated by fifty years the emergence of anthropology as a separate discipline. When a group of physicians, philosophers, colonial explorers, scientists, and teachers of the deaf joined together in 1799 in Paris to form the Society of the Observers of Man, they systematized and legitimized his imaginative improvisational methods. The centuries of "vain agitation in vain theories," they declared, had now ended. Through the study of "primitive" peoples, the new anthropologists could finally solve the old problem of human origins. By voyaging to distant lands, they would be able to travel back in time to set up "secure experiments on the origin and generation of ideas, on the formation and development of language, and on the relations between these two processes."[45]

In *The Observation of Savage Peoples*, published in 1800, the influential philanthropist, colonial administrator, philosopher, and educator of the deaf Joseph-Marie Degérando announced the program of the Society of the Observers of Man. For the "philosophical traveller, sailing to the ends of the earth," Eskimos, Hottentots, Laplanders, South Sea Islanders, Africans, and American Indians were living monuments of the primitive past. Just as studying the pyramids along the Nile could unlock the secrets of ancient Egypt, so observing these "savage" peoples would "recreate for us the state of our own ancestors, and the earliest history of the world."

For more sedentary anthropologists, there were "primitive" subjects closer to home. Among the most interesting were captured feral children—such as Peter of Hanover and Victor, the Wild Boy of Aveyron—who had apparently reared themselves alone in the forest. Disabled people, including "idiots," the blind, and the deaf, presumably also lived a kind of precultural existence. In their languageless isolation, the deaf provided especially rich speculative opportunities because, Degérando argued, "the deaf-mute is also a Savage." By studying the gestural language of people deaf from birth, the observant researcher could apprehend "in their principles the generation of our ideas."[46]

The most famous "primitive" subject of early-nineteenth-century anthropology was undoubtedly Victor, the Wild Boy of Aveyron. Discovered in 1800 digging for vegetables at night in a village garden, the

boy appeared to be a "wild savage," languageless, "unhousebroken," animalistic, completely unsocialized. Recognizing his potential importance
as a missing link between natural and civilized man, the Society of the
Observers of Man at first claimed the captured wild child for science and
humanity. Faced with the boy's apparent ineducability, however, some
members of the society concluded that the boy was not a wild child at all,
but simply a hopeless imbecile, useless to study. But Jean-Marc Gaspard
Itard, resident physician at the Paris Institute for Deaf-Mutes, where
Victor was housed, disagreed. A follower of Locke and Condillac, Itard
guessed that inadequate nurture, not defective nature, caused the boy's
apparent idiocy. Itard hoped that with proper stimulation, Victor could
be trained, and that the awakening of his apparently blank mind would
substantiate sensationalist theories of learning. If the Wild Boy could be
taught to use his perceptual apparatus, to construct meaning out of the
sensations of his eyes, ears, nose, and fingers, he would come to life like
Condillac's marble statue.[47]

At first, Victor performed surprisingly well. Once he had learned to
wear clothes, eat politely, and behave more or less conventionally, Itard
set about teaching the boy to use language. Proceeding by trial and error,
and using an elaborate system of flash cards and metal letters that Howe
would later adapt for his work with Laura, Itard within a year succeeded
in teaching Victor to associate a number of written words with objects
and to imitate a few sounds. While Victor seemed hopelessly unable to
comprehend or use speech, after a few more years of sustained work he
could recognize and write nouns, adjectives, and verbs of action, and
could even follow simple written commands, such as "pick up stone."

But then, to Itard's great disappointment, when Victor was about
seventeen he stopped progressing. In 1805, exhausted and discouraged,
Itard gave up, and Victor was pensioned off by the government to live
out his days in the care of an affectionate and motherly guardian.
Although the Wild Boy had learned to communicate by simple written signs and had shown evidence of emotional development, he
was, Itard concluded, incapable of further intellectual or emotional
growth. Considering where Victor started, he had come a long way, but

he would never fulfill the promise of Condillac's statue. Less developed even than many animals at the outset, he had been too damaged emotionally and cognitively ever to achieve anything like full humanity. The ideal experimental subject—an educable precultural being—remained to be found.

CHAPTER FOUR

Found

A DARTMOUTH COLLEGE student, James Barrett, revealed Laura's existence to the larger world in the spring of 1837. He spotted the little girl during a visit to the Bridgman farmhouse; Daniel Bridgman was serving his second term as selectman and Barrett had come on town business. Recognizing that a deaf-blind seven-year-old might have some scientific significance, he reported his discovery to the eminent physician and surgeon Dr. Reuben Mussey, a professor at the Dartmouth Medical School.

Mussey, a man of wide and eccentric interests that included vegetarianism, temperance, and the music of Handel, had evidently also read his Diderot and Degérando. He wasted no time in riding the seven miles to the Bridgman farm to examine the girl for himself. In a letter to a local newspaper he later detailed his findings. Despite her extensive disabilities, Laura could knit, sew, and correctly set the table. When presented with a silver pencil case, she quickly learned how to unscrew and reassemble its parts. Her disposition appeared kind and affectionate; she readily shared a piece of fruit with her little brothers and submitted cheerfully to her parents' direction. Throughout Mussey's visit she manifested a high level of energy and intelligence.[1]

When he came across Mussey's account in the late spring, Howe was delighted. Healthy deaf-blind children who did not suffer from more extensive brain or neurological damage were rare; in all his years working with the deaf, Abbé Sicard had never found one. But here, right in New England, was exactly the child Howe would need for his daring educational experiment. He wrote to Mussey at once, pointing out that Laura's case "might be made useful to science by throwing light upon some points of intellectual philosophy." Did Mussey agree that the girl should "be placed in some situation where the channels to her intellect will be widened, her mental powers developed & her life be made happier to herself & more useful to others?" The labor and expense of teaching her to converse and read would of course be considerable, but an attempt ought to be made, "for a human soul thus clogged & trammeled calls upon us as strongly for aid as a living man buried under ruins." Would Mussey second his proposal to educate the girl at Perkins?

Anticipating Mussey's reasonable objection that a school for the deaf would be a more suitable setting, Howe argued that, with her highly developed sense of touch, Laura would benefit from the apparatus for the blind used at Perkins. "I am confident," he wrote, "that with a child whose nervous system is well developed & whose brain in the perceptive region is of usual size & in good condition, much might be done." But would her parents have enough sense to hand her over to him? Were these simple farmers sufficiently intelligent "to perceive the advantages that might accrue to her & to science, from a course of instruction"? Could they appreciate the implications of his offer: that she would not only receive a free education, but also become an important experimental subject whose progress would be recorded with precision and care?[2]

Howe's excited and effusive letter elicited from Mussey a characteristically taciturn response. Ignoring most of Howe's questions and all of his theories, the New Hampshire doctor replied dryly: "Your Institution provides as much (I should think) as any other in such a case, & I cannot but hope you may have the opportunity of making an attempt to educate the girl."[3] Although Mussey could not himself summon much enthusiasm for Howe's project, he was willing to turn the matter back to Barrett, who agreed to revisit the Bridgmans on Howe's behalf. Taking his ambassadorial duties seriously, Barrett set out early in July both to gather more information about Laura and to sound out the Bridgmans on Howe's proposal.

Barrett, an amateur anthropologist of whom the Society of the Observers of Man could have been proud, planted himself in the Bridgmans' house for the better part of a day, taking note of all Laura's movements: she played with the pencil case again and opened his watch; she felt for the hooks and eyes on the sleeve of the dress of an unnamed lady who had accompanied Barrett; she went to a drawer, took out a box of hooks and eyes, and compared them with those on the lady's sleeve; she took off her own apron, which was pinned, and insisted that her mother replace the pins with hooks and eyes; she took out flatirons to press some muslin, but finding a bowl of potatoes in the back room, she laid aside her ironing, washed and rinsed the potatoes, and then resumed her ironing. Later she pounded mustard until it was time to set the table for dinner. When her mother signaled for her to continue pounding mustard, she inexplicably turned the pestle upside down and went on pounding with the top downward. "What these [facts] indicate relative to her mental operations you can as well determine as anyone," Barrett dutifully concluded in his report to Howe.

In addition to this catalog of trivialities, Barrett reported real news: the Bridgmans had no objection to sending Laura to Perkins. Since she had always learned easily and eagerly, they were confident that with systematic instruction she would improve rapidly. Howe could have her.[4]

FOR HOWE, THIS was the culmination of a three-year search. Diderot's *Letter on the Blind* had probably first set him off on his quest for a deaf-blind experimental subject. Howe admired the *Letter* so much that he translated it into English and had it printed at Perkins in raised letters for the blind; he could not have missed Diderot's offhand suggestion that the deaf-blind might not be the hopeless imbeciles they seemed. "Perhaps," Diderot mused, "they would acquire ideas if we could make ourselves understood to them while they were still children, in some fixed, determinate, and consistently uniform way; in a word, if we were to trace the same letters on their hands that we ourselves draw on paper and if the same meaning were invariably attached to them."[5]

As he thought about Diderot's brief hint and perhaps also about Martineau's challenge to American scientists, Howe realized that if he could find the right deaf-blind student, he would know what to do. He was, after all, an expert in teaching the blind; he had only to modify his methods to accommodate his student's deafness. Finding a suitable subject for his experiment was the real obstacle.

In 1834, just as he was beginning his search, word of a likely prospect—a young deaf-blind woman named Julia Brace—had raised his hopes. In the previous year or two she had become a minor celebrity, and when he read accounts of her, Howe thought she sounded right for his purposes. Fresh from studying Degérando's *On the Education of Deaf-Mutes*, he decided to travel at once to the American Asylum for the Deaf and Dumb at Hartford, where she lived, to see her for himself.

By the time he visited the asylum, Julia Brace's life story had been widely published. Born in Connecticut in 1807 to destitute parents, she had lost her sight and hearing after she came down with typhus at age four and a half. When her father died in 1825, shortly before her eighteenth birthday, Brace became a charity student at the Hartford asylum. After an initially stormy period of adjustment, during which "coercive measures were necessary," she yielded to the regimen of institutional life and grew docile.[6] By feeling the hands and arms of the deaf students and teachers at the asylum, she even learned to communicate in sign language. Despite her deprivations, she appeared to be perfectly content.

Lydia Huntley Sigourney, a relentlessly prolific poet who would later help make Laura Bridgman famous, was Brace's chief publicist and champion. Scorned nowadays for her cloying verses but adored in her own time as the "Sweet Singer of Hartford," Sigourney not only liked to write about children with appealing disabilities, but also (thanks to her rich husband) became one of the American Asylum's most generous and influential benefactors. In Julia Brace, Sigourney found her favorite kind of subject: an impoverished, pitiful, helpless young female whose plight inspired elevating thoughts. Moved by the idea of a deaf-blind girl more than by the flesh-and-blood young woman, Sigourney invented an idealized version of Brace about whom she produced a stream of didactic religious essays and what she called "poetic effusions."

In these writings, Sigourney elaborated a complex fantasy. On the one hand, as Sigourney imagined her, the deaf-blind girl was almost enviable. "Unchained by the senses that bind down to earth," she could commune directly with God and, like a Wordsworthian visionary, "Explore the regions whence she drew her birth,/And bathe in floods of everlasting day."[7] On the other hand, the poor girl was utterly, deliciously pathetic. Her abject dependence and her terrible isolation would inevitably move us to rise above our own petty unhappiness, to extend the helping hand of Christian charity—and, above all, to thank God that we did not share her afflictions.

Sigourney's Brace-inspired effusions struck a popular chord. In the 1830s, female victimization was becoming an increasingly familiar cultural theme in both England and the United States. Throughout the next decades, just as they would line up for exhibitions of Laura, throngs of spectators would weep over sculptures of captive women in chains, paintings of girls fading away from consumption, and melodramas in which young heroines lost—or nearly lost—their virtue or their lives. Because deafness, muteness, and blindness provided occasions for all kinds of dramatic situations and devices—pantomime, mistaken identities, miraculous cures—many Victorian novelists and playwrights could not resist adding their own creations to the sizable list of poor little blind girls and mute damsels in distress. In promoting Brace, Sigourney no doubt contributed to this trend and, at the same time, capitalized on it.

ENCOURAGED BY SIGOURNEY'S enthusiastic descriptions, Howe approached Brace with great anticipation. As soon as he saw her, however, he realized that she was useless for his purposes. Her value to the scientific observer depended on her ability to learn, but at twenty-seven, Brace was simply too old: her brain, as he explained to Sigourney, "had lost by long inactivity its flexibility."[8] Even as the embodiment of

Sigourney's sentimental fantasies, the real Brace fell short. She seemed torpid, inexpressive, and incurious; when left alone, she dozed by the hour. Like many blind people, she often sniffed objects to identify them—a useful but unattractive habit that Laura, with her damaged sense of smell, never adopted. Sigourney herself had to admit that visitors to the Hartford asylum, seeing Brace bent expressionlessly over her knitting or needlework, would "perceive nothing striking or attractive in her exterior."[9] To George Combe, Brace seemed bored and unhappy; the phrenologist William Ingalls, a subsequent visitor, reported that the "unfortunate young woman" was not only "morose and repulsive" in her aspect, but also selfish and vain in her character.[10]

The accusation of vanity is a bizarre but recurring theme in nineteenth-century accounts of blind women. Howe himself regularly criticized the "fondness for dress," fascination with ribbons and jewelry, and excessive self-esteem of some of the blind women he met.[11] As Laura approached adolescence, he began to worry that if admirers gave her trinkets or praise she, too, would succumb to this female vice: "It will require constant care and vigilance to prevent her perceiving herself to be a lion, than which hardly a greater misfortune can befall a woman," he warned in 1843.[12]

Perhaps the behavior of institutionalized blind women contributed in a small way to the perception of their vanity. Plainly dressed themselves, they naturally took an interest in the soft fabrics and intricate ornaments worn by visiting ladies. To vary the monotony of their days, female inmates may also have amused themselves (and each other) by changing their hairdos and adding decorations to their sober attire. But surely misogyny and puritanism, not anything the women did, led observers to characterize such behavior as "vain." Indeed, the accusation recalls the scene in Charlotte Brontë's *Jane Eyre*, when Mr. Brocklehurst, the director of the dismal Lowood School, commands—while his own ringletted daughters look on—that the students' hair be cut off, because curls and braids are forbidden in an "evangelical, charitable establishment."[13]

Julia Brace did take some interest in dressing fashionably, but to

Howe nothing else in her behavior suggested mental alertness. Studying
her, he found no evidence that the blind-deaf could be educated. Like the
Wild Boy of Aveyron, she had been trained—as an animal is trained—
to perform simple tasks and to obey, but Howe agreed with Itard that
real education entailed learning verbal language. True, she could communicate adequately with other deaf people in the early form of American Sign Language then used at Hartford, but for Howe, Sign was not
the real thing: a complete "arbitrary" language in which abstract ideas
could be expressed.

Like many other self-styled experts on the subject, he never understood that signs, as much as words, are fixed, complex, arbitrary sym-
bols; that Sign has its own grammar and syntax; and that it is capable of
generating an infinite number of propositions. To him, Sign was little
better than primitive pantomime, a barbaric "low" language that had the
pernicious added effect of encouraging the deaf to remain isolated from
general society in their own signing communities. Watching Brace converse in Sign at Hartford, he never doubted that although she had acquired a system of gestural communication useful in the small, tribal
world of the asylum, she had failed to learn language. For him, the great
question—"whether a blind-mute could be taught to use an arbitrary
language"—remained unanswered.[14]

Despite his disappointment in Brace, Howe did not lose faith in the
educability of the deaf-blind. She had not—as he saw it—succeeded in
learning language, but he nevertheless believed that "the trial should not
be abandoned, though it had failed in her case, as well as in all that had
been recorded before."[15] If he could only find the right student, he remained confident of ultimate success.

Howe's optimism was not simply characterological; it was also at
least partly the product of his college education. His studies at Brown,
lackadaisical as they may have been, had encouraged him to believe both
that the hand of a rational God could be seen in nature and that, in an orderly universe, scientific inquiry worked.

Howe had learned this doctrine in a course called "moral philosophy," which was taught by Brown's president, Asa Messer, a Baptist min-

ister whose real passions were engineering and politics, not theology.[16] Required for seniors by almost every antebellum American college, including Brown, moral philosophy was considered the crowning jewel of an undergraduate education. The typical course was based on a single textbook—usually, in Howe's day, William Paley's *Principles of Moral and Political Philosophy*—and set out to organize logic, philosophy of the human mind, natural and political law, and theology into a clear, consistent, ideologically moderate, and intellectually palatable whole.[17]

In his moral philosophy classes, Howe, like most other American college seniors, encountered the radical ideas of the Enlightenment, but only as tempered by a simplified version of Scottish Common Sense, a philosophy founded by the Aberdeen philosopher Thomas Reid and introduced into the United States in the late eighteenth century by John Witherspoon, the Scottish-born president of the College of New Jersey (later known as Princeton). By the beginning of the nineteenth century, Scottish realism had become the filter through which almost all American students learned philosophy.[18]

Common Sense philosophy proposed to correct the troubling excesses of post-Lockean thought: the materialism of Condillac, the radical skepticism of Hume, the idealism of Berkeley, and the scoffing of Voltaire. Rejecting the doubts of the skeptics as absurd, Reid and his followers appealed to common sense or "intuitive reason" as the ultimate tribunal of truth.[19] While Reid did not want to revert to Cartesian innate ideas, he did believe that God had furnished the human mind with faculties or powers, such as memory, reason, and perception, and with "original and natural judgments"—judgments that we cannot prove, but know to be true. Purely "the gift of Heaven," these fundamental judgments— the components of our common sense—allow all of us, Reid said, to recognize self-evident truths: mathematical axioms, moral principles, the existence of the objects we perceive and remember, the reality of causation, the existence of a divine Creator, and the testimony of our own conscience. These truths are equally apparent to all reasonable people, "the learned and the unlearned, the philosopher and the day-labourer."[20]

Common Sense philosophy flourished in American colleges in

part because it conveniently reconciled natural science with traditional morals and religion. Reid insisted that the trustworthiness of our God-given perceptions guaranteed the reliability of inductive evidence. And just as scientists could trust their experience of the material world, so also moralists and philosophers could depend on their observations of human nature. To Common Sense philosophers, the science of mind was no more speculative or mysterious than the science of body.[21]

Looking back on a Harvard education shaped by the bland precepts of Common Sense philosophy, Henry Adams would complain in 1904, when he was sixty-six, that he had reached manhood "with the certainty that dogma, metaphysics, and abstract philosophy were not worth knowing."[22] Perhaps because Howe and his friends had grown up a generation earlier and had regularly heard Channing preach, they had more respect for the usefulness of Scottish realism. College had taught them, as it had taught Adams, to scorn idle speculation. They, too, thought metaphysics a waste of time. But if their education suffered from what Emerson called "the American superficialness," it also buttressed their social optimism, stimulating them to study human nature and to reform and enlighten others.[23] For all its intellectual conservatism, Common Sense gave legitimacy to the kind of empirical psychological research that Howe wanted to do. It also guaranteed to him that the mind of a deaf-blind child would not be empty; the capacity for language and judgment would be there, waiting to be unlocked.

To Howe and his circle of Unitarian reformers, most of whom came of age in the first quarter of the nineteenth century, the quest for an experimental subject, an original human, had a Christian meaning and a practical application that it never had for European philosophers. Degérando, outlining his plan for the observation of "savage" peoples, had insisted that anthropology should be both scientific and vaguely philanthropic: "What more moving plan," he exclaimed, "than that of re-establishing . . . the august ties of universal society, of finding once more those former kinsmen separated by long exile from the common family, of offering a hand to them to raise them to a happier state!"[24] This lofty colonialist fantasy—French scientists offering the ripest fruits of enlightened civilization to their primitive brothers—had little in common with the aspirations of pragmatic social activists such as Howe, Dix, Sumner, and Mann. Paternalistic as they may have been in their own way, these Unitarian reformers wanted to use science to justify and enhance their ongoing humanitarian efforts: universal education of children, rehabilitation of criminals, and aid and education of the poor and the mentally and physically disabled. A successful wild child, an American improvement on poor Victor, would not only allow them to trace the development of judgment and language, as Martineau had suggested, but also show them the best way to educate and uplift the citizens of their own society.

THESE ALTRUISTIC AMBITIONS fueled Howe's excitement when he heard that the Bridgmans would let him try to educate their daughter. Hopeful that Laura would turn out to be the deaf-blind child he needed for his work, Howe hurriedly made plans to see her. He was eager, as he later explained, to seize the "rare opportunity" of not only helping one individual needy child, but also of trying out a plan that might benefit all deaf-blind people.[25]

Combining philanthropic business with pleasure, he set out for Hanover with a party of his friends: Rufus Choate and George Hillard, who were both up-and-coming lawyers and men of letters, and Longfellow, then a newly appointed professor of modern languages at Harvard. Since they planned to continue on through the White Mountains after Hillard delivered a commencement oration to a Dartmouth literary society, Longfellow had also invited fifteen-year-old Samuel Eliot, a cousin of the Harvard president, along for the trip. On commencement morning, July 25, Howe, energetic as always, rode out at dawn to the Bridgman farm, examined Laura, made firm plans with the Bridgmans for Laura to be sent to him in October, and returned to Dartmouth in time to spend the afternoon sitting through Hillard's oration.

Fifty-two years later, when the older men were all long dead, Samuel Eliot still remembered their trip to Hanover. Shortly after Laura's death in 1889, he described for Florence Howe Hall her father's "triumphant" return to the hotel after his successful first visit to the Bridgmans: "I perfectly recollect his exaltation at having secured her," Eliot wrote, "and the impression he made on me by his chivalric benevolence."[26]

For her part, Laura found Howe terrifying. When her mother tried to introduce her "to the noblest visitor," Laura recalled,

> I shrunk myself as hastily as I had strength. He took my tiny hand and greet[ed] me most cordially he seemed to be [such] a very unusually tall [man] to me, that it made me much repelled, because I never saw so tall a man before in my life.

Following Mussey's example, Howe tried to interest her in a silver pencil, but when he put it in her hand she became "agitated" and pushed it away. "I did not calculate his generosity and love in me," she explained.[27]

In their 1903 book, *Laura Bridgman: Dr. Howe's Famous Pupil and What He Taught Her*, Howe's daughters embellished Laura's characteristically frank account, transforming it into a scene from sentimental fiction. In their version, the little girl shyly enters the Bridgmans' parlor where the tall stranger awaits her; she trembles when he takes her hand tenderly in his, yet even in her fear she seems to understand that he is kind and gentle, and that her rescuer has come at last:

> Behind her lay the warm kitchen, the old fireplace near which stood her little chair, the cradle in which she had lain for weeks a helpless infant, kept alive through months of suffering only by her mother's care and devotion. If any prophet had foretold what a future lay before that little trembling child standing alone in silent darkness, linked to her kind only by the bond of a common humanity, who would have given him credence![28]

The more pedestrian reality—that during that first hurried encounter Howe made a rapid medical evaluation of Laura, came to financial terms with her parents, and settled on arrangements for her arrival—does not make the occasion less momentous. Although he did not then—or perhaps ever—fully realize it, in happening upon Laura, Howe had struck gold. Quite by luck he had found the ideal deaf-blind experimental subject. In later years, to prove that his teaching methods would work on most any deaf-blind child, he would look for others like her. But until the advent of Helen Keller, she would have no equal.

·⊰[CHAPTER FIVE]⊱·

Awakening

ON OCTOBER 12, 1837, two months before Laura's eighth birthday, the
Bridgmans brought her by horse carriage and stagecoach to Boston.
Overwhelmed with the burden of her care, exhausted by her demands,
and hopeful that Howe might somehow help her, her parents were ready
to part with her.

When the Bridgmans arrived at the Perkins Institution on Pearl
Street, Howe and his sister Jeannette, who kept house for him during his
bachelor years, were waiting. At the moment of separation, Laura panicked. Later, she remembered clinging to her parents until she was pulled
away from them: "They attempted to avoid me as quickly as possible. At
the very moment that I lost them I burst in bitterest tears." Hoping that
Laura might calm down if she discovered the treats her mother had
packed for her, Jeannette Howe dragged the screaming child toward her
trunk, but, Laura recalled, "my poor heart was too full of sorrow and
trouble."[1]

In her memoirs, Laura claimed that she had passed her early days in
Boston in an agony of homesickness and fear. She had shed "an abundance of tears," and time "elapsed so very heavily and painfully that I
did not know what to do with myself." Howe, on the other hand,
marveled at her swift and easy adjustment. In a letter to an institutional

benefactor written just ten days after her arrival, he exulted that his "very interesting" new charge was "as happy as a bird & apparently as intelligent as many children of her age with all the senses."[2] To the Bridgmans he wrote that although she had at first been "rather dull" and had cried two or three times, after two days she "became very lively & I do not think she repines at all for home now."[3] By early December, he could assure them that she was "always contented, generally cheerful & very often excited & mirthful, which she manifests by laughing and frolicking."

Perhaps there is truth to both versions. Separated from the routines of home, utterly disoriented at first, Laura no doubt lost all sense of time. Suddenly, inexplicably, her world—always somewhat unpredictable—had become chaotic: unknown hands pushed and pulled her about; unfamiliar food appeared under her nose; she stumbled against objects as she groped about strange passageways and rooms. Each of those early hours at the institution must have seemed to her an eternity. But faced with this terrifying new reality, she proved astonishingly resourceful. When homesickness overcame her, she soothed herself by taking up her familiar knitting. Recognizing a willing surrogate mother in the school matron, Mrs. Smith, Laura quickly learned to run to her for help if she dropped a stitch. Within a few days, Laura had also grown "strongly attached" to her twenty-two-year-old teacher and constant companion, Lydia Drew. As Laura began to feel safer, her curiosity awakened, and she started to investigate her new home. Before long, as Howe observed, there was no stopping her explorations: "Her little hands were continually stretched out, and her tiny fingers in constant motion, like the feelers of an insect."[4]

Soon Laura began to recognize a pattern to her days. At 6:00 A.M., Drew would put a china basin and a "nice sponge" on a chair in their small bedroom, and Laura would take a cold sponge bath. After Drew had dried her with a towel and combed her hair, Laura would dress, make the bed they shared, and help tidy the room. Next, out of deference to the squeamishness of the sighted, she would tie a green ribbon around her head to cover her damaged eyes: this "courtesy" was expected of all Perkins students. Once she had completed these preliminaries, she accompanied her teacher to the school assembly for morning prayers. At nine o'clock, lessons would begin, usually with Drew, but sometimes with "Dr." or with "Miss D." and "Dr." together. In accordance with Howe's philosophy that blind children needed vigorous exercise to offset their natural torpor, her studies were interrupted for periods of calisthenics, long daily walks with her teacher, and outdoor play with the other blind girls. At 6:00 P.M., the formal school day ended; bedtime was at eight o'clock.

Laura blossomed under this regimen. After only a few months, Howe was able to report to the institution's trustees that his new pupil— "a very pretty, intelligent, and sprightly girl"—had made astonishing progress. "An object of peculiar interest and lively sympathy," she was already running about the house, up and down stairs. She frolicked with the other children; dressed and undressed herself "with great quickness and precision"; behaved properly at meals; and not only could recognize "every inmate of the house by the touch," but also greeted each of them affectionately. Her sewing, knitting, and braiding equaled those of any other child. These achievements were "as nothing," however, compared to the interesting "mental phenomena" that she presented:

> a quick sense of a propriety; a sense of property; a love of approbation; a desire to appear neatly and smoothly dressed, and to make others notice that she is so; a strong tendency to imitation, insomuch that she will sit and hold a book steadily before her face in imitation of persons reading.[5]

Although Howe could not yet claim that she knew right from wrong instinctively, he was certain that she never took anything—not even an apple—without permission.

And miraculously, Laura was learning language. She had come to Perkins, as Howe said, "a human soul shut up in a dark and silent cell," with "all the avenues to it . . . closed, except that of touch."[6] From the day of her arrival, the door of that dark cell had slowly but steadily begun to open. Within three months, she had learned a hundred common nouns and was starting on verbs; after a year, using finger spelling, she could communicate in sentences; by the end of 1839, she was writing letters home. Together, she and Howe were making educational history.

From the beginning, Howe resolved to avoid the mistakes that he thought had been made with Julia Brace at the Hartford asylum. Laura had arrived in Boston already using a small number of gestures to convey her wants and to name particular people or things. She indicated her father, for example, by drawing her hand across her face to represent his whiskers; she mimed buttering a piece of bread when she was hungry. Although he could easily have built on this "natural" language, Howe refused that temptation. Signing, he believed, was a "poor and imperfect language" that "hampered and dwarfed" mental growth.[7] Even if Laura learned to sign proficiently, she would remain in essence a "primitive." Imprisoned in a world of "material existences and tangible qualities" and incapable of comprehending abstract ideas and moral principles, she would be little better than an imbecile, as useless to science as the Wild Boy of Aveyron. Only if she acquired verbal language could Howe make Laura the subject of the psychological research that Harriet Martineau had challenged Americans to undertake: Only by watching "this most interesting child" learn words would he be able to make "curious & valuable observations—upon the innateness of ideas—the succession of ideas &c."[8]

But teaching words to a child like Laura presented almost insuperable difficulties. Without sight or hearing, how could she possibly comprehend the nature of arbitrary language or the function of words? How could she make the connection between an arrangement of letters and the thing those letters symbolized? Where was the key that would unlock what Helen Keller later called "the mystery of language": that everything has a name and that each name gives birth to a new thought?[9]

Howe's solutions to these difficulties have rightly been hailed as ingenious. Adapting Itard's methods, Howe divided the learning process into sequential parts. The first step was to sensitize Laura's fingers. In anticipation of her arrival, he ordered the school's printing department to make up paper labels in raised letters for common objects—knife, spoon, key, bed, chair, stove, door, and the like—and pasted these labels on the objects that they named. During Laura's first lessons, he repeatedly moved her fingers across the labels, so that she could become accustomed to the feel of the embossed words. "So keen was the sense of touch in her tiny fingers," he reported, "that she immediately perceived that the crooked lines in the word 'key,' differed as much in form from the crooked lines in the word 'spoon,' as one article differed from the other."[10] Next, to begin to create an association between word and thing, he handed her the same words on detached labels. Before long, she could place the word "key" next to the labeled key and the word "spoon" next to the labeled spoon. As she worked, her teachers signaled to her that she had succeeded by patting her head or that she had erred by gently knocking her elbow.[11]

At first, in matching labels to objects Laura was only using her excellent memory to imitate what her teachers had done. But after a few days, she suddenly began to see that the pattern of lines on each slip of paper in some way represented the object on which it was placed. "This was shown," Drew observed, "by her taking the word 'chair' and placing it first upon one chair, and then upon another, while a smile of intelligence lighted her hitherto puzzled countenance, and her evident satisfaction assured us that she had mastered her first lesson."[12]

Howe's next step was to introduce the idea that each pattern of lines on the labels was made up of component parts—letters. He began by cutting the *book* label into four pieces, each with a letter on it. With Laura following his motions by feeling his hands, he arranged the pieces in their familiar order, b-o-o-k; then he scrambled the letters and let her rearrange them. Once she had mastered that skill, he ordered four sets of the alphabet for her in metal type, with the letters in high relief. These letters could be set in rows into a metal grid; by moving the letters around on the grid, Laura could begin to spell out words. Working with the metal type not only helped her to memorize the order of the alphabet, but also allowed her to practice arranging and rearranging letters into the words she had learned from the printed labels.

In her famous autobiography, *The Story of My Life,* Helen Keller claimed that awareness of language had come to her as a revelation, in a thrilling flash of comprehension. As Anne Sullivan held one of her hands under the pump spout and spelled w-a-t-e-r into the other, Keller had suddenly understood that the name for the "wonderful cool something" flowing over her hand was w-a-t-e-r: "That living word awakened my soul, gave it light, hope, joy, set it free!"[13]

Although there was no single word that triggered Laura's understanding, she, too, experienced a "eureka!" At first Howe had felt as if he were doing little more than teaching "a very intelligent dog a variety of tricks": the poor child "sat in mute amazement, and patiently imitated every thing her teacher did," but the process had seemed entirely meaningless and mechanical.[14] Still, he did not give up. Day after day, week after week, he and Drew kept Laura at work, arranging and rearranging letters and matching words to objects:

It was as though she were under water, and we on the surface over her, unable to see her, but dropping a line, and moving it about here and there, hoping it might touch her hand, so that she would grasp it instinctively.[15]

Then, after two months, Laura suddenly made the connection. The line "did touch her hand, and she did grasp it; and we pulled her up to the light; or rather, she pulled herself up." All at once "the truth began to flash upon her—her intellect began to work—she perceived that here was a way by which she could herself make up a sign of anything that was in her own mind, and show it to another mind." Now she was no longer a dog or a parrot: "It was an immortal spirit, eagerly seizing upon a new link of union with other spirits!" She had overcome the "great obstacle," and henceforth, Howe said, "nothing but patient and persevering, but plain and straightforward efforts were to be used."[16]

Laura made another leap forward in her third month of instruction, when she learned to finger spell. Unlike Sign, which is a complete gestural language, finger spelling is simply a method for using hand

shapes—the manual alphabet—to spell ordinary words. Purportedly invented in Spain by Trappist monks who wanted to converse without
breaking their vow of silence, finger spelling had proved useful to the
European deaf, especially for communicating with the hearing. It also
became popular as a means for inaudible conversation in girls' schools:
the British theologian John Kitto, who had come to rely on finger talking
after he lost his own hearing at age twelve, observed in his 1848 memoir
that at dinner parties he could count on most "educated ladies" to be fluent on their fingers.[17]

Gallaudet learned finger spelling during his studies at the Institution
for Deaf-Mutes in Paris, and later included the method in the curriculum
of the American Asylum, where it was used as a supplement to Sign, the
school's principal language. When Howe visited Julia Brace at Hartford,
he noticed some of the deaf children using the manual alphabet. Now
that Laura could spell with metal type, he was curious to see whether she
could also spell with her fingers. As an experiment, he sent Drew to learn
the technique from a deaf graduate of the Hartford asylum, George Loring, who taught it to her in a single afternoon. The next day, she began to
teach the manual alphabet to Laura, showing her the position of the fingers that corresponded to each of the metal type letters. Once Laura had
mastered the letters, Drew began teaching her words by presenting her
with objects and spelling their names into the palm of Laura's left hand.
To prove that she understood, Laura would then spell the new word in
metal type and place it next to the appropriate object.

As she learned to finger spell each word, Laura quivered with excitement. Placing her right hand over her teacher's so that she could feel
every change of position, Laura waited for each letter "with the greatest
anxiety": the moment she mastered the new word, "her anxiety changed
to delight." Once again she seemed to make a cognitive leap. "I shall
never forget the first meal taken after she appreciated the use of the finger alphabet," Drew wrote many years later. "Every article that she
touched must have a name; and I was obliged to call someone to help me
wait upon the other children, while she kept me busy in spelling the new
words."[18] With mounting elation, Laura realized that by means of the

manual alphabet she could not only spell words rapidly, but also for the first time converse with fellow human beings.

Howe had been away when Drew introduced Laura to finger spelling. As soon as he returned, he too learned the manual alphabet, and before long the other teachers and many of the blind girls had mastered the method. With so many people to talk to, Laura acquired new words with dizzying speed. To her vocabulary of a hundred common nouns, she quickly added verbs, and then adjectives. She used her first verbs, "open" and "shut," in her first sentences—"open door" and "shut door"—gleefully dramatizing the words with the action. Finally, Drew taught her proper nouns, and in a short time Laura knew the names of everyone at the institution.

Teaching her abstract and relational words of course proved trickier. Drew spent hours putting a ring *on* a box, *on* a hat, and *on* a desk; Laura finally seemed to get the idea, but became completely confused when her teacher then put the ring *in* the box or *in* the drawer. The idea that matron, too, was *in* the house only added to her bewilderment. But once again, after patient practice and repetition, she had a linguistic revelation. "In this case," Howe wrote, "perception seemed instantaneous, and the natural sign by which she expressed it was peculiar and striking: she spelt *o n* then laid one hand *on* the other; then she spelt, *i n t o*, and enclosed one hand *within* the other." Howe did not need to worry about whether she had really got the idea, for "when the true meaning dawns upon her mind, the light spreads to her countenance."[19]

Drew, who conducted most of Laura's lessons, marveled at her pupil's enthusiasm: "Such is her eagerness to find out one's meaning, such a zealous cooperation is there on her part, that it is a delightful task to teach her." One day Laura would be stuck on adjectives of quality; the next she would be dancing about the room pointing out objects that were *hard* or *soft*. After hours of puzzlement—at the notion, for example, that "left hand" did not mean only her own left hand—she would suddenly "catch" the general idea. All at once she could spell the name of her arms, hands, fingers, feet, and ears as they were touched and name them, *right* or *left*. But then she might baffle her teacher by pointing to her own nose and asking whether it was *right* or *left*. Drew was especially amused by Laura's coining of words. No sooner did her teacher make her understand the meaning of *alone*, for example, than Laura demanded to go for a walk with another little girl, *al-two*.[20]

By the end of 1838, Laura was intoxicated with language. She reminded Howe of "a child placed in foreign country, where one or two persons only know her language, and she is constantly asking of them the names of the objects around her."[21] Her growing vocabulary transformed her into a social being. Now, when she met a friend in the school's corridors, there would be "an inter-twining of arms—a grasping of hands—and swift telegraphing upon the tiny fingers, whose rapid evolutions convey the thoughts and feelings from the outposts of one mind to those of the other." Even in her solitary moments, Laura could entertain herself by using the manual alphabet to conduct imaginary dialogues, to recall "past impressions," or to practice spelling new words:

> If she spells a word wrong with the fingers of her right hand, she instantly strikes it with her left, as her teacher does, in sign of disapprobation: if right, then she pats herself upon the head and looks pleased. She sometimes purposely spells a word wrong with the left hand, looks roguish for a moment and laughs, and then with the right hand strikes the left, as if to correct it.[22]

In her second year at Perkins, Laura began to progress from simple two-word statements to longer and more complex sentences. At first she seemed to have no feel for English syntax. Recorded by her teachers, her early sentences resembled the pidgin English of congenitally deaf children, who often reverse standard word order: if she wanted bread, for example, she would say, "Laura, bread, give"; if she wanted water, she might finger spell "Water, drink, Laura."[23]

As her vocabulary expanded, however, she began to sound (in her finger spelling) less like a deaf child and more like an English-speaking toddler. Applying grammatical rules uniformly and logically, as small children often do, she regularized irregular verbs (*seed* instead of *saw;*

eated rather than *ate*), irregular plurals (*boxs* and *ladys*), and idiomatic prepositions (a sofa has sides, so the teacher must be sitting *in* it, not *on* it). Like most three- and four-year-old hearing children, she also had trouble using auxiliary verbs, especially in questions. Howe cited, "K. is sick. When will K. well?" as typical of her early errors.[24] But even such "mistakes" are proof of her progress. They show that she was not simply parroting sequences of words, but rather using internalized syntactical rules to create sentences of her own.[25]

After several months of constant drilling—many hours every day— Laura began to master standard English grammar, with all its exceptions, irregularities, and peculiarities. Since Howe had no experience teaching the deaf, he did not recognize the magnitude of her achievement simply in generating sentences in standard word order. Nor, of course, did he understand that she was using grammatical constructions that often baffle deaf children: plurals, negatives, comparatives, conjunctions, and subordinate clauses. After Laura's second year of instruction, Howe remarked that, at ten, she had the language skills of a three-year-old.[26] But a complex sentence from that period—"When Laura did go to see mother, ride did make Laura side ache"—shows a command of English syntax that sighted deaf students struggle to attain.[27]

Once Laura had learned the principal parts of speech—nouns, verbs, adjectives, prepositions, and conjunctions—Howe thought it time to teach her to write, "to show her that she might communicate her ideas to persons not in contact with her."[28] Teachers at the school had already had plenty of experience teaching writing to the blind, and Howe and Drew simply adapted their usual method of writing instruction to fit the needs of a deaf-blind child. To form letters, Laura learned to use a French writing board—a letter-sized sheet of stiff pasteboard with horizontal grooved lines. Blind students at Perkins wrote by inserting the board between two pages of writing paper so that the grooves could serve as guidelines. Holding the pencil in one hand, they used the other to control the point of the pencil and to keep the spaces between the letters and words. Laura learned the mechanics of writing fairly easily, but had more trouble understanding the purpose. She submitted to writing drills with a "mute amazement" and "docility" that her teachers found "amusing to witness," but "when at last the idea dawned upon her, that by this mysterious process she could make other people understand what she thought, her joy was boundless."[29]

Late in 1839, after a few months of instruction in writing, Laura, unaided, wrote her first letter home:

> laura will write letter to mother laura will ride with father. laura will make purse for mother laura will sleep with mother and father mother will love and kiss laura now laura will carry letter for mother laura will go see wales [Howe's sister, Maria Wales] laura will go home.[30]

Howe admitted that this was "indeed, a very rude and imperfect letter, couched in the language which a prattling infant would use." Nevertheless, it heartened him, for "it shadowed forth, and expressed to her mother, the ideas that were passing in her mind."[31] (If he noticed the expressions of homesickness and longing for parental affection in Laura's letter, he made no comment.)

By her twelfth birthday, Laura could manage long, complex sentences, including negatives, contrasting tenses, and, most surprisingly, conditional "if" clauses. Deaf children have so much difficulty using the English conditional that Howe's accounts of her achievements met with disbelief, especially among teachers of the deaf. In a public lecture, one skeptic, the director of a state school for the deaf, charged that Howe's reports savored of "humbug," and that Laura could not possibly "conceive the force of the word IF in a complicated sentence." "Tell this to the marines," the director scoffed, "for the sailors won't believe it." Howe, ever sensitive to criticism, fired back with an example of Laura's conversation, as recorded by Drew:

> I must go to Hanover to see my mother; but no, I shall be very weak to go so far; I will go to Halifax if I can go with you. If

doctor is gone, I think I will go with Jennette; if doctor is at home, I cannot go, because he does not like to be left alone; and if J. is gone, he cannot mend his clothes and fix all things alone.[32]

Let the doubting director read this sentence, Howe taunted, "and if he still thinks Laura talks like a parrot, let him come and see her, and watch her beaming and changing countenance as the sentences fall from her fingers, and he will be as glad to retract his uncharitable sentiment, as I shall be to forget the discourteous form in which he uttered it."

As Laura mastered more words and sentence patterns, she began to organize and categorize ideas, information, and perceptions. After her second year at Perkins, she could count to a hundred, add and subtract, measure time both in days and weeks, and divide the school day by recesses and mealtimes. In 1840, she began to study multiplication and geography. Although her damaged sense of smell had blunted her ability to taste, she learned to distinguish different degrees of acidity, and to tell cider from wine and wine from vinegar. She understood, at least in a rudimentary way, the concepts of comparative size and quality, the relationships between nouns and pronouns, and the names for different mental states: remembering, forgetting, expecting, hoping.

The more she learned, the more rapidly Laura improved. She seemed, Howe said, "to advance in a geometrical ratio, for every step which she takes aids her in that which is to follow."[33] After four years of education, she could summarize what she had read and invent short stories of her own. She kept a daily journal in which she noted "every little event which transpires in the institution" and maintained an extensive correspondence with friends and admirers. (As an adult, she even tried her hand at poetry.) An avid collector of long words, she soon commanded a vocabulary that, according to Howe, was the equal of any twelve-year-old's, "but more matured."[34] And she hardly ever made a spelling mistake.

Although her language never sounded completely idiomatic, at the age of twelve she was—according to the standards of modern linguistics—language-proficient. Obedient to fundamental grammatical rules, she could generate an infinite number of syntactically varied, context-appropriate sentences. Using either finger spelling or writing, she expressed emotions, asked and answered questions, responded to present events, remembered the past, speculated about the future, and simply mused.

By the end of 1840, Howe was ready to hail his experiment as a success. Publicly guarded (though privately confident) at the beginning, he had warned the Perkins trustees in 1837 that he could make "no sure prognostic" about Laura. While no pains or expense would be spared to develop the "moral and intellectual nature of this interesting child, and no opportunity lost, of gathering for science whatever mental phenomena her singular case may furnish," he could not promise results.[35] But after three years of instruction, no doubt remained. Though the "darkness and the silence of the tomb" had surrounded her; though "no mother's smile called forth her answering smile"; though "no father's voice taught her to imitate his sounds," she had emerged from isolation to join the human community. "By the cheerful toil and patient labor with which she gleans her scanty harvest of knowledge, she reproves those who having eyes see not, and having ears hear not." Rescued from a living death, she was a case study in the resilience of the "immortal spirit," the limitless potential of the mind, and the transformative power of enlightened education.[36]

Howe announced his scientific conclusions in his annual reports for the years 1840 and 1841. There were no surprises. Laura's education proved exactly what he and his progressive friends had believed all along: that human understanding is more than simply the product of experience. Howe had already been certain of this on October 21, 1837, just nine days after Laura's arrival in Boston, when he wrote to a friend:

> We have a very interesting little girl here who is deaf, dumb & blind. . . . The immortal spirit within her, although in darkness & stillness like that of a tomb, is full of life & vigor, is animated by innate power & triumphantly refutes the doctrine that the

soul is but a blank sheet upon which education & experience write everything.[37]

Now, three years later, he could make the claim publicly. Although Laura had been cut off from almost all sense data, she had learned to communicate with others, to exchange ideas through language. Her accomplishments showed that the mind is not simply passive, an empty slate. True, Locke had been partly correct when he wrote that if we observe how children learn languages,

> we shall find, that to make them understand what the names of simple *Ideas*, or Substances, stand for, People ordinarily shew them the thing, whereof they would have them have the *Idea;* and then and repeat to them the name that stands for it, as *White, Sweet, Milk, Sugar, Cat, Dog.*[38]

Deprived of sight and hearing, Laura had been excluded from the process that Locke described—and still she had learned language. To overcome her sensory deficits, she must have had dormant but inborn mental powers and capacities. These powers were not innate ideas as Descartes understood them, but, Howe claimed, the "innate intellectual *dispositions*" described by Common Sense philosophers.

Recapitulating the teachings of Common Sense philosophy, Howe argued that Laura's case proved that both the universal human tendency to use language and the basic elements of language itself were divine gifts: "When God created man, His son, an heir to so much of His own nature, He gave him the tendency to use language; He gave him even its rude elements, and endowed him with mental powers, by the right use of which he might improve and perfect them."[39] Howe explained that in some cases—"simple savages," the deaf, and the blind—physical or cultural deprivations stunted language development, but education could always activate latent mental capacities. Just as Molyneux's blind man, restored to sight, would eventually learn to judge distance and recognize color, so also the deaf could be taught to talk, read, and write, and the

blind to learn geography and arithmetic. While Laura's sensory deprivations had stalled her intellectual growth, they could not destroy her natural faculties. Once Howe had awakened her mind, her progress was
assured.[40]

To sympathetic audiences, Howe grounded this explanation of
Laura's mental growth in the popular nineteenth-century science of
phrenology—also known as craniology, or "head-reading." Like many
other Unitarian progressives of the period, Howe had embraced
phrenology as the key to human behavior. He claimed that before he
knew phrenology, he had been groping in the dark, as blind as his pupils,
and that he owed all his success at Perkins "to the light derived from
from phrenological views of mental philosophy."[41]

As Howe understood and practiced it, phrenology involved more
than measuring bumps on the head; it was a systematic and complete new
science of the mind. In 1800, the Austrian anatomist Franz Josef Gall
first postulated phrenology's basic tenet: mental activity originates in the
brain, which is the organ of the mind. The brain, as Gall and his disciples
described it, was not unitary, but made up of "congeries" of organs that
corresponded to thirty-seven innate and independent mental faculties,
including feelings (such as hope, combativeness, and veneration) and intellectual faculties (such as language and knowledge of form, size, comparison, and causality). Each faculty had its seat in a definite region of
the surface of the brain and, in any person, the size of a particular region
revealed the development of the corresponding faculty: religious people
had large organs of veneration, for example, and aggressive people,
large organs of combativeness.

Phrenologists claimed that the most up-to-date scientific methods—
brain dissection and case studies—supported their theories and, at the
same time, established the physiological basis for Common Sense psychology. By mapping onto the brain the mental "intuitions" and "dispositions" described by Thomas Reid, phrenologists aimed to free
psychology from the introspective tradition of Descartes and Locke:
anatomy could finally trump philosophy. And true to the spirit of Common Sense, phrenologists boasted that their teachings were unpreten-

tious, straightforward, and accessible to everyone. As Howe said, metaphysical authors and "mystical psychologists" gave him a headache, but phrenology was "clear, simple, natural."

ALONG WITH MANY other liberal New Englanders—progressives such as Edward Everett, George Bancroft, Henry Ware, George Ticknor, Horace Mann, and Channing himself—Howe had been converted to phrenology by Gall's German collaborator, Johann Spurzheim, who came to America in 1832, intending both to spread the phrenological gospel and to study the people and customs of the nation. An indefatigable proselytizer, Spurzheim stayed in Boston for six weeks, lecturing to full houses. When he suddenly collapsed from his exertions and died, Boston and Cambridge hailed him as a martyr to science.[42]

Spurzheim's protégé George Combe, an energetic and engaging Edinburgh barrister, quickly took up his leader's fallen mantle. To propagate the faith, Combe toured the eastern United States in the years 1837–1840, delivering scores of lectures to overflowing audiences. By the time of his American tour, Combe's *The Constitution of Man considered in Relation to External Objects*, published in Edinburgh in 1828 and a year later in Boston, had already become the phrenologists' Bible: more than 700,000 copies had been printed in English. Howe and his friends read *The Constitution of Man* with the enthusiasm of the converted. "I know of no book written for hundreds of years which does so much to 'vindicate the ways of God to man,'" Mann wrote in 1837; its doctrines "work the same change in metaphysical science that Lord Bacon wrought in natural." Howe admired Combe as "one of the first intelligences of the age," and praised his treatise as "one of the greatest of human productions." Until Combe's death in 1858, Howe turned to the benevolent Scotsman for advice; Combe was for him, as for Mann, a father figure, intellectual mentor, and trusted friend.[43]

Howe and his friends valued phrenology as a system for analyzing personal and social problems and prescribing remedies. They feared that theirs were perilous times: the masses showed a frighteningly "impatient and restless spirit," and the nation, under Andrew Jackson's rabble-rousing administration, seemed dangerously unstable. The spread of radically egalitarian ideas, the beginnings of Irish immigration, the rise of entrepreneurial capitalism and "Mammon-worship," and a wave of religious revivalism had overstimulated American brains. "There is no country on earth," Howe warned in 1837, "whence the brain and the nervous system of man is kept in such a state of turmoil and excitement, as in ours; . . . verily, we have sown the wind, and are already beginning to reap the whirlwind." Unless reformers, guided by phrenological principles, could strengthen social and political institutions and calm the fevered brains of an agitated, ignorant, greedy, and selfish populace, the "unhallowed and disgraceful scenes of riot, burning, and bloodshed, which have disgraced our land within the last five years" would inevitably portend "greater horrors to come."[44]

Phrenologists never spelled out precisely how their science would temper "extravagant notions of personal and political liberty" and quiet the religious frenzy aroused by evangelical revivalism. Perhaps they hoped that phrenology could change people's behavior simply by offering a scientific, organic justification for moderation and self-restraint. Howe always believed that a phrenologically informed society would inevitably be a good society. Protected from excessive cerebral action and unhealthy "nervous excitation," its citizens would learn to live harmoniously, with all their propensities, faculties, and sentiments "in their due proportion and natural order," and with all the organs of their minds in healthy equilibrium.[45]

For Howe, phrenology provided not only a recipe for individual and societal improvement, but also a complete explanation of Laura's intellectual progress. Of course she had learned language: directly behind her eyes lay her organ of language, ready to become active and grow larger. Because of this organ, she, like everyone else, had "an irresistible impulse" to "*exteriorise*" herself through language. A living human being "is necessarily a speaking being," Howe believed, and a deaf-and-dumb child must have "the same mental organization, the same desire for language" as a hearing child. Although Laura had come to him "hardly having more intelligence than a dog," he had never doubted that she shared the common human desire and capacity for associating names with things and thoughts of things.[46]

After measuring Laura's head in 1838 and again a year later, Combe verified Howe's explanation of her mental growth. Combe's initial examination of the contours of her skull had indicated to him that she had naturally vigorous moral and intellectual powers. Guided by phrenological principles, Howe had discovered a way to activate those latent powers by conveying knowledge to them. When Combe returned to Perkins the next year, he found that her continued education had, as expected, produced a "distinct increase" in the size of Laura's brain. The coronal, or moral, region showed particular growth, both absolutely and in relation to her animal region—the region of faculties common to humans and lower animals. The large anterior lobe of her brain indicated that her faculties of knowing and reflecting were well developed, as were her Self-Esteem, Love of Approbation, Cautiousness, Firmness, and Conscientiousness. Given the size of her organs of Order, her tidiness came as no surprise. In short, Laura had started out with a promising head, and as she acquired language, her brain had grown bigger and better.[47]

IN THE LIGHT of recent psycholinguistic research, Combe's phrenological approach is not quite as silly as it sounds. Neuroscientists today might laugh at his examination of cranial bumps, his list of mental faculties, and his fanciful map of the brain, but they would agree with a surprising number of his basic assumptions. Experiments in this century with apes, infants and children of various ages, the linguistically impaired, and the deaf, for example, seem to support the phrenological notion that humans have a species-specific predisposition for language, a kind of grammatical "mental software" located in the brain. Recent studies have also provided evidence for the phrenological view that in all children (including the deaf) language acquisition is a developmental imperative, like walking. In *The Language Instinct*, Steven Pinker speaks for most modern cognitive scientists when, updating the old anti-

Lockean phrenological line, he argues that "language is not a cultural artifact that we learn the way we learn to tell time," but instead "a distinct
piece of the biological makeup of our brains."[48]

Where psycholinguists today would disagree fundamentally with
Howe is in assessing the importance of Laura's first two years. Howe
wanted to believe that those years were lost. When some of his critics,
doubting the miracle of her rapid progress, argued that she must have
remembered some English, he insisted that she had long ago forgotten
the little she had known. For all practical purposes, she was no different,
he said, from a congenitally deaf-blind child.[49] A strong body of recent
linguistic literature on "critical periods" suggests, however, that when
Laura began her instruction she knew a great deal more than either she
or Howe realized. Comparisons of the congenitally deaf with those who,
like Laura, lost their hearing during childhood show that even a brief exposure to language (including Sign) makes subsequent language acquisition far easier. Laura's two years of hearing almost certainly made the
crucial difference.[50]

According to the critical-period hypothesis, children learn language—as they learn a variety of physical and cognitive skills—according to a maturational timetable. Successful language acquisition must
take place more or less on schedule. If there is too long an interruption
or delay, a window of learning opportunity closes. The critical period
for language is early childhood—perhaps before age six or seven. After
that, the capacity for language tends to wither away as the brain begins
to lose plasticity or whatever neural capacity it is that ordinarily pro-
duces children's explosive growth in language. By the onset of puberty,
it is too late. The cases of the congenitally deaf-blind, wild children, and
abused children locked in solitary confinement have shown that if crucial
linguistic milestones have not been reached by a certain age—probably
about twelve—the child can no longer catch up. An adolescent without a
mother tongue will never be capable of generating mature, grammati-
cally coherent sentences.[51]

Unlucky in many other ways, Laura was fortunate in the timing of
both her illness and her Perkins education. During her first twenty-six

months, with normal exposure to language, she passed through developmental stages on schedule. As an infant she learned to distinguish between meaningless background noise and the meaningful words spoken by members of her family. While she could still hear her own vocalizations, she developed from a cooing, gurgling, sound-imitating infant into a phrase-making toddler. Then, when her sudden and complete hearing loss deprived her of all auditory feedback, she began to sound and behave—as Howe said—like a congenitally deaf child. But her short experience of speech had left a neural residue. Although she had forgotten how to *use* language, her brain had been successfully "programmed" for grammar.[52]

Laura and Howe both believed that he had taught her all she knew, but in fact they had not had to start at the beginning: the foundation of her learning had been laid long before she arrived at Perkins. And when he reintroduced her to language in her eighth year, she was still young enough to make up for lost time. Her brain had not matured beyond the point of learning: the window was still partly open. Her language never sounded natural. There was something strange, almost eerie about it, as if it had been produced by an intelligent being from another world. (Contemporaries called it "quaint" and "Latinistic.")[53] But thanks to her initial two-year exposure to language and the timeliness of her Perkins education, she was able to express herself with clarity, fluency, precision, and even at times with eloquence.

Still, there are aspects of Laura's language acquisition that no cognitive theory has fully explained. As many linguists and psychologists admit, schematic models can go only a small way toward describing the enormously complex process of learning human language. One problem is that individuals vary. In 1986, after studying the language abilities of three deaf-blind adults, psycholinguist Carol Chomsky concluded that there are no "representative" cases: individual aptitude and personal characteristics such as inquisitiveness and drive turned out to be important but indefinable factors in the ability of each of her deaf-blind subjects to learn and use language.[54]

In Laura's case, a peculiarly "passionate" and "unquenchable" curiosity drove her to master language and find out about the world. Drew and Howe both remarked that she seemed compelled to know things. Like a preschooler in the throes of the "why?" stage, she besieged them with questions. Why do flies fly with wings instead of walking on the floor? Why don't fish have legs? Does the horse know it is wrong to go slow? Why don't horses and flies go to bed? Why do flies not have names like boys and girls do? Why do cows not draw? Is the worm afraid when the hen eats him? Why do cows have two horns? To push two cows?

Her teachers struggled to come up with satisfactory answers, for it was "painful" for them to arouse "such a vivid curiosity as now exists in her mind, and then baulk it."[55] Laura trembled with excitement during her lessons. Every new word, every bit of information, sent her darting from one thought to the next in a feverish hunt for understanding. Reluctant to dampen her enthusiasm or frustrate her, Howe sometimes let Laura seize control of the curriculum. "No definite course of instruction can be marked out," he admitted. "Her inquisitiveness is so great, that she is very much disconcerted if any question which occurs to her is deferred until the lesson is over." Often she led Howe and Drew "far away from the objects" that they had commenced with. If in a lesson on metals, for example, they told her about lead, she would want to know about the effect of eating it, about lead pencils and lead birdshot, and then about why people shoot birds. And it was hard to put her off. When she came upon a Latin book printed in raised letters, she made herself ill trying to make sense of it. Even after Howe explained to her that the book was in a foreign language, she pleaded to be told the meanings of the strange words.[56]

Waiting for answers was an agony. When one of her female teachers could not figure out how to explain the meaning of *Yrs respectfully,* a phrase that Laura had discovered in an embossed notice, Laura said that she could not bear the suspense of not knowing: "I will ask doctor, for I must know." Howe noticed that in reading, she refused to pass over a new word or guess its meaning from the context, but instead grew "very uneasy," and ran around, shaking her hands until she found someone to explain it. Mentally exhausted at times, Laura often wished she could stop her mind from racing. "I cannot help to think all days," she complained. But then, as if driven onward, she resumed her questioning: "Why cannot I stop think? do you stop . . . think? Does Harrison stop . . . think now he is dead?"[57]

Where did this inquisitiveness come from? Of course, the most obvious answer is simply that she was extraordinarily intelligent. Howe naturally preferred a phrenological explanation: he argued that the structure of Laura's brain made her so remarkably curious. Innately excitable, restless, and bright, she was deeply frustrated by her sensory deficits and correspondingly desperate to compensate for them:

> Her spirit, apparently impatient of its narrow bounds, is as it were continually pressing against the bars of its cage, and struggling, if not to escape, at least to obtain more of the sights and sounds of the outer world.[58]

When Granville Stanley Hall, the first American child psychologist, examined Laura in 1879, he found her "perpetual craving" for knowledge disturbing. Influenced by the pioneering German psychologists with whom he had studied, he came up with a clinical diagnosis: she suffered, he said, from "question-mania." (He even had a German name for this condition: *Grübelsucht*, a mania for racking one's brains.) Hall speculated that residual memories of seeing and hearing stimulated her compulsive inquisitiveness:

> We may recognize in Laura's strange and insatiable curiosity, especially about things which others see and hear . . . some sort of sub-conscious reminiscences flashing through the sad background of her childish recollections.[59]

Psycholinguists today might be inclined instead to search for a neurological explanation. They might, for example, hypothesize that the reawakening of Laura's "language organ" caused her brain to operate in a kind of compensatory cognitive overdrive.[60] Or, if they credited Stanley Hall's claim that Laura's curiosity seemed pathological, they might wonder if the streptococcal infection that robbed her of sight and hearing also triggered obsessive-compulsive symptoms. Considering her fanatical orderliness as well her inquisitiveness, a diagnosis of "Pediatric Autoimmune Neuropsychiatric Disorders Associated with Streptococci"—PANDAS—is not altogether far-fetched.[61]

Laura's questions could also have sprung from a reservoir of pent-up emotion. Perhaps confusion, anger, frustration, and anxiety fueled her burning need to know. Think of all she did not understand. She could not at first have comprehended where she was, what had become of her parents, or why they had abandoned her. She had lost Tenney. The familiar fields and streams of the New Hampshire countryside had vanished. When, if ever, would she go home again? Later, as she began to learn language, she must have asked herself why the other blind children could talk with their mouths when she could not. Surely she wondered why she did not sleep and study with the rest of the girls. And behind all her questions about the names and meanings there may have been a deeper and more painful bewilderment: why was she not like other children?

WHETHER ITS SOURCE was intellectual, neurological, or emotional, Laura's curiosity ignited an extraordinary gift for language. Once Howe gave her access to words, her powers of comprehension, memory, and concentration allowed her to become—and express—a more developed self. With language, she could name and assert that self, make requests, form complex relationships, and let her feelings be known. She learned to complain. Requesting and collecting information, she began to piece together a safer, richer, and more coherent reality. Language transformed her silent, unpredictable, invisible world into a place of causality and order. Asking questions, conversing with others, recording her thoughts and emotions, she could at last start to make sense of things. She could discover where she stood.

And language, of course, made Laura famous. Moved by Howe's reports of the early 1840s, admirers from around the world wrote to him, asking for specimens of her writing. A few lines from her hand represented to them the triumph of the human soul against "utter darkness." She was a living refutation of Calvinist determinism and Lockean materialism, an embodied argument, Howe said, "stronger than cold philosophy." Her acquisition of language proved that modern education worked, that humans were perfectible, and that the optimism of the reformers was neither naïve nor presumptuous. If Laura could be rescued, anyone could. Sporting "joyously in the light of knowledge," she was a beacon to others, for whom, Howe wrote, she shone "as a lamp set upon a hill, whose light cannot be hid."[62]

CHAPTER SIX

The Angel

IN OCTOBER 1842, Howe received a congratulatory letter from the great British historian and social critic, "the Sage of Chelsea," Thomas Carlyle. Although the two had never before met or corresponded, Howe, eager to publicize his work, had sent Carlyle a copy of his most recent account of Laura: the *Tenth Annual Report of the Trustees of the Perkins Institution* for the year 1841. Carlyle was deeply touched by the story: "Few things that I ever read have interested me more than this of your dear little Laura Bridgman;—probably one of the beautifulest phenomena at present visible under our sun." Howe's rescue of a child, "isolated, as within fivefold iron gates, from all men and all things," struck Carlyle as almost miraculous. "One knows not what act more like a god's the art of man can accomplish," he wrote, "and yet I believe it is rather, and first of all, the virtue of man; his love, his patience, his long-suffering mercy, fruitful in all manner of arts and expedients."[1]

Carlyle admired Howe for penetrating a "Labyrinth deep as the centre of the world" and, like Daedalus, giving wings to an imprisoned child. But it was Laura who fascinated him:

The good little Girl: one loves her to the very heart. No Goethe's Mignon, in most poetic fiction, comes closer to one than this poor Laura in prose reality and fact. A true angel-soul and breath of Heaven, imprisoned as none such ever was before.

Carlyle imagined that Laura's disabilities had protected her from worldliness. Deaf to praise and blind to the world's attention, she was as pure and innocent as Eve before the Fall. He counseled Howe to guard her against flattery, so that she would always remain a "poor, simple Grace Darling."[2]

THIS WAS JUST the enthusiastic response that Howe had been hoping for when he decided in 1840 to use his *Ninth Annual Report*—the report that would make Laura and him both famous—to begin publicizing her rescue. At eleven years old, she had advanced so far that he no longer needed to hesitate; he could confidently expand the brief accounts of her in his earlier reports into a complete history of her background and miraculous progress. Curiosity about her was already building. Intrigued by his preliminary reports of the late '30s, people were suddenly asking to see her and to know about her. "So general is the interest which she has excited, and so numerous are the inquiries concerning her," Howe explained in the introduction to his *Ninth Annual Report*, "that I have thought it would be showing proper respect to the public . . . to publish . . . a short history of her case."[3]

In the early '40s, Howe energetically publicized his work with Laura, sending copies of his annual reports around the world and enlisting the endorsements of well-connected friends. Recommending the reports as "a noble contribution to humanity," Charles Sumner, George Ticknor, Francis Lieber, and Horace Mann forwarded the reports to influential ministers, phrenologists, physicians, professors of moral philosophy, and writers in the United States and abroad.[4] Howe's old friend and mentor Edward Everett, while serving as ambassador to the Court of St. James's from 1841–1845, spread the word in England, as did George Combe, who wrote to Howe from Scotland in 1841 to assure him that his name was now well known throughout Great Britain. Laura's case, Combe said, was "spoken of with deep interest and admiration in every society," and the British public "very much admired" the "universally attractive" story of her rescue.[5]

The portrait Howe painted of Laura soon charmed the world. Within ten years, a Boston newspaper would claim that her name was probably known "to a larger number of persons than that of any female person in the world, unless we except the Queen of England."[6] Indeed, it is difficult to find any mention of her in the nineteenth or early twentieth century—whether in histories of Boston, the asylum movement, and deaf-blind education, or in biographies of the Howes—that does not attach the epithet "famous" or "renowned" to Laura's name. The testimonials to her reputation are too numerous to catalog: her education "has attracted more attention than that of any living person" (*Memorial History of Boston*, 1880); "to the benevolent of all lands the history of Laura Bridgman has been a familiar story" (*New York Times*, 1883); "her story is too well known to need repetition" (*Reminiscences* of Julia Ward Howe, 1899); her progress "was the theme of world-wide comment and discussion" (*Boston Post*, 1881); "Laura Bridgman has been the cynosure of public attention and interest" (record of the proceedings of a public meeting, 1881); "her name has become familiar everywhere" (*Encyclopædia Britannica*, 1911).[7]

After the publication of the *Ninth Annual Report*, articles celebrating her began to appear regularly in newspapers, women's and children's magazines, and evangelical miscellanies. As the editors of *The Mother's Monthly Journal* for January 1841 remarked, no mother could read a description of Laura "without having her most tender sympathies excited; and we could not furnish a more interesting story for children."[8] *The Youth's Magazine* hailed her as "one of the most touching exhibitions of early suffering that can well be imagined." With her cheerful demeanor, "little delicate hand," and winning ways, she was a "most affecting object."[9] Her pleasing appearance moved a correspondent of *The New York Commercial Advertiser* to ecstasies of overstatement: "Slender and delicately formed, with beautiful features and fair complexion, so graceful were her motions, so animated her gesticulation, and so full of life was her countenance, that but for the green ribbon bound over her sightless

orbs, you [would] have called her one of nature's most gifted children."[10] In *The Power of the Soul over the Body, Considered in Relation to
Health and Morals* (1845), a widely read and influential book of moral
philosophy, George Moore praised her as a "human spirit untainted by
the loveless experiences of this selfish world." "How rapid the progress
of this unshackled soul in divine learning!" he exclaimed. "How raptur-
ous its joy at the wonders of wisdom everywhere visible! how unutter-
able the fullness of its sympathy with heavenly affections!"[11]

Laura's sensory deprivations provided an irresistible opportunity for
popular poets, who lamented the music she could not hear and the flowers, mountains, rivers, and sunsets she could not see. "In vain for thee,
the Rainbow paints the sky,/Or Flora decks the smiling earth in green,"
one poet wrote in a typical evocation of her suffering. "Silence, and
darkness, in their sad embrace,/Thy mind entomb, and banish every
grace."[12] Like the tract writers, religious poets discovered Christian
meaning in her terrible plight:

> He, in mysterious Providence, with hand
> Of matchless love, commanded Light no more
> To visit thee, fair child, and the delicate air
> Forbade to play upon thine ear's soft harp.
> And yet, how happy thine imprisoned spirit!
> For in its heaven-born freedom it may hold
> Unveiled communion still with Him, of light
> The Fountain pure,—of melody and joy.[13]

And of course Lydia Sigourney, disability's most prolific lyricist, found
inspiration as well as delicious pathos in Laura's rescue from isolation
and darkness:

> So little daughter, lift thy head,
> For Christian love is nigh,
> To listen at thy dungeon-grate,
> And every want supply.

Say, lurks there not some beam from heaven,
Amid thy bosom's night?
Some echo from a better land,
To make thy smile so bright?[14]

ENTICED BY WHAT they read, sightseers began lining up by the hundreds to get a look at Laura: on July 6, 1844, at the peak of her popularity, a record-breaking crowd of eleven hundred came to get a look at her. Part of her appeal lay in her strangeness. Displayed at Perkins, she was a freak, as odd and amazing as General Tom Thumb and the Fiji Mermaid, on view at P. T. Barnum's museum. At the same time, she was a scientific phenomenon, a living monument to Yankee ingenuity. Her rescue not only fostered patriotic pride, but also encouraged enlightened reform. Above all, Laura provided the occasion for Christian sympathy. Helpless but cheerful, the little deaf-blind girl from New Hampshire could not fail to melt hearts and awaken soft feelings.

Howe framed his detailed reports of the early 1840s to capitalize on every aspect of the public's growing fascination with Laura. Hailed as both landmark documents in educational theory and as masterpieces of narration, his most famous reports—those of 1840, 1841, and 1842— wove together observations of Laura's physical, intellectual, and moral development with meditations on the spiritual significance of her progress.[15] Recognizing that her terrible privations aroused both "tender compassion" and "great curiosity," and that her achievements inspired wonder, he alternated scientific and sentimental rhetorical styles in these reports, writing by turns as the objective philosopher, the fond surrogate father, the tireless teacher, and the pious moralist.[16]

Howe's descriptions of Laura's life in New Hampshire, her adjustment to life at Perkins, and her attempts to master language read like anthropological reports of encounters with "savages": in a tone of interested detachment, he invited readers to marvel at a primitive but extraordinary creature. For the benefit of the learned, he included lengthy speculations on the nature of language and the workings of the human mind. Detailed explanations of his teaching methods not only demonstrated his own ingenuity, but also provided educators with a blueprint for teaching the disabled. And the sentimental passages in which he rhapsodized on Laura's delicacy, sweetness, and sincerity fed the general public's appetite for angelic heroines and uplifting pathos. By shaping Laura's life into a narrative of suffering, rescue, and redemption, he transformed her into an object lesson in the efficacy of enlightened benevolence and the power of the human spirit. Small, pitiful, pretty, and good, she offered "a beautiful and pleasing exhibition of the powers of the Soul . . . and the triumph of the mind over all material bonds & trammels."[17]

The emotional and literary centerpiece of Howe's narrative was his description of Laura's first visit from her mother, after an eighteen-month separation. Howe contrived his account to recall a venerable tradition of similarly harrowing parent-child recognition scenes: Telemachus and Odysseus, Lear and Cordelia, the biblical blind Tobit and his long-lost son, Tobias. Howe's tour-de-force depiction of the reunion moved his readers to tears. Subsequent newspaper and magazine reports would invariably excerpt it to illustrate the pathos of Laura's story.

Howe had staged the scene to heighten its emotional intensity. "Desirous of learning . . . all he could" of the workings of Laura's mind, he decided not to tell her of her mother's impending arrival. Like a spectator at a play, he simply watched the drama unfold:

> The mother stood some time, gazing with overflowing eyes upon her unfortunate child, who, all unconscious of her presence, was playing about the room. Presently Laura ran against her, and at once began feeling of her hands, examining her dress, and trying to find out if she knew her; but not succeeding in this, she turned away as from a stranger, and the poor woman could not conceal the pang she felt, at finding that her beloved child did not know her.

Gradually, after her mother gave her various articles from home, "a vague idea seemed to flit across Laura's mind, that this could not be a stranger." Feeling her mother's hands again, she turned first pale, then red. As hope struggled with painful uncertainty—"and never were contending emotions more strongly painted upon the human face"—the truth "flashed upon the child . . . as with an expression of exceeding joy she eagerly nestled to the bosom of her parent."

As a further test, Howe signaled Laura to leave her mother and follow him. She obeyed instantly, but with "painful reluctance," clinging to him in bewilderment and fear. The moment that he relented and returned her to her mother, Laura "sprang to her arms, and clung to her with eager joy." When the time came for Mrs. Bridgman to leave, Laura again showed her resolute but loving nature. Sobbing, she accompanied her mother to the door, where she stopped to search for the matron, Mrs. Smith, who could always comfort her. Grasping the matron with one hand, Laura held on "convulsively" to her mother with the other,

> and thus she stood for a moment—then she dropped her mother's hand—put her handkerchief to her eyes, and turning round, clung sobbing to the matron, while her mother departed with emotions as deep as those of her child.[18]

The valiant, anguished little Laura of this heart-wrenching scene was not entirely Howe's invention. In the sentimental British and American literature of the period, the suffering-but-happy child had long been a familiar figure. Whether blind, mute, consumptive, lame, orphaned, abandoned, captured by Indians, or enslaved on a plantation, the pathetic child featured prominently in the fantasies of suffering and rescue that animated many popular literary works. Sometimes the little sufferer was a boy, a frail Tiny Tim or a male Cinderella like Dickens's Oliver Twist or young David Copperfield. Later in the century it would be a mare, Black Beauty. But most often the victim was an uncomplaining girl, a Little Nell, Little Eva, Little Dorrit, Little Match Girl, or Little Princess. In general, little girls made the most appealing victims, for, as Howe explained, when the "sufferer is a child—a girl—and of pleasing appearance, the sympathy and the interest are naturally increased."[19]

In Howe's day, stories about lovable little victims were a staple of most American literary diets. While Hawthorne and Melville struggled to find an audience, the sentimental productions of Lydia Sigourney, Susan Warner, Harriet Beecher Stowe, and Maria Cummins were snatched up by readers (a growing number of them leisured middle-class women) who relished the pious emotionalism of domestic novels, moral tales, captivity narratives, and "poetic effusions." The popularity of such fanciful and lachrymose reading suggests how far Americans had strayed by midcentury from the intellectual rigor, patriarchal authority, and gloomy doctrines of colonial Calvinism. New England's fierce eighteenth-century divines would have recoiled from the pleasant literary moralizing that delighted their nineteenth-century descendants. But by the time Howe was in college, old-style American Calvinism had had its day. Changing religious practices and beliefs now encouraged the popular taste for sentimental fare.

Unconstrained by puritanical scruples about the pleasures of light reading, Unitarians were among the earliest, most inventive, and most prolific American purveyors of uplifting stories. Howe grew up hearing instructive anecdotes from the pulpit and reading didactic secular stories. He was steeped in the sentimental rhetoric of self-improvement literature and conduct books. Their characteristically florid metaphors—rudderless ships tossed on "the perilous oceans of life," and wrecked on the shoals of selfishness; beacons of light guiding lost souls through dark and stormy nights; seeds of goodness shriveling in the dry soil of greed—had taken root in his own figurative prose style.[20] In the popular moral tales of Maria Edgeworth, Catherine Sedgwick, and Hannah More, he had encountered dramatic accounts of the natural piety of orphans and the intuitive godliness of deaf and blind children.

These good little disabled children—cheerful, reverent, and unselfish—would become the fictional progenitors of his own version of Laura Bridgman. Like her literary counterparts, Laura was, Howe said, "the instrument of great good." By setting an example of self-improvement "under the worst difficulties" and joy "under the darkest cloud," she had the power to awaken "kindly emotions" in others. The

"silent show of her misfortunes" would furnish his readers with an opportunity to feel sympathy, act charitably, and thus prove "how much of
goodness" there was in them.[21] Laura herself was both victim and moral
exemplar, redeeming others from selfishness and inspiring them to emulate her own cheerful resignation. Rescued from a living death, she had
in turn become a rescuer.

ALTHOUGH HE HAD been raised on pious rhetoric, it is impossible to
know how seriously Howe took it. Even in his private correspondence,
he tailored his tone to suit the audience and occasion. (As the director of
a charitable institution, he understood the importance of appealing to the
religious sentiments of the wealthy and influential.) When addressing
devout benefactors, he wrote with a ripe religiosity. Joking with more
worldly friends, he could be sardonic and irreverent. He fiercely de-
fended the optimistic doctrines of liberal Unitarianism against Calvinistic attacks, yet he seldom went to church. Although he worked and
socialized with morally introspective reformers and intellectuals, he
never acquired the New England habit of agonized self-scrutiny. But
however shallow or tenuous his attachment to religion may have been,
he knew how to tell an inspirational story. Whether from conviction, cal-
culation, or literary custom, he tailored his account of Laura to suit the
conventions of that familiar genre.

TO TRANSFORM HER life into a pious fiction, Howe had to deny or explain away all Laura's imperfections and problems: unpleasant realities,
after all, could spoil a pleasing moral tale and disfigure an idealized heroine. For his purposes, Laura had to be perfectly and innately good. Accordingly, he claimed that she was "one of those who have the law
graven upon their hearts; who do not see the right intellectually, but perceive it intuitively." She gravitated to the right, he said, "as naturally as a
stone falls to the ground." In a navigational metaphor borrowed from
the conduct books, he compared her conscience to a compass: "As at
midnight and in the storm the faithful needle points unerring to the pole,
and guides the mariner over the trackless ocean," so did her conscience

"guide her to happiness and to heaven." Perhaps in compensation for her disabilities, God had endowed her with moral intuition to guide her "in her dark and silent pilgrimage through time."[22]

Although her privations were horrible, Howe insisted that Laura herself did not make an upsetting or depressing spectacle. Indeed, she accepted suffering joyfully. Despite her isolation from others, she delighted in banter, jokes, and "games at romp." With a warmhearted and "beautiful spirit of charity," she took pleasure in nursing the sick, to whom she was "most assiduous in her simple attentions, and tender and endearing in her demeanor." Sitting by the side of one of her little friends, whether at her needlework or her studies, she would "break off from her task every few moments, to hug and kiss them with an earnestness and warmth . . . touching to behold."[23]

Howe claimed that unlike ordinary children, Laura never complained or cried from selfish vexation and seldom from physical pain. The "fountain of her tears" flowed only for others, when her companions suffered or her teacher was grieved.[24] An example to those who take their sight and hearing for granted, she counted the blessings she had. In fact, her whole life was "like a hymn of gratitude and thanksgiving":

> She rises uncalled at an early hour; she begins the day as merrily as the lark; she is laughing as she attires herself and braids her hair, and comes dancing out of her chamber as though every morn were that of a gala day; a smile and a sign of recognition greet every one she meets; kisses and caresses are bestowed upon her friends and her teachers; she goes to her lesson, but knows not the word *task;* she gaily assists others in what they call housework, but which she deems play; she is delighted with society, and clings to others as though she would grow to them; yet she is happy when sitting alone, and smiles and laughs as the varying current of pleasant thoughts passes through her mind; and when she walks out into the field, she greets her mother nature, whose smile she cannot see, whose music she cannot hear, with a joyful heart and a glad countenance.[25]

Howe's relentlessly rosy description leaves out any mention of Laura's occasional willfulness, her furious impatience with slow finger spellers, and her outbursts of violence. The reports convey nothing of her fear and loneliness, or of how exhausting it was for her teachers to be constantly with her, spelling the answers to her endless questions, letter by letter, into her hand. Glimpses of the real child appear only in the letters and journals written by visitors, teachers, and Laura herself.

One of the many sad truths omitted by Howe was that the other blind children at Perkins did not always want to play with Laura. Many of them had learned finger spelling to communicate with her, but they naturally preferred spoken conversation with one another. Relying on sound for much of their own pleasure, they often rejected the company of a speechless deaf girl. Inevitably, Laura felt hurt and angry. On an evening visit to the school in 1839, William Ingalls, a phrenologist, saw her retaliate when a group of blind children refused to let her join their outdoor game. Enraged, she slipped inside and shot the bolt of the door, locking them out. When the missing children were finally discovered hours later, Drew punished Laura in the manner Howe recommended: she withheld all communication and affection until Laura, frantic with loneliness, showed sufficient contrition.[26]

Laura was less repentant in June 1841, when she wrote in her journal: "Saturday I bit Sumner because he squeezed my arm . . . he was very wrong." The "Sumner" she referred to was none other than the future senator from Massachusetts, Howe's best friend, Charles Sumner. "Sumner is not gentle like Doctor [Howe]," she later complained to her teacher. "Why does Doctor want Sumner to come here if he is not gentle? . . . I do not like or love Sumner; I do not care for him."[27] Did an important visitor like Sumner feel free to handle a blind girl roughly or take liberties with a mute who could not object? If so, Laura was apparently prepared to defend herself. When her teacher reproved her another time for running away from a visiting phrenologist, Laura would have none of it. "Man was not kind to me, and troubled me, and I did not like to have him put his hand on my head."[28]

In the light not only of Howe's idealizing, but also of the relentless pressure on her to live up to her image, Laura's feistiness is surprising. Although she could not read the letters she received, she objected on principle to Howe's opening her mail. "Doctor was wrong to open little girl's letters," she protested. "Little girls open theirself." Not all her teacher's exhortations could convince her that selfishness was a crime. Even the warning that "ladies do not love selfish girls, and she would not be loved when she grew old if she were selfish" failed to change her opinion that a little selfishness could be a good thing. Her teacher told her that her mother would be sorry if she misbehaved, but Laura resisted the emotional blackmail. Although in fact she seldom saw or heard from Mrs. Bridgman during this period, Laura insisted, "My mother will love me."[29] When one of her teachers explained that in her sentence, "I, & J[eannette], & Doctor went in the boat," the "I" should come after "Doctor," Laura balked at this grammatical self-effacement. "Why must 'I' come last? I rode *between* Doctor and Jennette."[30]

Behind the angelic mask that Howe had fashioned, the tough little farm girl survived. When a mouse came into the room where she was sleeping, she triumphantly reported that she had "walked on it, and stamped very hard . . . and he was very dead and could not move." (Drew had trouble believing this until she discovered the "very dead" remains.) Carlyle's little "angel-soul" was also not above pushing and pinching when she was impatient or irritated. Her teachers constantly reproached her for striking them and for pushing the blind children who got in her way or on her nerves. Under the pressure of lengthy moral exhortations or her teacher's refusal to speak to her, Laura would cry, repent, and apologize, only to lose her patience and sin again another day.[31]

Some of Laura's aggression surely sprang from frustration, but much of it must have been a reaction to an infuriating sense of vulnerability and a fear of abandonment. Her mother, overwhelmed by domestic responsibilities and exhausted by the birth of six younger children (five of whom survived), found less and less time to visit or write. Laura's tentative, imploring letters suggest how hurt she was by her mother's increasing neglect:

Dear My Mother:

   May I come with Miss Drew to Hanover if I will be very
good and not trouble mother? Do she want me come to see her?
I will try to be good at Hanover. . . . I send love to mother. . . .
Will mother be very glad to see me and Drew? . . . I can sew and
study and write and knit.[32]

But when Laura finally got to Hanover in October 1841, for the first time
since 1839, she found that no one could communicate with her: her father, as distant as ever, had no interest in learning finger spelling, and her
mother's attempts were halfhearted. When Tenney visited, he and Laura
happily resumed their outdoor excursions, but of course he could not
finger spell, either. Much as she loved being with him again, hunting for
eggs in the barn was not the enthralling activity it had once been.

   As Laura waited for the vacation to end, boredom engulfed her. She
missed Perkins and the intellectual stimulation that Howe provided. Ma-
rooned in Hanover, she could talk only of the prospect of a visit from
"Doctor":

   I think much about Doctor, I want to see him. I cannot wait till
   he comes. I am in hurry till Doctor come. Why did he go? Does
   he know I want to see him very much? I think Doctor does not
   love me to go away . . . he must come to see me quick. I think
   much about him at all times.[33]

In truth, despite his frequent absences from Perkins, Howe was now the
emotional center of her life. Overbearing and irritable with other adults,
he could relax around children, who always brought out the best in him.
For Laura, he was the most desirable of companions, playful, inventive,
and responsive to her questions.

   Her attachment had grown even stronger that year after she came to
live in the director's apartments with him and his sister. Howe's daughters claimed that between 1841 and 1843, when he married, his household
revolved around Laura: she "enjoyed his constant companionship" and

"was like a daughter to him, the pet of all the friends who visited him."[34] He frequently told Laura that she was his daughter, and she came to see him as an affectionate substitute for her own frightening and distant father.

Inevitably, Laura had lost the childhood home of nostalgic memory. Her stultifying time on the family farm made her count the days until she could return to "Doctor" and "the Institution." The next year, when her teachers proposed that she spend her vacation at home, Laura preferred to visit Drew's family in Halifax, Massachusetts, or to stay in Boston with Howe and his sister. Laura recalled that her mother had wept to see her go after the last vacation, and "was very sad" when they parted. But Laura no longer clung to comforting dreams of return and reunion: "Was [my mother] silly? She cannot teach me at home, I should be very dull and forget all."[35]

Despite Howe's fondness for comparing Laura's condition to imprisonment behind iron gates and entombment in an underground vault, neither he nor her teachers seem to have understood the emotional repercussions of her physical condition. While he was away on a five-week trip to South Carolina, Georgia, and Kentucky to promote education for the blind, Laura suffered agonies. When he finally returned, she "cried with joy; and her nervous excitement deprived her fingers for a while of the power of language."[36] Even short separations could undo her. Years after the event, she recalled panicking when Drew left her for just a few minutes in a Boston confectioner's shop. Finding herself alone among strangers, Laura had made a frightful "shriek noise." Drew rushed back in, mortified, and punished Laura for creating a public disturbance. The teacher's reproaches echo in Laura's reflection on the scene: "I doubt not," Laura later wrote, that the other people "must have felt disgusted to think that there was a wild beast who had entered into the shop."[37]

In fact, her teachers often criticized her expressions of strong emotion as animalistic. They reproached her for "wild" behavior and urged her to restrain her temper and moderate her nervous excitement. Most of all, they objected to the "uncouth," growling sound of her voice. Like

many other deaf children, Laura often vocalized, sometimes unconsciously and sometimes deliberately, to get attention, express excitement,
or simply let off steam. Her teachers scolded and punished Laura to
make her stop these "unladylike," "rude," and "disagreeable" noises.
They said her "bad" noises made her sound like a wolf and urged her to
please Howe by learning to stay "still and gentle."[38]

At first Laura objected to this silencing. "Some of my noises are not
bad, some are pretty noises. I must make noises to call someone," she argued, pointing out that "God gave me much voice." She also tried her
best to make her voice acceptable. One day, after promising to be quiet,
she made a whispered noise. "That was with my tongue," she explained
to her teacher, by way of justification: "I made your smooth noise." But
by 1845 it had become clear that Laura could not acquire a soft girlish
voice and would not—or perhaps could not—give up vocalizing. Forced
to compromise, Howe agreed that at set times she could shut herself in a
closet and "indulge" in making noise.

Perhaps she enjoyed this small victory, but it came at a cost. Despite
her early attempts to defend her voice, Laura eventually accepted the
view that her "bad" noises made her seem like a beast. In refusing to be
quiet and "gentle," she believed she had chosen wildness. It is not surprising then that on exhibition days, when her teachers barricaded her
behind settees to protect her from the press of the crowds, she assumed
that the spectators needed to be shielded from her. "Are ladies afraid of
me?" she asked.[39]

Laura's loud noises, so disruptive of her public image, were only one
aspect of a more general aesthetic problem. Howe wanted his readers to
appreciate the pathos of Laura's plight, but he did not want to frighten or
repel them. He understood that while the idea of a pitiful little deaf-
blind girl had sentimental appeal, the reality of severe disability was not
pretty. In fiction a heroine might have a slight (usually curable) lameness,
a picturesque wasting disease, or a self-imposed muteness, but she would
never display "shocking" or distasteful symptoms or behave in an unseemly fashion. If the heroine was blind, her eyeballs looked normal; if

she was deaf, she stayed completely mute. Enucleated eyes and "barbaric" noises like Laura's had no place in pleasingly pathetic stories.

Howe had directed a school for the blind long enough to know that manifestations of disability could be unnerving to "normal" people. He himself felt uncomfortable around the deaf, whose noises and "barbaric" signing repelled him. While he was not squeamish about blindness, he knew that the very idea of damaged eyes can be horrifying, the stuff of nightmares and Greek tragedy. Although he did not suffer from such primordial fears, he did share another common worry: that the blind, not seeing themselves seen, would behave strangely or embarrassingly; that they were, as Martin Luther had said, incapable of shame.[40] Diderot had made a similar argument, theorizing that those who cannot see have no reason to be modest in dress or behavior. Of course, Howe knew that in reality the blind are at least as concerned about their appearance as the sighted. But he had also observed understimulated blind children engaging in behaviors—licking and sniffing objects, and rhythmic, rocking body movements called "blindisms"—that some observers might find disturbing. (Deprived of visual stimulation, limited in their physical activities, and subject to boredom and loneliness, some blind children may, as the child psychoanalyst Dorothy Burlingham has put it, "make use" of their own bodies to compensate for a lack of experiences in the external world.)[41]

In painting his idealized portrait of Laura, Howe carefully addressed the fears of his able-bodied audience. He reassured his readers that she had none of the distasteful habits—real or imagined—of other deaf and blind people. He could say truthfully that after she learned finger spelling she had shown no inclination to use the "primitive" sign language of the deaf. And he simply denied that her voice bothered him. In his reports, he transformed her noises—the "bad" ones that he had tried so hard to suppress—into endearing and distinctive little sounds, intelligent noises that were nothing like the "meaningless" growling of other deaf people. Laura vocalized, he said, as a way of naming her intimate friends—"for one a chuckle, for another a *cluck*, for a third a nasal sound, for a fourth

a gutteral, &c." Although the sound of her frequent laughter was not always "agreeable," it was more "natural" than that of other deaf people.
In any case, it was healthful, providing her with the pulmonary exercise
necessary to prevent respiratory disease.

Howe admitted that "the shrivelled remnants of what were her eyeballs" did not make an "agreeable" sight, but he assured the public that
a "clean green ribbon" always concealed Laura's disfigurement.[42] No
clumsiness in her movements, untidiness in her clothing, or impropriety
in her behavior betrayed her blindness. Indeed, he said, few children
took so much care about their appearance:

> Never, by any possibility, is she seen out of her room with her
> dress disordered; and if by chance any spot of dirt is pointed out
> to her on her person, or any little rent in her dress, she discovers
> a sense of shame, and hastens to remove it. She is never discov-
> ered in an attitude or an action at which the most fastidious
> would revolt, but is remarkable for neatness, order, and propri-
> ety.[43]

Once Laura understood a rule of polite behavior, Howe said that she
never again transgressed. Informed, for example, that it was "disagreeable to others" for her to blow her nose at the table, she positively
blushed at having given offense and never repeated her faux pas. And not
once had she offended the sensibilities of others by uncovering her un-
sightly eyes in public.[44]

Howe also addressed the disconcerting possibility that a deaf-blind
girl might have—or, worse yet, display—erotic feelings and desires.
Many of his readers were well acquainted with Nydia, the beautiful blind
slave girl in Edward Bulwer-Lytton's wildly popular novel of 1834, *The
Last Days of Pompeii*. No doubt they had been shocked—but intrigued
and titillated, too—by Nydia's "fierce," "uncontrolled," and "passionate" amorousness. "As darkness . . . favours the imagination," Bulwer
had suggested, "so, perhaps her very blindness contributed to feed with
wild and delirious visions the love of the unfortunate girl."[45] Perhaps

they shared the fantasy (epitomized by D. H. Lawrence in his famous story "The Blind Man" and recapitulated by Raymond Carver in "Cathedral") that relying on the sense of touch makes blind people more sensual than the sighted, and that the "unspeakable intimacy" of their knowing touch has a "hypnotizing effect" on the sighted.[46] Howe himself worried that institutionalized children might "indulge" in masturbation or other forbidden sexual activities, the necessary "evils" of life in a sexually segregated institution.[47]

But in Laura's case, he insisted, there was no cause for anxiety. An "unsophisticated child of nature," she had absolutely no idea of sex. In fact, she was so naturally delicate, so refined, so utterly different from the "savages" with whom the deaf are sometimes compared, that she would not let anyone of the opposite sex even touch her. She showed affection to her female friends, "constantly clinging to them, and often kissing and caressing them," but with men she repelled "every approach to familiarity." Although she was fond of certain men, she refused to sit upon their knee "or allow them to take her round the waist, or submit to those innocent familiarities which it is common to take with children of her age." She was, in short, "as pure and spotless as the petals of a rose."[48]

UNDERSTANDING THE NATURE of Laura's appeal, Howe deliberately promoted this spiritualized version of Laura. What mattered to the public was not so much her actual character, appearance, or behavior, but her image, her effect "before the eyes" of others. As he explained to the English writer Mary Howitt, Laura's real significance lay in her ability to "call forth" sympathy and love. As "the poor diseased child" from "the wild mountains of New Hampshire" was brought, step by step, "into communication with other souls," readers of his annual reports "from all parts of the world" had "looked eagerly on, and uttered their words of encouragement." At last,

> when the child was raised by the hand, and came out, and walked with her fellows, all the people raised a shout of joy; and

poor little Laura Bridgman was received into the human family with a heartier shout of welcome than a "purple born" princess! Yes! This deaf, dumb, blind, and half taught girl is perhaps known more widely and looked upon with more kindly interest than any person of her age in the world.[49]

An international publicity campaign such as Howe's could not have occurred in 1820 or even perhaps in 1830. But by 1840, an emerging market in mass entertainment had begun to create popular interest in celebrities—people from all walks of life who fascinated not just because of their abilities, accomplishments, or rank, but simply because they were famous. For the first time, crowds of fans waited for their idols at railroad stations and outside theater doors, and devoured newspaper accounts of the personal and professional lives of writers and performers whom they might never actually see. Celebrity-watchers elbowed each other to catch a glimpse of Harriet Beecher Stowe, Jenny Lind, Charles Dickens, or Fanny Elssler because these public figures were "lions," objects in themselves of popular entertainment.[50]

A combination of forces contributed to the new cultural demand for celebrities in the midcentury period: higher rates of literacy, new technologies for cheaper printing and more extensive advertising, improved transportation, developments in engraving and photography, and the rise of a leisured middle class eager for diversion and spectacle. Paradoxically, Victorian sanctification of domestic privacy—the "feminine sphere" of the middle-class home—may have helped create a public appetite for the display of celebrities, including famous women.[51] The innovations of professional managers and promoters—P. T. Barnum and other impresarios, as well as enterprising book publishers such as J. P. Jewett, who "pushed" *Uncle Tom's Cabin* into "unparalled circulation"—shaped an audience that was attracted to the singular and surprising, "to the ideal as well as to the freak."[52]

Ambivalent about public exhibitions but hungry for recognition, Howe disdained the role of impresario, yet he played it well. Of course,

he did not have the commercial motivation—or the brash showman-
ship—of a Barnum. Nor, for all her popularity, did Laura attain the star
power of a Jenny Lind. But if the "Swedish Nightingale" had her ten
thousands, Laura had her thousands. Just as fans scrambled for souvenirs of Lind—her dropped handkerchiefs and gloves—admirers asked
for keepsakes of Laura—specimens of her handwriting or embroidery
and locks of hair. (Impatient with constant demands for her autograph,
Laura sometimes complained, "I do not like to write my poor name so
much.")[53]

Howe worked energetically to advertise Laura, but his campaign
benefited most lastingly and dramatically from an unexpected celebrity
endorsement. In 1842, on a visit to Boston, Charles Dickens, already the
most popular English novelist in the world, came to see her.

BOSTON WELCOMED DICKENS in January 1842 with almost hysterical excitement. The first real celebrity author, the beloved "Boz" was
mobbed by fans and feted by dignitaries wherever he went. More than
any writer of his day, he enjoyed, as he himself understood, "a particular
relation (personally affectionate and like no other man's)" with his public.[54] As soon as his ship, the *Britannia*, docked in Boston Harbor, a
swarm of editors and journalists rushed aboard to shake his hand, take
down his reactions, and look him over. Crowds of autograph seekers
waited at his hotel, where he agreed to hold daily receptions to meet his
admirers. (One woman reportedly begged him to walk entirely around
the room, "so that we can all have a look at you.")[55]

Thanks to Howe's publicity campaign in England, Dickens had
heard about Laura long before he docked in America. He probably got a
copy of Howe's famous 1840 report from a fellow mesmerist, Dr. John
Elliotson, who corresponded with Howe and took a phrenological interest in Laura's case. Even if Dickens had not already read about Laura, he
would inevitably have visited her during his two-week stay in Boston.
Since he made a practice of inspecting asylums, workhouses, and prisons
wherever he went, he would never have missed a tour of Perkins. More-

over, Cornelius Felton, Sumner, and Longfellow—the eminent young men who acted as Dickens's cicerones—were all members of Howe's circle, eager to show off their friend's accomplishments to their illustrious foreign visitor.[56]

Sumner, accompanied by Boston's mayor, Jonathan Chapman, escorted Dickens and his wife to Perkins on January 29, a week after their arrival. (To Howe's disappointment, he was still away on his southern tour at the time.) The entire school was in an uproar preparing for the visit. One Perkins teacher, Eliza Rogers, complained in her journal that with all the excitement, she had been forced to dust the schoolroom herself, "as no one else in the house could be found to do it." As for Dickens, Rogers remarked ruefully, "he did not deign to notice anything or anybody except Laura, who was there under Miss Swift's care." Mary Swift, who had the good fortune to be assigned to Laura that day, recorded that "Mr. Dickens seemed very much pleased with Laura." At first in the schoolroom, Laura had been "very still," and "did not appear at all as usual," but the illustrious guests had followed her into the parlor, "and there she was quite playful." Dickens "could hardly believe the evidence of his senses, and was much more surprised than people usually are." Laura herself, oblivious both to the momentousness of the occasion and the interest that she had aroused, simply recorded in her journal: "Ladies and gentleman came to see girls."[57]

Dickens spent two or three hours at Perkins, and then continued on to a whirlwind tour of South Boston's other charitable institutions: the State Hospital for the Insane, the House of Industry for paupers and orphans, a local hospital, the Boylston School for Neglected and Indigent Boys, the House of Reformation for Juvenile Offenders, and the Massachusetts House of Correction. As a humanitarian and reformer, he applauded these new, progressive institutions:

In all of them, the unfortunate or degenerate citizens of the State are carefully instructed in their duties both to God and man; are surrounded by all reasonable means of comfort and happiness . . . ; are appealed to, as members of the great human family, however afflicted, indigent or fallen; are ruled by the strong Heart, and not by the strong (though immeasurably weaker) Hand.[58]

But it was Perkins—and Laura—that captured his imagination. Later he would write to Howe that he had never in his life been "more truly and deeply affected" than he was by the sight of her.[59]

To the extent that she is remembered at all today, Laura is recalled as Dickens described her in *American Notes:* a "fair young creature," her face "radiant with intelligence and pleasure," her hair neatly braided "by her own hand and bound about her head," and her dress, "arranged by herself, . . . a pattern of neatness and simplicity." Although he confessed to feeling some discomfort in her presence—he, too, found her "uncouth" noises "rather painful to hear"—he nevertheless supplied the expert finishing touches to Howe's sentimental portrait.

Dickens may have been willing to overlook discordant realities because he recognized in Laura's story themes that were central to his own fiction—isolation and enclosure, transformation, and redemption. Perhaps he realized that Howe's narrative, with its images of surveillance, imprisonment, and loneliness, and with its pathetic but valiant little girl heroine, echoed aspects of his novel *The Old Curiosity Shop,* published only the previous year. In any case, for Dickens, as for most of Laura's admirers, Laura mattered mostly as a metaphor. Her voracious curiosity, retentive memory, lively wit, and powerful intellect interested him less than her pleasing appearance and cheerfulness. Like his own Little Nell, Laura was for him a curiosity and a symbol, living out "a kind of allegory."[60]

Echoing Howe's imagery, Dickens presented Laura's story as an inspirational tale of captivity and rescue. Without sight, hearing, or language, she had been "built up, as it were, in a marble cell, impervious to any ray of light, or particle of sound; with her poor white hand peeping through a chink in the wall, beckoning to some good man for help, that an Immortal soul might be awakened." Freed from her dark prison and summoned to life, she now had the power, through her example, to redeem the spiritually deaf and the morally blind. "Let that poor hand of hers lie gently on your hearts," Dickens concluded with a flourish, "for there may be something in its healing touch akin to that of the Great Master."[61]

IN "THE BIRTH-MARK," a short story by Nathaniel Hawthorne, a sorcerer wishes that his beautiful young wife were absolutely perfect. When he uses his magic to erase her single flaw—the tiny hand-shaped birthmark on her cheek—she dies. Together, Dickens and Howe performed a similar alchemy on Laura. In their narratives, the living child—argumentative, curious, irritable, impatient, noisy, and demanding—disappears, supplanted by a sentimental ideal.

Endorsed and elaborated by Dickens, Howe's portrait of Laura made her world-famous. Thousands thronged to see her, asked for keepsakes, followed her story in newspapers, and read paeans to her in evangelical journals and ladies' magazines. "It is well for *Laura Bridgman* that she cannot read all that has been written and printed about her," wrote the editor of the American Sunday-School Union's *Youth's Penny Gazette* in 1849, "for if she could, she would be very likely to be vain."[62] But idealizing Laura also imprisoned her inside an artificial and unchanging persona, a literary type, the Good Little Suffering Girl.

Mythologized and allegorized, what future could the real Laura Bridgman have? In his letter to Howe, Carlyle tried to envision an adult life for the "good little creature" whose story had so moved him. "My wish for this dear Laura were that, if you once taught her to read and to work, she were safe home with her good mother again," he wrote to Howe. "But then I suppose nobody could speak with her there? Alas, hers is a delicate, difficult case, and you will require all your benevolence and good sense in her behalf." Even the Sage of Chelsea was at a loss to imagine the ethereal little "angel-soul" as a flesh-and-blood young woman—a person who would need companionship, material support, and a measure of dignity and independence.

CHAPTER SEVEN

Second Acts

DICKENS BOASTED THAT *American Notes* was "a most complete and thoroughgoing success."[1] The book sold briskly. In England it went through four printings in two months; in New York fifty thousand copies of a pirated edition sold in two days.[2] Within a few months of its publication, hundreds of thousands of Dickens's readers on both sides of the Atlantic knew that Samuel Gridley Howe was the paragon of "Noble Usefulness" who had brought the miracle of Laura Bridgman to pass.

Inspired by Dickens's enthusiastic description of Laura, as well as by the increasingly famous Perkins annual reports, the newspapers hailed Howe as a scientific giant, a nineteenth-century knight-errant, and an instrument of God's will. "In this best of all periods in the existence of man," one journalist proclaimed, "our hero is the advocate of *good*," not "the man of blood and conquest." By rescuing Laura, Howe had proved himself "one of the great men of this age," a benevolent conqueror in the war against darkness and pain.[3] "Who," another writer asked, "would not rather have been the first who triumphantly planted the standard of intelligence and hope within the apparently impregnable ramparts of that dark and dreary citadel, than to have victoriously borne away the martial banners from the fields of Arbela and Waterloo?"[4]

To progressives, Howe was the very model of a modern reformer:

"he who enlightens the ignorant, ennobles the degraded, and in all his ways and works raises the type of humanity and assimilates it to that of the heavenly."[5] Religious writers praised him as a secular saint, a redeemer "actuated by a feeling of angelic purpose and charity," a Samaritan "whose name ought to be reverenced as one of the greatest benefactors of suffering humanity."[6] In freeing Laura from her prison-house he had "trodden . . . sublimely in the footsteps of his divine Master," giving, "as far as human aid could do it," sight to the blind, "language to the sealed lips," and "purifying and enlightening faith to the imprisoned and mourning soul."[7] For the educational movement, Howe represented the "miracle" of modern education. Horace Mann said that it was "wholly owing to the character of Dr. Howe, to his judgment, his knowledge, and the energy of his benevolent impulses" that a beautiful but lost child had been "rescued from a gloomy and miserable existence."[8] And in "To Laura Bridgman," W. Holmes imagined Howe as nothing less than a rationalist redeemer, opening new avenues of moral and scientific progress:

> Be thine the task, O! generous How[e], to guide
> The imprisoned guest, through Nature's ample fields,
> To draw the curtain of her wealth aside,
> And show the pleasure that true science yields;
> To tread the path by learning seldom trod,
> That leads "from nature up to nature's God."[9]

All this adulation failed to cure the unhappy restlessness that had plagued Howe for most of his life. As early as 1836, he had begun escaping regularly from Perkins, touring the country, lecturing, and putting on exhibitions to promote education of the blind. In the spring of 1841, just as Laura was beginning to make him famous, he applied to become ambassador to Spain, soliciting letters of support from friends—Prescott, Ticknor, Choate, and Abbot Lawrence—who had close ties to Daniel Webster, the newly appointed secretary of state. But office seeking proved humiliating: as Sumner later remarked, because Howe had neither political clout nor money, "no notice was taken of the application."[10] Mann generously consoled Howe for his disappointment, pointing out that Howe's "moral faculties would perish of inanition" in backward, priest-ridden Spain. "What can you do better than to go on in that beneficent ministration in which you are now engaged?" Mann asked. "What can you do better than to push forward any good cause, and to swing your thundering great battle-axe against any bad one?" Mann interpreted Howe's restlessness as an outbreak of his naturally adventurous spirit: "The nineteenth century is too late for your military knight-errantry. . . . You must tame your war-horse to work in common harness."[11]

But the Chevalier could not settle down. A few months after his failed attempt to go to Spain, he set out by stagecoach with Sophia and Abby Carter, his two most attractive and accomplished blind students, on a monthlong tour of Virginia and South Carolina, returning home in early January 1842, only because his girls were "not equal to the fatigue of it."[12] Later that month (shortly before Dickens's visit), he took off again with the Carter sisters, this time down the Ohio River to Kentucky, where he persuaded the state legislature to appropriate $10,000 for the establishment of the Kentucky Institution of the Blind. From Kentucky he took a riverboat down the Mississippi to New Orleans, stopping along the way to make speeches and exhibit the exhausted young women.

Traveling in those days before railroads was uncomfortable and sometimes dangerous, but even while his reputation was at its zenith, Howe longed for new challenges and adventures. His need to get away—as well as a genuine commitment to promoting education for the blind—spurred him to visit seventeen states during his first ten years as director of Perkins. After the glamour of his years abroad, the mundane life of a school director seemed stifling and tame. Satisfying his lofty ambitions within the confines of a complex institution was difficult: teachers did not always follow his orders; students sometimes failed to respond to his methods; politicians forgot to praise him or refused to support his work. And his personal credo—"Obstacles are things to overcome"—left little room for compromise.

In the early 1840s, Howe was especially frustrated by his inability to replicate his work with Laura. He believed that through his experiments with her, he had invented a universally applicable method for teaching deaf-blind children. Her awakening might have appeared miraculous, but in fact his pedagogical system—a "practical metaphysics" of his own devising—had saved her.[13] He and his admirers assumed that as soon as he recruited other deaf-blind students, he would be able not only to repeat his earlier success, but also to realize an even grander vision: the creation of a model deaf-blind school at Perkins. But to his chagrin, his educational magic only seemed to work on Laura.

When Laura was mastering conjunctions, irregular plurals, and the basics of arithmetic, Howe began his search for other deaf-blind students. In the fall of 1840, he pursued a Rhode Island boy named Oliver Caswell, who had been deaf and blind since the age of four. Although Howe visited and later wrote to the family's minister, urging him, "for the boy's sake and for the sake of science," to persuade Oliver's parents to send him to Perkins, the Caswells, "very poor and benighted people," refused to let their son leave home.[14] Then, in November he got word of another prospect: Lucy Reed, a deaf-blind girl from Danbury, Vermont, who was two years older than Laura. He wrote to Lucy's father at once to persuade him to send her to Perkins.[15]

On paper, Lucy sounded promising. Barely fourteen, she might still be young enough to learn. Her early childhood resembled Laura's. After developing normally for three years, she had lost her hearing, probably as a result of chronic ear infections. Over the next five years, she had suffered from some sort of eye disease, but did not become totally blind until her eighth year, "when she injured her eyes by a rosebush, the consequence of which was total extinction of vision."[16] (Perhaps this unlikely story was inspired by the fairy tale "Rapunzel," in which the prince loses his sight when he leaps from a tower onto a thorny bush.)

Howe promised Lucy's parents that by using his "systematic and scientific principles" he could do much for her. They could be reassured, he said, by his success with Laura, "one of the most interesting and intelligent little creatures you ever saw: as happy as a bird the live-long day;

and very much engaged in learning all those things which engage children's attention."[17] Lucy would fare much better with him than at a school for the deaf; because of Laura, the Perkins students knew finger spelling and were accustomed to a deaf-blind playmate. Moreover, Lucy's family would be required to contribute little or nothing for her Perkins tuition, since as a New Englander she was eligible for a state subsidy.

To Howe's delight, the Reeds agreed to his proposal. But when Lucy, accompanied by her younger sister, arrived at Perkins in February 1841, he was appalled. She was, he said, "in a lower stage of humanity than any human being I ever saw, excepting idiots."[18] A few weeks later he described her to an acquaintance as "a very wild and ignorant creature, differing not much in intelligence from a wild animal." Frenzied and uncontrollable, she "used her nails and her teeth in self-defense when touched exactly like a cat or leopard."[19] He admitted that she was "as nearly unnatural as you can well conceive a human being to be. She keeps her head enveloped in a kind of bag; and her parents even have not seen her features for two years."[20]

Howe had planned to separate her from her family immediately, as he had Laura from hers, but he could not pry Lucy apart from her sister. The two girls were literally attached: Lucy had pinned their dresses together. Once Howe managed to remove the pin, Lucy held on with her teeth. In the end, he had to allow the sister to remain at Perkins for several weeks until Lucy had calmed down.

Lucy's career at Perkins ended after only five months, with recriminations on both sides. When her parents, distressed by Howe's treatment of her and dissatisfied with her progress, removed her from the school in July, he protested angrily. His self-justifying reports about her are so transparently vindictive that they cannot be fully credited, but her teachers' journals and letters from Lucy's father provide a fuller story.

It is clear from these accounts that when Lucy came to Perkins she was more panicked than Laura had been and less resourceful at finding comfort. Perhaps because she had not had the benefit of a gentle companion such as Tenney, she did not know how to befriend people outside her own family. The affectionate hugs and approving pats that Laura craved meant nothing to Lucy, who ignored or repelled the caresses of strangers. At the same time, she was hardly a wild beast. Although her parents had not succeeded in teaching her table manners, they had trained her to be clean in her dress and to sew proficiently.

But unlike Laura, who came to Perkins a terrified but tractable eight-year-old, Lucy frightened her teachers. At fourteen, she was bigger, stronger, and more dangerous in her panicky violence than Laura had ever been. The "bag" that concealed Lucy's face was really nothing more than a large handkerchief draped over her head, but the "mysterious covering" gave her a strangely menacing air.[21]

To add to Howe's difficulties, Lucy's parents—unlike the deferential Bridgmans—intended to monitor their daughter's progress and well-being. An educated, prosperous, independent Vermont farmer, Timothy Reed had the time to take an active interest in his child's welfare and the confidence to question the eminent Dr. Howe.

Not surprisingly, there was trouble. In theory Howe opposed corporal punishment and physical coercion. He enthusiastically supported Horace Mann's efforts to discourage the whipping of students in the public schools. He agreed with the principle, advanced by home-management manuals of the 1830s and 1840s, that affection, not fear, is the true basis of authority.[22] But he could find no way to gain Lucy's trust and cooperation. Unable to coax her into remaining in her desk chair, he resolved to hold her down by force. She struggled fiercely against him, first digging her fingernails into his hands until she drew blood and then, "as if perceiving a more sensible spot," clawing at his face "so ferociously" that he feared for his eyes. To protect himself, he donned thick gloves and a wire fencing mask, but she deliberately reached under his coat sleeves to scratch his arms. When he continued to hold her, she tried to bite his hands. Although he exerted all his considerable strength to force her to sit down, she kept fighting him until they were both exhausted.

Faced with her stubborn resistance, he finally procured leather handcuffs and fastened her hands behind her back. After a few days, she so dreaded the handcuffs "that their touch was enough to make her yield."[23]

Losing the use of her hands left her utterly helpless, cut off from all perception of the outside world, as if she had entered a terrifying void. No wonder that the mere threat of this punishment could subdue her.

Howe's use of restraints may have been cruel, but it is not surprising that he resorted to a tactic that even he admitted was "severe." He had little patience for defiance and, in any case, as both Helen Keller and Anne Sullivan later testified, gentle persuasion does not always or easily win the cooperation of a frightened, frustrated deaf-blind child. Justifying Sullivan's use of corporal punishment, Keller recalled that as a languageless child, she too had acted "like a demon," responding to attempts to control her by kicking, screaming, and pinching. Keller claimed that when she was not yet seven years old, her tantrums had been so powerful that she had knocked out two of her teacher's teeth with her fist.[24] According to Dorothy Herrmann, Keller's most recent biographer, Sullivan had no qualms about responding in kind to Keller's violence. Like Howe, Sullivan at first engaged in "terrific tussles" with her pupil, and to subdue her tied her hands behind her back. Indeed, Keller admitted that Sullivan was considerably more punitive toward her than Howe ever was with Lucy: impatient and quick-tempered herself, Sullivan occasionally boxed Keller's ears or "whipped" her for misbehavior.[25]

Whether necessary or not, handcuffing Lucy worked. She became docile and would even allow her sister to leave her side, "moaning, however, sometimes most piteously." Although for months she made absolutely no progress in language, she would sit quietly at her desk and submit to "what was to her the incomprehensible efforts of her teacher."[26] Once she had calmed down, Howe said, Lucy seemed to be happier and more sociable. After a month, she even volunteered to give up her head covering. As Howe recounted the story, at bedtime one night, she used gestures to make one of the blind girls understand that if the girl would sleep with her, she would uncover her face. When the girl agreed, Lucy first stuffed cotton into her eye sockets, then put on a pair of eyeshades of the kind worn by some Perkins students, and finally removed her veil. Her face, Howe noted, "presented a singular appearance, being perfectly etiolated, as white and as inexpressive as the unexposed part of a person's arm or chest." Nevertheless, her features were "very good" and her countenance "pleasing."[27] Outwardly at least, she had been civilized.

Intellectually, however, Lucy remained a disappointment. Lydia Drew and Mary Swift, who at this point shared the teaching of Lucy and Laura, did their best to teach Lucy the alphabet, but without success. Occasionally, Laura tried to help, but more often she resented sharing her lesson time with Lucy, who was, she complained, a "very dull scholar."[28] After five months of relentless work, Swift reported some faint signs of progress. Lucy seemed more interested and alert, and in July, just before her parents decided to take her away, she astonished her teachers by spelling out the word "cake" at the dining table, instead of simply grabbing.

Howe always insisted that Lucy would have learned language if she had remained in his care. He complained to Mann that her teachers had just "broken through the crust & got at the living spring within" when Lucy's father came in mid-July to take her back home. The fault lay entirely with her mother, "a very ignorant & very nervous body," who had talked herself into believing that life at Perkins was killing her daughter. "The secret of the whole is, she loves her daughter more warmly & more blindly than does a cow her calf," Howe fumed; the silly woman had "teased the father day & night, untill the poor man, to make peace came down for the child." According to Howe, when Mr. Reed saw how well Lucy was doing, he had been reluctant to remove her but confessed that " 'he dared not face the old woman without the child.' "[29]

Explaining Lucy's abrupt departure in his annual report for 1841, Howe shaped her story into an object lesson in parental folly. Unlike Laura, the girl had arrived at Perkins overindulged, undisciplined, and untaught. Under her parents' care, she had degenerated into a wild beast who grabbed for food, climbed trees, and showed preternatural strength and aggression. The "bag" with which she covered her head was the product of grotesque and unrestrained vanity. In her absurd desire to look beautiful, she had imagined that the veil "increased her comeliness" by concealing her repulsive blind eyes. (A more reasonable conjecture might have been that Lucy had originally used the handkerchief to protect her painfully inflamed eyes from the light, and eventually grew accustomed to wearing it.) Instead of putting a stop to the nonsensical head covering, Howe charged, her parents had humored her "whim" by providing her with a supply of suitable handkerchiefs, which she could change as soon as they became soiled. The same foolish indulgence prompted the Reeds to remove Lucy from Perkins. Out of their own need to spoil her with "luxuries and delicacies," they had prevented Howe from providing "that food which nourisheth the soul, and which may be a source of enjoyment to her long after they are in their graves."[30]

Lucy and Laura might suffer from the same afflictions, but Howe insisted they were otherwise nothing alike. Laura was affectionate, expressive, and bright; Lucy, impassive and dull. Laura had clung passionately to her mother at their first reunion; when Mrs. Reed visited, Lucy showed more interest in the treats her mother had brought than in loving embraces. Despite Lucy's coldness, Laura had willingly acted the good fairy, cheering Lucy up when she cried and helping to teach her to spell. When the time came for Lucy to leave Perkins, Laura had embraced her warmly, despite Lucy's apparent indifference. Neglecting to mention that Laura had often been annoyed and impatient with Lucy, Howe quoted Laura as saying later to her teacher, "I am very alone, because Lucy is all gone. . . . Lucy will not come back more." Aiming one last arrow at the Reeds, Howe concluded: "Laura was not the only one to sorrow for Lucy's departure, and she is not the only one who would hail her return with joy."[31]

From his farm in Vermont, Timothy Reed had no way to respond publicly to Howe's attack, but he did reply privately.[32] The Reeds, in fact, had been nursing grievances of their own. Reed complained that he had been forced to write repeatedly to Howe, demanding reports of Lucy's progress. When her parents visited Lucy in June, they had found her looking neglected and disheveled, in old shoes and mismatched stockings. She had come to Perkins with seven pairs of stockings, Mr.

Reed pointed out indignantly, and had returned home with only four. He also questioned the privileged treatment given to Laura, who now boarded with Howe and his sister in the director's quarters. Why did Laura, who could communicate with others and make her needs known, usually eat with the Howes, while Lucy, who was completely helpless, had to manage on her own in the communal dining hall?

The Reeds' complaints were not simply expressions of parental overprotectiveness. In her months at Perkins, Lucy had lost a good deal of weight. She appeared unwell. Although Howe assured the family that it was "perfectly natural that the poor thing should be ill and pine during the first weeks or months she should be here," the Reeds did not share his indifference to Lucy's physical deterioration.[33] They wondered who, in a crowded dining hall, was making sure that she got enough to eat. Furthermore, although physical restraint may have been effective, Howe had neither sought their permission to handcuff Lucy, nor even informed them of his coercive methods, which they learned of only after their younger daughter returned home.

Finally, and most dishonorably, Howe had published an offensive letter about Lucy in a New York newspaper shortly after her arrival. The Reeds objected both to the inaccuracy and the unkindness of the letter, in which Howe described Lucy as "wild" and "nearly savage," and made fun of the "bag" on her head. That he chose to call the handkerchief a "bag" particularly rankled: it seemed a deliberate attempt to make their daughter's pathetic habit seem ridiculous. After seeing this letter in print, the Reeds lost faith in Howe's benevolence.[34]

Howe answered each of the Reeds' charges in a long letter, which he urged them to make public. He said he had nothing to apologize for. Lucy had been overly pampered at home, and it was good for her to be forced to take care of herself in the dormitory. She may have *seemed* to suffer, but sink-or-swim "is found to be the best way to make [blind children] capable & smart." Lucy's younger sister bore the responsibility for the missing stockings: she should have kept better track of them. The leather handcuffs "had a most excellent effect" and caused Lucy no pain.

He had been "fearful that there would be trouble" about his using them, yet he had not shrunk from his duty, knowing that his motives were "those of kindness." His conscience confirmed that he had done right.

Although he had sent the letter that offended the Reeds to a New York newspaperman, Howe protested that he had never intended it for publication. He admitted that it may have been written "in a hasty manner," but denied any mockery or malice:

> I might have said she wore a bag on her head, & I might have said she was nearly savage . . . : but my Dear Sir; if you reflect upon this in a charitable spirit, you will perceive that there was no untruth in saying so: Lucy wore a covering over her head which from the very first day she came here was *called* a bag even by the blind girls. . . . God forbid we should talk or think light of the poor thing! We used the word bag, as innocently as you talked about the handkerchief. As for the word "nearly savage" . . . savage you know means sometimes, *untaught, unpolished, rude* . . . as the poet speaks of "savage berries of the wood."

In any case, Mr. Reed was "too good a Christian" to blame Howe for the publication of a letter that he had believed would be kept private.

Lastly, Howe refused to countenance any criticism of his apparent favoritism toward Laura. He and Jeannette had decided to have Laura board with them as a way of forming her manners. His apartments and his table were his own, paid for at his own expense, and if he took one of the children to live with him, the parents of the others had no right to complain. It was true that he loved Laura as if she were his own child, but Lucy too might eventually have earned a place in his heart. If only the Reeds had not been so hasty in removing her, he "probably should have become very much attached to her in time." In fact, the blind girls already liked Lucy more than Laura. But he would be magnanimous and "make allowance" for Mr. Reed's unfair accusations, despite the "unbecoming" tone in which they were couched. Even the best of schoolmasters and the best of schools had to suffer from "the fondness and partiality of parents."[35]

AFTER THIS EMBARRASSING debacle, Howe was relieved to get another chance to prove himself with a deaf-blind student: Oliver Caswell, the Rhode Island boy whose parents had earlier refused Howe's entreaties. Perhaps the Caswells had waited to see how Laura turned out, or perhaps Oliver, now almost twelve, had grown too large and unruly to manage. In any case, Howe welcomed the boy joyfully when he arrived at the end of September 1841, two months after Lucy's departure. Although his parents had warned that Oliver could become "ungovernable" and violent "when thwarted in any way," he appeared pleasant and tractable, "a stout, thick-set boy, rather short of stature, with light hair, fair complexion, and a most pleasant expression of countenance." His manner was friendly and calm, Howe said, "and his intelligent look and eager gestures proclaimed that there was enough intellect within, could one but establish the means of communicating with it."[36]

Oliver, who was almost exactly the same age as Laura, had lost his sight and hearing when he was three years and four months old, following an attack of scarlet fever. Once his health returned, he learned to orient himself by eagerly sniffing, touching, and licking everything he could lay his hands on. On his first day at Perkins, when he felt the unfamiliar register of the furnace under his foot, he startled Howe by stooping down, moving the metal plates around, and then completing his inspection with his tongue. He also arrived at Perkins with a substantial vocabulary of pantomimic gestures to express his wants and feelings.

In his early days at Perkins, the otherwise placid boy had one defiant episode, which Howe easily quelled. Worn out by a long and frustrating lesson, Oliver threw something—probably one of the labeled objects used for instruction—on the floor. In accordance with the Perkins policy of correcting each and every fault, his teacher, Eliza Rogers, resolved to hold his hand on the object until he picked it up. When Howe happened on the scene, both the teacher, "thinking it necessary to conquer him," and Oliver's mother, who had not yet returned to Rhode Island, were trying to force him to obey. Howe took command at once. Oliver "had never been controlled, and his animal nature was now aroused," Howe recalled with a touch of admiration. "A colt could not start away more restive, when the saddle is first placed on his back, than did Oliver when I placed my hand on his head." Where Lucy had been an untameable wildcat, Oliver was simply a skittish horse. Howe had only to rein him firmly until he calmed to the saddle. Once he "seduced" Oliver's senses with the odor of some cologne water and forced him to submit to kisses and pats, the boy was "conquered." He never again gave his teachers any trouble. In the subsequent nine years that he lived at Perkins, he remained "perfectly docile," obedient, respectful of authority, cheerful, and calm.[37]

As a second Laura Bridgman, however, Oliver was undeniably a failure. Howe admitted that the boy, for all his good nature, simply did not have Laura's "keen zest," or "quickness of thought, and delicacy of organization." Oliver could manage to string words together, but he never grasped basic grammar. Despite intensive instruction, his "sentences" remained structureless: Howe cited, "Oliver, fish, boat, Thomas, Bradford," and "Wood, axe, cut, Thomas," as typical of Oliver's syntax. Even when he seemed to have mastered new words or concepts, he quickly forgot them; his teachers soon realized that he lacked Laura's tenacious memory. In arithmetic he was equally slow. Laura had to struggle with algebra, a subject she always disliked, but he could barely remember his numbers. Eventually, he learned to count as many as fifty objects, but only by holding up his fingers.

When Mary Swift, filling in for Eliza Rogers, took over Oliver's instruction for two months in 1845, she was stunned by his dullness. "I had no idea of the difference in his mind and Laura's until now that I have attempted to teach him," Swift noted in her journal. "He is so very slow compared with her and asks few questions, but seems perfectly satisfied with what I tell him, without inquiring further."[38] Howe's daughters, Florence and Maud, recalled that while Oliver cared only about "concrete objects," Laura pondered "abstract matters of right and wrong," wearying herself and others with questions about motives and responsibility.[39] Imperturbable, smiling, and incurious, the boy was lovable but, as Howe conceded, "lymphatic in temperament" and lacking "that rapidity of thought and action which characterises Laura in so remarkable a degree."[40]

UNWILLING TO ADMIT defeat after the Lucy Reed episode, Howe made the best of Oliver's slowness, portraying him as a sturdy working-class lad who had risen to the level of his innate abilities. The son of a ferryman, Oliver naturally excelled in the workshop, not in the classroom. Like the hearty laboring boys in Dickens's novels, he laughed uproariously, especially at his own mistakes, bore his injuries bravely, and hid his tender feelings. And when confronted by a bully, he showed his true "manly" nature, becoming "as bold as a little lion."[41]

The Old Curiosity Shop had just been published when Oliver arrived at Perkins, and Dickens's influence on Howe's characterizations is unmistakable. In the Perkins annual reports, he transformed Laura into a second Little Nell and Oliver into Kit Nubbles, Nell's comical, working-class friend. Just as in the novel Nell tries to show Kit how to form letters, their laughter barely concealing "a gentle wish on her part to teach, and an anxious desire on his to learn," so in Howe's much admired narrative, Laura helps the laughing Oliver learn the manual alphabet.[42]

> The two presented a singular sight; her face was flushed and anxious and her fingers twined in among ours so closely as to follow every motion . . . while Oliver stood attentive, his head a little aside, his face turned up . . . there was an expression of anxiety as he tried to imitate the motions—then a smile came stealing out as he thought he could do so, and spread into a joyous laugh the moment he succeeded, and he felt me pat his head, and Laura clap him heartily upon the back, and jump up and down in her joy.[43]

In his more fanciful moods, Howe hinted at an affectionate attachment between Laura and Oliver, like the one between Nell and Kit. But despite her occasional interest in his progress, Laura viewed Oliver primarily as a rival for her teachers' time and approval. Mary Swift fostered this competitiveness, pointing out to Laura that notwithstanding his duller wits, "the gentle Oliver" was more popular than Laura with the other students. While Laura pushed away the blind girls if their conversation bored her and challenged her teachers' authority, he became a universal pet, as friendly—and inarticulate—as a puppy.[44] As late as 1846, when Laura was almost eighteen, she wondered why he, who was so much slower intellectually, "does not do wrong as often as I do."[45]

HOWE'S DICKENSIAN PORTRAITS of the two children charmed his readers, but could not completely mask his failure to teach Oliver. By April 1842, when Julia Brace came to Perkins, Howe had given up the idea of creating other deaf-blind prodigies, and the prospect of teaching a middle-aged Brace held little interest for him. Eight years earlier, when he first visited her at the American Asylum for the Deaf and Dumb, in Hartford, Connecticut, she had already seemed ineducable, and the passage of time had not improved her in his eyes. He agreed to take her on only because her benefactor, the redoubtable Lydia Sigourney, pleaded with him to try his methods on her protégée, and Howe did not want to refuse so wealthy and influential a friend. Warning Sigourney that Brace's thirty-four-year-old brain might have lost "by long inactivity its flexibility and susceptibility," he promised to put aside his misgivings and do what he could.[46]

Although he expected little from his new pupil, Howe recognized an opportunity for publicity when he saw it. Unpromising as she was as a student, the torpid Brace would make a telling contrast to Laura, and thus reveal the destructive effects of sign language on deaf-blind children. To make this point, he took Laura to Hartford in November 1841, on a ceremonial visit intended to highlight Brace's hopeless inferiority.

Howe reported anonymously on this historic meeting in a newspaper article that was later widely reprinted. (In that account, the contrast he sets up between the adorable girl and the strange, impassive older woman eerily foreshadows the comparisons that observers would make almost fifty years later between the aging Laura and her charming young successor, Helen Keller.) Howe wrote that from the moment Laura walked into the Hartford asylum, she dazzled everyone with her "beautiful features and fair complexion," graceful motions, vivacity, and friendliness, "evidently enjoying the boon of existence, and speaking in dumb but expressive language the praise of Him who willeth the happiness of all whom He createth." Brace, in sad contrast, was "unprepossessing in her appearance," inexpressive and unresponsive. Even after she had been "made to understand, by placing her fingers on Laura's eyes and on her ears, that she was blind and deaf like herself, . . . her countenance changed not." Although Laura "clung" to the older woman, presented her with a chain that she had braided, and tried to kiss her, Brace "cooly" pocketed the present and walked away. Astonished and disappointed, Laura asked, "Why does she push me? Why does she not love me?"[47]

"Vain impulse of affection!" Howe lamented. The Hartford school's methods had ruined Brace. The contrast between the animated child and the inexpressive woman dramatized the superiority of verbal language over Sign, of Perkins over the American Asylum, of Howe over Gallaudet. "Such is the consequence of education; such the consequence of evolving the moral and social nature, as has been done in the case of Laura; or of exercising only the lower propensities, and allowing the human being to live as do the brutes," Howe concluded.[48]

He later reported that Brace had understood "perfectly" the purpose of her transfer to Perkins, and that she seemed "desirous of learning something in the school with the blind girls." Such informed acquiescence seems improbable. But even if she had some glimmering of where she was and why, Brace must have been disoriented and lonely. Uprooted from the signing community of the Hartford asylum, her only home since 1825, she had no way to communicate with others except through pantomime. She cooperated with the Perkins teachers, but could not remember any of the words they tried to teach her. When she was not in class, Howe observed, Brace chose to "lose consciousness" and would lie "flat upon her face, sleeping or dozing for hours together." After a month or two, her teachers gave up.[49]

Brace lasted a year at Perkins and then returned to the American Asylum. A small legacy from a benefactor allowed her to live there quietly until 1860, when she moved in with a married sister. She was buried in an unmarked grave in Bloomfield, Connecticut, in August 1884.[50] In 1850, seven years after Brace's departure from Perkins, Oliver's family decided that the time had come for him, too, to leave. Since his progress there "seemed slow if any at all at present," he might as well come home; his mother missed him. In addition, echoing the Reeds, the Caswells told Howe that they worried about their son's health. Without finding fault at all with Howe—"far from it"—they could not help observing that Oliver looked "thin of flesh" whenever he returned to Rhode Island for vacation. They were deeply grateful for Howe's "kindness and benevolence," but believed their "dear boy" could most safely and profitably live with his family, where he could occupy himself by making mats and doing simple chores.[51] Lucy Reed, too, lived out her days at home, quietly sewing, doing patchwork, and covering boxes. She died at seventyseven.[52] Outwardly at least, her adult life differed little from Laura's.

ALTHOUGH HIS PLANS for a school for the deaf-blind had failed, by 1842 Howe had a new, more exciting idea. If he could not replicate his success with Laura, he could raise the stakes of his original experiment. He would use her now to support a cherished belief that "man, from his very constitution, is bound to worship some supreme being."[53] By leading her to discover the existence of her Creator, he would demonstrate that even the most deprived and isolated child has an intuitive understanding of God and a natural inclination to venerate Him.

Laura was the ideal subject for an experiment on the innateness of religious faculties. Deprived of sense data and cut off from language, she had grown up completely unconscious of her Maker. According to Howe, even after she somehow learned the word "God" in 1841, she had no idea of its meaning.[54] In terms of religious knowledge, she remained a blank slate.

As a New England Unitarian, Howe believed that "we are made for God; all our affections, sensibilities, faculties, and energies are designed to be directed towards God."[55] Phrenology had taught him that this universal religious disposition had a physiological basis, in the cerebral Organ of Veneration. Although Laura's disabilities had blocked her religious development, she had both the intellectual capacity to infer the existence of a Prime Mover and the natural inclination to worship a Supreme Being. Just as Howe had awakened her capacity for language, he would now stimulate her disposition for knowing and revering God. After all, she had already shown a promising inclination to respect those with power and knowledge. She intuitively distinguished right from wrong, and seemed to have an active conscience. Her questions about "the origin of things" were incessant. Without ever giving away the right theological answer, Howe would use his famous pedagogical skills to lead her on until, with a flash of understanding, she put the pieces of the puzzle together for herself.

His plan was to drop a series of clues that would gradually guide her toward recognition of the Truth. As he explained to her the operations of nature and the relationship of cause and effect, for example, she would naturally wonder about the source of all this natural harmony. To help her think about a divine Creator, he would encourage her to distinguish between manmade things and natural objects, for which there were no human makers. Using magnets, he would convey to her the idea of "immaterial power." As she followed the growth of a plant with her fingers, he would prompt her to think about what made the leaves sprout. Guided step by step in this way, she would inevitably discover "the power and love of that Being, whose praise she is every day so clearly proclaiming, by her glad enjoyment of the existence which he has given her."[56]

At a time when Howe and his Unitarian (or "Liberal Christian") friends were immersed in a bitter feud with "orthodox" Calvinistic evangelicals, this experiment seemed momentous both philosophically and politically. If Laura somehow grasped the idea of God in the same intuitive way that she had grasped the idea of language, then Howe could claim to have struck a blow against orthodoxy. Her spontaneous recognition and veneration of her Maker would demonstrate that children were

not "the imps of fallen man," as Calvinists taught, but "wonderful" beings, capable of working out their own salvation.[57]

Howe's eagerness to teach this optimistic lesson had its roots in
a century-old sectarian rivalry within the established (that is, tax-
supported) Congregational Church of Massachusetts. In the first decades
of the nineteenth century, a growing faction of liberals, many of them
prosperous, enlightened Bostonians, began to question the pessimism
and provincialism of orthodox doctrine. At first, their disaffection had
little effect on the orthodox, who despite their dwindling numbers continued to control most of the state's Congregational churches. Around
1815, however, as the liberals finally declared their opposition more
openly, power struggles broke out in many parishes, especially in eastern Massachusetts. When a ruling of the liberal State Supreme Judicial
Court—the famous 1820 Dedham decision—gave the liberal majorities
in many towns the authority to wrest their churches (and church property) from the orthodox, a bitter formal breach inevitably followed.

Neither side was ready to forgive or forget until after the Civil
War.[58] Even as disestablishment, Catholic immigration, the rapid expan-
sion of other Protestant denominations, and an entrepreneurial economy
were making their old quarrels irrelevant, the two factions continued to
exchange blows, like boxers too intent on their struggle to leave the ring,
even after the audience has gone home. The Unitarian elite controlled
Harvard, the statehouse, and most of the wealth of eastern Massachusetts, but they nevertheless felt vulnerable and beleaguered, fearful that
the orthodox, in their desperate bigotry, could threaten rational free inquiry, refinement, and learning. And the orthodox, despite their own
corrosive internal divisions, never stopped attacking liberal heresy and
godlessness.

Most infuriatingly to Howe, evangelical "zealots" opposed Horace
Mann's efforts to make the common schools nonsectarian. Since 1837,
when Mann was elected secretary of the newly formed Massachusetts
State Board of Education, the orthodox had criticized him for refusing to
include creedal instruction in his plans for reforming the public schools.
On the floor of the legislature and in the press, as well as from the pulpit,

they argued that Bible reading and nondogmatic moral education (which Mann endorsed) would not suffice. If the schools failed to provide instruction in revealed religion, how would the children of wicked or indifferent parents learn the way to salvation?[59]

These attacks never seriously jeopardized Mann's work, but they made him sick with anxiety and frustration. "The orthodox have hunted me this winter," he complained to George Combe in 1844 at the height of the struggle, "as though they were bloodhounds, and I a poor rabbit."[60] Howe, on the other hand, always relished a good fight and enjoyed hitting hard knocks "on Satan's cranium."[61] "I sometimes think we should have been shipwrecked before this but for [Howe's] pilotage," Mann confessed. (In fact, Howe became so bellicose that at one point Mann had to beg him to control his wrath.)[62]

Laura was potentially a powerful weapon in this sectarian battle. If Howe could show that under his tutelage she had succeeded in finding God, he could use her to prove Mann's point: children did not require formal instruction in revealed religion to save their souls and did not have to be terrified into piety by the threat of Hell's fires. Innocent of all dogma, unafraid, and unconverted, Laura could offer living proof that children learn morality and reverence by example, inference, and "mind-expanding education," not through indoctrination and intimidation.[63]

AS A THEORETICAL approach, Howe's plan for Laura's religious education might have sounded plausible, but in practice it never made much sense. Perhaps Walt Whitman could "behold God in every object," and find "letters from God dropped in the street" (each one signed with God's name), but Laura did not have Whitman's eyes or ears.[64] Nor, short of keeping her in solitary confinement, could Howe insulate her for long from religious indoctrination. In an institution full of devoutly orthodox students and teachers from all over New England, many of them eager to impart the Good News to a benighted soul, preserving Laura's ignorance of revealed religion was simply not feasible. Yet, for the experiment to work, this sociable child, brimming with persistent questions, would have to be kept in the dark about the central reality of her teachers' and schoolmates' lives. Recognizing the danger, Howe gave strict orders that no one at Perkins was to discuss religion with Laura, but of course there was no way to enforce such a rule, especially now that she could converse with visitors and correspond with strangers.

Even if he could have found a way to shield her, Howe's scheme was impossibly vague, a muddled and grandiose fantasy that in reality he pursued only sporadically. What, after all, did he expect to happen? Did he really imagine that when Laura felt "the pushing of vegetation," she would posit a First Cause for the universe? That the mysterious "attraction of magnets" would lead her to discover the soul? That she would connect the twinges of her conscience to a divinely ordered moral system? Laura's agile, inquisitive mind worked by childlike free association, not Cartesian logic. Each bit of information that came her way released a torrent of loosely connected questions. Confronted with a growing plant, she was more likely to ask if animals liked to eat it, whether the plant minded being eaten, why some animals ate other animals instead of plants, and whether the animal-eating animals were bad, than to speculate about the Divine Creator of all vegetation.

Most likely Howe committed himself to such a nebulous and impractical plan without really thinking it through and later did not want to back down. Initially, he had been tentative about it, simply noting in his annual report for 1841 that he was experimenting with indirect methods "to convey to her some adequate idea of the great Creator and Ruler of all things." But when that announcement provoked a storm of reproach from the orthodox, Howe dug in his heels. His original vague notion suddenly became a crusade. By the time he wrote the next year's report, his tone had turned truculent: "It is said continually, that this child should be instructed in the doctrines of revealed religion, and some even seem to imagine her eternal welfare will be periled by her remaining in ignorance of religious truths." Although he did not doubt that she could "be made to give edifying answers, as are recorded of many other wonderful children, to questions on spiritual subjects," he refused to train her to parrot dogmas and creeds. "The conception of the existence of a Creative Power, . . . the last and noblest fruit of the growing mind," should not be forced prematurely.[65]

His "sense of responsibility to God" as well as his love for Laura dictated that he ignore the sniping of his evangelical critics. Mindful of the "high responsibility of the charge of a soul," and feeling as deep an interest "as the mother who bore her," he would stick to his plan of allowing her religious feeling to develop naturally. The "book of nature" would be his only guide: it had taught him that if he prepared Laura's mind for religious consciousness, he could gradually make her understand "every religious truth that it may be desirable to teach her."[66]

But even as he boldly asserted the rightness of his methods, Howe was preparing his readers for the experiment to fail. "Expressions dropped carelessly by others; as God, Heaven, Soul &c." had already confused the child, he complained. She had started to ask questions about religion before she was mentally and spiritually prepared to understand the answers. In their ruthless bigotry, the orthodox were poised to interfere with her behind his back. In fact, he suspected that they had already begun surreptitiously "to instil into her mind notions which might derange the whole plan of her instruction." If they persisted in their interference, he could not answer for the consequences.[67]

IN THE END, Howe's vaunted plan for Laura's religious education—like his school for the deaf-blind—came to nothing. Over the next few years, she badgered him and her teachers with anxious questions about birth, death, and morality, but her religious consciousness failed to develop according to his script. Perhaps no child, however clever, could have followed his trail of obscure metaphysical clues. Laura may have been delicate and pretty enough to make a credible sentimental icon, but she could not so easily be transformed into a Common Sense theologian.

The real Laura, bewildered by death, terrified of abandonment, and impatient with evasion, needed definitive and comforting answers. Even if she had been able to understand Howe's reasonable Unitarian God, that benevolent but distant abstraction might not have satisfied her. She wanted a warm, embracing deity who could work compensatory miracles in Heaven, a Savior who would ultimately open her eyes and ears and loose the string of her tongue.[68] After decades of soul searching, Bible reading, and religious discussion, she finally found her God. In 1862, to Howe's chagrin, she joined her parents' evangelical Baptist church and was baptized by immersion in a brook near the Bridgman farm.

CHAPTER EIGHT

Sea Changes

IN 1840, THE SCOTTISH PHRENOLOGIST George Combe proposed a cure for Howe's chronic restlessness: still a bachelor at forty, Howe should marry. Combe had observed that in addition to well-developed cerebral organs of Combativeness, Benevolence, and Love of Approbation, his friend possessed large organs of Affection. In denying these impressive organs "their legitimate gratification," Howe stood in the way of his own health and happiness.

Combe, who had himself married in middle age, recommended that Howe select as his bride "a Lady of mature years, in whom the moral and intellectual organs predominate." An ideal mate would be someone "with just such a brain" as Howe's taciturn but efficient older sister, Jeannette. Wed to a similarly self-effacing middle-aged woman, Howe would, Combe promised, discover that the "constant quiet play" of marital affection has "an inexpressible charm . . . which relieves and cherishes all the better faculties of the mind . . . and makes them wear longer."[1]

On April 23, 1843, at the age of forty-two, Howe finally took Combe's advice. But his bride, Julia Ward, a New York heiress eighteen years his junior, was hardly the sort of sedate helpmeet that Combe had in mind. Indeed, it would be difficult to imagine a more ill-suited couple than Samuel Howe and Julia Ward. The daughter of a rich Wall Street banker, she had grown up in a mansion, liked parties and pretty clothes, could not make a decent meal, and hated domestic chores. Howe, who had always vowed he would never marry a rich woman, lived on a small income at the Perkins school in drafty apartments that stank of water closets. Ward, outgoing and vivacious, had an impish wit and loved to tease; Howe had little sense of humor, and none at all about himself. He demanded attention, praise, and obedience, but Ward had an iron will and ambitions of her own as well as an independent income. She was also better read and better educated than her intellectually insecure husband. Longfellow, who had some misgivings about the match, described her as "a fine, young, buxom damsel of four and twenty, who is full of talent,—indeed carrying almost too many guns for any man who does not want to be *firing salutes* all the time."[2]

When he married, Howe was almost certainly not the sexually repressed celibate that Combe took him for. In 1829, while he was in Greece, there had been rumors of his carrying on with young women in his employ.[3] Although he hotly denied these "vile" stories, the numerous adulteries that he later confessed to his wife suggest that he did not stumble into marriage completely ignorant of women.[4] A man of the world, perhaps he should have followed the example of some of the men in his circle by looking for a wife who enjoyed domestic submission. (Ralph Waldo Emerson found two such wives: the first, on her deathbed, told him that she would do him "more good by going than by staying"; the second wrote that "Husband knows best" was her creed.)[5] Howe thought he preferred a woman of spirit and intellect. After they were married, however, he used all the weapons in his arsenal—"argument, silence, infidelity, and indifference"—to undermine his wife's confidence and thwart her ambitions. Yet Julia Ward proved irrepressible.[6] Besides caring for six children (one of whom died in early childhood), she wrote essays and poetry, read German philosophy, lectured—in open defiance of Howe—at public meetings, and achieved immortality as the author of

"The Battle Hymn of the Republic." Once her husband was out of the way permanently, she went on to distinguish herself further as a feminist leader and suffragist spokeswoman.

IT WAS LAURA'S celebrity that first brought this unlikely couple together. In the summer of 1841, when Laura was eleven years old, Julia Ward and her two sisters were spending the season in Dorchester, near Boston. Longfellow and Sumner, friends of Julia's brother Sam, came to call and proposed an excursion to the Perkins Institution to see the miraculous deaf-blind girl. Howe was absent when the visitors arrived, but a Perkins teacher conducted them to Laura, who was seated at a desk beside Lucy Reed. Fifty years later, Julia Ward Howe still recalled that Lucy had flashed a smile "so beautiful as to call forth from us an involuntary exclamation."[7] About Laura, however, she said nothing: throughout Julia Ward Howe's long life, she maintained a curious silence on the subject of her husband's most famous pupil.

Just as the visitors were preparing to go home, Sumner looked out the window and spotted Howe on his black horse. Julia Ward Howe, who waxed hagiographic about her husband once he was dead, memorialized the moment. "I looked out also," she wrote in her memoirs, "and beheld a noble rider on a noble steed." When one of the women in their group wanted to give Laura a small gift—just a trinket—Howe, always concerned that fame might spoil the child, "forbade this rather sternly." Ward was impressed, she recalled, by his display of "unusual force and reserve."[8]

Almost two years later, despite a stormy courtship during which Howe wrangled with the Ward family for control of his future wife's fortune, the marriage finally took place. On May 1, 1843, the newlyweds set sail for Europe, accompanied by Julia's sister Annie. (In that period, brides, often unaccustomed to the company of men, welcomed the companionship of their female relatives on honeymoon tours that might last many months.) Howe, who was himself most comfortable in an all-male social world, invited Horace Mann along, with the idea that the two of them could take excursions together to investigate European schools and

Laura Bridgman in adolescence. Her teachers complained that she refused to smile for photographs. (COURTESY OF THE PERKINS SCHOOL FOR THE BLIND)

Laura reading to Samuel Gridley Howe from an embossed book. The artist has made Laura's cheeks more pleasingly round than they were in photographs.

Mary Swift and Laura, c. 1845. Their right hands are joined so that they can finger spell to one another. (COURTESY OF THE PERKINS SCHOOL FOR THE BLIND)

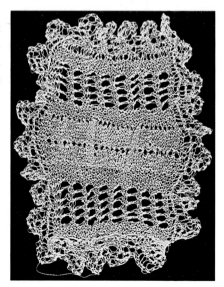

laura will write letter to mother laura will ride wi with father. laura will make purse for another laura will sleep with mother and father mother will love and kiss laura now laura will carry letter for mother laura will go see wale, laura will go home.

Laura's first letter home, written in 1839, betrays her homesickness. The letter reads: "laura will write letter to mother laura will ride with father. laura will make purse for mother laura will sleep with mother and father mother will love and kiss laura now laura will carry letter for mother laura will go see wales [Howe's sister, Maria Wales] laura will go home." (FROM MARY SWIFT LAMSON'S *LIFE AND EDUCATION OF LAURA BRIDGMAN*)

An example of the fine lace that Laura made to present to friends or to sell in the Perkins shop. This piece belonged to Mary Swift Lamson. (COURTESY OF THE MASSACHUSETTS HISTORICAL SOCIETY)

Formerly the Mount Washington House, a South Boston hotel, this building became the home of the Perkins Institution in 1839. Except during vacations, Laura lived here until she died. (COURTESY OF THE PERKINS SCHOOL FOR THE BLIND)

Laura teaching Oliver Caswell to read, from a painting signed "D. Fisher," c. 1841. (FROM PRO-CEEDINGS AT THE CELEBRATION OF THE ONE HUNDREDTH ANNIVERSARY OF THE BIRTH OF DR. SAMUEL GRIDLEY HOWE, NOVEMBER 11, 1901)

Laura reading an embossed book, c. 1850. Books printed in raised letters were difficult for many blind people to decipher and too large to hold comfortably. Nevertheless, Laura read whatever she could get her hands on. (COURTESY OF THE PERKINS SCHOOL FOR THE BLIND)

$\mathcal{S}$amuel Gridley Howe in middle age, c. 1858. (COURTESY OF THE PERKINS SCHOOL FOR THE BLIND)

$\mathcal{C}$reated in 1889, shortly after Laura's death, this fanciful image is based on earlier portraits of her and Howe. He was, of course, much younger than this when he first taught her, and he did not use toy blocks to instruct her in the alphabet. (COURTESY OF THE PERKINS SCHOOL FOR THE BLIND)

Laura threading a needle with her tongue, c. 1885. In the early 1870s, she was happy to replace the green ribbon that had earlier covered her eyes with the more fashionable opaque eyeglasses shown here. (COURTESY OF THE PERKINS SCHOOL FOR THE BLIND)

In the foreground is a plaster cast of Laura's autopsied brain, made under the supervision of the neurologist Henry H. Donaldson. Sophia Peabody sculpted the bust in the background in 1841, the year before her marriage to Nathaniel Hawthorne. Horace Mann, who would later marry Sophia's sister Mary, suggested that Howe give Sophia the commission. (COURTESY OF THE PERKINS SCHOOL FOR THE BLIND)

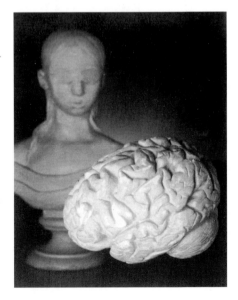

asylums. At the last minute, Mann decided that he, too, should combine honeymoon pleasure with philanthropic business and, after years of vacillation, married Mary Peabody on the morning of the day they sailed.

The two couples had planned to remain abroad for about six months, but when Julia became pregnant, the Howes were forced to extend their stay. While they waited out the winter in Rome, Howe simmered with boredom and impatience. "Give my love to our circle,—to all of them," he wrote plaintively to Sumner in February. "Oh, how I wish I were in the midst of it again! And again at work. . . . Life without labour is nothing,—nothing."[9] Free to resume their travels after the birth of their first child, Julia Romana, in March 1844, the Howes began the long trip home, returning to Perkins in September. They had been gone sixteen months.

LAURA DEPENDED ON Howe for affection and intellectual stimulation, and his marriage and long absence were hard on her. She had been living in the director's apartments with him since 1841, when Drew resigned, and was used to being his pet. Naturally, the change in his domestic arrangements—the displacement of the familiar Jeannette Howe by the unknown Julia Ward Howe—threatened Laura's position in the household and made her feel anxious and a little jealous. Instructed to think of Mrs. Howe as her new mother, Laura at first protested. If anyone should be her surrogate mother, it was Howe's sister. "I cannot love Mrs. Howe . . . because I do not see her often; she is a stranger."[10] Mary Swift reported that, struggling with jealousy, Laura asked: "Does Doctor love me like Julia?" Swift, never one for coddling, answered with an unequivocal "no," but Laura as usual pursued the problem. "Does he love God like Julia?" "Yes," replied Swift, who by that time should have known him better.[11]

As the day of the wedding approached, Laura begged to be allowed to attend, but Howe refused. Perhaps his bride did not care to be upstaged by a deaf-blind celebrity, or perhaps he feared that Laura's unseemly noises might disrupt the ceremony. Deploying her extraordinary powers of self-consolation, Laura cheered herself up by cleaning out the closets in the director's apartments and by memorizing the names of all the cities that Jeannette Howe would pass through on her way to the festivities in New York. Bowing to the inevitable, she also began to practice saying "Mrs. Howe" with her mouth, "because I shall want to call her." But Laura's disappointment and anger took their toll. Three days after the wedding, she reported to Swift a terrible dream. "My heart ached, I was very much frightened last night. I do not know what made my blood make a noise. . . . I did not know dreams could make my heart afraid." Her bad dream had felt "very hard and heavy and thick": in it, another Perkins teacher had come into her room with a horrible pig, which had run downhill on a board onto her bed and climbed over her as she slept.[12]

Worse for Laura than the marriage itself was the prospect of Howe's long absence. Months before his engagement had even been announced, she came to him with a "disturbed look" to report another of her nightmares. "I cried much in the night because I did dream you said good bye to go away over the water."[13] Perhaps to soften the blow of his departure, Howe encouraged a group of Perkins teachers to take Laura and Oliver to Boston Harbor for a tour of the Cunard steamer that would carry him and his bride to Europe. Two days before the sailing, the Perkins party boarded the ship and inspected the staterooms, saloons, and cabins. Curious as always, Laura asked where the molasses and flour were stored, where the cooking was done, and if the food was good. When she arrived in the galley, the cook offered her a piece of cake as proof of his culinary skill. Laura, true to form, demanded to know how he got milk for the cake. After she had visited the ship's cow, Laura insisted on walking the entire length of the ship, to get an idea of its size.

But the excitement of touring an oceangoing steamer was small consolation. Struggling to cope with her own grief at Howe's departure, Laura offered to comfort Swift: "Do not be very sad," she told her teacher; "I will make you happy." (In fact, Swift, who disagreed with Howe about religion and resented some of his edicts, was probably more relieved than sorry to see him go.) When Swift tried to cheer Laura up by bringing Oliver into the room, Laura again responded with heart-breaking pluck: "I will try very hard to make him happy. He must not be sad." Taking Oliver by the hand, she led him into Howe's room and pointed out all the things that had been taken away. Swift recorded in her journal that after talking with Oliver for the rest of the afternoon, Laura "became more quiet."[14]

The pain of other recent abandonments no doubt intensified Laura's misery over Howe's departure. In 1843, she had still not recovered completely from the loss of her beloved first teacher, Lydia Drew. Drew had resigned in September 1841 to marry a middle-aged doctor, Cyrus Morton, a neighbor of Drew's family in Halifax, Massachusetts. He was the widower of Drew's older sister, Lucy, who had died in childbirth two years previously, along with the stillborn child. The bereaved Dr. Morton needed a wife for himself and a mother for his two surviving sons, and it was not unusual for an unmarried young woman to shoulder her dead sister's responsibilities—especially when she had no brighter prospects. Two years earlier, Drew had suffered the embarrassment of a broken engagement; by 1841, at age twenty-six, she might have welcomed the chance to marry her brother-in-law and leave her exhausting work at Perkins.[15]

Until Lydia Drew Morton died in 1887, she remained Laura's steadfast friend. Even after the birth of her own two children, Drew corresponded with Laura and often invited her to spend vacations in Halifax with the Drew and Morton extended families. (Drew's great-grandson, Lloyd Morton, still living in Halifax, recalls handed-down stories about Laura's visits, when family members would summon her to breakfast by banging on the wall, so that she could feel the vibrations.)[16] But much as regular reunions with Drew cheered Laura, she would always regret the departure of her first Perkins teacher. Years later, she still fondly recalled how Drew had taught her to read, sew, and "make the blind letters." "Miss D. had a long piece of patience in me in many respects," Laura wrote in her memoirs. "I was very strongly attached to her."[17] Other remarkable women would have charge of Laura later but, with all their virtues, they did not have Drew's steady good nature, flexibility, or sense of humor. None of Drew's successors would laugh so heartily at Laura's jokes or fully appreciate her sly wit.

At about the time that Drew left, Laura's parents also disappeared from her life. Preoccupied with a growing brood of younger children, Mrs. Bridgman had gradually stopped responding to Laura's letters, and Mr. Bridgman, of course, had never shown any interest in his daughter. In the summer of 1841, just before Drew resigned, she accompanied Laura to New Hampshire for summer vacation; after that trip, no further arrangements were made for Laura to return home until January 1846. In the intervening four and a half years, Laura spent her vacations either in the homes of her teachers or on her own at Perkins. Her family was so entirely out of touch with Laura that a few months after Howe's departure, the normally uncommunicative Jeannette was moved to write a letter remonstrating with Mrs. Bridgman:

> I wish you would write to Laura. There will be some danger of losing her interest in home, unless she hears or sees some of the family. We hoped you would have come this Spring, perhaps you will in the Autumn or Winter.[18]

When the Bridgmans received this letter in August 1843, they had not had any news of their daughter for at least nine months and had no idea who was teaching Laura or caring for her while Howe was abroad, if, indeed, they even knew that he was gone. They seemed to have simply let her drift away.

Laura's feelings of loss run through her letters of this period like a sad refrain:

> Miss Ward is married,—Mrs. Howe. Miss J. [Jeannette] went to see Dr. married. . . . I am very sad to have Dr. & Mrs. Howe go & stay many months, one year. They will go three thousand miles, far off. . . . Mrs. Howe can talk with her fingers, she goes away in May. . . . Dr. and Mrs. Howe went away in the ship Monday. They will come next spring, very long.[19]

The passage of time did not help Laura forget. Eight months after Howe's departure, on January 1, 1844, she greeted Swift with the news "It is new happy year day" and then, extending her hand to the east, added wistfully, "Doctor cannot know I say so."[20] Sometimes she liked to pretend that he had returned. Addressing his empty chair, she would ask, "Are you tired of going very far? Did you want to come back?"[21]

Howe added to her distress by ignoring most of her letters. "Why do you not write a letter to me often?" she demanded at the end of March. "Do you always pray to God to bless me? I think of you often. . . . I have not seen you for ten months, that is very long. . . . I want you to write a letter to me."[22] Trying to make sense of his silence, she asked Swift to explain what had gone wrong: "Doctor loves wife best of any. . . . I love him best of any, why does he not love me?"[23]

Faced with Howe's neglect, Laura did her best to establish a bond with his wife. She proclaimed her newfound devotion to Julia Ward Howe in a series of unusually ardent and obsequious letters. "I want to see you very much," Laura wrote in April. "When you come home, I shall shake your hands & hug & kiss you very hard, because I love you & am your dear friend. Are you very glad to receive letters from me? One night I dreamed that I was very glad to see you again. I hope you do not forget how to talk with your fingers."[24] After she learned of the birth of the Howes' baby, Laura's letters to Mrs. Howe became almost frantic. Her pleas to remain a member of their family show how clearly she understood the precariousness of her own situation:

> I love your baby very much, & am your precious. I shall make a present for you to remember me many years. I should like to live with you and your husband & dear baby. While you were away one year I was in great misery, & had to miss you many times. I did not like to have you go away with Dr. Howe. As soon as you come home, I shall run to you & kiss & hug you very hard, & shall take my very dear baby & kiss it very softly & take off her things. I shall always set her a good example. I want to see her very much. I should like to make a very nice clothes to help you.

. . . I want you to come back *now;* if you do not come quick, then
I must send a long string to pull you over the sea to South
Boston. I thought of you & [baby] Julia & Doctor many times,
that they would love me very much, because I love them & you
so much.[25]

The desperation in this letter suggests that Laura already sensed that
Howe's new wife was not predisposed to be an ally. During her engagement, Julia Ward had made a show of learning to finger spell, but after
the marriage all pretense of affection for Laura stopped. As the Howe
daughters later admitted, their mother felt "a physical distaste to the abnormal and defective" and "a natural shrinking from the blind and other
defectives with whom she was often thrown."[26] Laura, whose uncanny
ability to "read" the moods and characters of those around her was legendary, would have been well aware of Mrs. Howe's aversion. (Laura's
teachers believed that she possessed telepathic powers, and Howe conceded that it was impossible for her companions to hide their emotions
from her.)[27] Sensing Julia Ward's physical antipathy must have terrified
Laura. What would become of her when the Howes returned?

During this period of loneliness and uncertainty, Laura had nobody
to comfort her. Mary Swift and Jeannette Howe shared responsibility for
Laura's care during Howe's absence, but neither was in a position to offer her much reassurance about the future. Indeed, Jeannette Howe, who
had spent the past decade keeping house for her adored brother, may
well have been worrying about her own fate. No doubt she had benevolent feelings toward Laura, but her icy reserve made it difficult for her to
form emotional connections with anyone. Even Howe's daughters, who
usually painted flattering family portraits, had to admit that their aunt,
married by then to her widowed brother-in-law, was strange and cold: "a
shy and silent person," ponderous in her movements, with a large,
"closely corsetted figure" and an alarming want of tact.[28] Laura always
spoke of "Miss J." with respect, but never with much warmth or interest.

Although younger and more sociable than Jeannette Howe, Swift
provided Laura with little more in the way of solace or affection. The

top graduate of a teachers' seminary, Swift regarded herself as a professional teacher, not as a surrogate mother. In her meticulous journals, Swift often noted and analyzed Laura's moods, but she did not consider her pupil's emotional state her main concern, except insofar as Laura's irritability or sadness got in the way of her lessons.

Under the conscientious supervision of Jeannette Howe and Swift, Laura was seldom alone during the sixteen months of Howe's absence, but she was often lonely. Isolated from the other blind children at Perkins not only by her deafness, but also by her privileged status, she slept and ate in the director's apartments, with only "Miss J." for company. During the day, she followed Swift's strict schedule of lessons:

6:15 TO 7 A.M., *arithmetic;*

7 TO 8 A.M., *breakfast and housekeeping chores;*

9 TO 10 A.M., *student-teacher conversation;*

10 TO 11 A.M., *geography;*

11 TO NOON, *writing;*

NOON TO 1 P.M., *reading and discussion of books;*

1 TO 2 P.M., *knitting or sewing;*

2 TO 3 P.M., *calisthenics with the blind girls;*

3 P.M., *dinner.*

After dinner she and Swift took their daily five- or six-mile walk, during which her teacher made sure that "not a moment was wasted"; finally, Laura would knit until bedtime at six. Laura's favorite time in the day was nine o'clock in the morning, the "much-loved" hour when Swift allowed her to bring up her own subjects for conversation.[29] Only during that single precious period each day could Laura try to spell out with her fingers what was on her mind.

Of course, she longed for Howe's return: he would reintroduce some spontaneity into her regimented schedule, indulge in occasional "romps," and perhaps tell her again that she was his dear daughter. But much as she looked forward to their reunion, Laura also felt anxious and uneasy. In August 5, 1844, just a month before Howe was due home,

Laura recorded in her journal the details of a lonely day and another ominous dream:

> company came to see the schoolars i thought of dr. howe and his wife and the baby all the time that I should be very gay to see them. my teacher was very sick with her lungs all the morning so that she could not teach me any so i knit a purse all day. i staid a little while in mrs. howe's room and it made me think much about her and doctor and the baby. and i dreamed of them last night that his coat was made of velvet in europe and he did not ask me how i did.[30]

No doubt the infrequency of Howe's letters or a new coolness in their tone led to her premonition that when he returned, her beloved "Doctor" would no longer care very much about how she did.

LAURA'S DREAM PROVED prophetic. When Howe came home to Perkins in September, he turned on her with a sudden and surprising vehemence. He announced that he was disenchanted with his famous pupil, bitterly disappointed in the adolescent who had replaced the delightful little girl he had left behind. "I hardly recognized," he later claimed, "the Laura I had known."[31] The thirteen-year-old whose soul, Howe could say in 1843, had "put forth the buds of the brightest virtues," whose character was one of "amiable simplicity," and whose passion for knowledge was so ardent as to be almost dangerous to her health, now seemed limited in intellect and flawed in character. He lamented that his high hopes for his creation, his Galatea, his great experiment, had been shattered. For him, the great romance of her rescue from darkness was over.

Howe frequently promised that he would someday write a book about Laura, but he never did. After his return from Europe, he discussed her in five more of his annual reports, but always in a tone of disappointment. The paeans to her charm, joyfulness, goodness, and brilliance that had punctuated his earlier accounts were replaced in these later reports by analyses of her shortcomings of character and intellect, by complaints about the mistakes others have made in dealing with her, and by testy justifications of his own actions.

Howe's list of frustrations and disillusionments was long. Laura's intellect no longer dazzled him. Her celebrated accomplishments—accurate spelling, a large and mature vocabulary, thorough mastery of geography—struck him now as amounting to very little. At fifteen, the little girl whose progress had astonished the world appeared to him "without so much acquaintance with language as a common child of six years old."[32]

He suddenly realized that he had been unreasonable in his high hopes for a child with her terrible disabilities. Laura had come to him too late, past "the season of life when the vernacular tongue should be learned." "Five precious years, in which, perhaps, as much, if not more, is learned by children than in any other five years of life, had been to her a dark and silent blank." She could never have made up for that lost time. Long disuse had probably weakened "the natural *disposition* for speech" permanently. When, with his help, she finally did begin to acquire language, she was impelled not by the "sportive playfulness" of a young normal child, but by a "conscious desire for light."[33] Howe was ready now to concede that in Laura's case nature's decree was immutable. Because she had not been able to learn effortlessly and spontaneously at the time and in the way that other children learn, she was doomed to learn imperfectly.

Laura's character and temperament also began to strike Howe as hopelessly deformed. In his naïve early enthusiasm, he had been blind himself, he said, to "important considerations": her "hereditary disposition" and "deranged constitution," and the "undue development" of her nervous system. The high spirits, sportiveness, and intensity that before had enchanted him now made him uneasy. There was something uncontrolled, almost savage, about her. Her family background, perhaps, had tainted her. Owing to the legacy of her mother's volatile disposition or to her humble origins, the Laura he reencountered in 1844 was not "so happily organized as many other children"; she suffered from "constitutional disturbing forces which do not affect others." By nature, he noted a few years later, she was subject to "sudden paroxysm[s]" and "nervous explosion[s]":

> Let it not be supposed that her usual gentleness, her affectionate disposition, and her cheerfulness, come altogether from a happy constitutional temperament, for it is not so. On the contrary, she inherits a constitutional disposition to irritability and violence of temper.[34]

Near the end of his life, Howe's conclusions about Laura were even more scathing: in 1874, he recalled that when she was young, the expression of anxiety on her face had sometimes been so intense "as to beget the thought that she might be a wild young witch, or be going mad."[35]

Now that the scales had dropped from his eyes, Howe realized that Oliver Caswell was actually the more successful of his educational experiments. Despite Oliver's failure to grasp the fundamentals of language and notwithstanding his "smaller brain," he was placid, submissive to his teachers, cheerful, and thus in the end "much more satisfactory" than the alarmingly volatile Laura. Howe's report for 1844 concludes with unprecedented praise for the uncorrupted and incorruptible—albeit slow-witted—Oliver. Howe could now say of him what he could no longer say of the flawed adolescent, Laura: that a child "more gentle, honest, true-hearted" than Oliver "exists not."[36]

WHAT EXPLAINS HOWE'S angry disenchantment with the little girl who made him famous? Why, after a separation of only sixteen months, did she seem to him so altered—and so disfigured? Howe repeatedly, and at great length, tried to justify his change of heart. At the root of his disillusionment, he claimed, was his horrified discovery that his cherished plans for Laura's religious awakening had been sabotaged. While he was away, ignorant and selfish persons, "more desirous to make a proselyte than to keep conscientiously their implied promise of not touching upon religious topics," had filled her head with "pestilent catchwords and sectarian shibboleths." Recklessly disregarding his attempts to "prevent her forming such [religious] notions as would seem unworthy to her more developed reason," they had made her into an absurd, dogma-reciting automaton:

> She could not understand metaphorical language; hence the Lamb of God was to her a *bona fide* animal, and she could not conceive why it should continue so long a lamb and not grow old like others and be called a sheep.[37]

By forcing upon her doctrines that she was not ready to understand, these zealots had forever blighted the "natural and harmonious development of her religious nature" and impaired her capacity for reverence, gratitude, and love.[38] He had looked forward to coordinating her moral, religious, and intellectual development,

> to lead her wondering mind to the perception of the higher attributes of God, as her capacity for such perception was unfolded, until, her moral nature being fully developed, she might have been as much impressed with love for his tender mercies as she had been with wonder at his Almighty Power.[39]

But while his back was turned, the orthodox, with their perplexing and frightening doctrines, had bent and twisted her native inclinations out of their natural shape, like the twigs of an espaliered tree.[40] At the same time, they had wantonly destroyed her usefulness to science. Laura's mind was now so contaminated by dogma that she could no longer serve as the subject of his cherished experiment on the innateness of religious dispositions.

More infuriating, almost, than the damage done to Laura's character and to Howe's philosophical aspirations was the flouting of his clear and explicit orders. To guard against the very kind of interference that had occurred, he had given strict instructions before he left that no one, including Mary Swift, had permission to discuss religion with Laura. If, in her voraciously inquisitive way, Laura raised questions about spiritual matters, she should be told to wait for his return. If she would not be put off, her teachers were to tell her to address her concerns to him in a letter. Howe claimed that he never doubted that his wishes would be honored. According to his daughter Laura Richards, he "sailed to Europe with his bride in May, 1843 . . . with cheerful confidence that on his return he would be able to continue his course of leading the child of his spirit, through paths which could be made clear and smooth to her, onward and upward."[41]

Howe said that when he discovered that orthodox proselytizers had destroyed his cherished plans, he felt mutilated, as if they had stolen something from him. "It is painful," he explained, "to be forced to relinquish ideas which by long possession have become regarded as much one's own—as much a part of one's self, as one's property, or one's limbs."[42] Among his friends and family, his rage and disappointment became legendary. Sixty years later, his daughters Maud and Florence retold the story with undiminished indignation:

> Laura was much interested in religious ideas, as is very evident from numerous passages in the journals. But the expansion of her mind in this direction was unduly and inconsiderately hastened, if not forced, by those who interfered with more zeal than wisdom. To whom did it of right belong to give this poor child the crown of all knowledge, the knowledge of her Creator and His laws? Did it not belong to the man who had first brought the light of human life and thought into her strange prison, who had planned out the whole wonderful scheme of her education, with its novel and successful methods? . . . Dr. Howe was much troubled upon his return from Europe to find that the mind whose opening development he had watched with such wise care had been turned aside from the high paths where he hoped to lead it. His disappointment was very great.[43]

YET, DESPITE HOWE'S well-publicized fulminations, it is hard to avoid the suspicion that he had been complicit in his own betrayal. By proclaiming in 1842 that Laura would discover God on her own, Howe had backed himself into a corner. Except for some hazy ideas about using magnets and flower buds, he had never formed a realistic plan for leading Laura toward religious consciousness.[44] If the orthodox, fearing for her salvation, had in fact "interfered" with her while he was abroad, they had also provided him with a face-saving way out of an embarrassing predicament.

Laura's indoctrination could not have taken him completely by surprise. Even before he left for Europe, he had acknowledged that visitors and other students were talking to her about religion. From Mary Swift's journal he must have known that Laura was "reading about God" and regularly attending church with one of her orthodox teachers, Eliza Rogers. He would also have seen reports in her teachers' journals of her many questions about religious matters, as well as the entry in Swift's journal for March 27, 1843, when Laura announced, "I have been reading about God."[45] And he must have understood that at this period of intense religious revivalism—the Second Great Awakening—when evangelical enthusiasms were fueling missionary activity, orthodox Christians could not in good conscience allow his famous pupil to remain in the dark about her own salvation. If bearers of the Good News could voyage to the wilds of Africa and Asia to instruct the "savages," they surely could—and determinedly would—travel to South Boston to instruct his benighted little student.

Moreover, Howe had left his prize philosophical chicken in the care of Mary Swift, an evangelical fox. He could have chosen a Unitarian teacher instead—several were already employed at Perkins—but he entrusted Laura to a devout, orthodox Congregationalist. (On Sundays, after church, Swift used her remarkable memory to transcribe the weekly sermon into her journal, apparently word for word.)[46] In later years, Swift always denied Howe's accusations of disobedience, claiming that she had strictly—if reluctantly—kept silent about religion. Possibly she had. There is no doubt, however, that she regarded his experiment as "disastrous" for an inquisitive, impatient, high-strung child such as Laura.[47]

Howe's depiction of Laura as a pathetic religious primitive, struggling to make literal sense of figurative religious language, is also problematic. Of course, her deafness sometimes caused her to misunderstand
or misuse words. As a blind child, however, she was all too accustomed
to metaphors. For her, *most* words were mere figures of speech. The
terms she studied in geography, for example—river, mountain, city,
ocean—were the emptiest of abstractions, utterly detached from anything in the object world that she could apprehend. Such words could
make sense to her only by analogy. "God" and "soul" might have been,
if anything, less disconnected from her inner life and experience than
most of the words she regularly used in imitation of her hearing and
sighted teachers. For a child as amazingly adept as Laura was at mimick-
ing the language of a world that she could not see, smell, or hear, understanding inaudible and invisible religious mysteries would have posed no
greater difficulty than learning about the moon, or France.

Contrary to Howe's claims, Mary Swift, who kept meticulous notes
on Laura's questions and comments, insisted that religious concepts
came relatively naturally to Laura:

> It was far more difficult to teach her many common things of
> life than to teach these [Christian] truths, which indeed she
> learned so easily that we could not determine when and how she
> obtained her knowledge of them. Her soul seemed to be pre-
> pared for them, receptive of them. . . . It may be she could not
> receive them all clearly; neither did she receive all clearly in her
> other studies, but we did not delay the teaching on this ac-
> count.[48]

Swift, of course, had her own religious ax to grind. Still, her teaching
journals provide detailed, daily evidence that Laura had a remarkable
ability to grapple with religious ideas. From the time in 1842 when Laura
first began to think about God, she showed that her restless mind was not
susceptible to the rote indoctrination that Howe dreaded. Her questions
were original, quirky, searching, incessant, and unorthodox. Why did

God not make her fingers all the same length? Why did God not give animals souls? If God can see us, does He have eyes? Why did God allow another Perkins student, little Orrin, to die? Does God know our thoughts? Does God know Latin? Do all people love God? Why did God make some people black? Is God ever surprised? How could God talk to men and women and tell them what to write in a book?

While Howe was abroad, Laura peppered him by mail with questions that reveal the intensity of her struggle to make sense of religious ideas and her impatience with pat answers. On January 28, 1844, she wrote:

> My very dear Dr. Howe:
>
> What can I first say to God when I am wrong? Would he send me good thoughts & forgive me when I am very sad for doing wrong? Why does he not love wrong people, if they love Him? Would he be very happy to have me think of Him & Heaven very often? Do you remember that you said I must think of God & Heaven? . . . Is God ever ashamed? . . . Why did you say I must think of God? You must answer me all about it, if you do not I shall be sad. Shall we know what to ask God to do? . . . How did God tell people that he lived in Heaven? How could He take care of folks in Heaven? Why is He our Father? . . . Why cannot He let wrong people to go to live with Him & be happy?[49]

As one of Howe's more moderate critics noted at the time, such questions showed anxiety and confusion, not moral or cognitive incapacity.[50]

The inquisitive young girl who demanded answers to her often irreverent questions bears no resemblance to the uncomprehending, robotic convert that Howe had portrayed. Indeed, Laura's insistent questioning suggests that on his return he might justifiably have heralded his philosophical experiment as a great success. Did Howe really fail to see that the intensity of her interest in religion could be construed as evidence of a natural religious inclination? Did he not understand the implications of what Mary Swift had told him: that Laura's soul was amazingly "receptive" to religious truths?

HOWE'S INSISTENCE ON seeing Laura's religious development as a catastrophe, even in the face of abundant evidence to the contrary, raises the question of why he was *really* fed up with her. After all, her story was his to write. If he had wanted to hail her religious education as a success, he had plenty of evidence to offer. Instead, he chose to create a melodrama of treachery and spiritual defloration, of innocence warped and virtue lost. In his rancorous and self-pitying narrative, he, not Laura, became the victim. Her failure to fulfill her angelic promise had wounded him, he said, and he could respond only with bitterness and regret.

Although Howe had a lifelong pattern of falling out with friends over political differences, it is difficult to explain his rejection of Laura. She was, after all, a child who depended on him not only for her physical care, but also for emotional nourishment. But Howe was not given to self-analysis or self-doubt. Complex feelings of which he was unaware might have fueled his anger, aggression, and sense of aggrievement. For reasons that he did not acknowledge even to himself, and that we can only guess, he may have been ready to distance himself from Laura. Perhaps he wanted—or needed—to see her as a failure, sullied and diminished.

One explanation is that Laura was simply a target of Howe's more general frustration. After the excitements of travel, he had returned to South Boston depressed and irritable at the prospect of resuming his work as the institution's director. By 1844, some of his fondest hopes for educating the blind had already been disappointed. When he reluctantly established the Perkins workshop in 1840, he had been sure that the Perkins graduates who found employment there would be able to sell enough of their manufactured goods to earn their own keep. Now, however, he had to admit that the workshop was likely to remain a drain on the Perkins treasury indefinitely. Despite his earlier optimism, the blind workers he had educated could not support themselves in the real world.[51]

To his disillusioned eyes, the blind themselves suddenly seemed al-most repulsive—not in their sightlessness, but in their physical weak-ness. A new tone of disgust and disapproval entered his descriptions of their inadequacy:

> If a person should compare the cadets at a good military acad-emy with the boys who have just entered a school for the blind, he would almost conclude that they were two distinct races of beings—so strongly would the florid complexions, the erect fig-ures, the expanded chests, the muscular limbs, the vigorous mo-tions, and the firm tramp of the young soldiers contrast with the pale faces, stooping forms, puny limbs, feeble motions, and hes-itating tread of the blind.[52]

Disenchanted with his students, he began to think he had been misguided in his earlier estimation of their potential. It seemed to him now that those born blind were almost hopelessly stunted, intellectually as well as physically. By 1848, he was ready to declare in capital letters in his an-nual report, that "THE BLIND, AS A CLASS, ARE INFERIOR TO OTHER PERSONS IN MENTAL POWER AND ABILITY."[53]

The unexpected—and probably unjust—accusation of racism that confronted him when he returned from Europe exacerbated Howe's an-gry, bitter mood. In 1833, he had refused admission to a "colored" blind boy on the grounds that at a time when Perkins was struggling to sur-vive, "more harm might be done if the admission of the boy kept others away, than good could be done to him." Soon after that, however, the board voted unanimously to remove racial bars to admission. When a black woman brought a blind child (Howe could not recall whether it was a boy or girl) to the institution a few months later, Howe received her cordially, but told her that the child, who was only four, was too young. She seemed satisfied at the time, but ten years later, a "pathetic description in verse, of an imaginary interview between the mother and the Director" appeared in the abolitionist press. In the poem, the mother says:

They told me—and scornfully bade me go back,
They'd have nothing to do with a child that was black.[54]

Howe, who traveled in abolitionist circles even before he became fully committed to the cause, was understandably infuriated by this libelous doggerel.

Other, more personal disappointments may also have contributed to Howe's angry rejection of Laura. The timing of his sudden impulse to spurn her, immediately after his honeymoon, raises the suspicion that he was displacing onto her some of the frustration and rage that he felt toward his new wife. Howe's marriage had got off to a rocky start. Although he and his bride enjoyed many pleasant moments during their honeymoon travels, the conflicts that had plagued them during their courtship erupted repeatedly after the wedding. Having chosen a wealthy, artistic, and ambitious young woman, Howe was disappointed when she not only failed to metamorphose into a self-effacing helpmeet but also grumbled about his neglect and resisted his authority. He was impatient with her moods and hated her barbed teasing; she, in turn, complained that he had no interest in her ideas, discouraged her writing, and had "scarcely half an hour in twenty-four" to give her.[55] Her fear of sharing her own mother's fate, and dying in childbirth—a fear with which Howe had absolutely no sympathy—almost certainly strained their sexual relationship, as it did that of many other nineteenth-century couples.[56] Laura, with her insistent needs, questions, and demands, might not only have been an intolerable emotional burden for Howe, but also perhaps the scapegoat for his marital frustration and anger.

In turning against Laura, Howe may have been redirecting other, unrelated angers and disappointments, but telling his tale of religious treachery gave him the additional satisfaction of advancing Horace Mann's cause. Howe had returned to Boston to find his friend in the thick of a ferocious battle of broadsides with the orthodox. Although the liberals had really already won the war for nonsectarian common schools, Mann continued to feel vulnerable to every attack. (His biographer, Jonathan Messerli, has pointed out that Mann—like Howe in this re-

spect—could "never emancipate his mind from a conspiracy and perse-
cution complex when even the slightest opposition to him appeared in
print.")[57] "I look upon my cause as desperate," Mann wrote to Howe in
October 1844, in a characteristically overwrought letter, "but am determined to have one fight for it, and if I die, I will die *game*."[58] Howe,
sharing Mann's sense of aggrievement, jumped at the chance to join the
fray. "Now is the time for your friends to come to your aid," he replied,
"and I for one will do what little I can."[59] One of the ways Howe helped
was by publicizing the story of Laura's botched religious education.
Her frightened and bewildered response to Calvinistic indoctrination
showed, he said, that sectarian education was a sham.

MUCH AS HOWE may have enjoyed using the story of Laura's deterioration to embarrass his orthodox enemies, it is unlikely that he fabricated it
purely out of spite or because his mood was angry. In withdrawing from
her, he must have been reacting at least in part to some alteration in her
manner or appearance. Whether or not her exposure to religious orthodoxy had done her any harm, Laura had undoubtedly changed in the sixteen months he was away.

It would be surprising if she had not disintegrated emotionally. The
strain that she suffered during his long absence would have shaken any
child. Abandoned first by Drew and then by her parents and Howe, and
left to the chilly ministrations of Mary Swift and Jeannette Howe, Laura
might well have grown nervous and irritable. She could not even comfort herself during Howe's absence with the knowledge that her life
would return to normal when he returned. Now that he was married,
with a child of his own, she had no idea whether she would continue to
live with him as a member of his family. Months of anxiety, anger, and
grief must have taken their toll on the sprightly child that Howe remembered. Laura's supposed "derangement" might simply have been rage at
the adults who had abandoned her and panic about what would happen
to her next.

Howe's disenchantment with Laura may also have been a response
to her physical transformation. Although in the nineteenth century

menarche occurred late, Laura, at fifteen, was beginning to undergo puberty. Photographs suggest that by September 1844, her nose and chin
had begun to lengthen, and her body to take on its adult proportions.
The angelic little girl who had seen Howe off on his travels was about to
be replaced by a young woman—a severely disabled young woman—
who would inevitably elicit from him, as from any observer, a more
complex and ambivalent response. Howe himself recognized that as long
as they are young, the disabled have a special appeal: "Human sympathies are always ready to be poured out in proportion to the amount of
human suffering. . . . When the supposed sufferer is a child—a girl—and
of pleasing appearance, the sympathy and the interest are naturally increased."[60] No longer a child and no longer of such "pleasing appearance," Laura may simply have lost her charm for Howe. Worse, as a
sexually maturing young woman, she may have heightened a guilty un-
easiness that had always been there. While a little blind girl would "naturally," as Howe said, awaken sympathetic interest, the sight of a blind
young woman could stir up insistent and troubling fantasies.

"Normal" people, of course, sometimes wonder about the sexual
feelings and experiences of the disabled. Blind people in particular can
arouse in the sighted an intense combination of fascination, titillation,
and voyeuristic guilt. But from the beginning, Howe had vehemently denied that Laura could be imagined as a sexual being. She was, he had
proclaimed, as innocent as a newborn and as spotless as a rose. An ethereal angel, she could not be the object of sexual curiosity or desire. It was
impossible to be curious about her sexual feelings, because she had none.
Now that Laura was fifteen, however, the physical evidence of puberty
made this reassuring idealization hard to sustain. Perhaps the sight of her
maturing body forced Howe to acknowledge not only that she was becoming a flesh-and-blood woman, but also that he himself had noticed
that fact.

He had always taken pains to establish his own sexual restraint toward the little girl who lived with him during his last six years as a bachelor. In his report for 1841, in one of the strangest passages in all of his

writing about Laura, he documented her fastidiousness and his elaborate propriety:

> From the time she came here, she has never been accustomed to be in company with any man but myself; and . . . I have, in view of the future, very carefully refrained from even those endearing caresses which are naturally bestowed upon a child of eight years old, to whom one is tenderly attached. . . . When she meets [a man], she shrinks back coyly; though if it be a lady, she is familiar, and will receive and return caresses; nevertheless she has no manner of fear or awe of me. She plays with me as she would with a girl. Hardly a day passes without a game at romps between us; yet never, even by inadvertence, does she transgress the most scrupulous propriety, and would as instinctively and promptly correct any derangement of her dress as a girl of fourteen, trained to the strictest decorum. Perceiving, one day, that I kissed a little girl much younger than herself, she noticed it and stood thinking a moment, and then asked me gravely, *"Why did you kiss Rebecca?"* and some hours after, she asked the same question again.[61]

This passage, for all its ingenuousness, betrays a peculiar erotic tension in their relationship. Howe records Laura's reiterated question, but is silent about his reply. Why indeed did he kiss little blind Rebecca while "carefully" refraining from kissing Laura? What "view of the future" inhibited him in her case? Perhaps, bizarre as it may seem, he reasoned that Rebecca, blind but not deaf, would be more marriageable than Laura, and that it would therefore be acceptable to accustom her to male caresses. Possibly he imagined that his kisses would be more likely to arouse Laura sexually than the much younger Rebecca. Yet earlier in the same passage he says that "Laura is still so young, and her physical development is yet so imperfect—she is so childlike in appearance and action, that it is impossible to suppose she has yet any idea of sex." Or perhaps his "view of the future" included the notion that although Laura was perfectly pure and innocent in childhood, she might later be vulnerable to corruption, and that he should therefore avoid planting seeds of adult lasciviousness.

In Howe's wildly inconsistent account, Laura is on the one hand as innocent as a much younger child, and on the other hand as coy around men as a fourteen-year-old girl. He is the only man allowed to touch her, but, for reasons that remain unclear, he refrains from kissing or caressing her as he does the other little blind girls. She "romps" with him as she would with a girl, yet is keenly aware that he is a man. To bolster his case for the purity and propriety of their relationship, Howe goes on to tell a story—he calls it presenting some "facts"—that, quite to the contrary, dramatizes an unmistakeable eroticism:

> During the last year, [Laura] received from a lady a present of a beautifully-dressed doll, with a bed, bed-clothes, and chamber furniture of all kinds. Never was a child happier than she was; and a long time passed in examining and admiring the wardrobe and furniture. The washstand was arranged, towels were folded, the bureau was put in place, the linen was deposited in the tiny drawers; at last the bed was nicely made, the pillows smoothed, the top sheet turned trimly over, and the bed half opened, as if coquettishly inviting Miss Dolly to come in; but here Laura began to hesitate, and kept coming to my chair to see if I was still in the room, and going away again, laughing, when she found me. At last I went out, and as soon as she perceived the jar of the shutting door, she commenced undressing the doll, and putting it to bed, eagerly desiring her teacher, (a lady,) to admire the operation.[62]

Howe's little tale is told with a cloying archness, like a parody of Dickens. It purports to be about innocence, but is really about a shared knowingness; Howe and little Laura both understand that a kind of striptease is in progress. The "coquettish" invitation to Miss Dolly to come to the half-opened bed; the laughing rediscoveries of Howe, still watching from his chair; the teasing accumulation of detail as the undressing of Miss Dolly is slowly prepared for and then repeatedly deferred; the unavoidable inference that Howe opened the door and peeped at the naked, blind Dolly after all. These aspects of the narrative belie Howe's assertions of perfect purity on Laura's part and unyielding self-restraint on his own.

Once Laura became a woman, however, the naïveté of these self-consciously charming early accounts could not be sustained: the sexual issues and tensions, unacknowledged but latent in Howe's narratives, would have to surface.[63] The fifteen-year-old who awaited Howe on his return in 1844 was too old to figure in an innocent pedophilic comedy of the kind he had recounted in 1841. She had outgrown childish "romps" and coy games with dolls and, if for no other reason than the changes in her own body, could no longer claim to be totally ignorant of sexual matters. It may be that Howe turned against Laura in part because he could no longer imagine her—and himself with her—as naïvely, and therefore as guiltlessly, as he had before. She had spoiled his stories simply by growing up.

He might also have been ashamed, or even frightened, of directing the same intense curiosity—philosophical and medical but also sexual—toward the young woman that he had directed toward the little girl. For six years, he had observed the child Laura with what he described as a purely objective, though benevolent, scientific eye. But watching a sexually mature blind woman could have been far more problematic psychologically.

Even for someone in his position, looking at the blind—who cannot look back or see themselves seen—is inescapably voyeuristic. (The poet Denise Levertov speaks of the "strange joy" of gazing her fill at a blind stranger's face, "ashamed, shameless.") As Freudian theorists have pointed out, however, this freedom to stare can awaken unconscious fears that ocular punishment will be exacted, an eye for an eye, for ocular

pleasures. In Howe's case, watching a grown-up Laura might have provoked feelings of guilt or anxiety that retribution would somehow be
visited on his own prying, penetrating eyes.[64]

Intriguing as such psychoanalytic speculations may be, they are at
best conjectures. What is certain is that Laura had outlived her emotional
usefulness to Howe. During his last bachelor years, when she filled the
role of surrogate daughter, Laura was a source of liveliness and affection
in his otherwise somber household. But Howe had returned from his
honeymoon with a girl child of his own, and three more baby girls were
eventually to follow, as well as two sons. Whatever emotional needs he
had for family life were amply filled—indeed, considering his frequent,
extended absences from home after his marriage, perhaps overfilled—by
his own wife and children.

By the end of 1844, Laura had also outlived her professional usefulness to Howe. Hundreds of sightseers still came to Perkins on exhibition
days to see her, but her days as a major tourist attraction were numbered:
an amazing little girl might draw large crowds, but a deaf-blind woman,
as she got older, would be less and less appealing. Besides, Laura had already established Howe's international fame as an educator, reformer,
and humanitarian. What more could she contribute? Anything that she
learned or accomplished as an adult would not significantly enhance his
career or increase his fame. The excitement—the miracle—was in the
drama of her rescue; Howe had got from it, and from Laura, nearly all
that he could.

He may also have grown tired and even a little resentful of having
his star tied to Laura. For a man who disliked sharing the limelight, the
public's adoration of her must have rankled. After all, the throngs of
Saturday visitors to Perkins wanted to see her, not him. Because of
Laura, doors had opened to him throughout Europe. On his honeymoon
tour, he had received invitations to meet Thomas Carlyle, Maria Edgeworth, William Wordsworth, Sydney Smith, Florence Nightingale, Richard Monckton Milnes (later Lord Houghton), Lord Morpeth (later the
earl of Carlisle), the marquess of Lansdowne, the duke of Richmond,
and the duchess of Sutherland. All these celebrities expected Howe to re-

gale them with tales of Laura Bridgman.[65] Like an actor associated with a single role or a writer recognized for only one book, Howe, by the end of his European tour, must have felt overshadowed by his own creation.

After his return to Boston, Howe threw himself into a host of new causes and interests, as if in pursuit of a different kind of glory, a fresh renown. He had always been the sort of person whose enthusiasms wax and wane: Greek and Polish independence, schools for the blind, the common-school controversy. The education of Laura Bridgman would be only one—though the most famous—in a long career of noble enterprises that he took up with excitement and eventually abandoned. In the decades following his marriage, he threw himself into virtually every reform movement that came along: improvement of lunatic asylums and institutions for the feeble-minded, penal reform, the Free Soil Movement, John Brown's raid on Harpers Ferry, the establishment of "oralist" schools for the deaf, the Cretan insurrection, the attempted annexation of Santo Domingo. Laura would never again be the focus of his work or, except in passing, the particular object of his interest. To his credit, he took full responsibility for her custodial care until his death in 1876, and even provided for her in his will. But after 1844, he no longer thought her important.

AS SOON AS she and Howe were reunited, Laura, famously skilled at reading "the natural language of the emotions" on the faces and hands she touched, must have realized that his feelings for her had changed.[66] But if she recognized Howe's emotional withdrawal, she never spoke of it. Nor did she complain when she was told to move out of her old room in the director's apartments and into the girls' section of the institution. As long as she lived, her silence about her fall from grace remained absolute. She spoke of "Doctor" only with awe and gratitude. He was, she always said, her dear and beloved benefactor. When he died, she wrote that she missed him sadly, having loved him "as a father."[67]

Teachers and Teaching

WHEN HOWE WAS honeymooning in London, Sydney Smith, the celebrated wit, dubbed him "Prometheus." The nickname of course delighted Howe: according to Greek mythology, Prometheus was the
benevolent titan who first created humans out of clay. By educating
Laura, Smith's flattering joke implied, Howe had given a soul to an inan-
imate body.[1]

If her education at Perkins in fact resembled an act of creation,
Howe did not accomplish the miracle by himself. From the beginning, he
depended on a staff of female workers who not only carried out his
teaching plans, but also chatted with Laura, corrected her behavior, took
her on walks and outings, helped her with needlework, read to her, made
notes on her progress, and invited her to their homes during school vacations. Between 1838 and 1850, Laura generally had a teacher to herself—
first Lydia Drew, then Mary Swift, finally Sarah Wight—but the others
also had a hand in her care. These women were Laura's most constant
companions; they shaped her values, helped form her opinions, and
taught her most of what she knew about the world.

BEFORE 1845, HOWE never said much about any of the teachers he employed. Drew worked closely and amicably with him for more than four

years, but he did not mention her by name in his annual reports until 1841, even though he always included lengthy excerpts from her journals. He singled her out only after she had resigned, in a valedictory tribute praising her "unwearied patience and ever-watchful kindness" toward Laura.[2] Howe's reticence, self-aggrandizing as it may seem, could have been prompted as much by propriety as by egotism. The genteel women who taught at Perkins were not public figures, and he may have thought it indiscreet to talk about Lydia Drew in print.

But when he returned from Europe to find that Laura had been "damaged" during Mary Swift's watch, Howe was too outraged to keep silent. In his report for 1844 (published in 1845), he blamed her teacher publicly for Laura's failures. Regardless of whether Swift had given the nod to orthodox proselytizers behind his back—she denied it, but he implied she had—she had applied Calvinistically punitive methods in her teaching. Instead of using affection to soften Laura's heart, Swift had tried to break the child's will. No wonder Laura was now angry, obstinate, and troubled.

Perhaps blaming Swift helped distract Howe from any guilt he might have felt about Laura. It was he after all who had abandoned her—first physically, by going abroad, and then emotionally, after he returned. But like many of us, Howe preferred wrath to self-recrimination. An aggressive man of action, he tended to tranform his inward qualms and misgivings into rage at the bad faith of others.

Howe laid out his grievances against Swift in a lengthy and detailed critique. Although she had proved skillful and industrious at "intellectual instruction," she had warped Laura's moral development. For example, misled by her own religious belief in the depraved nature of children, Swift had interpreted Laura's unpleasant vocalizing as a moral failing, an expression of rudeness or defiance. A more enlightened teacher would have seen these noises for what they really were: explosions of pent-up nervous energy. Laura did not make her "disagreeable" sounds out of ill temper or perverseness; she lacked self-control. By constantly reprimanding her, Swift had merely succeeded in making Laura more irritable, and the once tractable child had turned stubborn. The correct way to get her to restrain herself, Howe argued, was to appeal to her desire for approbation: "Children always resist the unconditional surrender of their own will to that of another, unless the summons be made in the irresistible language of love—which is the *open sesame* to every child's heart."[3]

Howe said that when he returned from Europe, he had read Swift's teaching journals "with grief equalled only by surprise." In his annual report, he illustrated his point by quoting her journal entries for three days in February 1844. According to her own account, she had spent those three days in a fierce struggle with Laura over a handkerchief. Laura liked to keep her handkerchief on top of the desk; Swift wanted it hidden away inside. This was an old quarrel, but in the past Laura had grudgingly submitted to her teacher's authority. On February 2, Laura finally rebelled:

> To-day when I told her to put it in the desk, she hesitated as usual, and put it in her lap, saying "I prefer to put in my lap," and then held up her hand for me to continue with the [lesson]. I said, "I told you to put in the desk, and now I want you to do it." She sat still for about two minutes, and then lifted the lid very high, threw the handkerchief into the desk, and let it fall with such a noise as to startle all in the school-room. Her face was growing pale and she was evidently getting into a passion.[4]

When Swift demanded that she open the desk, replace the handkerchief, and shut the lid again gently, Laura, crying by now, replied that she would take out the handkerchief, but only to wipe her eyes, not to please her teacher. Swift rose at once to the challenge: Laura would not be allowed to wipe her eyes until she first went through the motions of replacing the handkerchief properly. Angry enough now to declare war, Laura slammed the desk lid a second time, and Swift retaliated by restraining Laura's hands to prevent her wiping her eyes. "She sat still awhile," Swift noted, "and then uttered the most frightful yell that I ever heard. Her face was perfectly pale, and she trembled from head to foot."

At this point, Swift left Laura alone, hoping that a dose of isolation would subdue her. Laura feigned indifference and talked on her fingers to herself at first, but by the end of a lonely day she was ready to apologize. Swift, however, was not convinced that her contrition was sincere: "She . . . *said* she was sorry, but her countenance indicated anything but sorrow." On the next day, February 3, Swift resorted to punishment, and told Laura that she would not be allowed talk to her friends or attend a Perkins party "because only good girls went." When Laura remained obdurate, Swift, at a loss, confided to her journal: "I do not know what to do, and never felt the need of counsel more." Faced with Laura's "spirit of defiance," Swift finally decided to try solitary confinement. On February 4, a Sunday, Laura spent the day alone in the basement, coming upstairs only for dinner. By evening, her misery seemed genuine, and Swift agreed to forgive her. "Why do I feel so very sad after I ask God to forgive me, and when you forgive me?" Laura asked. Swift replied that it was because Laura felt sorry "that she had done wrong at all."

Howe was outraged by this story. "Every reflecting person must see and lament the error of treatment," he said, even though "the best might have fallen into it." Swift had failed to understand that a good teacher does not break a child's will, but gently and lovingly leads her student "to break its own will." A wiser teacher—a religious liberal, perhaps—would have taken advantage of Laura's tears to win her over with love, instead of scolding and punishing her:

How many softening hearts do we harden by our own sternness; how often are rising sobs suppressed by harsh reproofs; how many by their Gorgon aspect turn the just forming tear of contrition into stony hardness, and leave it the nucleus of selfishness and rage! And if these things are done even by parents, who would "coin their hearts, and drop their blood for drachmas" to promote the real good of those whom they punish, how much oftener are they done by teachers who, when roused by opposition, forget there there may be great selfishness in their determination to carry their point.[5]

Howe not only criticized Swift publicly in his annual report, but also apparently complained about her privately to his friends and acquaintances. A commiserating letter from Maria Edgeworth, the Anglo-Irish educational theorist and children's book writer, survives among his papers. "I feel with you, & for you, and for her [Laura], all that you have so feelingly, so judiciously described of regret for the mistakes that were made in her education during your absence," Edgeworth wrote. She confessed that she even felt sorry for Swift, "the mistaken, imperfect tutoress—who yielding to her own temper conceived she was reforming the temper of her pupil—a mistake most frequently made by self love in education." Worse even than this "mistake of the temper" was Swift's "fatal error" in "unduly straining the tender conscience" of a fragile child. "A child should be strengthened up to its conscience & its conscience strengthened up to it instead of either being made to feel that they have failed towards each other," Edgeworth argued. Making a child feel sinful and weak could destroy the natural "blest sense of shame" with which it was born.[6]

Edgeworth and Howe agreed on the principle, derived from Locke's *Some Thoughts Concerning Education,* that discipline should be based on affection, not coercion.[7] During the 1830s and 1840s, popular home-management manuals directed to middle-class women, as well as more learned books on educational reform, promoted this philosophy, which was espoused in the antebellum period by growing numbers of religious moderates and liberals. Rejecting the old "spare the rod, spoil the child" injunction so often invoked by Calvinists, American advocates of affectional discipline—including Lydia Sigourney, Catharine Beecher, Lydia Maria Child, Louisa Hoare, Catherine Sedgwick, Helen Hunt Jackson, Horace Mann, and his wife, Mary Peabody Mann—maintained that children should not be hedged in by rules, but cradled in tenderness.[8] Raised with love (in a home, needless to say, where the child was free from heavy labor and the mother had leisure to devote herself to child care), the child would naturally and spontaneously absorb the parents' moral values. In time, the child would "enshrine" the adored parents in its own mind, so that even when they were absent in body, they would always and everywhere be present: their loving supervision would become part of the child's very self. For children reared in this way, punishment would be redundant. Using self-examination and self-reproach, they could—and would—discipline themselves.[9]

As Howe pointed out in his report, this self-disciplinary process could only develop in children who identified authority with tenderness. Swift, he argued, should have tried harder to win Laura's love, instead of concentrating so single-mindedly on her intellectual progress. For all Swift's advanced training, she had not known the way to her pupil's heart. There were others at Perkins, "with far less intellect and acquirement" than Swift, who had succeeded in gaining "more complete dominion over [Laura's] affections," and whose will and pleasure had therefore become Laura's "delightful law."[10]

HOWE'S CRITICISMS OF Swift were unforgiving—she was, it should be remembered, an underpaid, overworked, unsupervised twenty-three-year-old—but they were not inaccurate. In truth, she was too rigid and exacting for the job he had given her. Her orderly schedule of ambitious lessons did not match Laura's needs. Desperate to make sense of the world, Laura demanded immediate responses to her questions. Her hunger for finger-spelled conversation never let up. She also wanted Swift, who was not the cuddly type, to provide her with physical affection. Touch was the only sensuous pleasure available to Laura, and she craved caresses. Deprived of stimulating sights and sounds, tantalizing smells and subtle tastes, she constantly—and perhaps oppressively—tried to kiss and hug her female companions, clinging to them as they talked and walked, fingering their jewelry and dresses, and stroking their hair.

Swift had needs and goals of her own. Only three months after putting her in charge of Laura, Howe had gone to Europe, leaving the young teacher to manage and educate his most famous student as best she could. Swift had to assert authority; otherwise Laura, with her intense personality and frantic curiosity, would have seized control. A perfectionist, Swift wanted to do what she had been trained for. Her job, she

believed, was to harness Laura's restless energy and discipline her rov-
ing mind by providing her with a structured curriculum of important
academic subjects: mathematics, geography, natural history, reading, and
writing. Swift expected to encourage good moral habits in her students
and check bad ones but, as an educated professional, she wanted obedience, respect, and achievement from her pupil, not love.

Laura's memoir of 1849 captures their incompatibility. Swift would
not allow her, she complained, "to have the pleasure of sitting or conversing with . . . any one else." Instead, her teacher would insist that she
work "so assiduous for a few hours." The problem, as Laura saw it, was
that Swift provided too much instruction and not enough companionship:

> She was very firm and particular and impatient that she made me
> obey her very quickly to work industriously. I felt in my heart I
> ought not to regard her wishes but I determined to do my duty
> for her I did not always like to be with her. I used to wish to be
> all solitary in the sink closet which I wash in now.[11]

What Laura had really needed, she said, was someone "very loving and
kind."

Swift recognized that she and Laura were not a particularly good
combination. She had noticed that Laura was "especially attracted to
those who have a gentle, timid nature."[12] Disciplined, assertive, and efficient, Swift could not be—and did not wish to be—the tender, motherly
companion that Laura craved.

But Laura was not, as Howe charged, simply the helpless victim of a
repressive teacher. Out of loyalty or discretion, Swift never revealed
how difficult Laura could be to manage. In 1846, during a self-critical
moment, Laura confessed to another teacher that she had often pinched
Swift's arms, bitten her neck, and "hugged her very hard to hurt her."
Another time, Laura's conscience "reprove[d] her severely" for complaining to others that she did not love her teacher. Laura guiltily re-

called that Swift, discouraged and exhausted, "sometimes told me she was so tired of trying to make me better."[13]

On May 1, 1845, shortly after Howe published his criticisms of her performance, Swift resigned from Perkins. She waited until Howe was dead, however, before publishing her side of the story. In her 1878 biography of Laura, *The Life and Education of Laura Bridgman*, Swift finally made her case: if Howe had found Laura tense and fractious when he came home from Europe, the fault was not her teacher's. It was he, not Swift, who had injured the child. He had been so intent on justifying his own Unitarian views that he had willfully underestimated Laura's ability to understand religious doctrine. By forbidding all discussion of religion during a crucial time in Laura's development, he had succeeding only in frustrating her. Although Laura, obedient to his wishes, had dutifully refrained from asking religious questions "save when her soul was so full it must find utterance," this unnatural self-restraint had taken a toll on her delicate constitution. "There was, especially in the last year of my intercourse with her," Swift observed, "an impatience in waiting that extended to other things." Troubled by religious confusion, Laura could not concentrate on her studies, and Swift complained, "When I supposed she was absorbed in our conversation on other topics, she surprised me with questions on religious topics, for replies to which she must wait."

Swift charged that Howe's ban on religious instruction had not only contributed to Laura's tension and volatility, but also prevented her teacher from appealing to "the highest motives." Forbidden to invoke religious doctrines or exemplars, Swift had no alternative but to punish and scold. The benighted child "was living under the old dispensation," Swift explained, "and had not even the example of Christ as a model; for until my last month with her, she did not even know his name." Of course, Swift added diplomatically, she made "these statements with no design to censure Dr. Howe, but merely to answer questions regarding the difference of my opinions from those entertained by that eminent philanthropist."[14]

The irony of Howe's falling out with Swift is that he had once prized her as his most intelligent and highly qualified teacher. She had been recommended to him originally by Lydia Drew, who met Swift in 1839, at the newly opened Massachusetts Normal School in Lexington, the first publicly funded teachers' seminary in the country. Swift was one of seven young women (including two of Horace Mann's nieces) who had enrolled when the school opened in July 1839; in November, Drew joined the class, which eventually grew to twenty-five. Although she remained at the school for less than six months, that was time enough for Drew to spot Swift as the brightest, most mature, and most energetic girl in a class of poorly prepared sixteen-year-olds.

An experienced teacher who had already worked wonders with Laura, Drew, at twenty-four, could not have had much to gain from a brief stay at a struggling new school in the company of adolescent girls. The class records note that she enrolled because "Dr. Howe sent her . . . to learn some of the Normal methods, with the hope that they would assist in her difficult task of teaching."[15] Whatever his actual expectations for improving Drew's teaching, Howe was eager to signal his support for the struggling Lexington school, one of Horace Mann's pet projects. Mann had envisioned this normal school as a model, the first of many that he planned to scatter throughout the state to train a professional staff for his common schools. Luckily, he had succeeded in hiring a gifted founding director, the Reverend Cyrus Peirce, a Unitarian minister and former principal of a private high school in Nantucket. The new Lexington school, however, was built on almost nothing: it had no admissions criteria, no established curriculum or standards, few books, no apparatus, weak public support, and a tiny enrollment.[16] According to Peirce, most of the girls in his first class were appallingly ignorant, undisciplined, and silly (Swift was an exception). The presence of a teacher of Drew's experience and reputation amounted to a public endorsement of the school. By sending her as a student, Howe showed not only that he believed in the concept of teacher education, but also that he had confidence in Mann's wobbly and underfunded new enterprise.

Four months after Drew arrived at the Lexington school, Howe wrote her to ask who among her classmates he should recruit to teach at

Perkins. She replied that although the other students were an unimpressive lot, there was one young woman who stood out. "I wish you could get Miss Swift;—she is *the right one*."[17] Not only was Swift physically healthy and emotionally steady, she excelled in the rigorous studies that Peirce required: composition, geometry, algebra, physiology, natural history, botany, political economy, bookkeeping, vocal music, intellectual and moral philosophy, and the art of teaching.[18] Her daily journals—mandatory for all the Lexington school students—were a model of clarity and precision. (Indeed, her school journal, published in 1926 by Harvard University Press, has become a classic in the history of education, providing scholars with a complete transcription of virtually every word of every lecture that Peirce delivered.)[19]

Swift was also unusually proficient—for a female of that period—in Greek and Latin. Peirce himself had taught her classical languages at his school in Nantucket, where she had been his top student. When she followed him to Lexington, he continued to take a special interest in her studies and, she later recalled, "told me that he regretted that I should, in this year in the Normal School, with only English studies, forget what I previously had of Greek." (For her impeccable Latin, she said, "he had no fear.") Determined that this exceptional student not lose ground, he volunteered to spend three evenings a week tutoring her. In her memoirs, Swift paid tribute to "Father" Peirce's dedication to her achievement:

> What a picture it would have made! that corner of the schoolroom nearest the black stove, with one candle on his desk, and the old man and the young girl studying the Greek Testament! The Old Master might truthfully have written beneath it "Devotion."[20]

Her classical training made Swift a particularly strong candidate for employment. In 1840, when she graduated, Howe was looking for a teacher trained in Greek and Latin, and Swift's first assignment at Perkins was to prepare a gifted blind boy, Joseph Smith, for admission to Harvard.

To get Swift to come to Perkins, Howe first had to overcome the objections of her father, a doctor who had recently moved from Nantucket to Philadelphia to become a professor of medicine at Haverford College.[21] Paul Swift worried that the physically and mentally taxing work of teaching the blind might be too much for a young woman of Mary's overly conscientious temperament, but in the end he relented. His daughter, he explained to Howe, was "ardently devoted to the profession which she has chosen and for which we have endeavored to qualify her."[22] If she thought that teaching at Perkins was her vocation, he would not stand in her way.

As it turned out, Dr. Swift's fears were well founded. In the fall of 1841, after a year as a regular Perkins classroom teacher, Mary Swift collapsed from exhaustion and her parents insisted that she come home to rest. Alarmed by her condition, they wanted her to remain with them in Philadelphia and find a job in a "select private school," but she preferred to go back to Perkins. This time, Dr. Swift was more firm. Before he would allow her to resume her duties, he insisted on new terms of employment. Given her tendencies to perfectionism and "morbidity" (by which he may have meant what we would call anxiety or depression), she needed more protection and more care. In the future, she would have to be excused from participating in public exhibitions; the strain of them was too great. And her work deserved more recognition—tangible recognition in the form of an increased salary.[23] Howe wanted to keep Swift enough to give in. By the end of 1841, she was back in Boston, presumably with promises of a lighter workload and a raise.

When he agreed to Dr. Swift's demands Drew had just resigned, and Howe may already have decided that he wanted Mary Swift to replace her. Now that the scientific importance of Laura's education had been established, he was looking for "some intellectual person" not only to teach Laura, but also to keep exact and detailed records of her progress. Although Drew had done her best to maintain her daily journals, her other responsibilities had often interfered: tutoring Laura had not been her only job at Perkins. If information "of the greatest value to science" was to be preserved, Howe needed to raise enough money for a full-time teacher-companion who would have the time and the skill to create a complete record of Laura's development.[24] Swift, the most meticulous of diarists, was the logical choice, and at the end of 1842, Howe proudly announced that, thanks to some generous benefactors, Laura would have "the entire time and services" of Mary Swift, "a young lady of great intelligence who is devotedly attached to her."[25]

WITH A COMMAND of classical languages, unusual intelligence, and a prosperous, articulate, and assertive father on her side, Swift was in a stronger bargaining position than most of the female teachers at Perkins—or at any other school, for that matter. In the 1830s and 1840s, young women were flooding into the teaching profession, which before 1825 had been a male preserve, considered unsuitable for women. By 1838, according to Mann, the profession had been transformed. Sixty percent of teachers in Massachusetts were female, and the proportion would soon grow even higher.[26] Between 1825 and 1860, a quarter of all native-born New England women were schoolteachers for at least some portion of their lives.[27]

Complex economic and social forces propelled these young women into the classroom. At the same time that an expanding population and the creation of common schools were increasing the demand for teachers, industry was drawing more heavily on the pool of employable young men, who could find better wages in shops and factories than they could in schools.[28] Moreover, the labor of female teachers was a bargain for taxpayers. In *Notes on the United States of America*, George Combe observed that in Massachusetts, male teachers were paid $15.44 per month, exclusive of board; females received $5.38. These poorly paid women cost much less than men to feed: the state legislature estimated the monthly board for male teachers at $2.50 a week, for female teachers at $1.50. (This was at a time when a common laborer, according to Combe, earned $1.00 a day.)[29]

Changing ideas about the nature and role of women supported the feminization of teaching, just when the demand for cheap female labor was growing. Horace Mann promoted this new ideology enthusiasti-

cally: women should not waste their talents and "generous, philanthropic" impulses by staying idly at home, he said. Instead, they should
be encouraged to take up "the sacred and peaceful ministry" of teaching.
By nature gentle, tender, and loving, women were uniquely and ideally
suited for service "in the sacred temple of education":

> Is there not an obvious, constitutional difference of temperament
> between the sexes, indicative of a preärranged fitness and adapta-
> tion, and making known to us, as by a heaven-imparted sign, that
> woman, by her livelier sensibility and her quicker sympathies, is
> the forechosen guide and guardian of children of a tender age?
> . . . To breathe pure and exalted sentiments into young and tender
> hearts—to take the censers which Heaven gives, and kindle
> therein the incense which Heaven loves—this is her high and
> holy mission. . . . In camps or senates she could shine but for a
> day, and with a fitful light; but if, with enduring patience and fi-
> delity, she fulfills her sacred duties to childhood, then, from the
> sanctuary of her calm and sequestered life, there will go forth a
> refulgent glory to irradiate all countries and all centuries.[30]

Not only did the schools need talented, intelligent women, but these
women, Mann argued, needed enlivening work. Without it, they would
be driven, "from mere vacuity of mind, and the irritation of unemployed
faculties, to the frivolities and despicableness of fashion, to vain amusement, or to reading silly books, merely to kill time, which, properly understood, means killing oneself."[31] Catharine Beecher, the founder of the
Hartford Female Seminary and a renowned educator, agreed that teaching provided women with a sure path to self-improvement. She pointed
out that teaching not only allowed them to fulfill their religious obligation to be of service to others, but also gave them a measure of re-
spectable independence.[32]

MORE THAN THE meager salary, the moral imperative of usefulness drew
Swift to Perkins. Like most of the women employed there, she believed

that teaching the blind was God's work. Even after 1846, when she married Edwin Lamson, a successful Boston merchant to whom she may already have been betrothed when she left Perkins, she continued her philanthropic activities. In addition to raising their three surviving children (a fourth died in early childhood), Swift taught Sunday school at the Congregational Church of the Messiah in Boston, and served on both the Winchester, Massachusetts, school committee and the board of trustees of the Industrial School for Girls at Lancaster.[33] In 1858, alarmed by the plight of the unprotected rural and immigrant girls who were pouring into the city to find work, she began to lobby for the establishment of a Boston Young Women's Christian Association; largely as a result of her persistence, the Boston YWCA was organized in 1866. For the next thirty years, Swift devoted herself to the moral and physical protection of working-class women and to the growth of the YWCA movement.[34] Aware of the historic significance of the year she and her classmates had spent at the Lexington Normal School, she also organized class reunions and wrote most of the class records. If it were not for her diligence, we would know little about the pioneering women who enrolled in Mann's first normal school.

Swift was more than a public organization woman. Like Drew, she continued to feel privately responsible for Laura. Although at Perkins she and Laura never claimed to have loved each other, Swift, busy though she later was, always kept in touch, and Laura came to depend on her friendship. As long as Laura lived, Swift (who died in 1909 at eighty-seven) invited her home for visits, stopped in to see her at Perkins, supplied her with little gifts, and kept up their voluminous correspondence. After most of Laura's old friends had died or lost interest, Swift remained faithful.

SWIFT'S DEPARTURE ON May 1, 1845, left Laura adrift, without a teacher of her own or a clear direction for her studies. Although Howe, absorbed in new humanitarian projects, had little time for Laura, he could not simply send her home. The public still thronged to see her and expected to continue reading of her progress in his annual reports; besides, he had already raised the money for her to have her own teacher. After a few months of indecision, during which time Laura received no instruction, Howe finally came up with a plan. Perhaps, under his guidance, another, more enlightened teacher could correct some of the damage done to Laura during Swift's regime. If he protected Laura from corrupting outside influences while the new teacher strengthened her conscience, Laura's defective character might improve. In this way, he could demonstrate the effectiveness of enlightened, nonpunitive discipline.

The dangerous influence of bad companions was a constant theme in Howe's writing of this period. He was preoccupied almost to the point of obsession with the problem of controlling "vicious associations" in institutions. As a member of the Boston Prison Discipline Society, in which he became active soon after he returned from Europe, he had joined forces with Sumner and Mann in a fierce debate between advocates of two rival penal philosophies: the "congregate" or "silent" system used at the Auburn (New York) State Prison, where inmates worked and ate together in enforced silence, and the solitary confinement system used in the Eastern State Penitentiary in Philadelphia.

Howe championed the solitary system, and when the Boston Prison Discipline Society decided to endorse the congregate model instead, he was outraged. In a vitriolic minority report, he argued that because "mutual contamination is the great evil to be cured" in any prison, "*total abstinence* from bad company" was the obvious remedy.[35] With Laura clearly in mind, he pointed out that if the "imprisoned souls" of those deprived of sight, hearing, taste, and smell could "struggle out through the narrow aperture of the touch" to communicate with others, then surely convicts under the congregate system would find a way to converse, "though they may never utter an articulate sound."[36] To have any chance at rehabilitation, penitentiary inmates would have to be walled off completely from their peers and introduced only to companions who could exert a good influence.[37]

The principles that could reform a criminal might also work for a deaf-blind girl gone wrong. Hoping to rehabilitate Laura, Howe decided that she would no longer be allowed to mingle freely with the other

Perkins students. Instead, two or three suitable blind girls, selected by him, would be permitted to call on her from time to time in her private room, for play or conversation. She was to sleep, eat, and study with a carefully chosen new teacher, who would be her constant companion. "By this means," Swift dryly observed, Laura "was prevented from receiving any new ideas, except through the medium which he approved."[38]

As part of his program of isolating Laura, Howe made a new rule: even on vacation visits to her teachers' homes, she was no longer allowed to share a bed. At a time when only the most affluent families had an extra bed for guests, and when young women commonly snuggled together on cold nights, this was a puzzling proscription. Eliza Rogers, a teacher who often took Laura home to Billerica, Massachusetts, with her during vacations, told Howe that she was astonished to receive his new instructions:

> I am very glad that you wrote me with regard to her [Laura] sleeping alone . . . for I had not the slightest idea of your wishes on this point & when she was here last autumn my practice was totally different, she having either myself or one of my sisters for a companion every night. Before I read your letter I had made a similar arrangement, as I found it a very pleasant one for her; and when I informed her of the change I would give no reason why, save that you prefferred [sic] it.[39]

Howe issued his edict about Laura's sleeping arrangements on May 26, 1845, only a week after the prison-discipline controversy exploded into open warfare. At the May 18 meeting of the Boston Prison Discipline Society, Sumner, encouraged by Howe, had seized the floor and fiercely denounced the pro-Auburn faction.[40] This unexpected attack unleashed the Furies: once again, Howe was trading insults, this time not only with his usual orthodox adversaries, who favored the more overtly punitive congregate system, but also with the conservative Brahmins who thought the solitary system too expensive. In the heat of this angry moment, Howe's mind was naturally fixed on the benefits of Philadelphia-style moral quarantine. Filled with zeal for the separation cause, he apparently resolved to seal Laura off from every possible contamination, even while she was in the homes of her teachers.

Howe never spelled out exactly what he feared would happen if Laura shared her bed with other girls. To assume that he was worried about homosexual activity would be anachronistic; the word "homosexual" was not even in use at the time. Antebellum Americans did not suffer from modern anxieties about homoerotic feelings, and same-sex crushes, romantic letters, embraces, and endearments were the norm.[41] (Sumner's friend and law partner, George Hillard, jokingly complained to Longfellow in 1842 that Sumner was "quite in love with Howe and spends so much time with him that I begin to feel the shooting pains of jealousy." And before Howe's marriage, whenever Sumner spent the night with Howe in the director's quarters at Perkins, they left the doors between their rooms open so that they could talk until they fell asleep.)[42]

Most likely, Howe feared that cuddling with another girl might be too stimulating for a female of Laura's defective character. Perhaps he imagined that physical closeness could awaken lascivious desires, encourage masturbation, or arouse hysterical passions in such a vulnerable young woman. As he saw it, living in the all-female world of a large institution had already put Laura at risk: "All establishments, in which a large number of persons of one sex live long together, are unnatural, unfavorable to the growth of social virtues and graces, and injurious to the moral nature in a greater or less degree," he said.[43] If the "secret histories" of nunneries, monasteries, armies, navies, and boarding schools were ever exposed, they would all be condemned as morally vicious. And the most undesirable, unwise, and hazardous single-sex establishment of all was "a congregation in one great household of young girls." Because of the "peculiarities of the female character," too much contact with their peers threatened the moral growth of girls, who should ideally be raised separately, each under the surveillance, supervision, and guidance of a virtuous, religious woman.[44]

Convinced now that Swift had been the wrong choice for that all-important role of female moral guide, Howe wanted to find for Laura a teacher-companion who agreed with his views on religion and discipline. In the summer of 1845, he finally settled on Sarah Wight, a quiet, diffident woman who had begun working at Perkins in 1843, when she was twenty-one years old. Although Wight had not attended a normal school, her Unitarian credentials were impeccable. Patient, gentle, and deeply (but liberally) religious, she was the ideal mentor and role model for Laura. And, unlike Swift, Wight needed the job.

RAISED IN THE shadow of her father's professional failure and the family's subsequent impoverishment, Sarah Wight was well schooled in humility. Her father, John Burt Wight, a Unitarian minister, had been a casualty of the Massachusetts sectarian wars. Born in Bristol, Rhode Island, in 1790, he graduated from Brown in 1808 at the top of his class and, notwithstanding his Calvinistic leanings, received a master's degree from the liberal Harvard Divinity School. Immediately following his ordination in 1815, he was called to the Congregational Church of Christ in Wayland, Massachusetts. At first his ministry went smoothly, but after a few years the liberal winds blowing westward from Cambridge and Boston began to push him toward Unitarianism. "With increasing knowledge and experience," Reverend Wight explained, "my religious views . . . gradually became more enlarged, consistent, excellent, and delightful."[45]

In the 1820s, as many of his congregants were responding to the revival movements of the Second Great Awakening by demanding a more emotional, evangelical Christianity, John Wight adhered steadfastly to his new liberal convictions. Inevitably, his ministry began to disintegrate: some members "signed off" to join Baptist and Methodist churches in nearby towns, and others withdrew to form an orthodox congregation, where they could hear "the plain preaching of the Gospel Agreeable to the creed exhibited by . . . Pastor [Wight] at his Ordination."[46]

In the religious free market that followed disestablishment, John Wight had more and more trouble attracting paying customers to his church. Although his admirers praised him as "a man of amiable disposition, of meek and quiet temper, and truly catholic spirit," he was a dull preacher.[47] Forced by his congregation's dwindling membership to give up $100 of his salary in 1833, and another $200 in 1834, he finally had no choice in 1835 but to resign his position after twenty years of service. His four children (of whom Sarah, born in 1822, was the third) probably remained in Wayland with his wife, a local woman. For the next thirty years, Reverend Wight led an itinerant life, occupying pulpits for short periods in Castine, Maine; Milford and Amherst, New Hampshire; and North Dennis, Massachusetts. Returning regularly to Wayland, he subsisted on occasional gifts from former parishioners and on fees for substituting for the regular Unitarian preacher and officiating at marriages and funerals.

For all its liberalism, the Wight family's religion was not quite the same as Howe's. His was the rationalistic, freethinking, public-spirited Unitarianism of affluent, cosmopolitan Boston; theirs, the earnest, introspective, morally exigent Unitarianism of the rural village. Pastor Wight and his children may have spurned orthodoxy, but they continued to fear that "the least of God's commandments cannot be transgressed without incurring a corresponding penalty," and that every fault or deficiency, no matter how petty or insignificant, required acknowledgment, repentance, and correction.[48] Sarah Wight grew up convinced that the struggle for perfection required relentless self-examination and painful self-sacrifice.

The strain of their economic hardships and the demands of their religion told on John Wight's children. Of the three that survived, two—Sarah and her older brother, Henry—suffered emotional breakdowns in their fifties. Both were committed to Boston's most up-to-date mental hospital, the McLean Asylum, and both died there of mental disease.[49]

When he chose her to become Laura's teacher-companion, Howe, recently returned from his travels, had not had the opportunity to spend much time with Sarah Wight. He formed his opinion of her in part from reading her teaching journals, the daily accounts of lessons and student progress that all Perkins teachers kept, both for the director's information and for their own records. As Howe leafed through the matter-of-fact, routine reports from his staff, her thoughtful comments must have stood out. Unlike the other teachers, she not only provided notes on lessons in algebra, natural philosophy, reading, and geography, but also included reflections on teaching, character analyses of particular students, and detailed accounts of her attempts to improve the "bad" girls.

Wight was a perceptive teacher. She liked her classes to be spirited, but if competition became intense, she watched for signs of "painful anxiety" on her students' faces. When "a cloud seemed to hang over the class" during a Saturday morning grammar lesson, she asked herself if her pacing was off. "I am only anxious to go so fast and only so fast as is necessary to maintain the interest of the class," she mused, reminding herself that students generally lose interest "because they are hurried on faster than they can comprehend" or because "they learn a few words & fancy they know all about it." Forcing the girls to sit through formal lectures in astronomy struck her as counterproductive: "Attendance upon these lectures will not in reality be any benefit but rather an injury to the members of my class. . . . Trying to grasp so much that is new to them they learn little get discouraged and I fear they will lose all the interest with which they commenced the study." Better to be less ambitious and more realistic. When her students were sleepy in the morning, she neither scolded them nor forged ahead with the lesson. Instead, she had them walk outdoors on the piazza for five "very profitably spent" minutes.[50]

Howe, who subscribed to what educators nowadays like to call the "whole child" philosophy, approved of Wight's pedagogy. Her quasi-phrenological methods of evaluating her students also pleased him. She believed, as he did, that everyone has an essential, organically based nature or disposition. By analyzing each troublemaker's character, Wight sought to formulate an individualized program for moral improvement, which she believed was always possible, even in the most intractable cases.

This was precisely the approach that Howe favored in disciplining convicts. One of the great advantages of solitary confinement, he believed, was that it allowed "moral treatment" to be adapted to each inmate's particular weaknesses.[51] He was no doubt glad to note the care with which Wight tailored her responses to wrongdoing to fit the doer, not the deed. Taking into account past behavior, natural disposition, and any signs of contrition, she reproved some girls in private for their mischief, but required others, if they seemed naturally stubborn, to stand before the class and "confess the wrong" publicly.[52]

Her attempts to correct Julia, the most difficult girl in the class, reveal the intensity of Wight's commitment to moral education. Caught with several clusters of stolen grapes in her hands, Julia claimed at first to have found the forbidden fruit on the steps, but eventually confessed, explaining that she had lied because she feared her teacher's disapproval. Less worried about the crime than the criminal, Wight speculated phrenologically about Julia's motivations: "Her cautiousness is so large that it seems almost diseased & this has probably been the cause of her habitual disregard of the truth."[53]

The girl showed penitence for her first offenses, and Wight forgave her. A few weeks later, however, Julia lied again, denying—despite the telltale crumbs—that she had taken a piece of cake from another girl's desk. This time Wight had to try harsher measures:

> She has been talked with, hours after hours but there seems but little good to work upon her. . . . Told her that as her word could not be believed & she could [not] use her hands as they were intended I would confine them that she might have leisure to think for what purpose they were given her. Besides it was not safe for her to have the use of her hands.[54]

Having her hands tied had terrified Lucy Reed into submission, but Julia refused to repent. After a week, Wight noted, "Julia has given me no excuse for liberating her hands." Eventually—Wight did not say when—she untied Julia's hands but then, only three weeks later, she had to tie them again for another three days. In rage and frustration, the girl had torn up her own new bonnet. Still, the struggle did not end. On August 31, 1844, just before the journal breaks off, Julia was sent to her room for telling falsehoods. "It is *very* discouraging," Wight noted, weary but apparently not yet beaten.

Her relentless moral surveillance of students like Julia might strike us as oppressive, but Howe approved of it. Indeed, he found Wight's approach to discipline far more enlightened than Swift's. Where Swift demanded obedience, Wight wanted goodness. By imprisoning Julia's hands, Wight intended to free the girl's mind for reflection and self-knowledge, not to punish her. Prevented from doing mischief for a long enough time, the natural thief might find the "leisure" to think about doing good. Wight's conscious goal was neither to exercise her own power nor to break Julia's spirit, but to foster gradual moral growth in a naturally weak and disordered child.

Wight's phrenological orientation, her dedication to moral treatment, and her tenacity with a difficult student like Julia gave Howe hope that this gentle but zealous teacher could correct Laura's deficiencies. Although Laura had failed as a religious experiment, there was still a chance that she would succeed as a disciplinary case study. This was the crucial moment. At sixteen, she was entering a critical period, one of "great difficulty and great danger . . . when the natural tendency of every human soul to separate and independent individualism becomes very strong." Her unfortunate exposure both to orthodox doctrine and to Swift's punitive methods had already damaged her, and her constitution was unfavorable to begin with. If Wight, guided by his principles, could nevertheless teach Laura to grow calm and gentle, what a "rare attainment" in moral training that would be.[55]

ONLY FOUR MONTHS after Wight took charge, Howe was ready to proclaim the experiment a success. Just as he had predicted, affectionate, nonpunitive discipline worked:

> There have been a few moments . . . when, either from the developing tendency to independent individualism . . . or from constitutional irritability, or both, Laura has manifested a spirit

which threatened violent explosions of temper. I am certain, that, if at such times she had been treated with the slightest sternness, or even with coldness and indifference, the effect would have been most unfavorable. But her teacher, never for a moment losing her temper, never ceasing to manifest the tenderest interest in her pupil, yet not *obtruding it upon her,* or making it the pretext for overruling her will, has succeeded in making Laura *judge* and *condemn herself;* so that, without being accused, she has perceived her fault, and, without being punished, she has come out of the trial stronger and better than before.[56]

Wight—self-sacrificing, vigilant, and mild—had proved to be exactly the sort of female role model and mentor that he recommended for young women. "No one," Howe said, "has conceived so high an idea of woman's patience, devotion, tenderness, and capacity, that it would not be raised, if he could see . . . the whole of them exemplified in the daily intercouse between Miss Wight and Laura."[57] Together, he and Sarah Wight were mending a broken, morally defective child. Because of her unfavorable natural disposition, Laura would never be perfect, but she could learn to grow better.

CHAPTER TEN

Attachments

LAURA HAD ALWAYS longed for "a very loving and kind teacher," and her "poor heart" was "filled with delightful emotions" when she learned that Howe had chosen Sarah Wight to take Mary Swift's place. Ever since Wight had arrived at Perkins three years before, Laura had felt drawn to her. (As Swift had observed, gentle, timid women always appealed to Laura.) "I was so much exhilarated to think of W's teaching me," Laura later recalled, "for I loved her so very much as long as she dwelt here."[1] Laura also liked Wight's family. She had already spent several school vacations with them in Wayland, rediscovering the pleasures of her rural childhood: searching for eggs in the barn, digging dandelions for dinner, riding on a donkey, and calling on neighbors.[2]

When her new teacher took charge of her on August 29, 1845, Laura marked the occasion in her journal:

> I was very much gratified when miss wight commenced to teach me to day & she taught me at nine about artumetic [arithmetic] & to cypher at ten oclock i should desire to be good & do what she advise or to forbid or to require me always we should be very happy together.[3]

Two weeks later, she wrote to Wight's mother to report delightedly on their progress:

> miss wight is my excellent teacher. She supplies me six hours she teaches me decimals fractions & meaning of new words & write & history & geography & stories & we go to boston frequently & to walk every day. . . . I resolve to [be] good & kind to wight always & she loves me exceedingly i love her also. . . . we are verry happy togetherr in our room.⁴

No wonder Laura was pleased. For Swift's inflexible schedule, Wight had substituted a varied program that allowed for more spontaneity and recreation. Although Wight offered plenty of academic instruction, she always made time for the sort of meandering conversation that Laura relished. Wight would entertain even the most speculative questions. What did Adam eat when he was a baby? Why cannot people do right always as Jesus Christ did? Why did Laura herself sometimes ignore her conscience and do wrong? Why do the sun and the moon not fall to the earth? If crippled people have muscles, why are they unable to stand up? Was God as wise as Jesus? Where did God get a body for Christ?⁵

With her warmth and responsiveness, Wight had no trouble winning Laura's heart. In her journal, Laura soon began referring to her teacher as "My dear Dove," "Miss Dove," "My dearest teacher," and "My beloved W." Wight recorded many of Laura's frequent declarations of affection. Struggling with some difficult arithmetic problems, Laura confessed, "I used to be impatient when my questions were so hard but now I laugh & try as you advise me." After an hourlong discussion of good and bad impulses—just the sort of theoretical discussion she most enjoyed—Laura said to Wight, "I love you so dearly for teaching me many new things about thoughts." Two months after Wight began to teach her, Laura declared, "I love you very much; I love you like God."⁶

Wight soon became Laura's entire world. Teacher and pupil were alone together day and night, even during vacations, and Laura's contact with other people was strictly limited. From time to time three girls, chosen by Howe, were invited to converse with her for periods of half an hour. If Laura asked to visit the girls' sitting room, Wight almost never objected. "I go there with her & show her the flowers & let her speak a few minutes with any one who may be there. She is very soon ready to go to our own room." Laura did not find this arrangement oppressive; on the contrary, Wight observed, she "feels that I am here all the time & that keeps off the sense of loneliness. It is very seldom that she is alone more than one hour in the 24."[7]

Yet, for all her satisfaction with her teacher, Laura continually misbehaved. Wight filled the pages of her journal with detailed accounts of their battles. On October 3, 1845, Laura, told to sit by herself, wandered off to find someone to talk to. Three days later, angry when she didn't get her way, "she clasped her hands very tightly her face grew very red & she made a sound in her throat." On November 3, she was too rambunctious. A few weeks after that, she shook Wight's arm and then, half playfully, punched her. Just before Christmas, in an impish mood, Laura hid her hairbrush, pretended it was lost, and got Wight to look for it. On February 9, 1846, annoyed by her teacher's nagging, Laura grabbed Wight's hand, "twisted it over very violently," and then dug her fingers into Wight's arm. In addition to many such serious misdemeanors, there were also minor outbreaks of defiance. Protesting that she was too old to be ordered around all the time, Laura regularly—sometimes furiously—rebelled, defying Wight's injunctions to wear gloves, change into dry stockings, put on galoshes, pin her shawl closed against the wind, and stop making disagreeable noises.[8]

Wight resolved to adhere to her principle "of never allowing even the slightest fault to pass without some notice of it at the time or afterward."[9] She believed that although Laura was essentially good, she lacked patience and self-control. Her privileged status at Perkins had encouraged excessive self-esteem: "She has a seat apart from the other pupils in the schoolroom," Wight noted, "and she knows that she is an object of more interest than any other. . . . Her friends and strangers love to show her particular attention and are not always judicious in the man-

ner of doing it." Overestimating her own abilities, Laura balked at obey-
ing orders with which she disagreed.[10]

In disciplining Laura, Wight's goal was to transform an excitable, willful child into a docile, industrious young woman who would
never lose her temper, challenge the wisdom of those in authority, or
entertain "bad thoughts." Wight's journals show how conscientiously
she set about her task. Her method was to make Laura suffer inwardly
for each act of misbehavior. The pain of guilt and remorse, Wight
believed, would soften—and thus gradually strengthen—Laura's
conscience. No matter how sorely Laura tried her patience, Wight
remained calm, loving, and patient. She refrained from punishment and
scolding, even when Laura slapped or pinched her. "Reproof would
have hardened the child," Wight said, and she wanted Laura to melt with
contrition.[11]

WIGHT BASED HER disciplinary program on the precepts of the innovative educators who visited Perkins regularly: Horace Mann; his wife,
Mary Peabody Mann; and her sister, Elizabeth Palmer Peabody, a disci-
ple of Bronson Alcott. These progressives believed, as Mann argued in
his famous 1844 lecture, "On School Punishments," that wayward students can best "be led to inward repentance, and to resolutions of
amendment" by "kind advice, by affectionate persuasion, by a clear display of the nature of the offence committed." Frequent chastisement
would only frighten children into paralyzing timidity or provoke them
into open defiance; it could not induce them to honor their parents, love
their brothers and sisters, respect their fellow citizens, or venerate God.[12]

In the years—1826–1831—that Mary Peabody Mann kept a school,
she developed strategies for nonpunitive classroom discipline. Children,
she argued, should be made to "feel the natural consequences of doing
wrong": the withdrawal of their teacher's approval, the displeasure of
their classmates, and the pain of self-reproach. Often, Mrs. Mann said,
she had been able to teach a naughty pupil to hear "the voice of God"
simply by asking, "Is there not something in you, that makes you feel
very uncomfortable when you have done wrong?" Above all, Mrs. Mann

stressed the importance of inspiring trust and affection. She had observed again and again that when children love their teacher (who for Mary Mann was ideally a woman), they value her opinion, wish for her approbation, and naturally adopt her principles.[13]

AS MRS. MANN recommended, Wight used sorrowful but gentle leading questions to awaken Laura's conscience. Did Laura know why she felt angry toward her teacher? Had Laura refrained from bad thoughts? What was she thinking about when her teacher left her alone to reflect on her naughtiness?[14]

Combined with gentle exhortations, these probing questions almost always prompted a tearful confession and abject apology. Laura was in no position to resist: she depended on her teacher for everything—intellectual stimulation, physical affection, emotional sustenance, access to a safe and stable world. Fearful that Wight would withdraw, Laura constantly used her fingers to "read" her teacher's expression. "I do not want you to look sad, I want you to be happy," she would say, trying to get Wight to smile; "I will try *very* hard, I will not do wrong again."[15] Sensing a change in Wight's finger spelling frightened her. "You talked sadly as if you were not loving me," she would complain.[16]

Their moral struggles quickly fell into a pattern. After one of Laura's angry outbursts or moments of defiance, Wight would say nothing about the offense, but act mournful; soon Laura would begin to look troubled and Wight would know that her pupil's "conscience was doing its work."[17] Sometimes Wight elicited even more remorse than she had bargained for. After a long day of moral questioning and resistance, Laura would have trouble sleeping or become alarmingly agitated. At times, Wight could not help being "completely disarmed by her pale distressed countenance":

The tears passed down her cheeks as she embraced me most affectionately. I felt instantly that nothing that I could say then would add anything to the effect produced by her own conscience.[18]

Bouts of repentance might end with Laura mending Wight's clothes, presenting her with little gifts, or straightening her teacher's room. After a particularly bad day, Laura insisted that Wight take her most cherished possession, a pincushion.

Wight disapproved of punishment, but her benevolent discipline was in its way as oppressive as the ferrule or cane. Laura often had to struggle to please her teacher without fully understanding the rules. So many different things that she did were called "bad"—keeping secrets from Wight, disobeying orders, making disagreeable noises, hitting and pinching, bragging, thinking angry thoughts—that it was hard to see a pattern. She knew that during the American Revolution, the British had been "bad," but hostile Indians, slaveholders, the killers of Christ, and girls who refused to wear their warm mittens were "bad," too. She knew that she was supposed to control her "bad" noises, but unless she kept her hand on her throat to feel the vibrations, she could not always tell when she vocalized. Sometimes she was unsure whether she had been wrong or only rambunctious. In her excitement over a friend's visit, for example, she shook Wight's arm, but then grew afraid she might have transgressed. "Does it make you cross to have any one shake your arm?" she asked, putting her hand to Wight's face. "Perceiving I was laughing," Wight noted, "she laughed also."[19]

Laura rarely complained about her physical limitations, except in the context of her moral perplexity. "I want to do right but I cannot hear with my ears what every body says about it what they think is right and best to do," she explained. A few months later, after an irritable outburst, she tried to make Wight understand her frustration. "If I could hear you speak or see your face always I do not think I should be angry but I do not like to feel of your countenance always."[20]

Although Laura struggled to follow moral lectures, she often ended up bewildered. When Wight, on Howe's instructions, tried to teach her about benevolent motives, Laura could not reconcile the principle of emulating Christ with what she had previously been told about his superhuman powers. "We cannot be benevolent as [Jesus] was," she reasoned. "I cannot . . . do kind things to crazy people, and blind and deaf people, and cure them."[21] During Bible lessons, Laura paid close attention, pressing Wight's fingers intently "so that no letter could escape her." She became proficient at parroting Wight's religious rhetoric, but could not always make sense of ethical abstractions or figurative language. Bible stories baffled her. Why wasn't Jesus wrong to grieve his parents by going off to Jerusalem when he was only twelve? What sense did it make to call people—who aren't made of salt—"the salt of the earth"? If Christ was perfect, how could he be tempted? If he was all-powerful, why didn't he simply escape from his murderers? If Jesus had been around when she was small, would he have cured her of the fever that made her deaf and blind? And if he cured people, why did he let them get sick in the first place?

To add to Laura's confusion, Howe occasionally intervened directly in her religious instruction. Wight may have been a Liberal Christian, but she did not share his scientific rationalism, and he worried that she might lead Laura into superstitious error. If he happened to read something in Wight's journal that struck him as unenlightened—and if he had the time—he would suddenly step in to set Laura straight.[22] After a session with Howe, Laura would return to Wight agitated and perplexed. Did Wight agree with "Dr." that there were many mistakes in the Bible? Did she, too, believe that accounts of miracles might be false or mistaken? "Why do you not teach me as Dr. does about the Bible?" Laura demanded. When Wight explained that she and Howe did not "think exactly alike about all things," Laura looked troubled. "Her color changed and she looked very serious for a few minutes." "Why is your manner more diffident and timid than Dr.'s when you talk to me about God and the Bible and when you talk about wrong things you speak more gently and sad and not so firmly?" she wanted to know.[23]

Wight, of course, resented Howe's intermittent intrusions, which put her in an awkward position when Laura asked religious questions. "I am sure that Dr. Howe can teach Laura infinitely better than I can," she wrote with thinly veiled annoyance, "yet important as his instructions may be to her they cannot take the place of the words that Laura craves daily and hourly from a friend who is constantly with her." When

Wight, fearful that Howe might later contradict her, tried to avoid spiritual topics, her constraint alarmed Laura, who then felt driven to ask questions of everyone she met. Overwhelmed by the contradictory responses she got, Laura would either grow frantic or begin to dwell on morbid thoughts of sickness and death.[24]

Laura also had trouble sorting out the mixed messages that Wight seemed to be sending. On the one hand, Laura was told to govern herself; on the other, she was expected to obey authority unquestioningly. Wight lectured her constantly about self-control, yet would allow Laura no autonomy. Every request, no matter how unreasonable or intrusive or infantilizing, must be obeyed: Laura was never allowed to draw the line. As a child, she had been able to resist the head-rubbings of a visiting phrenologist, but as a young woman she had forfeited control even of her own body. Just before Laura's seventeenth birthday, Wight, wanting to encourage a younger blind student, Lizzy, to pull a loose baby tooth, ordered Laura to open her mouth so the girl could touch her teeth. When Laura flatly refused, insisting, "I will not mind. I must be very firm," Wight was astonished. To her, such willfulness seemed incomprehensible.

Laura held out against her teacher's silence until the afternoon of the next day, a Sunday, which Wight spent sitting mournfully by the window. When Laura finally approached her, Wight took her on her lap. "As she sat down," Wight wrote, "my eye fell on a beautiful rose which had just unfolded itself. I said to Laura see this beautiful fragrant rose that God has given us He wants us to be good and happy today. The dear child was completely over come. Bursting into tears she embraced me then opening her mouth wide she turned to Lizzy saying I want to show Lizzy my teeth. We wept together for I was so much relieved and so happy I felt as much as she."[25]

Infuriated by Wight's demands, yet utterly dependent on her, Laura increasingly turned her rage inward. She could not risk alienating her beloved teacher, the source of all comfort and affection, and in any case it was impossible to fight with someone who responded to anger only with quiet disappointment and who forgave her with kisses and hugs. If she could neither understand the moral instructions she was supposed to follow nor resist Wight's suffocating tenderness, Laura could maintain a modicum of control by hurting herself.

Wight's descriptions of Laura's self-punishing episodes make painful reading. One November day, for example, after they had been together for most of the day, Wight was exhausted from hours of finger spelling. When she wanted to go upstairs to take a break, Laura protested, "I love you too much I want to be with you *all* the time." Wight explained that she needed to be alone, but Laura would not stop following her, insisting, "I want to go with you always." Deploying one of her conscience-awakening questions, Wight asked Laura if she wished to disobey. Abashed, Laura retreated. Fifteen minutes later, Wight found her hiding in the sink closet. "Did you see what I was doing in the closet?" Laura asked. "My left hand harmed me to blame me for doing wrong, to make me sorry."[26]

Physical self-punishment seemed to comfort Laura. "Do you ever harm your body when you do wrong?" she wanted to know. Wight, apparently more intrigued than disapproving, responded by asking whether hurting herself made Laura feel more "gentle and amiable." "No," Laura replied, "but I was gentle afterwards."[27] Although Wight was vague about exactly what Laura did to "harm" herself, she noted from time to time that "Laura had punished herself so severely & had suffered so much" that her own best course was to offer the poor child encouragement for the future.

In her early years with Wight, Laura also discovered self-starvation. In November 1845, Laura stopped eating anything but a little brown bread and milk, and her weight dropped from about 113 pounds to 79. During the spring of 1846, she became so nervous and weak that Wight often had to excuse her from lessons.[28] By early summer, Howe began to worry that Laura's life was in danger. In his report for 1846, he prepared his readers for the possibility of her death:

During the most of the past year she has been weak and sickly. In the spring especially, she became very much emaciated, her appetite failed amost entirely, and she could hardly be persuaded to take nourishment enough to keep her alive. . . . As she grew thinner, and paler, and weaker, she appeared to be laying aside the garments of the flesh, and her spirit shone out brighter through its transparent veil. . . . She walked without a shudder upon the brink of the grave.[29]

Recently she had shown some signs of improvement, he said, but she continued nevertheless to be "at a fearful crisis in her life."

Howe's report provides a clear picture of a disorder that we would recognize at once as anorexia nervosa. Laura, he noted, denied the evidence of her growing physical weakness. Insisting that she felt fine and resisting all entreaties, she refused to vary her meager diet:

She does not wish to change her food at all, but, when meal-time arrives, she sits down cheerfully to her simple bread and milk, morning, noon, and evening; and having finished that, she disregards all the dainties and the fruits with which the capricious appetite of invalids is usually tempted.[30]

Attuned, as always, to the connection between mind and body, Howe sensed that emotional turmoil, not organic disease, had led to Laura's illness. The passage from childhood to womanhood was, he believed, inherently perilous. When Laura fell ill, her soul had been in the process of transformation. Under Wight's tutelage, her conscience was awakening, and "the germ of religious feeling" had begun to grow upward and expand into worship and love of God. But the strain on her had been severe. "Great and continual activity of the brain and nervous system" posed a special danger for a child with her physical disabilities and high-strung temperament.[31] Her mental constitution made religious and moral subjects intensely interesting to her, but she could not withstand the excitement of pursuing them.[32] "If we did not hold her back," he observed, "she would kill herself in a short time."[33]

In *Fasting Girls: The History of Anorexia Nervosa,* historian Joan Brumberg connects the increase in anorexia nervosa in the Victorian period to the middle-class ideology of unreserved love. Family intimacy, Brumberg argues, could become stifling and manipulative, leading to "debilitating forms of psychological interdependence" between mothers and daughters. Deprived of privacy and autonomy—all in the name of love—middle-class Victorian girls might resort to nonverbal forms of behavior to express their rebellious feelings. When their mothers' possessiveness and relentless surveillance left them no other freedom, these girls could assert themselves—as Laura did—by refusing to eat.[34]

Laura and her teacher were locked in a relationship more exclusive and suffocating than that of any Victorian mother and daughter. Out of loving concern, Wight read Laura's diaries and mail, monitored her conversations, determined her daily schedule, tucked her into bed, told her what to wear, and evaluated the moral worth of her every action. Her total commitment to Laura meant that Wight had little time for a life of her own—and that Laura never escaped her teacher's tender, reproachful gaze.

Because abstaining from food—especially meat—fit the Victorian idea of female decorum, Laura's limited diet caused concern, but Wight did not label it "bad."[35] At a time when an etherealized, sylphlike look was fashionable for women, Laura's emaciation was acceptable, if worrisome.[36] More than her lack of appetite and loss of weight, Laura's stubbornness bothered Wight, who felt her authority challenged. She first ordered and then tried to coax Laura into eating some meat and vegetables, but without success. Responding with "a most unamiable emphasis," Laura had refused even to discuss the matter. "I was no less surprised than grieved at such an answer," Wight wrote. "Heretofore although she has frequently differed from me in opinion she has been ready to yield to me." In this "little thing" and in this alone, Laura asserted her autonomy.[37]

Refusing food also allowed Laura to toy with her suicidal fantasies. Death terrified and at the same time fascinated her. When she was angry at herself, it even seemed inviting. Despising herself for her angry thoughts and doubtful that she would ever live up to Wight's expectations, Laura entertained fantasies of dying. On December 24, 1845, after mischievously hiding her hairbrush and then suffering agonies of remorse, Laura told Wight of a strange dream:

> I thought I was but fifteen years old & that I was very sick & was going to die. At last you and Dr. put me in the ground & I was so happy to be in Heaven. My soul was in Heaven, but when you put the earth on me it gave me life again.[38]

In August, and again in September, she reported other, more seductive dreams of death: "I dreamed I wrote a letter to God, and tried very hard to get some one to carry it. I told him that I wanted to come to visit him very much. I dreamed that I was in heaven once, and saw God with my eyes."[39]

Laura's self-punishing diet nearly killed her, but by the winter of 1846 the danger had passed. Howe deserves much of the credit for saving her life. On the theory that nagging her to eat would do more harm than good, he left her to her bread and milk, prescribed a course of sea bathing and horseback riding, and insisted that her teachers divert her "from all exciting trains of thought" and hide their own concern about her health.[40] Surmising perhaps that Laura was reacting to the many abandonments and losses she had endured, he arranged for Wight to take her to Philadelphia to visit Mary Swift. When that failed to improve her appetite, he decided that the time had come for Laura to reestablish her connection to her own family.

Accompanied by Wight, Laura traveled to Hanover in June 1846 for the first time in over three and a half years. She found her family transformed. Namesakes had replaced her dead older sisters. Collina, the newest arrival, had been born sixteen months earlier, and Mary, an infant when Laura last visited, had turned into an active four-year-old. Laura's brothers, Addison, fourteen years old, and John, twelve, had been afraid of her during her last visit, but now they were old enough to learn finger spelling and to converse. Addison especially showed interest in his famous sister, and she immediately chose him as her favorite.

After so many years, Mrs. Bridgman, too, seemed different to Laura, who suddenly felt critical of the mother she had once clung to. "Laura came to me much excited," Wight reported during the visit. "Her mother had been punishing Collina & her mother did not smile often &c."[41] Quick to anger, Mrs. Bridgman had probably always swatted her children, but now, after an enlightened Perkins education, Laura noticed—and disapproved. Laura also objected to Mrs. Bridgman's unhealthy indulgence in stimulants. "You must exert yourself not to drink Tea or Coffee," she admonished her mother in a letter, "but have some Milk & Water. . . . I shall be so very much gratified if you will resist your inclination to drink Tea. . . . You must break the habit off & never to drink any Tea & Coffee so as to please me."[42]

Only Asa Tenney remained unchanged. He visited frequently during the two weeks Laura spent at home; each time, she asked to go to the barn in search of eggs, as they had when she was small. "She would take his hand & go off alone with him with a childish confidence that I have rarely seen her manifest towards a gentleman," Wight noted with surprise.[43] Later, Laura wrote that meeting Tenney again when she was a young woman, she appreciated his "beautiful character" more even than she had as a child.[44]

AFTER LAURA'S VISIT to New Hampshire, her health slowly returned. Perhaps, as Howe had hoped, renewing her ties to home had restored her appetite. With Wight's encouragement, Laura began to correspond regularly with her relatives and to keep track of news from Hanover. Shortly after their reunion, Laura told her mother how happy she was to have found her family again:

> i constantly imagine what you are doing every day. to day i
> thought you were having two kinds of bread at five this morning

> & at ten oclock you were preparing luncheon for the family. . . .
> it gives me a great deal of pleasure to think of you all. . . . i am
> very earnest to hear from you & the rest of the family.[45]

Reconnected to home, Laura had more to think and talk about. She worried about her mother's illnesses and Collina's naughtiness, remembered her siblings' birthdays, noted the comings and goings of hired girls, and followed the activities of the Bridgman aunts, uncles, and neighbors. With her family back in her life, Laura's world had become larger and more populous; it was no longer inhabited by her and her teacher alone.

Her teacher's deepening affection may also have contributed to Laura's recovery. During their first two years together, Wight's dutiful devotion had gradually been transformed into genuine attachment, so that her work with Laura no longer felt like self-sacrifice. By 1847, Wight could announce that Laura was "becoming more of a companion every day more gentle and joyous more quiet and thoughtful."[46] A year later, Wight noted that Laura "grows continually more affectionate more lovely and at the same time more sensitive."[47] Despite Laura's stormy episodes, Wight believed that she and her pupil had become spiritually attuned to one another: "Any thing that interests me deeply seems to suggest a corresponding train of thought in her," Wight remarked. "It is often the case that I can scarcely believe it to be the effect of accident merely."[48]

As her relationship with Laura matured, Wight's own moralism softened. When she thought of "the thousand little kindnesses" she received from Laura continually, Wight admitted to feeling "almost condemned" for dwelling so much on Laura's misdeeds. She began to think of her pupil not just as a disciplinary problem needing to be solved, but as the victim of complex psychological forces. Instead of simply reforming Laura, she wanted to figure her out.

Wight came to believe that Laura suffered from an incurable "infirmity of temper." Her self-control was naturally fragile and poor health or insufficient exercise could push her over the edge.[49] Physical disability exacerbated Laura's constitutional weaknesses. While other children benefited "insensibly" from daily intercourse with others, "she poor child received very little" beyond the words that Wight spelled into her hand.[50] After seeing Mrs. Bridgman resort to corporal punishment, Wight also surmised that Laura's propensity for violence had been nurtured in early childhood. Perhaps Mrs. Bridgman had whipped and shaken Laura, just as she now whipped Laura's siblings.[51] In light of the mother's volatility, Wight could not, she said, expect perfect self-restraint from Laura: "A parent may strike a child in anger and it is called a punishment for the child[;] Laura obeys the same impulse for the moment regardless of persons."[52]

By 1848, Laura's irritable rebelliousness bothered Wight less as a moral transgression than as a practical problem. Wight did not plan to remain at Perkins forever. She worried that once she was gone, Laura's excessive "self-esteem"—her obstinate independence—would make her unhappy.[53] In December, when Laura in a fit of temper struck her twice on the back of the head, Wight was not so much angry as alarmed. Who, she wondered, would put up with such behavior in a grown woman? What would become of Laura if she did not learn self-control? "Such an outbreak as this makes me more anxious for her future than anything else in her situation. As she grows older and is irritable from sickness or provocation who will bear with her and soothe her[?]"[54]

WIGHT AND LAURA remained together five years. For Laura, this was a period of emotional and intellectual flowering. Stimulated by constant conversation with a patient and devoted teacher, she developed greater powers of expression. Her vocabulary became more varied, her stories and letters more sophisticated. She finally learned to use capital letters. Although her angry, violent outbursts never completely stopped, they became less frequent. Wight believed that Laura's self-control improved steadily, and Howe agreed, observing that "the flowing tide" of Laura's "animal spirits" had subsided as she grew older: "Without being less cheerful and happy, she is in her usual mode more quiet and subdued"[55]

During her years with Wight, Laura occasionally confessed to feeling unwell or cross, but by 1848 she most often spoke of her joy. Along

with the details of many "delightful" days with her "lovely teacher"—
lessons in history and moral philosophy, pony rides, invigorating shower
baths, long walks, Bible reading—Laura recorded her own happy feelings: "I have had many kind feelings & did not feel like doing wrong
which increases my happiness constantly"; "I derived much pleasure
from meditating upon our best friends"; "I have had a very happy day I
thought much of Christ & his beautiful character & his disciples"; "I
have had numerous very pleasant ideas"; "I am naturally very fond of
mirthfulness"; "I have had a very pleasant day. I have been hilarious &
vivacious."[56] Her life, as Howe remarked, was "to her a boon, and she so
considers it, for often, in the fulness of her heart, she says—*I am so glad
I have been created!*"[57] Wight, too, marveled at Laura's happiness: "I can
compare her with nothing more readily than the singing birds, deriving a
portion of her joy from the same source with them—healthy animal life
but partaking too of a far higher character, that of an immortal being ex-
ulting in life strength and progress."[58]

Nourished by her happiness, Laura's imagination soared. Pleasur-
able dreams and fantasies replaced her childhood nightmares of menacing animals. For the first time, she reported comforting daydreams about
her family:

> I have been thinking about my Mother & Brother A today. . . . I
> could enjoy such a long excursion to my house so much. Mother
> would rush to the front door to meet me. She would salute me
> with much cordiality I am extremely anxious to visit her for a
> month. . . . I could assist Mother as much as possible. I should
> not have to have her work incessantly. She could sit with my lit-
> tle cosy Miss W. I could prepare her a very luxuriant luncheon
> every day.[59]

Sometimes Laura imagined sprouting wings and flying to Hanover to
surprise her "dear family." As she grew more attached to Addison, she
especially enjoyed picturing his astonishment if one day she walked into
the school he attended in East Hartford.[60]

By 1849, elaborate fantasizing had become one of her favorite forms of play. Planning an imaginary party for a hundred imaginary friends kept her amused for two days. She dreamed up a "new spacious parlour," so crowded with her guests that "the air would be scanty or breathed up totally." A big table, richly set, would be loaded with all kinds of pies and cake and fruit. After her friends had eaten, she would make them "laugh very heartily by my most comical remarks" and then play a borrowed music box to give them "the pleasure of hearing very sweet & loud & soft sounds." They would all sit up late—until eleven or twelve—and then stay the night. If there weren't enough beds for everyone, Laura would spread blankets on the floor or have some of her guests sleep on shelves. Of course, it was all only a daydream, Laura said, but she enjoyed building castles in the air.[61]

In her most exciting fantasies, Laura endowed herself with superhuman powers. She imagined having half a dozen wings along her back:

> My legs would be so powerful to leap a great distance as well as the kangaroo. My arms could be of much utility. . . . I wish so much to run of my [own] accord as swiftly as my strength will allow me. I could visit all of my good friends. . . . I should carry many little things to them for Miss Wight & our friends with great pleasure.[62]

No longer helpless and dependent, Laura's imaginary self could fly, jump, or swim great distances in the service of love. And the friends of her daydreams welcomed her visits joyfully, lifting her in their arms, kissing her "very ardently," and clasping her in warm embraces.[63]

Laura wrote in her journal of her affection for many people—Addison, her mother, Howe, Tenney, and various Perkins benefactors, teachers, and students. In the spring of 1849, she began to speak fondly of Edward Bond, a young Unitarian minister who often visited and sometimes wrote her letters. Without fully understanding the implications, Laura knew—or guessed—that he was courting Wight. Laura's greatest, most absorbing love was for her teacher. The pages of Laura's journal are filled with her thoughts on Wight's health, plans for Wight's happiness, and praise for Wight's virtues.

Laura worried constantly about her teacher's bouts of illness and melancholia. On June 1, 1848, chilly weather made Laura resolve to defer an excursion because, she said, "I was very unwilling for my dove to expose herself to the cold & damp evening to call for me. She is very poor & feeble & thin & yellow. It might be very perilous that she should take a bad cold." What Wight needed, Laura concluded, was a restorative vacation. "I shall be highly gratified to have my dove go home for a week."[64] In March, when her "lovely teacher" fell ill again, Laura wrote that she felt "very anxious & agitated while my invalid was in such distress. I felt as my tears could flow over my face like the dew." Laura not only missed her teacher's company, but also hated to see Wight suffer:

> The time passed so heavily & sadly along by me. I was so very sadly seeing her suffer much from the cold & fever. . . . I was very willing . . . to deliver her from her pain. . . . I sat in my rocking chair by her. She reclined herself on the sofa all day. I took a book & began to study natural philosophy. I anticipated every necessary liking for her.[65]

Although she longed to remain beside Wight's sickbed, Laura understood that her ministrations only made things worse. Her well-meant compresses and massages—her very presence—added to her exhausted teacher's distress. One day, hoping to relieve Wight's suffering, Laura ran to get her music box. "I thought the music would divert her as it made very sweet sounds," Laura explained, but Wight "announced to me it hurt her head so badly."[66] Laura realized that "I was not of service . . . because I might torment her by my least motions, partly because I felt so sorely grieved to see her so feeble and unloquacious."[67] For Laura, leaving Wight in peace was always the most difficult of love's austere and lonely offices.

When she considered her own future, Laura assumed that she would always remain with Wight. Laura's "most pleasant thought," Wight said, "is that she may keep a nice little house in good order for me."[68] Imagining this "tiny house" gave Laura a sense of purpose: to manage it, Wight would need her assistance. "I could give her all my aid," Laura wrote in her journal. "I could help her wash & wipe & put all her dishes so very nicely. I could sweep my little chamber & dust & keep it very nicely every day." Together, she and Wight would pick out furnishings, choose "nice & delicate dishes," and take care of each other forever.[69]

LAURA'S SECURE AND happy world began to fall apart in the spring of 1850. After an extended visit to Wayland with Laura, Wight returned to Perkins to find that Howe's annual report for 1849 had just appeared. Although the report included a lengthy and laudatory description of her work, Howe had neither consulted with Wight in preparing his account nor shown her a draft before publication. She was devastated when she read what he had written.

It seemed that notwithstanding his lavish praise of her gentleness, patience, devotion, and virtue, Howe had filled his report with careless falsehoods and subtle insults.[70] She objected to his characterizing her influence on Laura as "wholesome"; the word sounded coarse to her. She resented his implication that she had gone along with his radical brand of Unitarianism and endorsed his religious experiments: she would never have agreed to leaving her beloved pupil in spiritual confusion or religious uncertainty. And his casual description of her disciplinary methods made Wight sound rigid and authoritarian:

> After breakfast her teacher . . . takes a sort of review of . . .
> [Laura's] conduct and actions the day before, making such re-
> marks in commendation or criticism as may be desirable. Her
> diary is then examined and criticized. Her letters also are exam-
> ined . . . to see if they are legibly written.[71]

For years she had nurtured Laura's conscience by scrupulously refraining from direct criticism. Now readers of Howe's report would believe that Wight had been no better than Mary Swift.

The most humiliating feature of Howe's report was the passage describing Wight that he had chosen to quote from Laura's journal. From the scores of excerpts he could have picked—passages expressing Laura's love, admiration, and appreciation of her teacher—he chose the only one that mocked her. And then, as if for good measure, he italicized the most embarrassing sentence:

> I had a very pleasant day. I have been very hilarious. I could not help laughing incessantly. My mind is so very full of drollery and mirthfulness. *I wish that my dear teacher would have a little share of my mirthfulness.* She does not like fun as well as I do.[72]

This was the sorest of sore points. Painfully sensitive, Wight struggled against her tendency to succumb to "sad thoughts."[73] Yet, for no apparent reason, Howe had used Laura's playful journal entry to expose this private weakness to the world.

Overcoming her timidity, Wight wrote Howe a letter of protest. Inevitably, his reply added calculated insult to offhand injury. He said that he had chosen not to show her the report before printing it because he preferred that what he put before the public should "really" be his. Perhaps she could have written a better report, but "had you done so, & done it with tenfold more care and labour than I did, you would have found that there would have been room for criticism." To his mind, "wholesome" was a "most excellent" word. In fact, he had selected it expressly. Nor would he make any apology for including the passage from Laura's journal about Wight's inability to have fun:

> As touching what I said about your cheerfulness, Dear Miss Wight, I think I was not far from the truth: you are not a melancholy person, *not deficient in cheerfulness,* that is . . . but you are not remarkable for that light hearted gaiety which constitutes what is called a *cheerful* character. . . . Let me say one word though it may seem uncalled for: . . . being human, you are not perfect, & yet probably it would not be possible for me to point

out a single instance of short coming which you would not be disposed to object to.[74]

Why did Howe treat Wight—the most submissive and devoted of employees—so unkindly? Sheer fractiousness, perhaps. Frustrated at this period by the bitter Free Soil party politics in which he had immersed himself, he was in an especially irritable and combative mood. (Longfellow remarked at the time that Howe reminded him of Orestes driven by the Furies.)[75] Possibly Wight had annoyed Howe by befriending his wife, who, at a low point in her marriage, had taken to confiding her troubles in affectionate notes addressed to "Bestest of all Wighties," and "My little dear Wightie."[76] Or perhaps Howe had simply grown tired of paying for Laura to have her own special teacher, and wanted to give Wight a push toward the door.

In fact, Howe had framed his report as a valediction. Laura had just turned twenty, and he announced this was to be the final chapter of her story. "The great point of interest" in her life had been at the beginning: "It was the first step that was most difficult and most interesting." Now Laura's case could yield nothing further to science, religion, or philosophy. Howe's only remaining concern was to provide for her future. Of course, she could go home to live with her family, but he feared that "she could not find in their remote village the means of continual culture and improvement, which are to her the bread of life, and the appetite for which grows by what it feeds upon." Although Laura worked diligently at her needlework, she could not sell enough of her crocheted bags and purses to pay for her keep in Boston. "Perhaps by a little effort on the part of her friends," he concluded, "money enough might be raised to buy for her a life-annuity, which would place her beyond the reach of pecuniary want, and secure to her the attendance and companionship of some young lady, who could be to her what Miss Wight has so long been."[77]

Reading this appeal for her replacement must have come as a shock to Wight, who at the time had no immediate plans for leaving Perkins. She did have a suitor—Edward Bond—and they had discussed marriage.

But swept up in the missionary fervor of the day, he had set sail for the Sandwich Islands (Hawaii) in December 1849, determined to save native souls, and she had not gone with him. Until he returned or could send for her, Wight intended to keep her job.

If Howe's intention had been to speed her departure, he succeeded. At the end of July, Wight suffered an emotional and physical breakdown and went home to recuperate. She returned to work two weeks later, but remained, according to Laura, "very troubled & weak."[78] On August 18, after much soul-searching, Wight formally resigned. "I must accompany Laura home as I have promised," she wrote to Howe, "but after it is very desirable that I should give up all care of Laura."[79] Wight informed him that she planned to join forces with another Perkins teacher, Mary Paddock, to open a small private school for girls in Boston. In that way, she could remain nearby in case Laura were sick or in trouble.[80]

Wight left Perkins on November 7, 1850. Dreading a painful scene, she had kept her departure a secret from Laura until the previous day. But at the moment of parting, it was Wight who burst into uncontrollable tears. Later, she explained that in leaving Laura she felt "as if I had lost a part of my very self."[81] Guilty anxiety added to Wight's misery. She regretted now the unflattering tales she had told about Laura.[82] With a reputation for violent misbehavior, how would Laura find another teacher to love and care for her? "I have some fears for Laura when I remember how often she requires a soothing word, but she loves new persons and new things," Wight wrote to Howe a week later, as if to comfort herself. "I must believe that she will be happy."[83]

But Laura was never really happy again. She had loved Wight "half as much as if she was my wife," and for the rest of her life mourned the loss of her "best & greatest teacher."[84]

CHAPTER ELEVEN

Lamentations

LOST WITHOUT HER beloved teacher, Laura poured out her grief in letters to Wight. "My poor eyes are having a heavy shower of rain now while I write to you. I beg of you that you must come to console me & to arouse my poor spirits." Never, Laura wrote, had she expected to meet "so great & violent trials." In the absence of her greatest, dearest friend, time passed "very heavily and painfull." Every week felt as long as a long year.[1]

Laura complained that she was too sorrowful to eat and began to waste away, as she had five years before. Hoping to talk reason to her, Howe invited her to stay at his house until she could calm down. He explained that it grieved him to see her so disconsolate. She owed it to him to accept her new, more independent situation cheerfully. To please him, Laura tried to appear tranquil and resigned, but she confessed to Wight that her private agony had not diminished:

Last Monday in the P.M. I was obliged to leave the warm sitting room. . . . I staid in my cold room for an hour. I shut my door & put a chain on the hook so that no one could open the door. I burst into tears for a full hour. I was so much agitated that my heart might be inilated [annihilated]. I put my shawl around my neck. . . . It seemed to me as if I could escape so abruptly from my room & throw myself in your arms for safety.[2]

If Laura could have visited Asa Tenney, the other gentle good angel in her life, he might have offered her some solace, but he too was gone. She had received the news of his death on a Sunday morning in February 1846, in a letter from her mother. "Very feeble and ill from the cold weather," he had died on December 29—Laura's birthday—at the age of sixty-three, only a few days after taking to his bed.[3] He had been thinking about Laura until the end. Neighbors recalled that a day or two before he fell sick, he tried to get enough money to buy a basket from an Indian woman "for the deaf dumb and blind child." As his strength ebbed, he struggled to write Laura a last letter, but could not summon the strength to finish it.[4]

Fortunately, Wight had been there to help Laura mourn. "I am very sorry that my oldest friend is dead that I never can see him again," Laura had said, turning first red, then pale, as Wight spelled out Mrs. Bridgman's letter. Wight did not contradict her when she added, half inquiringly, "I think Mr. Tenney can see us now."[5] Feeling the vibrations of the bell ringing for church, Laura announced that she wanted to wear mourning, and Wight, sympathetic to the impulse, helped her find a crepe badge—one that Drew had used years before. After services, teacher and pupil read and discussed comforting passages from the Bible, and Wight listened as Laura reminisced about "Uncle Asa": how he used to "trot" her in her little chair every day, take her for walks over the mountain and to the barn, help her find berries, and caress her "in a great many different manners."[6]

In the following weeks, Laura's sleep was disturbed and she often looked sad, but she did not want to talk about Tenney again until the end of May, when she and Wight returned to Hanover for vacation. As soon as Laura stepped off the train in Concord, she began asking questions about her old friend. Had he been sad not to see her before he died? Could he see her now and know her thoughts? How could she know when it was her time to die? Would Wight go with her to see Tenney's grave?

To help Laura recover from her grief, Wight suspended their regular lessons in arithmetic and geography for several weeks. Instead, she and Laura talked "quietly and gently of Gods love and care for all things he had made." Wight told her "how he took care of the birds and the bees all living things and how sure we might be that he would do all that was best for us." Despite the risk of Howe's doctrinal disapproval, she reassured Laura that "her friend who was kind to her was not in the ground that he was still living and more loving than ever and much happier than when he was in his poor sick body." Consoled, Laura "grew calm and even cheerful by degrees."[7]

WHEN WIGHT RESIGNED, Laura had no close friend or companion left at Perkins to comfort her. Eventually, with no one else to turn to, she confided her sorrow to her mother. "I shuddered so much & worried so sadly," Laura wrote home on January 2, a few days after her twenty-first birthday; "I could not credit of renouncing my best & wise teacher."[8] Alarmed by this pitiful letter, Mrs. Bridgman wrote to Wight in early February, begging her to remain in touch:

Write me again when convenient think you will write often to L she said she had written you 3 or 4 letters always tel me about L think she will write to you oftener than to me . . . hope you may come with Laura again. I will keep your mantle until you come again.[9]

Mrs. Bridgman feared for Laura, but she was also worried about herself. She dreaded above all the possibility that Howe, distracted by other interests and impatient with Laura's grief, might send her home for good. As Mrs. Bridgman explained in her letter to Wight, life on the family farm was already too hard to bear. The weather was bitterly cold. Her hired girl had quit and the boys could not help: Addison was away, boarding at the Kimball Union Academy in Meriden, New Hampshire, and John would soon follow him. Laura's father, now over fifty, suffered from rheumatism, and they feared he might grow lame. To add to her troubles, Mrs. Bridgman, at age forty-six, had given birth to a new baby, Ellen, in April 1850. Mary and Collina, now nine and five, looked after the baby when they could, but they also went to school. ("I pitty those who may have little ones when are quite in years to take care of and no older ones to help," Mrs. Bridgman said.)[10]

All her worries and responsibilities had worn Harmony Bridgman out. She told Wight that in addition to her usual chores, she was rising at three in the morning to wash the boys' school clothes and sew their shirts. To get any work done during the day, she had to tie Ellen in a rocking chair, but soon the child would be too big for that. If Laura were to come home now, how would the family manage? They could only pray that Howe would not force the issue. "I wont talk no more about the dark side," Mrs. Bridgman concluded ruefully, "I have lookt so much on the dark side the year past it hardly seems sometimes there is any bright side."

Six weeks later, she also wrote a supplication to Howe, sweetening her appeal with an enclosure of some money toward Laura's expenses. Wight's departure, Mrs. Bridgman explained, had increased the family's anxiety about Laura's future:

> I can but hope that she will stil be cared for as she has been. I hope I am not alltogether unthankfull for what Dr. Howe and others have done for Laura. I think I have great cause for gratitude to God and Man that so much could and has been done to make her happy and comfortable.[11]

Knowing that Howe had "many cares," Mrs. Bridgman would nevertheless "hope and trust Laura will not at presant be foregotten by Him." Perhaps, busy as he was, he could provide a way for Laura to be happy—"more so than she can at presant . . . be at home."

MRS. BRIDGMAN HAD good reason to worry about Howe's "many cares." His schedule in 1851 was more frenetic than ever. Besides overseeing a large and complex institution for the blind, he was absorbed in a new philanthropic project: establishing a school for the "feeble-minded," who until then had often been left to languish in almshouses. At Howe's urging, the Massachusetts legislature had appropriated money in 1848 for him to operate, on a trial basis, a school for ten mentally retarded children. Three years later, impressed by the progress the children had made, the legislature officially created the Massachusetts School for Idiotic and Feeble-Minded Youth, naming Howe the general superintendent.[12] Now he had two schools to fund, staff, and oversee.

His immersion in the tempestuous politics of the day added to Howe's frenzy. After the Mexican War, when tensions between North and South over the status of slavery in the newly acquired territories began to mount, he had thrown himself into the free-soil crusade. When the antislavery "Conscience Whigs," disgusted by their party's attempts at Southern appeasement, bolted in 1848 to form the new Free Soil party, he went with them. Outraged by Southern perfidy, indignant at Northern temporizing, and horrified two years later by the Compromise of 1850 and the Fugitive Slave Act, he was determined to do his part to destroy the slavocracy.

As the struggle to prevent the westward spread of slavery intensified in the 1850s, Howe's abolitionist and free-soil activities consumed him. When Mrs. Bridgman wrote to him about Laura in the spring of 1851, he was feverishly campaigning for Charles Sumner's election to the U.S. Senate; writing for *The Commonwealth*, a free-soil newspaper that he had helped organize; and meeting regularly with the Vigilance Committee, an ad hoc group dedicated to helping fugitive slaves and thwarting slave catchers.

Even among the ardent abolitionists in the Free Soil party, Howe stood out as a radical. He identified passionately with the "degraded, wretched, and hopeless slave," and despised those who, under cover of the Fugitive Slave Act, "used the wealth and influence which God gave them to kidnap and enslave a fellow-man—a poor, trembling, hunted wretch."[13] At first, he thought that aggressive political activism would contain and ultimately end slavery, but by 1856 he no longer saw any alternative to violence. The intransigence of the South had finally persuaded him that John Brown was right: the crimes of a guilty land would "never be purged *away;* but with Blood."[14]

DESPITE THE EXTRAORDINARY pressures and excitements of the moment, Howe found time at the end of March to reply reassuringly to Mrs. Bridgman's appeal. For all his irascibility, he almost always responded chivalrously to a humble plea such as hers. Moved by Laura's sorrow and her mother's desperation, he promised Mrs. Bridgman that he would continue to do everything in his power for Laura's welfare. He agreed that for the moment she was "more happy and advantageously situated" in Boston than she would be in Hanover.[15] Much as he wished to be spared the trouble and expense of keeping Laura, he did not have the heart to send her away.

In any case, for the moment, the question of Laura's future could be postponed. Wight's plans for starting her own school had failed to materialize and she needed to earn money. Until she figured out her next step, she was willing to keep Laura with her in Wayland as an occasional boarder. Relieved to be with her teacher again, even temporarily, Laura spent the spring and summer that year shuttling between Wight's home, where she was happy, and Perkins, where she was miserable. In April, Wight reported to Howe from Wayland that Laura was delightedly following her everywhere, "like my very shadow." Back in Boston at the end of May, Laura begged Wight for another invitation:

I still feel so feeble & languid. I shall be glad to come to Wayland. I shall be so very happy to be under your tender care for a long time. I cannot sleep so soundly for many nights. I wake very often in the night. I cannot taste anything for my poor appetite is penalized. My brain is so very active & irritable. . . . My poor tongue has lost its coat very sadly I cannot taste any thing. I suffer so greatly from thirst when ever I take a morsel in my mouth. I have to drink a full cup at a time. I do not feel any better.[16]

Although Howe maintained that Laura was adjusting to Wight's absence from Perkins, Laura herself was unequivocal about the sadness of her altered situation. After five years of living with her own beloved teacher, sequestered from the other blind girls, Laura did not see how she could be happy as an ordinary inmate of the institution. "I cannot content myself here," she complained to Wight from Perkins. "I used to love to stay with you too much to run among so many people."[17]

By July Laura realized that her happy visits to Wayland would soon end. Wight's vague understanding with Edward Bond had ripened into a formal engagement. In September she planned to meet him in San Francisco, where they would be married. From there, the newlyweds would go on to Kauai, in the Sandwich Islands, to spread the Unitarian gospel.

Laura hoped at first that she could go, too. She pleaded with Wight not to leave her behind:

I abhor too much to have you steal your sweet hand from my sight. I am so passionately anxious to be put in the thought of going with you & I shall surely die of a violent & vast grief during your saddening departure. . . . I wish so much to live with you always. . . . I love you as much as myself.[18]

If she were allowed to accompany them to the Sandwich Islands, Laura promised to make herself useful. "I should love to have the care of your snug cosy house. I could put all things in apple pie order for you & your family."

When Wight discouraged this fantasy, pleading the difficulty of the journey, Laura appealed to Bond. "I should like to come & live with you very much indeed," she wrote; "I shall come & meet you with great effort & spirits."[19] If he agreed to her joining them, he would save the expense of a housemaid; Laura would do all the work. Wight needed her, Laura warned. After their many years together, Laura knew and loved her teacher better than anyone else possibly could. "I feel as if W's heart must burst into a great sorrow & solitude in the ship. . . . She will think of my great loss & my society & my spirits." And Mr. Bond should take mercy on Laura, too. How would she survive the great trial of separation from her Angel, Miss W.? What if Laura died, and Wight did not hear of it until long afterward?[20]

A few days before Wight's departure, Laura, as if to comfort herself, composed and sent to Bond one of her most elaborate fantasies. She imagined hiding in Wight's wardrobe until the ship sailed. When Wight opened the wardrobe, she would be amazed to discover the stowaway. Or perhaps Laura would hide in the ship's hold and creep into Wight's cabin one night. In the morning, "It will astonish her very much to find me sitting in a nice rocking chair. She would be so strongly tempted to lift me in her arms." Laura also dreamed of proving her love by showering Wight with astonishing gifts: fifty hogsheads of maple molasses, cologne, and salt; a beautiful alarm clock; a fur cloak; a pair of gloves. If the newlyweds wanted a house for themselves in Honolulu, she would send a capable beaver, full of energy, to build it for them. Did they want transportation? Help carrying heavy burdens? She would give them an elephant.[21]

On September 24, Wight embarked, alone. "I always expected to dwell with my best Wight for numerous years but my hope became wrecked," Laura confided to her mother two months later. "My disappointment was so vast & sorely. My wishes were drowned & spoiled." Laura could only ease her pain with happy daydreams. She imagined swimming across the ocean until she caught up with Wight's ship. How delighted her teacher would be to see her!

> Miss W. would come rushing toward me first & take me in her slender arms like a Babe. She would wish so passionately [to] conduct me to the Sandwich Islands. She will talk with me incessantly. We would sit up all night for our own pleasure.[22]

Memories of Wight—of the touch of her hand, "so very gentle & soft"; of their long talks and warm embraces—came "very naturally & pleasantly" to Laura. "I love to think of her & talk of her so much," Laura explained to her mother. "I would prize to die with her."

WITH WIGHT FINALLY and irrevocably gone, the problem of Laura's future loomed larger than ever. She was almost twenty-three now, too old to be enrolled in a school for blind children. Her days as a public attraction were also behind her. Sightseers who had flocked to marvel—and weep—at the spectacle of a pathetic little girl were not interested in watching a gaunt and nervous adult woman. Nor, at her age, did Laura have anything further to offer as a scientific exhibit; she had no new tricks to perform for visiting educators and psychologists. The newspapers and magazines, too, thought of her as old news. They had run their Laura Bridgman stories years ago.

In her twenties, Laura was not likely to attract admiring new benefactors. Unlike Helen Keller, who fifty years later would grow up to be an appealing young woman, with a smiling rosebud mouth, round cheeks, softly waving hair, and bright blue (glass) eyes, Laura was neither winning in manner nor especially pleasing in appearance. Fastidious, birdlike, and intense, she seldom hesitated to criticize visitors for dirty hands or poor spelling, and made no effort to charm those who failed to charm her.

As sociologists have pointed out, social adjustment is a slippery concept, especially when applied to the disabled. "Assertion of individuality may all too readily be interpreted as maladjustment in a society in which the pressures on a cripple are to accept submissively a dependent role."[23] Undoubtedly, Laura's stubborn "self-esteem" made her seem difficult and odd. At the same time, her sensory deficits inevitably isolated her from cultural and social influences. Without sight or hearing, she could not always successfully imitate ingratiating feminine behavior, and Howe's policy of protecting her from bad influences had exacerbated her peculiarities. Sequestered from the other blind girls, who tended both to resent her special status and to look down on her for her deafness, Laura had not learned to conform to a group or to keep quiet about her own demands and complaints.

Wight's exclusive attention had fostered Laura's self-absorption. Pupil and teacher, living virtually alone together during Laura's adolescence, had spent hours every day for five years discussing nothing but Laura: her good and bad deeds, her thoughts and feelings, her moral progress, her diet, and her health. Wight seemed to belong to Laura totally. In losing Wight, Laura lost an extension of herself. No wonder that the separation devastated and enraged her.

Howe was surely right to want Laura to establish an adult identity. But even if she somehow acquired the emotional maturity to do so, what role, in the middle of the nineteenth century, could a severely disabled, genteel young woman assume? Laura's first choice—housekeeper and permanent companion to Wight—had been denied her. As an alternative, Laura sometimes wondered about becoming a wife.

She had noticed of course that most young women, including many Perkins teachers, sooner or later took on that role. In 1845, blushing and laughing, she inquired about her own matrimonial prospects. "Do you think," she asked Wight, "I shall ever be married with a gentleman whom I love best & most?" Wight responded with a firm "no."[24] Like most people then—and some people now—she found the idea preposterous. As Howe's daughter, Laura Richards, put it in 1928, in *Laura Bridgman: The Story of an Opened Door,* "the crown of earthly life" was simply not for deaf-blind girls. "In this relation, as in every other," Richards proclaimed, Laura "stood apart from other women."[25]

Despite Wight's discouraging prediction, Laura was reluctant to rule out marriage. (Perhaps her own sexuality—to the extent she understood it—was not as unthinkable to her as it was to others.) She reminded Wight that they both knew blind women who had married. Besides, Laura argued, notwithstanding her disabilities, she would make a competent wife: "I can sweep & fix things very nicely & do many things."[26] Not surprisingly, however, suitors failed to appear.

If she was not destined to marry, Laura believed that at least she could work. She always liked the idea of supporting herself and for years had earned spending money by selling her handiwork—crocheted bags and doilies. Some Perkins graduates—those who could not find paid employment and whose families were too poor to support them—went to work in the Perkins adult workshop. But consigning Laura to a lifetime of stuffing mattresses simply never occurred to Howe: he had not educated her for mindless labor. While her mother toiled on a farm, Laura ironically was reared to be a middle-class girl, too delicate and refined to work every day at a menial job.

Wight always favored the idea of Laura's becoming a teacher, responsible for the care and education of a deaf-blind child.[27] In 1847, Laura had tried tutoring Lizzie Alden, a deaf and partially blind girl, but the experiment did not work out. Laura was too impatient, impulsive, and needy herself to succeed in managing difficult younger children.[28]

WITH WIGHT GONE and no lessons, regular work, or purpose of her own, Laura drifted through her days at Perkins. She sent long letters to her mother and to Wight, complaining of sleeplessness, loss of appetite, fits of weeping, and agonies of grief. Alarmed, Mrs. Bridgman wrote to Howe again in May, suggesting that he find a home for Laura with some "quiet private family" that could provide her with "suitable attention." A return to Hanover was still not a good idea. Although Laura enjoyed coming home for visits, she was used to the mild climate of Boston and would find New Hampshire winters unendurable. "Glad should I be if our place and Family were such as to make her happy," Mrs. Bridgman concluded, "but at present they are not."[29]

Howe was not so sure. While he recognized that the Bridgmans had problems, he hoped that living in familiar surroundings among those who loved her might restore Laura's equanimity and encourage self-reliance. He had always believed that congregate living was unhealthy and that disabled people were happiest living with their own families. When Laura returned to Hanover in October for vacation, he announced that the moment had arrived for her to decide for herself where she wanted to live permanently.[30] In a letter of extraordinary tact and tenderness, he presented Laura with her choice:

> My Dear Laura,
>
> I do not call you as I used to do my dear *little* Laura for you are now grown to woman's stature in body.
>
> Your mind also has grown to sufficient maturity to enable you to judge for yourself in most matters.
>
> I want therefore for you to decide whether it is best & most agreeable for you to remain in Hanover this coming winter or to return here. If you decide to return here, please let me know soon that I may make arrangements about your room & about a young lady to be your companion & friend.
>
> We shall do every thing we can to make you comfortable & happy if you come.
>
> If you stay in Hanover we shall want to hear often from you & always feel great interest in your welfare & happiness.
>
> Your old friend
> Doctor[31]

Laura decided to remain at home. She explained that she was enjoying her daily walks with her sisters, Mary and Collina, who had learned to talk with their fingers, as had John, Addison, and some of the Bridgmans' neighbors. Although her parents could barely communicate with her, Addison and Mary were lively manual conversationalists. Returning to Boston at this point had little appeal. Howe kept promising to look for a replacement for Wight, but even if he found one, Laura could not face adjusting to a stranger. Laura also understood herself well enough to admit that in some ways she liked thinking about her Boston friends more than actually being with them: "I appreciate them the more & more I am separated from them. I can love them so much [better] in our absence than while I am with them constantly." Finally, away from Perkins, Laura felt her spirits improve. Although she still loved Wight "the most of any one else in this world" and missed her badly, at home Laura could be "more uniformly cheerful." She hoped that she would hear often from Howe and her other Boston friends, but she was ready now to remain with her own dear mother.[32]

ALTHOUGH LAURA HAD become a burden to Howe, once she chose to live in Hanover, he half wanted her back. She had often disappointed and irritated him, yet his attachment to her was deep as well as ambivalent. At the same time that he wished her gone, he could not quite let go. Worried suddenly that without him she would regress, he reminded the Bridgmans to provide her with "some regular occupation; and also some regular daily instruction." Because she would probably outlive her parents, it was essential, he urged, that they keep her alert, informed, and in constant touch with other people.[33] He also sent instructions to Laura. She must try to find "a variety of minds to commune with" outside of her own family circle, or else, like an unused sword, her mind would grow rusty. And if she felt unhappy or understimulated in Hanover, she should return immediately to her "sunny home" in Boston. "I still keep your room, for I do not know but you may want it," he concluded, hoping—and fearing—that she would not be able to stay away for long.[34]

If Howe intended to shake Laura's fragile resolve, he succeeded. In fact, as she confessed to Wight, Laura had never been sure where she would be happiest—or whether she could be happy again anywhere. "Oh my dearest Mrs. Bond, I am so much confused in my feeble brain that I can scarcely think," she wrote, only a week after telling Howe that she intended to stay in Hanover. At home, when the sun shone and Addison and Mary had time to talk to her, Laura was "most highly delighted to be at H. with my blessed family."[35] But life on the Bridgman farm was not always so pleasant.

Laura understood her family's problems with surprising clarity. Her mother had borne many children, but had no idea how to cope with their demands, Laura said. Annoyed and exhausted by Ellen's constant pestering, Mrs. Bridgman failed to see that the little girl simply needed some toys to keep her amused. After two months at home, Laura was so upset by the turmoil that she commissioned Mary Swift Lamson to buy a few playthings for Ellen in Boston, and arranged for someone to bring them to Hanover. Laura recognized that her father also contributed to the tension of the household. A grim and chilly presence, he watched his wife struggle to manage Ellen, but refused to help. "My Father never likes to caress or pacify her as Mr. L[amson] does his only little daughter. . . . He does not like to go near my little birdie Ellen & she never approaches him when he comes into the house."[36]

As the winter deepened, Laura began to slip into a depression. Ice and snow made walking outdoors too treacherous; for exercise, she had to pace up and down inside the house. The neighbors who had visited frequently in the fall no longer wanted to brave the weather to come and chat with her. Laura's days passed more and more monotonously. With no one to teach her, she could only reread her few embossed books, knit, sew, and try to pitch in by dusting and wiping dishes. Her mother, unable once again to find household help, was staggering under the burden of her own cares. She had neither the time nor the finger-spelling skill to read to Laura or engage in conversation. "At present [Laura] cannot in our family have that attention that she needs," Mrs. Bridgman informed Howe at the end of December. "I could wish that it were otherwise, but must try to think it is all for the best."[37]

By Christmas Laura had begun to starve herself. On a diet of rye gruel mixed with milk and sugar, she rapidly lost her strength.[38] "I do not think you know certainly the consequences of my low health," Laura reported to Howe in mid-January. "I have the dispepsia. I subsist upon very simple & few victuals. I eat so sparingly."[39] Mrs. Bridgman was fatalistic about her daughter's chances: "I dont know what a cold winter may do for her but she wont probably live many years unless her health is better," she wrote, prepared for the worst.[40] Howe read these letters with mounting alarm. Emphasizing the danger of Laura's symptoms, he urged Mrs. Bridgman to persuade her to return to Boston, where her diet could be properly managed. He also wrote to Laura, reassuring her that her room at Perkins was still unoccupied and promising that he would hire a new teacher-companion for her—"a most sweet & sensible young lady much like your good Wight."[41]

Perhaps because she did not completely trust Howe's promises, Laura remained ambivalent. He had told her before that he would find a suitable replacement for Wight, but instead he had assigned one of the older Perkins students to keep Laura company. She had been indignant. What could she learn from a blind girl—someone who could neither read unembossed books nor describe the world? This time, Laura told Howe that before she agreed to return to Perkins, she would need more definite guarantees about her new teacher: "I should like to know what the ladys name & where she resides is she already prepared to come & be my constant friend."[42] Laura also feared that she could never love her new teacher as much as Wight—and that the new teacher would not love her. Worse yet, the teacher might win her heart, and then leave because the work was too exhausting. Laura could not face the prospect of another loss. Immobilized by misgivings, she put Howe off with vague talk about returning to Boston when her health improved.

In late February, Howe made her decision for her. Fearing that Laura was near death, he dispatched Mary Paddock to New Hampshire to bring her back to Perkins. As Paddock later told the story to Howe's daughters, she got off the train in Lebanon, New Hampshire, only to discover that a storm had made the roads impassable. After four snowbound days, she finally managed to get through to the Bridgman farm, where Laura lay bedridden, too weak to walk. Daniel Bridgman (sobbing loudly, in Florence and Maud Howe's implausibly embellished account) carried Laura out to the sleigh for the trip back to Lebanon. By the time they reached the railroad station, Laura seemed almost lifeless. Paddock recalled the train ride to Boston as one of the most trying experiences of her life. "She despaired of getting Laura to the institution alive, and when she was at last carried into the little white chamber where she had lived so long, it seemed for a moment that all was over."[43]

After a few weeks in Boston, Laura began to recover: she reported an improved appetite and more energy. Although she still could not stomach meat or potatoes, she was enjoying two hearty meals a day of rye gruel with toast dipped in milk.[44] In April a visit to Lydia Drew Morton in Halifax further restored Laura's health and spirits. Once again, Howe had saved her life.

YET NOTHING HAD been resolved. Although the crisis was over, Laura still had no work, no goals, no direction. As her strength returned, she resumed her supplicating letters to Wight, complaining that the passage of time only intensified her suffering:

> I get so languid much more easily than when you first left me. I cannot be so happy & healthy without you for I am in the darkness from you. It is your mystery or a miraculous spirit in you which strengthens my health and increases my happiness. It seems almost like our Lord Christ. I have always faith & confidence in you much more so than any one else in the earth.[45]

Months after her return to Perkins, Laura continued to lament her loneliness, ill health, and lack of appetite. She told her mother that she did not expect ever "to feel strong & well again as I was."[46]

Now that Laura was back in Boston, Howe had once more lost interest in her. Although she begged him to get her the "kind & sweet" lady he had promised—someone with whom she could read and converse—he paid no attention. Finding a candidate for the job might, of course, have been difficult. Even in those days, there was no surplus of gentle, self-sacrificing Unitarian females eager to devote their lives to a demanding, sometimes violent, deaf-blind woman in exchange for low pay and long hours. But in truth Howe was not looking.

In the fall of 1853, Dorothea Dix, the crusader for public insane asylums and Howe's sometime reformist ally, got wind of Laura's troubles. Dix claimed that her interest in Laura's plight had been "sadly quickened" by the remarks and criticisms of "strangers and casual visitors" to Perkins. This explanation rings false, and Howe did not buy it. More likely, Dix heard about Laura's suffering from Wight, with whom she occasionally corresponded.[47] Or Laura herself might have complained: in the course of her asylum investigations, Dix visited Perkins frequently and Laura considered her one of her "great & intimate friends." ("I love Miss Dix very dearly like a Sister," Laura noted in her journal in January 12, 1853; "She is a very estimable & lovely Christian.")[48]

Anxious, in her officious way, to solve Laura's problem, Dix made Howe a generous offer. She had canvassed prospective donors and secured pledges of enough money to create an endowment that would pay for Laura's permanent, full-time companion. Howe no longer had any reason to put off hiring Wight's successor. The only condition of the gift was that he employ an American: in other words, no Irish need apply.[49]

Howe bristled at Dix's temerity. What right had she to interfere in his management of Laura's life? Whoever had reported Laura's difficulties to Dix should instead have spoken "openly & plainly" to him. Laura was his creation; he knew what was best for her. "It is undoubtedly true that Laura's situation & surroundings during the past two years have been, in some respects, disadvantageous," he conceded, "but, it is equally true, that they have been, in other respects, advantageous." Although Wight's departure had pained Laura, he believed that in the long run she would benefit from the separation. Her teacher's companionship, "so suitable in many respects during the period of Laura's life during which it existed," would not have been suitable much longer.[50] At her age, Laura needed to be weaned from such infantilizing relationships. Instead of clinging to a teacher, she ought to get out into the world and meet more people.

The requirement that only an American be hired also irked Howe. Dix, like many "native" Americans at the time, was alarmed by the flood of Irish immigration and appalled by the transformation of cultured, Brahmin-controlled Boston into a crowded city, full of Irish peasants and increasingly dominated by an Irish political machine. (In the decade after 1846, 100,000 Irish immigrants arrived in Massachusetts; by 1855, more than half the population of Boston was Irish.)[51] Dix's legendary humanitarianism did not deter her from embracing nativist policies and opposing the employment of immigrants.[52]

In reality, Howe would no more have entrusted Laura to an Irish Catholic than to a Hindu, but he could not accept an explicit prohibition against hiring an immigrant. He wanted no part of Dix's nativism: his fight was against slavery. At this period of intense sectional rivalry, he feared that the nativists would undermine the unity of the North and thus strengthen the South politically. He also objected on principle to any "national prejudice or proscription." In hiring any teacher, he told Dix, "I must have in view her fitness & not her birth place."

Thanking Dix for her kind intentions, Howe said that he would gladly accept the money, but not on her terms. Donors could not presume to dictate the conditions of their gifts or make financial arrangements for Laura on their own. If and when he chose to hire a companion for her, the decision must be his and his alone. "The contributions which you promise from various persons," he concluded, "should be made to the *general* funds of this Institution, & without any restriction as to the mode of their application."[53]

Howe understandably resented Dix's highhandedness. But his rejection of her offer meant that Laura would have no paid companion. Even if he later wanted to hire one, he would not have enough money. After a year or two, Laura gave up asking about the "sweet & sensible" lady she had hoped for. Mrs. Bridgman was more persistent. As late as 1857, she was still gently prodding him to deliver on his promise: "I wish a suitable Lady could be procured who could devote a portion of time for Lauras bennefit that she may not grow dull and unhappy as she grows older."[54] Howe responded with excuses, reassurances, and evasions, but not with a suitable Lady.

THE 1850S WERE Laura's homesick years. To her, home always seemed to be where she wasn't. Wandering the halls of Perkins, she missed her family and longed for New Hampshire. "You can not imagine how very anxious I am to come home & be your guest," she wrote to Mrs. Bridgman in a typical letter of complaint. "I feel so miserable & strange of mind of late. . . . I wish to describe to you some details when I see you but it is so difficult for me to make a friend comprehend about my feelings & some of my own thoughts."[55]

Yet once Laura returned to Hanover, the isolation soon drove her to despair. If her oldest sister happened to be home, Laura felt cheerful. Mary was growing up to be a kind, attentive companion and a good conversationalist. Unfortunately, Mary was usually away, boarding at a school in Meriden. Left alone to amuse herself, Laura would begin to pine for the more sociable world of Perkins, stop eating, grow steadily weaker, and take to her bed. When she seemed near death, her parents would send her back to Boston to recover her strength. After a month or two, feeling adrift among children and busy strangers, Laura would again yearn for home, and the cycle would start over.

During this period, notwithstanding her recurring bouts of misery, Laura never completely abandoned hope for her own happiness. In her most sorrowful moments, a secret fantasy sustained her. She dreamed that her brother Addison was her true love. Someday he would rescue her from her loneliness; her real home would be with him.

The Addison of Laura's dreams was almost entirely the creature of her own wishful thinking. Although he was the more amiable of her two brothers and occasionally wrote her a letter, he never spent much time or energy on his sister. Brighter and more ambitious than John, Addison was often away from home and usually busy studying, first at Kimball Union Academy, and then at Dartmouth, from which he received a medical degree in 1856. He said pleasant things to Laura—that he was delighted to see her and that he thought of her often—but never showed the slightest interest in devoting his life to her.[56]

Wight knew that the affectionate relationship between brother and sister existed only in Laura's mind. "She thinks she loves him very much," Wight observed tartly in 1850, adding that the best way to get Laura to smile for her photograph was to have Addison in the room.[57] Like Wight, Howe found Laura's giddy affection for her brother annoying. When Laura pressed him, Addison tended to tell her whatever she wanted to hear, and Howe finally had to scold him for leading her on:

> You should be particularly careful in writing to her, to have your words express *exactly* your meaning *& nothing more*. In your letters to her, I understand you to express great desire to have her

come home & to come yourself to fetch her, while in the present letter to me, you . . . seem to speak as if it was doubtful whether she had better come.[58]

But Laura was no fool. She noted in her journal that although she liked to imagine Addison's pleasure at seeing her, in fact, when she went home to visit, he never reciprocated her "warm welcome."[59] In a long letter to him, she admitted that much as she loved him, she had no illusions about his feelings for her:

> I should love to come & study with you much, alone sometimes. I fear that you would drive me out of your presence. For I think you did not like to sit & commune with me in the least. You used to avoid me many times when I wished to be with you with all my heart. . . . I think you like to receive letters from me better than to see or talk with me.[60]

Laura did not have to believe her daydreams in order to be nourished by them. Regardless of the real Addison's actual sentiments, imagining an idealized brother's love gave her pleasure. She liked to picture his astonishment if she were magically to appear in his schoolroom. Wanting to be alone, the two of them would go off for a long, private talk. "It would seem as if we were like a family," she mused. "I shall have such a glorious time with him alone & quietly."[61] When she came to surprise him, she would look beautiful, wearing a dark cloak, blue bonnet, elegant scarf, and a nice pair of fleece gloves. He would be confounded at the sight of her, "his dearest Sister L whom he loves the most of any one else on this blessed earth."[62]

Naïvely but passionately, Laura even imagined marrying her brother. On an undated sheet of paper, she recorded an extraordinary dream, suffused with emotional and erotic longing:

> I was dreaming that i was living with my own family, mother & Father & Brothers Addison & John. In a little while i was ex-

ceedingly delighted to receive a such pleasant proposal from
Addison. I married him. After we took the marriage we were so
very happy & merry in coming together. Our hearts were ex-
tremely full of the affection & gratitude & joy & loving. We
were very social together. Some of my dear excellent friends
who were in the house to see us be married sympathized with us
in our joy. One night they came & gazed upon us both slumber-
ing together in a nice warm bed. My excellent husband embraced me & encircled my waist to show me the greatest
affection & love.[63]

In this gratifying fantasy, Laura reversed their real-life roles: Addison
was the needy one; she was independent. "As i was going to abandon my
husband he clung [to] me so as not to let me go . . . but implored me to
stay with him constantly."

At the age of twenty-four, Addison moved to Bascom, Georgia,
probably to practice medicine. Although he was too far away to visit,
Laura could still enjoy building her "castles in the air"—so long as he remained unmarried. When he wrote to her in June 1860 to announce his
engagement, her dream of making her home with him shattered. Now
she could only beg him not to forget her:

You must not abandon me in your heart. I should mourn & re-
pine to death if you felt icy & dusty in your heart toward me. It
is true that I love you as myself.[64]

In choosing to settle in Georgia, Addison did more than simply leave
home: he crossed the Mason-Dixon line. When the Civil War broke out,
he volunteered to defend the Confederacy, fighting for four years under
General Joe Johnston in the 25th Georgia Volunteers. At times, he must
have fired on fellow New Englanders, perhaps even on neighbors from
Hanover. After the war, he came home with his wife for a brief visit and
then returned to Georgia, where he served for almost ten years as a town
postmaster; in 1874 he moved to Decatur, Illinois, to work as a doctor.[65]

He may have written occasionally to Laura; if he did, his letters have not survived.

In June 1860, when Laura learned of Addison's marriage plans, she was still reeling from an earlier blow. Her sister Mary had died of scarlet fever seven months before, at the age of seventeen. Laura lost her just as they were growing close. In the last year of Mary's life, she and Laura had begun a lively correspondence. In long, confiding letters, Laura opened her heart to her sister, gossiping about mutual acquaintances, complaining about Addison's neglect, and describing her own anxieties and physical ailments.[66]

Mary's sudden illness had lasted only a week. She was packing her trunk to come home after the fall school term when she first complained of a sore throat. During the night, she developed a high fever and the symptoms of dysentery. When her condition worsened, her mother and her aunt, Augusta Bridgman, came to Meriden to nurse her. They said later that Mary had not seemed to suffer. "She had her senses up to the moment of her death," her brother John reported, "& appeared conscious that she could not recover." On the morning of November 14, she "expressed a willingness to die" and expired soon afterward. The funeral took place the next week in Hanover. As Mary lay in her coffin, with a wreath of flowers on her brow and a bouquet in her hand, she appeared "more like one under the quiet influence of sleep than in the icy embrace of death."

John Bridgman begged Howe to break the news to Laura. His parents could not face telling her: they feared that she would take the loss too hard. Mary was "the support & comfort of Laura while at home . . . the most acquainted with talking with & looking after Laura," John explained. Understanding Laura better than her own family did, the Doctor would know "the way in which such sad intelligence should be portrayed to her."[67]

HOWE WAS NOT in Boston to receive John's letter or carry out his wishes: he had fled to Canada the week before. Although he pretended to be there promoting the education of the blind, in fact Howe was running for his life. On October 25, 1859, John Brown had been indicted for treason after his raid on the federal arsenal at Harpers Ferry, and Howe had reason to fear that a federal warrant might be issued for his own arrest as a material witness. If that happened, and he was extradited to Virginia, he could wind up on trial for conspiring with Brown.

Though too weak from his wounds to stand, Brown, under interrogation, steadfastly refused to implicate the Massachusetts abolitionists who had financed him. Unfortunately for them, the diaries and letters in his possession revealed their names and addresses. Howe's was conspicuous among them. Along with other radical abolitionists—George L. Stearns, Theodore Parker, Gerrit Smith, Thomas Wentworth Higginson, and Franklin Sanborn—he had been a member of the "Secret Six," a group dedicated to supporting Brown's antislavery guerrilla activities. In the years leading up to the Harpers Ferry raid, Howe had given Brown weapons, raised funds for Brown's militia, and donated money from his own pocket.[68] Just weeks before the raid, he sent Brown fifty dollars.[69]

Howe's political opposition to slavery had turned militant on May 21, 1856, after Congressman Preston S. Brooks of South Carolina, goaded by one of Charles Sumner's notoriously vituperative speeches, used his gold-headed cane to club the Massachusetts senator almost to death in the Senate chamber.[70] The attack convinced Howe that the Union in its present form could not—and should not—hold, because the South would never be moved by moral suasion.

Sumner's nearly fatal speech had been about Kansas. In a three-hour oration, "The Crime Against Kansas," he denounced the South's "rape of a virgin territory." The Kansas-Nebraska Act of 1854, Sumner charged, was nothing but a Southern "swindle." By empowering the settlers of the western territories to decide the issue of slavery by popular vote, Congress had in effect authorized proslavery squatters from neighboring slave states to invade a free territory and seize control through fraud and intimidation. The only just remedy was to admit Kansas as a free state immediately. Otherwise, he feared, slavery could spread not only into the vast western territories, but ultimately, as the number of slave states increased, into the free states as well.

As infuriated as Sumner by the passage of the Kansas-Nebraska Act, Howe had thrown himself into organizing committees to send settlers to Kansas, so that a free-state majority could be maintained. In 1855, when the Northern newspapers began reporting bloody depredations by the Southern sympathizers who were also pouring into the territory, Howe helped raise $10,000 from outraged Bostonians to arm the free-staters. Once again in chivalric glory, he traveled west in July to deliver the money and assess the situation. His interviews with the frightened and angry emigrants he met in Kansas confirmed his conviction that slavery would be eradicated only by force.[71]

Howe first met John Brown, the most celebrated—and violent—of the Kansas antislavery guerrillas, in Boston. The Puritan of the Puritans (as Julia Ward Howe described Brown) had come east in 1857 to raise money for his small army of Kansas defenders, and Howe found him thrilling.[72] Although Brown, born in 1800, was only a year Howe's senior, Howe saw him as a figure out of America's heroic past—"honest, keen, and a veteran backwoodsman." Here was the uncompromising moralist, the man of action, the military leader who could deliver the slaves from bondage. Howe did not always agree with—or even know— the details of Brown's mysterious plans, but he had faith that Old Brown could stir up and lead a slave insurrection powerful enough to put an end to slavery. "He is an enthusiast, yet cool, keen, and cautious," Howe wrote in boyish wonder. "He has a martyr's spirit."[73]

Much as Howe admired martyrdom, he did not, at his age, aspire to it. (The month he spent in a dank Prussian prison in 1832 had doubt-less cured him of any illusions about the pleasures of self-sacrifice.) For two years, he had offered advice, sympathy, and material support to Brown, but when that "new saint" was arrested and condemned to the gallows, Howe panicked.[74] On November 14—the day Mary Bridgman died—Howe wrote to the newspapers, disclaiming prior knowledge of Brown's plans. "The outbreak at Harper's Ferry was unforeseen and unexpected by me," he declared. "It is still to me a mystery and a marvel."[75] By November 16, when the letter appeared in the press, Howe was in Montreal; he did not come home until early December, after Brown had been hanged. At the end of January, not daring to defy a congressional summons, Howe reluctantly appeared before a Senate committee appointed to investigate the raid. With the country in a violent mood, the committee chose not to pursue its inquiries too strenuously. Howe's explanations and denials satisfied the senators, and he returned to Boston, his escutcheon somewhat blotted, but his life and liberty intact.

WITH HOWE UNAVAILABLE, Laura's mother finally had to be the one to tell her that Mary was dead. "It was on a Sabbath day in December that I learned her sad fate," Laura recalled. "My heart was almost broken." After all that Laura had suffered, this seemed too much to bear. She burst into tears, unable to say a word. Although it was early in the day—the bell had just rung for morning prayers—the matron, Marie Moulton, thought it best to put her straight to bed. Laura remained in her room for a long time; it was months, she said, before she could resume her normal activities. She never remembered feeling more hopeless and alone. "It seemed as if I could not be worthy of comfort, or happiness."[76]

AFTER SHE LOST the people she had loved best—Tenney, Wight, Addison, Mary—something in Laura broke. Her imagination withered; her sense of humor dimmed; she stopped dreaming of herself as powerful. A querulous note crept into her journals and letters, and she began to enjoy talking about her ailments. In her thirties, despairing of the pleasures of the world, she turned increasingly inward, devoting herself to religious meditation and prayer. Dreams of heaven replaced her earlier fantasies of flying through the air into the welcoming arms of friends. At times, Jesus seemed closer to her than anyone she knew on earth. As she sat reading her Bible in lonely silence, Laura comforted herself with the thought that he spoke "down from his throne" and into her heart.[77]

CHAPTER TWELVE

Legacies

ON A HOT Sunday in early July 1852, Mrs. Bridgman and Sarah Herrick, the minister's wife, dressed Laura in her baptismal robes and led her to a nearby brook, where the members of the Hanover Baptist church waited. Laura was trembling violently. When she complained of feeling faint, someone fetched her a chair. Mrs. Herrick fanned Laura during the the long opening prayer, and then led her down to the brook. As Reverend Herrick clasped her hand to help her into the water, Laura felt, she said, "a thrill of crying joy."[1] Understanding her terror of drowning, the minister immersed her gently. Later, she remembered that as soon as she was on her feet again, he wiped her face.

Daniel Bridgman, a deacon of the church, helped Laura climb back up the bank; she had trouble moving under the weight of her wet robes. Some of the men offered to carry her home, but she insisted on walking. After the women dried her and she changed her clothes, she and her mother went to church and stayed until the last sermon was preached. Rejoicing and humility filled Laura's heart. "Joyfully buried with Jesus Christ" at the moment of her baptism, she had shared the "holy grief" of his sufferings and the delight of his resurrection. "I believe in the name of Christ," Laura proclaimed. "I put my strength in him . . . I am not afraid."[2]

IN THEIR 1903 biography of Laura, Florence and Maud Howe argued that Laura would never have resorted to baptism if their father had not been so busy, first with free-soil activities and then with his Civil War work. Toiling early and late and often on the road, he simply had not had a moment after Mary's death to soothe Laura's grief or to change her mind when she began to contemplate joining her parents' church.[3] Even in his sixties, he had remained so dedicated to his public work that he had little time for Perkins or his family, and none at all for Laura.

As long as Wight was her teacher, Laura took a lively interest in the political struggles that preoccupied Howe. In November 1848, Wight observed that "few voters have made more earnest inquiries into the character of the candidates for the presidency" than Laura had. When Wight tried to convince her that Zachary Taylor had some good qualities, despite his history as a slaveholder, Laura stuck to her abolitionist principles and refused to agree.[4] But after her teacher left, Laura lost touch with the great events taking place around her. As her thoughts turned more and more toward religion, the world seemed to recede. Although no record remains of her ever mentioning the Civil War, she must have known something about it. Perhaps in the light of her conversion, distant battles did not seem terribly important: her mind, after all, was on eternity.

HOWE, ON THE other hand, devoted all of his energy and talent to the war. As a sanitary inspector for the governor of Massachusetts and, later, a member of the United States Sanitary Commission, he traveled to inspect military camps and hospitals, and campaigned in Washington for more health officers and for higher standards of personal hygiene for the troops. Ever practical, he proposed combating lice by increasing soap rations, providing free laundry service to the soldiers, and hiring laundrymen. To maintain cleanliness, he urged that "Yankee ingenuity" be employed to produce light portable stoves suitable not only for cooking, but also for boiling wash water and drying the soldiers' clothes. "If a tithe of the science, skill, and care which are so liberally given to improving all the means of killing the soldiers of other armies were devoted to the means of keeping our own soldiers in health, the present mortality of war would be greatly lessened," he observed, foreseeing the terrible toll that disease would take on soldiers throughout the Civil War.[5]

Beginning in early 1862, as a vice-president of the Emancipation League and later as a member of the American Freedmen's Inquiry Commission, Howe also turned his attention to the plight of newly freed slaves, many of whom were living essentially as refugees under the uncertain protection of the Union troops. Averse to color lines, he lobbied for the arming of black soldiers and even opposed the creation of separate black regiments. After Emancipation, he campaigned for programs to benefit newly freed slaves and for laws guaranteeing them full civil and political rights.[6]

Howe's war work not only allowed him to use his still formidable energies, but also gave him an excuse to stay away from Boston at a time when home held few attractions for him. By now, all his old friends were gone: Summer, still pained by his wounds, spent most of his time in Washington, attending to his senatorial duties; Mann, who had moved to Yellow Springs, Ohio, in 1853 to take on the presidency of Antioch College, died of fever in 1859, at the age of sixty-three; and Theodore Parker, Howe's closest ally and mentor during the free-soil struggle, succumbed to tuberculosis a year later. His stormy marriage offered Howe few consolations. After "The Battle Hymn of the Republic" made his wife famous, they quarreled more fiercely than ever—about money, household management, sex, and her ambitions.[7] (Howe had twice asked Julia Ward Howe for a divorce—in 1854 and again in 1857—but she was unwilling to take such a scandalous step.)[8] When she openly defied him by undertaking a public lecture tour in 1863, he was furious, but powerless to stop her. Life in Boston became even more dismal for him that year when his beloved three-year-old son, Sammy, died of diphtheria.

Physically sick with grief, Howe took to his bed for almost a month; his health was never fully restored.[9] Longfellow, always perceptive about his friends, observed to Sumner: "It is a very heavy blow; as you know Howe's tenderest point is his love for his children."[10]

IN ASSUMING THAT their father could have talked Laura out of her conversion, Howe's daughters underestimated her attachment to her parents' church. Laura did not join the Baptists simply because Howe was not around to comfort her for Mary's death, nor did she undergo the frightening ritual of immersion on an impulse. Years of questioning, doubt, and reflection preceded her baptism.

From the beginning, the Bridgmans, whom Howe characterized as "pious and intelligent people of the Orthodox faith," had given him complete control over Laura's religious training. "They paid me the compliment of leaving me to be the teacher of their child in what I am sure they consider, as I do, to be the most important part of her education," he boasted in 1847, in a rejoinder to his orthodox critics.[11] Of course, Laura's parents did not have much choice at the time: unable to care for her at home, they depended on his goodwill. In any case, they had no reason to believe that she would ever be a candidate for baptism. When they turned her religious education over to Howe, she had neither the abstract understanding nor the verbal ability to make the necessary profession of faith.

By the late 1850s, the situation had changed. Under Wight's tutelage, Laura had blossomed intellectually and emotionally. She now had the maturity and linguistic competence to understand, desire, and qualify for baptism. Howe, meanwhile, had shown no curiosity about her religious views in almost a decade. Busy with projects of national importance, he had long ago written her off as a subject for experimentation. But as he lost interest in Laura's religious development, Mrs. Bridgman was becoming increasingly concerned about her daughter's soul. In 1858, when Jonathan Herrick, a dynamic new minister, was called to the Hanover Baptist church, Laura's mother confided to him that she "longed for the conversion of her afflicted child."[12]

The Bridgman family's Baptist roots went deep. In 1791, when a small congregation of dissenters, convinced that immersion was the only proper mode of baptism, separated from the established Congregational church, Daniel Bridgman's father, Asa, and his uncles, Abel and Isaac, were among them. Since Baptist ministers did not need formal training, Abel and Isaac Bridgman could help preach the word in their new church. Abel declined ordination when a council of ministers from Vermont and New Hampshire offered it to him, but Isaac, a popular and persuasive preacher, accepted ordination in 1801.

In their early years, the Hanover Baptists suffered the quarrels, upheavals, and schisms typical of small-town churches of the time. In May 1796, Abel Bridgman withdrew from the church because his religious views had changed; in May 1798, he saw the light again, retracted his errors, and was restored to fellowship, but not to the pulpit. The congregation split in 1806: one faction founded a new church in nearby Lyme, with Thomas Whipple as preacher; the other, "because Bro. Whipple had taken too much and too often of the ardent," preferred to stick with Isaac Bridgman. Bridgman remained as the Hanover pastor until he died in 1815 at the age of fifty-eight, but he frequently had to yield the pulpit to his congregants, most of whom regularly felt the call to sermonize.

Membership in the church fluctuated, dropping from 123 in 1811 to 49 in 1820, and then, as more energetic ministers appeared, rising to 139 in 1823. The Hanover Baptists met in barns, schools, and private houses until 1827, when they completed the construction of a brick church near Hanover Center. Among those who preached in the new building was Edward Mitchell, a Dartmouth student and Creole "mulatto" from Martinique. (The first black man to graduate from Dartmouth, Mitchell was ordained as an evangelist in the Hanover Baptist church in 1829, the year Laura was born.) In 1841, along with many other Northern Baptist churches, the Hanover congregation took a stand against slavery, resolving "that we have no fellowship with slavery, neither do we as a church regard any slaveholder as a member of good standing in the church of Christ." During the next two decades, acrimony—both personal and doctrinal—weakened the church, but by the time of Laura's baptism, Reverend Herrick had restored harmony.[13]

When the Herricks first met Laura in the summer of 1858, they did not know how to use the manual alphabet to converse with her directly, but they suspected that "she had her thoughts on religious things."[14] Their intuition proved sound. Tentatively, and without revealing her own thoughts and feelings, Laura had been questioning her mother about baptism. "I felt so timid, that I pondered every word in my heart," Laura said, by way of explaining her reticence.[15] The next time she was in Hanover, in the summer following Mary's death, Laura approached the Herricks on her own initiative. Recruiting her little sister, Ellen (Nelly), as her guide, Laura walked to the parsonage, sat Mrs. Herrick down, took her hand, and began to teach her the manual alphabet. "She then had me spell boy and cat, then Ellen and Laura," Mrs. Herrick recalled. "She then put me to talking, encouraging me by a good deal of praise, so that it was not long before I could converse with her quite satisfactorily."[16]

The minister's wife soon understood the urgency behind this finger-spelling lesson. Laura needed a sympathetic and intelligent interpreter so she could describe to Reverend Herrick the transformative religious experience she had recently undergone. Through Mrs. Herrick, Laura told the minister her story. Anguished and dejected after Mary's death, Laura had despaired of everything she had ever believed in: religion, the power of prayer, her own worth. "I did not feel myself in the care of God, or the Savior," she said. Then suddenly, after weeks of silent suffering, she felt her heart opened by the hand of Jesus. "I beheld his face boldly," she reported to the Herricks. "I let my soul fall into his hands."[17] She asked the minister if this meant that she had entered into fellowship with God. Should she now be baptized in her parents' church? "I have been baptized with the Holy Ghost," Laura explained, "but I have not been baptized with water."[18]

Convinced of the authenticity of her conversion, Herrick was eager to baptize Laura immediately. Mrs. Bridgman, delighted with "a marked change" that she perceived in Laura, did not want to delay, but Mr. Bridgman, perhaps fearing Howe's wrath, decided that they ought to wait. Laura reluctantly agreed to a postponement, as long as Herrick promised to baptize her as soon as she came home again for vacation. Before she returned to Boston, she asked him to describe every detail of the ritual, so that while she was gone, she could think about all that would be said and done when the day finally came. "I cannot hear, but I shall think of the words of the Savior," she told him after he had answered her questions. "I shall not be afraid."[19]

Laura did not return to Hanover until the summer of 1862. During her two-year absence, her determination to be baptized never wavered. Enough time had gone by at this point for her father to overcome his misgivings: with the Civil War raging, and with his pressing new national responsibilities, Howe would not know or care what Laura did during her vacation in Hanover.

ACCORDING TO HOWE's daughters, when their father eventually learned of Laura's baptism, he was more sad than angry. Despite all his enlightened efforts, Laura had ended up embracing the primitive faith of her parents. In later years, he always maintained that her conversion had caused an "extraordinary" and "painful" change in her personality. He said that he could scarcely recognize "the girl whose clearness and simplicity of mind had so fascinated him," in the "conventional and professing sectarian" that Laura had become. Howe's daughters, scornful of Baptist superstition, agreed that after Laura joined her parents' church, she lost her "elastic bird-like quality and her old spontaneity of feeling. Her mind became self-conscious. Her conversation, like her letters, was full of pietistic cant."[20]

Yet Laura's religious conversion served her well. At a crucial moment, it saved her from the isolation and purposelessness that psychologists call "social death."[21] At the time of her baptism, her life was at a standstill. Losing Wight and Mary had severed her closest ties. Like a chronic invalid consigned to a nursing home, Laura had no prospect of advancing, of earning money, acquiring new skills, or forming new attachments. "Warehoused" at Perkins, she might pass her time more or less pleasantly, but her accomplishments were all behind her. Disconnected from a social network and deprived of any practical role or function, she was in danger of drifting into the condition that social scientists describe as "a kind of limbo in which one has been written off as a member of society but is not yet physically dead."[22]

Becoming a Christian gave direction and meaning to the monotonous passage of her days. When she felt lonely or bored, Laura thought about the world to come and tried to "rest in the love of the almighty Lord." Her daily life did not seem so empty in the light of the joyous eternity ahead of her, when the finger of God would open her eyes and ears and unloose the string of her tongue.[23] Indeed, after her baptism, Laura said she was "like a new being." She had "beheld the great mercy of the Lord above," and felt, for the first time in her life, safe and strong.[24]

Moved by religious feeling, she even tried her hand at devotional verse. Her best-known poem, "Holy Home," originally composed in 1867 and revised several times, celebrates the glory she believed awaited her:

> *Heaven is holy home*
> *Holy home is from everlasting to everlasting.*
> *Holy home is Summerly.*
> *I pass this dark home toward a light home.*
> *Earthly home shall perish,*
> *But holy home shall endure forever.*
> *Earthly home is Wintery.*
>
> *With sweeter joys in Heaven I shall hear and speak and see.*
> *With glorious rapture in holy home for me to hear the*
> *   Angels sing and perform upon instruments.*
>
> *When I die, God will make me happy*
> *In Heaven music is sweeter than honey, and finer than a diamond.*[25]

Laura took particular pride in "Holy Home," and made painstaking copies of it to present to her visitors and correspondents.

At a school for children, Laura, now in her thirties, had neither the opportunity nor the social skills to make real friends. Joining her parents' church brought her into a new adult fellowship. As a "sister" in the Hanover congregation, she, who was everywhere else so singular, for the first time became part of a community. "All who beheld her baptism seemed deeply moved," Mrs. Herrick recalled, "and tears were seen in eyes unaccustomed to weep. It was an occasion long remembered."[26] Afterward, her Baptist neighbors did not forget to visit Laura when she stayed in Hanover. Jonathan and Sarah Herrick continued to correspond with her and invite her for visits, even after he was called to Troy, New York, in 1863. The new minister, Franklin Merriam, and his wife also befriended her. Like other Hanover Baptists, they made it their business— whether out of Christian duty or genuine affection—to write to Laura when she was in Boston and call on her when she was home. And during the winter months, when she was at Perkins, local Baptists stopped in to talk religion with her and to ask for copies of her devotional poems.

Baptism brought her closer to her mother, too. Delighted and relieved by Laura's conversion, Mrs. Bridgman proclaimed that faith had improved her daughter.[27] But the change, if there was one, may have been as much in Mrs. Bridgman's heart as in Laura's disposition. After years of coping with a demanding disabled child, Mrs. Bridgman finally got something in return. Just when her sons were repaying her many sacrifices by leaving—Addison to the South, John to Chicago—she had the satisfaction of seeing her daughter publicly embrace the family's faith. Although Mrs. Bridgman felt, Laura said, "so envious for her dear children to be christians & do right in the sight of God," the others, after leaving home to board at non-Baptist schools, refused to be converted.[28] Perhaps that is why in the years that followed Mrs. Bridgman began to see Laura less as another of her terrible burdens and more as an ally in her struggles.

LAURA LIVED UNTIL 1889. After her baptism in 1862, her story dwindles. She made no more major decisions, and her life underwent few outward changes. Gradually, the world forgot that she was still there.

During the nine or ten months of each year that she spent at Perkins, she followed a regular, rather undemanding routine. Like many genteel "normal" women, she devoted her mornings to light domestic work: cleaning her room, mending her clothing, and knitting or crocheting the souvenirs that she could sometimes sell for a little money. When she had time, she reread her few books, wrote letters, and received occasional calls from friends or curious strangers.[29] Sometimes in the afternoon she would drop in on sewing classes to thread the needles for the blind girls. (Laura could quickly thread even the finest needle by placing the twisted thread and the eye of the needle on the sensitive tip of her tongue.) She ate her meals in the common dining room and attended Sunday morning prayer services; otherwise, since the Perkins students were in class nine hours a day, she spent her time alone.[30]

Visiting and corresponding with her former teachers provided Laura with her greatest pleasure: she always longed for intelligent conversation. She looked forward to her regular visits to Lydia Drew Morton, who until her death in 1887 remained a loyal friend. Laura also grew close to Eliza Rogers, the only one of her teachers who fully shared her religious views. They were, Laura said, "sisters in the name of J.C."[31] In 1862, when the Bonds returned from the Sandwich Islands and settled in nearby West Newton with their three small children, Laura was, as she said, "in raptures" at being reunited with her "chosen friend Wight."[32] With the passage of time, their relationship had lost its old intensity, but Laura looked forward eagerly to visits. "I shall have a grand time with our old friend Wight in [the] country," Laura told Lamson in 1868; "it will enlighten my heart to meet her & have old talks & chatting also."[33] Although she did not see the Bonds often, Laura took an interest in their children, worried about Wight's precarious health, and, until Wight's death in 1878, continued to write her confiding letters.

Over the years, Laura's relationship with Mary Swift Lamson deepened. In 1884, Laura confessed in a rush of affection her gratitude for Lamson's constancy: "I trust that you can never forget nor throw your dear old pupil Laura out of your treasure of heart as long as you live on the earth."[34] Laura especially appreciated the condolence letter Lamson sent after Howe's death. "There is a good deal of comfort in it much sunshine," she said. When Lamson's husband died six months later, Laura, in turn, did her best to console her teacher. "You have all of my sympathy in your deep affliction & trials & ills," she wrote:

> How I wish that I could have an interview with you. I trust in God's mercy that your Husband is so happy with him & Jesus in a holy home which is Heaven. Jesus will not leave you comfortless. He will come to you. God is gentle in all his dealings.[35]

As she grew more worried about Wight's health, Laura turned to Lamson for news, and in the end it may have been Lamson who informed her that her dearest teacher had died. The fatal illness apparently came on gradually. In 1875, Laura reported a delightful surprise visit from her "beloved teacher WB," who had been too ill to make the trip before, but was now "well and in fine spirits." The two of them had ginger beer, crackers, and lemonade—"a real refreshment"—and caught up on each other's news. Wight did not leave until evening, promising to invite Laura to West Newton in a few weeks.[36] By the next year, however, Laura had begun to fear for "poor Wight," bedridden from an attack of "knee water."[37] Two years after that, Wight died at the McLean Asylum at the age of fifty-five; the causes listed in the Newton and Somerville town records were "melancholia" and "nervous exhaustion."[38]

All McLean patient records are forever sealed, so there is no way to know when Wight was admitted to the McLean Asylum or exactly how she died. (Howe, of course, had pointed out twenty-five years earlier that she suffered from a melancholy disposition.) Laura may not have understood the exact circumstances of her teacher's death, but she apparently sensed that the less said about it, the better. Her only comment afterward was uncharacteristically cryptic: "Mrs. Bond died in Oct. I felt so sad. She is happy in Zion."[39]

IN 1924, WHEN Edward Allen, then the director of Perkins, solicited recollections of Laura from former teachers and graduates, some of them, thinking back as much as fifty years, spoke of her cheerfulness and cordiality.[40] Others remembered her as difficult and strange. Cora Davis Gleason, a sighted teacher, told Allen that Laura's excessive neatness had been "painful" to observe. Always on the lookout for dust, missing buttons, and bric-a-brac in need of readjustment, Laura, as Gleason remembered her, was fastidious to the point of obsession.[41] The girls dreaded her visits to their sewing classes, because she would rip out their stitches if she found them faulty.[42] Still, they did not have the heart to break the school rule against playing tricks on the peculiar, deaf-blind woman in their midst.[43]

Laura, in middle age, had trouble befriending the hearing blind girls around her, but she did develop brief, intense crushes. "Sometimes a girl was her favorite for a week—then again for a month," one Perkins graduate remembered. "Laura's flames or favorites were to sit beside her at the table and communicate her desires to the head of the table and this was considered a great honor." But then, for no particular reason, her mood would change and she would choose another favorite. Laura's sudden explosions of anger disconcerted some of the girls. Once at dinner, when a teacher was too busy to speak with her, Laura "let out a yell that greatly alarmed us," Estella Blackmur recalled. Another time, Laura was furious at being served a dish she disliked. "Do you think," she demanded, "that I am so obstinate I would eat mince pie?"[44] Emma Coolidge Weston, a Perkins graduate who returned as a teacher in the early '80s, believed that long hours of solitude exacerbated Laura's peculiarities. "Laura had too much time to think, and too little of new interests," Weston concluded.[45]

The observations of G. Stanley Hall confirm many of these recollections. Hall, an innovative psychologist who would later become president of Clark University, came to Boston in 1878 to examine Laura shortly before leaving for Germany to study with Wilhelm Wundt, the father of experimental psychology. Shaped by Wundt's teachings, Hall's analysis of Laura provides the most complete and "scientific" portrait of Laura in middle age.

Like the Perkins graduates and teachers who knew her, Hall was

struck by Laura's "remarkable" cheerfulness. He marveled at her affectionate nature, her "native modesty and conscientiousness," and her love
of jokes and play. Her mental powers and "wonderful" memory amazed
him. Education, he believed, had not so much created her extraordinary
intelligence as revealed it.[46] But he, too, could not get over her strangeness. Anticipating by forty years Freud's definition of the "uncanny" as
something that is at once familiar and hidden or mysterious, Hall said
that Laura created in others an eerie sense of disquiet.[47] "Her strange
consciousness," he said, "is at every point so like yet so unlike our
own."[48]

Hall argued that Laura's physical disabilities could explain much of
her oddness. Although her "excessive" facial mannerisms and expressions disturbed some spectators, these habits were not unusual among
the blind. Because her deafness cut her off from the nuances of spoken
language, her "narrow" emotional range did not surprise him either. Her
feelings, like those of many of the deaf, he said, were intense, but "few
in kind."[49] Her sensory deficits had also stunted her sexual instincts,
which had failed to mature, "either in the waking or the sleeping consciousness." (Hall pointed out that the same was true of birds and rab-
bits, "in which the sexual instinct is destroyed or weakened if the eyes
are destroyed.")[50]

The infant science of psychology could not so easily account for
other aspects of Laura's oddness, however. She showed no signs of hys-
teria or melancholia, Hall noted, but nevertheless reminded him of the
madwomen on exhibit at Salpêtrière, the famous Paris clinic run by the
neurologist Jean Charcot. Like some of those mental patients, Laura had
"in the hands and face a sensitiveness to ordinarily imperceptible and
sometimes imaginary dust, which very closely resembles, save in degree,
that described by Charcot and Westphal as one of the characteristic signs
of incipient mania." Her touch was so preternaturally acute that she
could correctly guess the age, mood, and character of visitors by feeling
their faces.[51] The suddenness of her insights and the voraciousness of
her curiosity mystified Hall. It seemed as if buried knowledge from some
earlier life were breaking into her consciousness.[52]

Hall drew his conclusions about Laura at time when mental illness was increasingly defined as a woman's disease, caused by biologically based female vulnerabilities.[53] Trained in Europe to look at women with an eye to their psychopathology, he naturally assumed that Laura's "strangeness" came from something abnormal in her; he never stopped to consider whether the problem might really be his. Although he pre-, sented himself as a detached, clinical observer, he may have underestimated Laura's effect on him. Perhaps the uncanniness that he felt in her presence arose as much from his own dread of her condition as from anything she said or did.

THE SENSE OF strangeness that Laura often awakened in others may have influenced Howe's decision to exclude her from the new girls' cottages he established at Perkins in 1870. After years of worrying about the pernicious effects of congregate living, he had finally raised enough money to move the female students out of the overcrowded main building and into four homelike cottages, each with its own matron. Although leaving Laura behind meant that she would remain in the main building with the boys, moving her to a cottage was riskier. Because she made many people uncomfortable, she was not likely to contribute to the family atmosphere he hoped to re-create in the cottages.

Disenchanted with asylums and residential schools, including his own, Howe had fought hard for the funding for his new cottage system. As institutions like Perkins were opening throughout the United States, he had become increasingly convinced that congregate living was an inherently bad idea: "Wherever there must be separation of the sexes, isolation from society, absence of true family relation, and monotony of life, there must come evils of various kinds, which no watchfulness can prevent, and no physician can cure."[54] He realized now that walling off the weak was wrong in principle as well as practice. "What right have we to pack off the poor, the old, the blind into asylums?" he wrote in 1857 to the director of the Philadelphia Institution for the Blind. "They are of us, our brothers, our sisters—they belong in families."[55]

Howe admitted that this was one of the few subjects on which he had ever changed his mind.[56] Starting out as director of Perkins, he had assumed that residential schools would benefit disabled children by removing them from their overprotective mothers. He had thought that exchanging the smothering isolation of family homes for a structured, sociable setting would foster their independence and self-confidence.[57] But over the years, experience had taught him that no institution could replace the child's own home; only in families could children learn the habits of order, obedience, and discipline required for good citizenship.[58]

By the 1840s, Howe, along with many middle-class Victorians, sentimentalized the family, seeing it not only as the primary agency of morality, but also as the warm center of domestic feeling. Although in reality many Perkins students came from poor or working-class households, with struggling parents who had neither the resources nor the time to live up to this ideal, Howe apparently never questioned the popular myth of the sheltering, nurturing, morally uplifting family home.

He believed that in the best of worlds, disabled children would live at home and go to local schools with their able-bodied neighbors.[59] Although the common schools were not yet up to the job, he foresaw a time when they could serve all children, including the disabled. Until that day came, he resolved to look for temporary alternatives that would protect children from the corruption, alienation, and infantilization that institutionalizing them often entailed.

He had tried initially to transform Perkins into a day school by boarding students with neighboring families. When that proved impracticable, he hit upon the idea of simulating "normal" middle-class family life by moving students into small cottage residences. This innovative plan, soon widely imitated by other institutions, seemed to offer several advantages. First, it guaranteed complete separation of the sexes. Because the blind naturally wanted to touch one another, Howe said, physical separation was the only way to keep contact between the boys and girls within the bounds of propriety: "When both parties are blind," he explained, "even if the thought is pure and the purpose innocent . . . the innocent salute is liable to grow insensibly but irresistibly into a caress."[60] Second, dividing the students up into smaller housing units allowed for "proper classification" by age and social class. Children of "tender years and gentle culture" could live and study together, protected from those "of low tendencies and habits."[61] Finally and most important, each cottage resembled a "normal" middle-class Victorian family, "with its ties of kith and kin; with its tender associations of childhood and youth; with its ties of affection and of sympathy; with its fireside, its table, and its domestic altar."[62]

THE BLIND GIRLS may have welcomed the cottage plan, but moving out of the main building did not appeal to Laura. At the age of forty, she had no wish to leave her cozy private room with its "nice straw carpet & a very nice & costly sink & a very enormous bureau . . . & a nice looking glass & a table within 2 little drawers & a low couch & a gifted rocking chair & chair with a cane seat & a towel stand & nice closet."[63] Although she disliked having the boys nearby, the prospect of family-style living in close quarters with a group of girls seemed far worse.[64] By staying where she was, she could not only remain in familiar surroundings, but also enjoy the adult company of the teachers, many of whom had rooms near hers and spent their evenings, as she did, in the main parlor.

But in 1872, Laura committed an offense severe enough to get her evicted from the main building. The senior matron, Marie Moulton, persuaded Howe that Laura could not continue to receive such privileged treatment. In the future, she would have to live each year in a different cottage, so that no single cottage matron would bear the whole burden of care. This punishment terrified Laura. "I did not mean to commit evil," she explained in a frantic appeal to Howe:

> I feel sick in mind at time & also very sad. Will you have mercy
> on your Child Laura & preserve me in your heart I will resolve
> to do better & right at the blest Inst[itute]. I am so very anxious
> to return to the [main building] next term to abide with Miss
> M[oulton] & others & give aid to them. I was so happy until a

few days ago. . . . My heart aches with grief in having done wrong. Will y[ou] forgive me & have mercy on me.[65]

Laura's misdeed—probably one of her violent outbursts—may have given Moulton and the other teachers an excuse to end a trying situation. At the end of long days of working with blind children, they could not have enjoyed sharing their parlor with someone as demanding as Laura. Her transfer to the cottages relieved them of her constant questions, odd noises, and occasionally querulous intrusions. After she moved, she was allowed to call on her favorite teachers, but she had to limit herself to formal weekly visits.

Although Laura had trouble adjusting at first, her "natural right-mindedness and cheerful temperament soon reconciled her to her new home," Howe's daughters claimed.[66] Howe eased the transition by promising her a room to herself and allowing her to decorate it with furniture and rugs that could be moved with her as she rotated among the cottages, so that her surroundings would always seem familiar. In the end, the new arrangement probably did her good. She gave herself a title—"the house assistant"—and carved out a new role. In addition to doing her share of the housework, she rang the morning wake-up bell and served Sunday tea.[67]

Unlike Helen Keller, whose determination to count her blessings would become legendary, Laura liked to complain. She went on at length in her letters about her physical and emotional ailments: her scratchy throats, headaches, toothaches, lassitude, loneliness, poor appetite, dyspepsia, "violent" colds, weakness, liver congestion, and nervousness. If friends visited too seldom or too briefly, or busy teachers tried to avoid her in the halls or the parlor, she protested vehemently, bemoaning her solitude and the scarcity of good conversation.

Yet, as nineteenth-century women's lives went, Laura's was reasonably comfortable and secure, despite her many sorrows. Food always appeared on her table; a doctor came when she fell sick; new clothes arrived as needed. She had her own small collection of books and, unlike many of the immigrant women flooding into Boston, she knew how to read them. She was spared the heavy labor that wore out her own mother. Unlike many married women, she did not have to dread unwanted pregnancies or pray that her husband would be industrious and sober. She did not even have to put up with the low pay and long hours of the Perkins teachers. Of course, she was infantilized and dependent, but for a middle-class woman of the period, that was not so unusual.

After 1863, Laura owed some of her material comfort and security to Abigail Rand Loring, the widow of Elijah Loring, a wealthy Boston banker, and Abigail Matilda Loring, their unmarried daughter. The two Loring women, who died within months of each other, bequeathed $2,000 to establish the Loring Fund for Laura's support. Their own family experience with deafness and blindness prompted this benevolence: an acute illness had cost the Lorings' third son, George, his hearing and the sight of one eye when he was two and a half.[68] (In 1817, at nine years old, George Loring had become the youngest student in the first class of Gallaudet's Hartford school for the deaf, where he remained for sixteen years, eight as an outstanding pupil and eight more as a teacher.) Before his untimely death in 1852, at the age of forty-four, George Loring had served as the "acknowledged head" of the Boston deaf community. And back in 1838, it was he who taught Lydia Drew the manual alphabet, thus opening the world of language to Laura.[69]

The income from the Loring Fund relieved some of the financial pressure on Howe and the Bridgmans, who had worked out the terms of Laura's material support in 1858. They agreed at that time that if her parents contributed their fair share toward her expenses, Laura could make her home at Perkins during the colder months. (The exact amount that Howe required of the Bridgmans may not have been fixed: he asked for $150 a year; they claimed they could only afford $50, and he said he would try to solicit charitable contributions to make up the difference.)[70] With regular payments from the Bridgmans, the interest from the Loring Fund, some institutional funds, and the proceeds from the sale of her needlework, Laura could live at Perkins in comfort and ease.

When Laura's father died on November 28, 1868, these financial arrangements fell apart. Whether naïvely or by fraudulent design, Daniel Bridgman had divested himself of almost all his assets before he died. After his will was probated, not enough money remained in his estate to continue the payments for her support.

Over the years, the Bridgmans had often complained to Howe of their financial struggles. Like most farmers, they were probably strapped for cash now and then, but in fact they owned considerable property. Between 1833 and 1848, Daniel Bridgman had added steadily to the hundred or so acres his father had left him, buying more than two hundred acres from neighbors at a cost of almost $2,400. By 1860, however, all this land had become too much for him. His health was failing, and neither of his college-educated sons seemed interested in farming: Addison had opened a medical office in Georgia and John was practicing law in Chicago. No longer able to manage a large farm on his own, Daniel Bridgman sold his three-hundred-acre homestead for $4,500, and then, for $3,350, purchased a house on 104 acres two miles closer to town.[71] He held the mortgage on the property he sold, but may have had enough money to buy his new, smaller farm outright: there is no record of his ever mortgaging any of his own land, although he might have borrowed money from relatives.[72]

When Laura's brother John returned to Hanover sometime in 1863, he found his parents settled in a roomy house on land that they no longer had the strength to work. Apparently unsuccessful at lawyering, John moved into his enfeebled parents' house, worked the farm, and three years later married a Vermont woman, Harriet (Hattie) Taylor Bridge. In December 1867, Daniel Bridgman, an invalid by now, sold the farm, along with all the equipment and his personal property, to John and Hattie for $3,500. The price must have been low because the deed came with strict and explicit conditions. The entire transaction would be void unless John and Hattie "well and truly" maintained Daniel and Harmony Bridgman

in a kind and affectionate manner; to have the use of a suitable team for their use and accommodation; to be provided with suitable food, medicine and clothing; also to have free use of the house and furniture for the accommodation of themselves and company.[73]

The deed also required John and Hattie to provide Laura with a home "suitable for her condition in life—room food and medicine suitable for her support and comfort whenever she shall be at home—also transportation . . . to and from the Institution." Since Collina had married a few weeks earlier, the deed did not protect her, but it guaranteed Ellen "a home and the comforts thereof" as long as she remained single. (The deed made no mention, however, of payments due to Perkins.)

Eleven months later, Daniel Bridgman expired. In his will, signed on his deathbed in a faltering hand, he bequeathed $1 to each of his children, including Laura. The $2,000 that remained in his estate—most of it presumably the profit from the 1860 sale of his first farm—went to his wife, whom he named executrix. (It is puzzling that the will makes no mention of the $3,500 that John paid—or more likely still owed—for the farm. Perhaps, confident that under the terms of the deed his wife and dependent daughters would be well treated, Daniel Bridgman forgave the debt.)[74]

Howe always suspected that John pressured his dying father into selling him the farm as a way of protecting the estate against claims from Perkins.[75] It is also possible that Daniel had reasons of his own for transferring his property before he died. In *A Midwife's Tale: The Life of Martha Ballard, Based on Her Diary, 1785–1812,* Laurel Thatcher Ulrich notes that New England farmers often bequeathed their houses to a married son, with the stipulation that he provide his widowed mother with a room, food, medicine, and transportation. Martha Ballard's story, as Ulrich tells it, also shows that mothers did not always live harmoniously with their resentful sons and daughters-in-law.[76] Daniel Bridgman may have imagined that binding John to the conditions of a deed would be more effective than leaving the farm to him on the same terms in a will. If so, he was mistaken.

The moment that John acquired the property, Laura—who never

missed much—sensed trouble. In the summer before her father died,
while she was in Hanover for vacation, she told Wight of her forebod-
ings:

> Mother do not have much care of the house nor works much.
> Hattie does all cooking &c. Dear Papa has given his property
> into the hands of John. He will take care of Ma & Pa & me, but
> he will never support Nelly. J is not a Christian nor is H.

Laura noted apprehensively that Hattie, who was pregnant by that time,
"does not show much fancy for our society as last Fall nor sits in the sitting room with us."[77] With her father incapacitated and John in control,
Laura must also have realized that her mother had no access to money.
That year, Mrs. Bridgman had been unable to send Howe even enough
for Laura's clothes.[78]

After Daniel Bridgman's death, all pretense of civility in the household ended. To escape the unpleasantness, Nelly went to live with Collina and her husband, Timothy Dwight Simmons, a local farmer, and
married her brother-in-law, Carlos Simmons, within the year. Mrs.
Bridgman, left behind with John and Hattie, now found herself an un-
welcome boarder in her own home, relegated to a single room, where
she was supposed to live, sleep, and take the solitary meals that were sent
up to her. John also expected his mother to share her room with Laura
during the Perkins summer vacations.[79]

Laura's letters provide a clear picture of her mother's unhappy situation. "John & Wife never sit with my poor & deserted Mother," she reported indignantly to Wight in early 1869.[80] Their old house was now "a
dismal home," a "poor & unpleasant place on account of John and his
Wife who are unamiable folks."[81] Laura's mother spent as much time as
possible with her sister in Vermont, or visiting Collina and Nelly. "It is
the source of happiness for her to be absent from John and his family because they are not as happy & social folks as my own Sisters & their
Husbands," Laura explained to Mary Swift Lamson.[82] Whenever Mrs.
Bridgman returned home, she was "not treated with a cordial welcome

from Hattie . . . no doubt that was very uncivil in H to act so coldly & short. . . . H & John are not a happy or social family for us."[83]

When she visited Hanover, Laura felt the chill. "It is so very lonely to Ma & me at home," she complained to Eliza Rogers in 1870. "I miss N[elly] sadly."[84] Her old home was broken up, she wrote from Hanover a year later. "I cannot enjoy this life much on account of my Brother John & Wife they are not as good or kind as many families."[85] Sixteen years after Daniel Bridgman's death, Laura reported sorrowfully that although she had grown fond of John's children, the tensions at home had still not eased. "How sad in this family that John & Hattie are not happy & social nor amiable which is not a sunny home for Mother & me."[86] The problem, as Laura saw it, was that John had never learned to be a gentleman, despite his Dartmouth education.[87]

Laura also understood the humiliating financial implications of the deal that John had struck with her father. Julia Ward Howe said that when she met Laura shortly after Daniel Bridgman's death, Laura, "making that little pathetic sound of grief we all knew so well, said: 'I have been disinherited!' "[88] Left utterly destitute, Laura realized that she continued to live comfortably at Perkins only as a charity case, dependent upon Howe's loyalty and the "kind care" of others for her "expensive home."[89]

Howe was naturally outraged by the trick that John and Daniel Bridgman had played not only on him, but also on Laura and her mother. Although he had never thought much of Laura's father, he respected Harmony Bridgman and sympathized with her struggles. John's refusal to contribute even enough money for Laura's clothes seemed to Howe a violation of the most sacred ties "of kin & justice."[90] Equally galling was John's self-justification: that Laura benefited the institution by her presence and reputation. Howe pointed out angrily that her reputation, such as it was, came "from what the Institution has done for her; not from anything she has done for it; or ever can do."[91]

Howe never got any money out of John, but he took his usual revenge. In his widely circulated annual report of 1874, he published a scathing account of Laura's treatment by her family:

Laura is now about forty-four years old. Her father has recently died; and the little property which he thoughtfully left for his widow, and this, the most dearly beloved of his children, has been very selfishly, ungenerously, and, as I think, unlawfully misappropriated by some relatives; so that Laura and her aged mother must bear such unkind treatment in the old homestead, that they continue to live in it only through the lack of means of living elsewhere.[92]

But his fury at John did not affect Howe's kindness to Mrs. Bridgman. Knowing that she was terrified about Laura's future, he wrote her one of his most tender and chivalric letters:

I am very sorry to hear that . . . you feel uneasy and unhappy about dear Laura's prospects in life. Pray do not be unhappy on that account. She will not be allowed to suffer after you have gone . . . be at rest in your mind about poor Laura's being provided for.[93]

Although the income from the Loring Fund—$120 to $150 a year—could not pay the cost of her board, Howe promised that he would find the money to keep her. Of course, he desired "as a matter of justice to her, that those who enjoy the advantages of her father's property (to part of which she has just claim) should contribute to her support." But "if neither filial duty, nor brotherly affection, nor sense of justice" could move them to do it, other, more charitable people would help. As long as Laura lived, she would have a home at Perkins.[94]

WHEN HOWE DIED of a brain tumor on January 9, 1876, after two years of gradual deterioration, he left nothing to his wife. Although he had long ago squandered most of her fortune on reckless real estate speculation, he claimed in his will that she had "ample means of her own."[95] As a result, Julia Ward Howe was forced to support herself by giving public lectures for money—the very activity, ironically, that her husband had most strongly disapproved of for a woman. But he made good on his promise to Mrs. Bridgman. The income from the $2,000 that he bequeathed to Laura, added to the interest from the Loring Fund, guaranteed her board and a private room at Perkins for the rest of her life.[96]

Howe's other, more ambivalent legacy to Laura was his famous valedictory 1874 annual report, in which he said his farewells, summarized his achievements at the institution, explained his views on the education of the blind, and retold Laura's story. In this, his final account of her education and progress, he praised the power of her mind, the quickness of her perceptions, and the intensity of her thirst for knowledge. But his strange closing sentences about Laura—the last words he ever published on the subject—reveal his own conflicted feelings. Looking back now, and comparing her to the dull-witted Oliver Caswell, he said that "although comely and refined, in form and attitude, graceful in motion, and positively handsome in features, and although eager for social intercourse, and communion of thought and sentiment with her fellows," Laura did not have "that truly sympathetic nature which distinguished Oliver."

For all her brilliance, Howe concluded, Laura was fundamentally abnormal, emotionally and sexually. Oliver "might, and possibly did, unconsciously love her, a little; but she never loved him, nor (as I believe) any man; and never seemed to pine for that closer relation and sympathy with one of the other sex, which ripens so naturally into real and sympathetic love between normal youth, placed in normal circumstances."[97]

This parting shot is baffling. In the past, Howe had always praised Laura's sexual purity and innocence. And since he had thought of her all along as unmarriageable, why blame her now for not desiring a husband? One possible explanation is that her preference for women—whatever that may have entailed for her sexually—bothered him. Even if he never imagined that her feelings for women had an erotic dimension, her physical distaste for men might have irked him. Or perhaps he simply displaced onto her his anger at his own wife, who, fearful of pregnancy and furious at his imperiousness, frequently barred him from her bed.[98] Like

Julia Ward Howe, Laura, as he described her, fell short in womanly feeling. The world might once have hailed the miraculous Deaf-Blind Girl, just as it hailed the author of "The Battle Hymn of the Republic," but for Howe both women had turned out to be disappointments.

A DAY OR two before he died, Julia Ward Howe, who specialized in scripting lachrymose scenes, led Laura upstairs to Howe's sickroom to say good-bye. "The pathos of Laura's last meeting with her great benefactor was almost beyond description," Mrs. Howe elegized subsequently, in a specimen of her more overwrought prose:

> The man who, at cost of heroic effort, had delivered to her the keys of life, lay helpless in the grasp of fatal disease, his closing hour drawing nigh. He was surrounded by those nearest to him in ties of affection and kindred, but in all this sorrow, it was felt that a place belonged to this spiritual child, this creature, who, from childhood to mature womanhood, had been guided by his counsel and shielded by his love, owing him in the first instance the revelation of her own humanity. She could not see—she never had seen him, but she knew that she was in his presence for the last time. She was allowed to touch his features very softly, and a little agonized sound, scarcely audible, alone broke the silence of the solemn scene. All who were present deeply felt the significance of this farewell.[99]

In fact, Laura had found the experience terrifying as well as sad. She told Wight a few weeks later about the dreadful moment when her hand was placed on the dying man's unconscious head. "His flesh felt warm & moist with perspiration. I said, He is half dead." Laura's pain and grief made it difficult to talk, but "they consented for me to kiss him farewell."[100]

Laura shed no tears for Daniel Bridgman, but she truly mourned Howe. Despite his frequent absences and his inconstant affection, he had been to her a benevolent, mighty, and wise deity who provided her with food, shelter, medical advice, and comfort. He had given her language and rescued her from Hanover when she lay near death from self-starvation. Although her father and brother betrayed her, Howe remained true. His stimulating company had always delighted her, and his visits, though increasingly rare over the years, were great occasions. If she minded his emotional withdrawal in 1845, or his failure to hire a companion for her in 1851, she never let on. After his death, she said that she thought of him "day & night with sorrow & gratitude & love & sincerity."[101] He had been her "dearly beloved & adopted Father."[102]

CHAPTER THIRTEEN

Revisions

IN 1878, MARY SWIFT LAMSON infuriated Howe's widow and daughters by publishing her own biography of Laura: *The Life and Education of Laura Dewey Bridgman, The Deaf, Dumb, and Blind Girl*. Of course, Lamson's book was nothing but "a dry record of facts," too boring to take seriously, but her temerity was nonetheless galling.[1] Howe had been the author of Laura's life. Her story rightfully belonged to him and, after his death, to his heirs—certainly not to the orthodox teacher who years before had ruined his religious experiment.

Intending to write Laura's story himself, Howe had always fended off biographical poachers. When an editor approached the Bridgmans in 1854 with an offer to help Laura write her own life story, Howe vetoed the idea immediately. Despite the project's potential lucrativeness, Howe insisted that nothing should be done about a "Life" until it could be done "well & properly. It cannot be done now, or by her alone."[2] In 1868, a Dartmouth professor also tried to get permission to publish Laura's biography, but again Howe put a stop to it. "I intend to set about writing her life very soon," he told Harmony Bridgman, by way of explanation.[3]

Howe's failure to complete the book is puzzling. After all, in his annual reports he had already written nearly two hundred pages about Laura; he had only to weave the separate accounts into a unified whole.

For a man of his prodigious energy, that would not have taken long. The notes about Laura that he jotted down from time to time—ideas for chapters of the book he planned to write—provide a clue to his problem. Howe did not want to produce a straightforward biographical narrative; he aspired to philosophical profundity. He planned to discuss Laura's education in the context of momentous scientific and epistemological questions: the structure of language; the physiology of the brain; the developmental consequences of sensory deprivation; and the origins and nature of human volition, compassion, and the ability to measure time.[4]

As John Jay Chapman remarked, Howe was a man of action, not a deep or systematic thinker.[5] He could write forcefully and with feeling, but he had neither the academic training nor the analytical powers to debate Locke and Rousseau. His notes for Laura's biography consist mostly of disconnected philosophical maunderings. Howe may have realized himself that his preliminary thoughts led nowhere and that he could not use his experience with Laura to sustain an argument about the human mind.

Although he hated to admit it, he also knew that his experiments with Laura lacked scientific validity. In 1842, when critics suggested that she might have progressed so quickly because she remembered some language, Howe replied firmly that that was impossible, since she had been deaf and blind since "her tender infancy."[6] But six years later, he had no answer to John Kitto's compelling argument that Laura's mind had not been a blank slate. Kitto, a renowned biblical scholar and member of the British Society for the Diffusion of Useful Knowledge who had lost his own hearing at the age of twelve, politely pointed out that Howe's annual reports exaggerated Laura's mental and spiritual deprivations and that the image of her as a person buried alive was "too highly coloured." In the first two years of life, Kitto said, when Laura could still see and hear, "a vast number of ideas derived from the eye and ear must enter the mind . . . and supply, through all the rest of life, some materials for comparison and thought."[7] At the time Howe began to teach her, sensory impressions and ideas still remained in her mind, even if her conscious memory of them was dim. Her education had been a great triumph of pedagogic skill and benevolence, Kitto argued, but it could not settle any questions about the innateness of mental capacities or the relationship of nature to nurture in human psychological development.

Howe's inability—or reluctance—to compose Laura's biography before he died left the field clear for Lamson. A well-to-do widow with grown children, she had time for the job and access to the relevant papers. Since 1845, she had maintained continuous, affectionate contact not only with Laura, but also with her former colleagues, Lydia Drew Morton, Eliza Rogers, and Sarah Wight Bond, all of whom readily entrusted her with their teaching journals and correspondence. In addition, Lamson had received and saved many of Laura's most revealing letters. (Although Laura's correspondence, as she aged, increasingly consisted of complaints about her aches and pains, recitations of religious sentiments, and reports of visits with old friends, she continued to write newsy and perceptive letters to Lamson, the most intellectually demanding of her teachers.) To tell Laura's story, Lamson could thus draw on a variety of rich materials: her own memories, journals, and letters; the journals and letters of Laura's other teachers; and Howe's published annual reports.

In dismissing Lamson's work as a "dry record of facts," Julia Ward Howe and her daughters nevertheless had a point. Most of the biography is simply a chronologically organized collection of lengthy excerpts from teachers' journals interspersed with passages from the annual reports; no personalities, other than Laura's, emerge. Indeed, Lamson announced the modesty of her intentions in her preface: "My aim will be simply to state facts, and in making selections from the daily reports of her teachers to omit nothing which can be of service in any department of science."[8]

Yet, despite its narrow purpose, the book sends a subtly subversive message. By reprinting the teachers' meticulous, sometimes tedious records, Lamson demonstrated that she, Drew, and Wight—not Howe—did almost all the real work of educating Laura. The documents bear witness that it was these three extraordinary young women who day after day answered Laura's questions, found ways to explain abstract concepts, drilled her in arithmetic, took her for walks, disciplined her, prepared her for exhibitions, read to her, and ate and slept next to her. Howe looked in on her lessons, made suggestions, came up with some useful ideas, set policy, and of course paid the bills, but the intelligence, imagination, humanitarianism, and determination of Perkins teachers brought Laura, step by step, into the light.

Except for a few paragraphs criticizing Howe's handling of Laura's religious education, Lamson discreetly allowed the letters and journals to speak for themselves. However, in choosing Edwards A. Park, an orthodox minister and professor at the conservative Andover Theological Seminary, to write the book's introductory essay, she attacked Howe more directly. Although Park, who had interviewed Laura twice in the early '60s, embraced a moderate, forgiving brand of Calvinism— as Lamson herself did—he naturally sympathized with her view that Howe's religious experiments on Laura had been cruel as well as foolish. Laura's mind, he explained, "was like a child led without a lantern by a tenuous thread through the catacombs, the thread often broken, the leader often lost." Her constant questions were "a real *wail* for clearer thoughts; they were loud *cries* for the removal of her mental perplexities." But Howe, deaf to Laura's calls of distress, had withheld essential knowledge. "If her curiosity had been earlier gratified in receiving a knowledge of God," Park concluded, "her mind would have been more rapidly as well as more symmetrically developed."[9]

Howe's second daughter, Florence Howe Hall, who had adored her father, immediately thought about writing a rejoinder. Searching for ammunition, she and her husband wrote to the Bridgmans for letters in which Laura had discussed religion and asked the Herricks for copies of Laura's religious writings.[10] Disheartened perhaps by the documents they received, neither Florence Hall nor any of Howe's other survivors ever replied directly to Lamson, but over the years they shot arrows in her direction whenever they could. In a typical sally, published in the annual report of 1887, Michael Anagnos, Howe's son-in-law and successor, remarked that of Laura's teachers, only Sarah Wight could match Anne Sullivan in "breadth of intellect, in opulence of mental power, in fertility of resource, in originality of device and in practical sagacity." It was "a great pity," he added pointedly, that Laura "was not placed under the broad, quickening and vitalizing influence of this most excellent woman at an earlier stage of her education, when her mind was more plastic and susceptible to lasting impressions of generous views and liberal ideas."[11]

ANAGNOS, A GREEK patriot, journalist, and lawyer, had met the Howes in Athens in 1867 during the Cretan insurrection against the Turks. Howe had returned to the scene of his youthful glory to distribute the supplies provided by sympathetic Bostonians for the relief of the suffering Greeks. Anagnos (originally Anagnostopoulos) volunteered to serve as his unpaid secretary and assistant. Before long, Howe, Julia Ward Howe, and their oldest daughter, Julia Romana, had all fallen for the ingratiating young man. Howe invited him back to Boston to be groomed as his successor. Julia Ward Howe, who referred to Anagnos in her journal as "my darling," took tête-à-tête Greek lessons from him; and Julia Romana, painfully shy and emotionally unstable, married him in 1870.[12] As Howe's health failed in the 1870s, Anagnos gradually took over the administration of Perkins; when Howe died, his son-in-law's de facto directorship became official.

Anagnos, who liked to deliver his eloquent appeals for money holding a blind child in his arms, proved to be a brilliant fund-raiser.[13] Notwithstanding Laura's increasing frailty and reclusiveness, he trotted her into the public eye from time to time when she could be useful. In 1881, at a meeting to raise money for printing books for the blind, she was led out on the stage to demonstrate her ability to read the Bible in embossed letters. According to one newspaper account, she had not completely lost her power to amaze and move an audience. As she traced the raised words with her left hand, and spelled them out to an interpreter with her right,

> the countenance of the remarkable lady was almost lit up with the intelligence and emotion accompanying the consoling words she read from the Scriptures . . . a breathless interest was displayed by all present, and the blending of ingenuity, patience,

and philanthropy by which such results were wrought, made the strongest possible plea for the object of the meeting.[14]

Laura again helped with fund-raising in 1884, when Anagnos decided to establish the Howe Memorial Fund for a kindergarten at Perkins. With his help, she wrote an appeal that was published in newspapers throughout the state. At the opening ceremony for the kindergarten in 1887, Laura, accompanied by a blind translator, appeared onstage to plead with the audience for more donations.[15]

Anagnos brought Laura out one last time in December of that year, for an elaborate celebration of her fiftieth year at Perkins and her fifty-eighth birthday. (One Boston newspaper noted sardonically that to many people, the announcement of Laura's jubilee "will be a surprise from the fact that they have supposed that she was no longer among the living.")[16] Julia Ward Howe, whose interest in Perkins suddenly blossomed after her husband's death, presided over the ceremonies in the institution's music hall. Halfway through the orations, a group of little blind children from the kindergarten trooped onstage to present Laura with a basket of flowers and sing her a song composed for the occasion:

The birthday queen we children greet,
And offer roses, fresh and sweet.
May fortune never cease to bless
And crown her days with happiness.[17]

Later in the program, Marie Moulton led Laura up to a Christmas tree laden with gifts that stood in the middle of the platform. "She fluttered about the branches like a sober brown butterfly," Howe's daughters wrote afterward, "touching one and another of her pretty things, and uttering her expressive cries of joy." A gold bracelet and a music box gave her the greatest delight: she laughed aloud when she felt the music box vibrate.[18]

The crowd of students and Boston dignitaries heard speeches from an impressive group of philanthropists and liberal ministers, including

Edward Everett Hale, A. A. Miner, Phillips Brooks, and of course the widowed Mrs. Howe. The orators pressed all the usual stops: Howe had taken a wild little girl from her country home and restored her to her humanity; in leading Laura out of darkness, he had proved the power of faith, hope, and love; fearless and noble, he had been like a knight in the old days of chivalry; her education revealed the perfectibility of the human mind and soul, and provided knowledge of "the great unseen."[19]

Of the many speakers that day, only Laura avoided banality. In the letter that she had written to be read aloud, she recalled growing up on an "immense" farm in New Hampshire. When Howe first came to see her, his "long hands" felt frightening. She had been happy living with him and his sister Jeannette, especially after he bought her a "little costly chair with a stuffed seat . . . also a nice low and narrow bed, which could be made for sitting up in." Studying spelling, arithmetic, algebra, geography, history, astronomy, philosophy, and geometry had been a "joyous privilege." She was grateful not only to Dr. Howe, but also to her other teachers, some of them now dead, and to Mrs. Smith, the dearly loved first matron of the institution, who had first taught her how to thread a darning needle.[20]

The festivities concluded on a slightly jarring note. Anagnos seized the occasion of Laura's jubilee to publicize two new, up-and-coming deaf-blind girls: Edith Thomas, a nine-year-old pupil who had recently enrolled in the kindergarten, and Helen Keller, just seven, who was being taught at her home in Tuscumbia, Alabama, by a Perkins graduate. It seemed, Anagnos announced, "a singular coincidence that Laura's semicentenary should mark the advent of two little hapless pilgrims to the beneficent care that had given to her life all its brightness."[21]

DEAF-BLIND CHILDREN were hard to find, but the "advent" of these two promising little "pilgrims" was not entirely coincidental. Anagnos had been on the lookout for a new deaf-blind prodigy. Although Laura could still serve as a living monument to Howe, she was too old and strange to attract new benefactors to Perkins. The kindergarten, a costly venture that required the construction of special cottages on a separate campus in Jamaica Plain, Massachusetts, needed a younger, stronger, more endearing "poster child"—not a run-of-the-mill blind girl, but a second, more spectacular Laura Bridgman.

When Edith Thomas enrolled at the end of 1887, she seemed a likely prospect. She had lost her sight and hearing to scarlet fever and diphtheria at the age of four, and afterward gradually stopped speaking. Her teachers thought her intelligent, although she did not show much interest in learning finger spelling and often misbehaved, perhaps because pain or pressure in her ears annoyed her. Unfortunately, she was no beauty, but after her first year at Perkins Anagnos noticed that her face showed the refining effects of the "educational influences" surrounding her. She had a sweet smile, he said, and fortuitously her "drooping eyelids and long eyelashes" entirely concealed her sightless eyes.[22]

Although Edith was making steady progress, Anagnos had far higher hopes for the other little deaf-blind girl, Helen Keller. Reading about Laura Bridgman in Dickens's *American Notes*, Keller's mother had realized that her daughter might be helped. At the suggestion of Alexander Graham Bell, a self-styled expert on education for the deaf, the desperate parents had written to Anagnos asking him to recommend a tutor versed in Howe's methods. In March 1887, Anagnos sent them his top Perkins graduate and personal pet, Anne Sullivan.

From Tuscumbia, Sullivan sent back glowing reports of Helen's extraordinary abilities, along with a photograph of her lovely pupil. The child's pretty face and endearing first letter to Anagnos convinced him that he had found his deaf-blind star:

> dear mr. anagnos I will write you a letter . . . photographer does make pictures. carpenter does build new houses. gardener does dig and hoe ground and plant vegetables. my doll nancy is sleeping. she is sick. uncle frank has gone hunting deer. we will have venison for breakfast. . . . I did read in my book about fox and box. fox can sit in box. I do like to read in my book. you do love me. I do love you. good-by[23]

After only seven months of instruction, Keller showed more fluency in writing than Laura had attained in three or four years. Compared to Laura's "gradual advancement," Keller's progress seemed, Anagnos later wrote, "a triumphal march—a series of dazzling conquests."[24]

In the annual report he published shortly after Laura's semicentennial, Anagnos formally proclaimed the arrival of "A Second Laura Bridgman." Howe's heroic work with Laura, blazing upon the pathway "like a column of holy fire," had lighted the way for Anne Sullivan, Anagnos said.[25] She had studied Howe's reports and imbibed his spirit. His golden words and shining example had "passed into her thought and heart and helped her on the road of usefulness." Applying his methods, she had in less than a year unlocked the mind of a "phenomenon." Already Helen Keller had proved herself Laura's equal in "intellectual alertness, keenness of observation, eagerness for information, and in brightness and vivacity of temperament." And although she was not yet eight years old, this Second Laura Bridgman clearly surpassed her "prototype" in "quickness of perception, grasp of ideas, breadth of comprehension, insatiate thirst for solid knowledge, self-reliance and sweetness of disposition."[26]

TO ANNE SULLIVAN, Laura was more than a "prototype." The two had lived in the same cottage at Perkins for several years in the early '80s, and at a lonely, unhappy time in Sullivan's life, Laura, always eager for good conversation, welcomed her company. After Sullivan learned the manual alphabet—probably from Laura herself—the two spent many hours talking. Perhaps even then something about the condition of deafblindness intrigued Sullivan.

The oldest daughter of impoverished, illiterate Irish immigrants, Sullivan had come to Perkins at the age of fourteen as a charity case, after a wretched childhood. When she was five, trachoma, a chronic, contagious inflammation of the eyes, left her almost completely blind. By her eighth birthday, her tubercular mother and two of her four siblings were dead. Her father, a shiftless alcoholic, subsequently abandoned her and her ailing but beloved younger brother to the infamous state poorhouse at Tewksbury. Under the appalling conditions there, her brother soon died. Sullivan arrived at Perkins, after four years in the poorhouse, unable even to spell her own name.[27]

Seven years later, her vision partially restored by surgery, she graduated at the top of her class, Anagnos's favorite student. Even so, especially during her first years at Perkins, Sullivan did not fit in. The other girls, most of them Protestants, scorned the Irish girl and laughed at her shabby clothes. During those difficult days, Sullivan found Laura's company soothing. Later, she would fondly remember the older woman sitting beside her window "quietly like Whistler's mother as we know her in the picture, with her sightless eyes turned towards the sun, a frail woman with fine features and delicate hands which wove their way in and out through the intricacies of beautiful needlework."[28]

In her first efforts with Keller, Sullivan profited from studying Howe's reports, but she soon recognized his mistakes and moved beyond him. Although Anagnos and Howe's daughters insisted that "the finger of the illustrious liberator of Laura Bridgman" had pointed her way, the years she had spent observing and talking to Laura probably helped Sullivan more. After a month or two in Alabama, she realized that it was "absurd" to teach a deaf-blind child language in an artificial classroom setting, as Laura had been taught. "Normal" children do not learn to speak by memorizing lists of words and studying grammar. To develop natural-sounding diction—as opposed to the peculiar, otherworldly dialect that Laura used—the child needed continuous immersion in language.

Abandoning Howe's scheduled lessons and formal curriculum, Sullivan decided simply to talk into Keller's hand "as we talk into a baby's ear." She used complete sentences, supplemented as necessary by gestures, to keep her pupil interested and engaged and to stimulate her to assimilate and imitate language.[29] Although Sullivan insisted that Keller write to sighted people in pencil, she also taught her to read and write in Braille. (In 1929, Keller observed, not unreasonably, that if Laura had had Sullivan as her teacher, "she would have outshone me.")[30]

IN MARCH 1888, Anagnos traveled to Tuscumbia to see Helen Keller for himself. Two months later, she and Sullivan came to Boston for six months as his guests. Keller's winning ways, dazzling accomplishments, and beauty made her an instant celebrity. Articles about her began to be published in Christian magazines, as they had about Laura years earlier, and sentimental poems on the latest deaf-blind angel appeared in ladies' journals. By the end of 1888, the advent of a new Laura Bridgman had restored Perkins to its place as the cynosure of the philanthopic world.[31]

Sullivan had set off for Alabama carrying, as a gift for her new pupil, a doll dressed in clothes that Laura had sewn, and when Keller arrived in Boston the next year, she was naturally curious to meet her doll's dress-maker. "Laura was one of the first persons whom Miss Sullivan took me to see when I visited the Institution," Keller later recalled. "We found her sitting by the window crocheting lace. She recognized my teacher's hand instantly, and seemed very glad to see her." To her little visitor, Laura seemed "like a statue I had once felt in a garden, she was so motionless, and her hands were so cool, like flowers that have grown in shady places."[32]

From the beginning, the historic encounter between the first Laura Bridgman and her successor went comically awry. Always fastidious, Laura was by now almost phobic about the unwashed hands of children, and refused to let Keller finger any of her needlework or touch her face. The girl's "strong, impulsive movements" also made Laura uncomfortable: "You have not taught her to be very gentle," she complained to Sullivan. When Keller, afraid at this point to touch anything, tried to sit on the floor, Laura jerked her up and scolded her. "You must not sit on the floor when you have on a clean dress. You will muss it. You must remember many things when you understand them." At the conclusion of the visit, the exuberant Keller, eager to kiss Laura good-bye, stepped on the frail old woman's toes.[33]

A YEAR LATER, Laura was dead. In late winter, she had complained more than usual of weakness, dizziness, and a "thorny throat." Perhaps because her "poor bones" ached, she had trouble sleeping. Recurring but mild attacks of erysipelas—a streptococcal skin inflammation—kept her in bed during April. By the middle of May, she was too ill to be left alone. She asked to have *The Imitation of Christ,* which she called her "Peaceful Book," beside her, and the matron spelled short selections of it into her hand from time to time. Dr. John Homans, the Perkins physician, attended Laura throughout her illness; he was one of her great favorites, and she always managed a smile for him.

As she weakened, Laura liked to have one of the teachers or older girls perform little services for her: bathing her forehead, combing her hair, or simply sitting by her bed and holding her hand. They knew she was failing when she no longer asked if her comb and brush had been returned to the proper box in the proper corner of the proper drawer. On her last Sunday, Laura suddenly realized that she had not yet packed her woolens away from the moths, but the matron persuaded her to wait until she felt better. By Thursday, her two sisters, Collina and Nelly, and her oldest friend, Mrs. Smith, had arrived for the deathwatch. At midnight, Laura seemed to rally and sat up to drink a little wine and milk; fifteen minutes later, she lost consciousness again. At nine o'clock on Friday morning, May 24, she tried to spell out a word, but her hand was already stiffening and she could only form four letters. Mrs. Smith guessed her meaning and slowly spelled into her hand: m-o-t-h-e-r. Laura nodded twice and relaxed. She stopped breathing just before noon.[34]

Funeral services took place the next afternoon in the institution's hall. Laura lay in an open white coffin, surrounded by spring flowers. At the head of the coffin stood a bust of Howe, a laurel garland from the bier draped across its pedestal. Laura's sisters were seated nearby, but Mrs. Bridgman had been unable to come: at eighty-five, feeble and mentally confused, she could no longer manage the trip to Boston.[35]

According to the newspapers, the "farewell rites" presented a scene "for which no humanitarian home may ever find a counterpart."[36] The Perkins student chorus sang, and Laura's minister, D. B. Jutten, pastor of the South Baptist Church, addressed the congregation. Forgetting— or perhaps forgiving—Howe's disdain for Baptists, Jutten eulogized Laura's rescuer, comparing Howe yet again to "one of those knights errant of the middle ages, possessed of all their chivalry, setting himself down before some castle whose triply-barred gate refused him entrance, and then laying siege until the gate was forced and the imprisoned captive released."[37] No record remains of what, if anything, her minister said about Laura.

Reverend Hale spoke next. The Laura he described was a symbol of the human capacity for progress and the power of education. Deprived of sight, hearing, and smell, she stood for the great truth "that we are not the creatures of the senses, that we do not depend on the things that perish, that we can live here with God, for God's children, in God's heaven, and as we live so we enter into the very joy of our Lord." Despite her disabilities, Hale said, Laura had also served a purpose. Through her, educators had discovered new methods for educating the blind, deaf, and weak.[38]

When it was all over, Collina and Nelly took Laura's body back to Hanover for burial in a graveyard near the Bridgman farm. Their sad homecoming brought neither peace nor reconciliation to the Bridgman family. Within four days of Laura's death, her sisters were fighting with John about money and appealing to Anagnos to intercede. True to form, John had flatly refused to pay either the medical bills for Laura's last illness or the cost of her funeral.[39] Anagnos probably paid for the small gravestone, which was engraved with a discreet advertisement for Perkins:

LAURA DEWEY BRIDGMAN

DECEMBER 21 1829

MAY 24 1889

DEAF DUMB AND BLIND

FROM TWO YEARS OLD

EDUCATED AT THE PERKINS INSTITUTION

SOUTH BOSTON MASSACHUSETTS

In 1890, Laura made the newspapers one last time, when Henry H. Donaldson, an eminent neurologist at Clark University, reported the results of his dissection of her brain. Immediately after her death, Stanley

Hall had requested that her body be autopsied and her brain preserved for scientific analysis. Dr. E. S. Boland of South Boston performed the autopsy eight hours later. Carefully removing the brain, with the eyes still attached, he stored it in a "moderately cool place" for the next seventeen hours, but did not weigh or measure it. At that point, a professor from the Harvard Medical School took charge, and in the interests of preserving a usable specimen, submerged the brain in a solution of Müller's fluid and alcohol. On July 10, according to Dr. Donaldson's infelicitously phrased account, the "brain in question was obtained and was put . . . in my hands for description."[40]

Donaldson was remarkably thorough. Aiming, he said, "to give as full a description as the material in my hands would warrant," he proposed to apply every possible test to determine "whether the peculiar mental existence of Laura Bridgman, which was the result of her defective sense-organs, has left any trace on her brain." This research was a "special study," he explained, in the more general field of the interrelation of brain structure and intelligence.

He began by photographing the brain from six angles. Because of the specimen's deterioration—seventeen unpickled hours having done the gray matter no good—Donaldson could not make a plaster cast, but he secured the services of a skilled craftsman to sculpt a clay model from which a number of plaster casts were made. (Visitors to Perkins can still admire one of these casts, displayed in a glass case in the school library.) Satisfied, Donaldson returned to the specimen itself, which he measured, weighed, dissected, and described in painstaking detail in a forty-five-page report, illustrated with drawings and charts.

He had not anticipated "appearances such as are recorded for microcephalic, criminal, or low-type brains belonging to the least civilized races," and he did not find any.[41] Although he had hoped to observe unmistakable organic traces of her disabilities, he could make no definite claims: some preserved brains swell and others shrink, so measuring and comparing their size is tricky. Still, he thought that Laura's left lobe—the "presumptive speech centre"—looked underdeveloped. Otherwise, however, her brain appeared unremarkable, just a "typical female" brain. In death, as in life, Laura could not supply definitive answers to scientific questions.

WITHIN MONTHS OF Laura's death, Florence Howe Hall and her youngest sister, Maud Howe Elliott, announced their collaboration on a new biography. According to their release to *The New York Times,* their plans rivaled their father's in intellectual ambition.

> To what degree mental faculties are the result of inheritance, and to what degree they are the product of development and acquirement, was the problem that attracted the great philanthropist in his work with Laura Bridgman. It enlisted the sympathy and the interest of the whole scientific world, and it is the nature and development of this great problem on its scientific and psychological side, that Mrs. Hall and Mrs. Elliott will present their work.[42]

For their research, the Howe daughters needed the cooperation of Laura's family, who still had many of Laura's papers, including letters, journals, and memoirs. By now, however, the Bridgmans were wary of biographers. In Howe's last regular annual report on Laura—the report for 1849—he had offended them by remarking that she had inherited a "constitutional disposition to irritability and violence of temper."[43] He had insulted the family again in a short biographical sketch of Laura, published in *Barnard's American Journal of Education* in 1857. Instead of characterizing Laura's parents as he usually did—as humble but virtuous country folk—he substituted a new portrayal: "The father's temperament inclined to the nervous, but he had a small brain; while the mother had a very marked development of the nervous system, and an active brain, though not a large one."[44] Although this sentence made little sense, even by phrenological standards, it was picked up and repeated by other writers, especially after eugenics became popular in the 1880s. In his report on Laura's brain, Donaldson still thought it necessary to re-

mind his readers that her parents had small heads and nervous dispositions.[45]

Before Laura's relatives turned any documents over to the Howes,
they wanted some assurances. On behalf of the family, Collina Bridgman Simmons asked that out of "respect to the feelings of an aged
mother and the sacred memory of a deceased father," Florence and
Maud "refrain from putting in print that Laura's parents had a 'small
brain.'" She pointed out that the Bridgmans were of "high blood"; indeed, one of their relatives had been among Queen Victoria's brides-
maids. Laura's family also insisted that the new biography correct one of
Howe's earliest misstatements. Contrary to what he had written, Laura
had never had severe fits, although she may have fainted once or twice.[46]

Even after Howe's daughters agreed to her conditions, Collina Simmons continued to be ambivalent about the project. Copying Laura's
journals and memoirs took time, she complained, and she and her sister
had learned never to part with originals. They regretted their generosity
in lending Laura's fragmentary memoirs to Stanley Hall. Ignoring Mrs.
Bridgman's repeated written requests, Hall had kept the manuscript for
ten years, denied that he had it, and finally returned it only after it had
been "so shamefully handled & marked by him as to be literally ruined."
Laura's sisters agreed to send eighty-one of her letters to Boston, along
with some other materials, but they wanted them back, since they had
not altogether ruled out writing a biography themselves someday. For
the moment, however, they would defer to the Howes, especially since
Mary Swift Lamson's book had failed financially.[47]

Laura Bridgman: Dr. Howe's Famous Pupil and What He Taught Her
finally appeared in 1903. Although the authors often sacrificed historical
truth to literary effect, the book was livelier and more readable than
Lamson's. The Howe family promoted it aggressively, sending review
copies to a long list of literati, ministers, journalists, philanthropists, and
scientists, including William Dean Howells, Thomas Wentworth Higginson, Julian Hawthorne (son of Nathaniel), and William James.[48]
Anagnos plugged it as a "rare and precious union of history and ro-

mance," and the Howes' friends did what they could to place favorable reviews.[49] Nevertheless, the book attracted little attention.

It might have found more readers if another, more compelling book about deaf-blindness had not appeared the same year. But no biography could have competed with Helen Keller's *The Story of My Life*. Although some critics had trouble believing that Keller could write so well on her own, *The Story of My Life* became an instant and enduring classic, praised for the beauty of its prose and the hopefulness of its message.[50] In 1996, the New York Public Library included it in a list of the twentieth century's hundred most important books and the centennial issue of *The New York Times Book Review* named Keller an author whose writing had changed the world.[51] *The Story of My Life* remains in print today.

Passing

FORGOTTEN EVEN WHILE she lived, Laura has vanished from public memory, eclipsed by Helen Keller. Pretty, self-sacrificing, cheerful, and good, Keller made a far more convincing sentimental icon than Laura ever had.

But Keller was not just a cardboard Victorian angel; she was a twentieth-century New Woman, too. She mastered French, German, Latin, and Greek; read Roman history, German philosophy, and English literature; graduated from Radcliffe College; wrote numerous books and articles; traveled around the world; and worked indefatigably for humanitarian causes. When she needed money, she earned it by writing, lecturing, and even appearing with Anne Sullivan on the vaudeville stage. A suffragist, pacifist, Swedenborgian, and radical socialist, Keller was not afraid to embrace unpopular ideas, although she usually did so sweetly.

She built her public identity on the assertion that for her anything was possible. At her college graduation, echoing Howe's maxim that obstacles are things to overcome, she proclaimed, "I grow stronger in the conviction that there is nothing good or right we cannot accomplish if we have the will to strive. . . . The doors of the bright world are flung open before me and a light shines upon me, the light kindled by the thought that there is something for me to do beyond the threshold."[1] With the encouragement—or "merciless prodding"—of Anne Sullivan, Keller ignored or made light of her disabilities, refusing to let them restrict her activities and achievements.[2] "I'm trying with all my might to be like everyone else," she said. "I want to forget my limitations."[3]

Her fierce determination—and phenomenal memory for the words and phrases that Sullivan continuously poured into her mind—allowed Keller to become the best deaf writer of English in history. Although people who lose their hearing in early childhood seldom get a feel for the rhythms of spoken language, Keller developed a remarkable ear for English.[4] As the poet Donald Davie has written in "To Helen Keller," she became, "by force" of her afflictions, "the most literary person ever was":

> No sight nor sound for you was more than a ghost;
> and yet because you called each phantom's name,
> tame to your paddock chords and colours came.[5]

Of course, Keller had editorial help for some of her books, but even in her personal letters, she composed graceful, lively, imaginative prose. *The Story of My Life* outsold and outlasted *Laura Bridgman: Dr. Howe's Famous Pupil and What He Taught Her* not only because Keller had a more moving and dramatic story to tell, but also because she was a better writer than Howe's daughters.

After Mary Swift Lamson told her of a deaf-blind Norwegian girl who was learning speech, Keller resolved that she, too, would strive to talk "like other people," so that she could "enjoy the sweet companionship" of those from whom she would otherwise be cut off.[6] Unfortunately, however, teaching a deaf person to speak is, as John Kitto put it, like teaching a bear to dance, or a man without hands to weave baskets.[7] Keller spent years training her voice, but speech proved to be the one obstacle that she could not pretend to overcome. For her, speaking intelligibly was a never-ending, self-punishing struggle, requiring an hour and a half of practice every day of her life.

According to one listener, Keller's voice always sounded "like that of a Pythoness." Maud Howe Elliott thought it was "the loneliest sound" she had ever heard, "like waves breaking on some lonely desert island"; Thomas Edison said it reminded him of a "steam exploding."[8] Yet Keller never stopped trying to perfect her imitation of "normal" speech. "One can never consent to creep when one feels an impulse to soar," she explained. "No effort that we make to attain something beautiful is ever lost. Sometime, somewhere, somehow we shall find that which we seek. We shall speak, yes, and sing, too, as God intended we should speak and sing."[9]

Despite her unnatural voice, Keller's impersonation of a hearing, sighted person was convincing enough to be inspiring rather than absurd. Her glass eyes looked almost real. In company, she kept an attentive, pleasant smile on her face, as if she could hear what was going on. Before public performances, she practiced her speeches over and over until they were intelligible. To prove that she could enjoy "normal" pleasures, she made a great show of appreciating music, art, and nature. And almost always, she maintained that she was deeply happy—at least as happy as anyone else. "The gladdest laborer in the vineyard may be a cripple," she insisted.[10]

Bruno Bettelheim has argued that millions of people adored Keller because she allowed them to fool themselves about disability. By pretending that her life was full and that her handicaps did not grieve her, she relieved the anxieties of the able-bodied about losing their own sight or hearing. At the same time, her resolute happiness freed her public from the obligation to be their "handicapped brother's keeper." If, as she insisted, she was not excluded from life, not lonely, and not suffering, then the world owed her—and others like her—no special compassion or extra care.[11]

For people with disabilities, however, Keller has always been a more problematic heroine. On the one hand, her independence and achievement have demonstrated that with suitable accommodation the disabled can excel in school and at work, that they need not be segregated, sheltered, and infantilized. On the other hand, the example of her triumphant, cheerful "normality" may create a burdensome expectation. As the visually impaired writer Georgina Kleege testifies in "Blind Rage: An Open Letter to Helen Keller," disability is sometimes infuriating and exhausting:

> I rage at myself, my body, my eyes, tears welling up in them, reminding me how useless they are. I rage against the world for being inaccessible to me. I rage against technology for offering the promise of access and then breaking down, being cumbersome, leaving me stranded.[12]

In private, Keller occasionally confessed to such feelings, but her public face always smiled, as if she knew that "nobody likes a grumpy cripple."[13] Becoming "the best damn poster child the world has ever known" enabled Keller to lead a useful, interesting life. But her uncomplaining courage may have made it harder for other disabled people to fall short.

Perhaps because she was so loved—and so lovable—the sign language activists who condemn Alexander Graham Bell, Horace Mann, and Samuel Howe for their advocacy of oralism, have tended to avoid blaming Keller. But in truth, as example and proponent, she helped advance the controversial cause of speech training in schools for the deaf. With the kindest of intentions, she encouraged the denigration of Sign, never fully understanding that not all deaf people had her ability, motivation, or access to private speech tutors. To those deaf people who still fight for Sign to be recognized as a complete language, Keller left at best a complicated and disquieting legacy.

UNLIKE KELLER, LAURA never aspired to "normality" or fostered reassuring illusions. She fully reported her loneliness, frustration, and anger. Unless something pleased or amused her, she saw no reason to smile. Passing for able-bodied never occurred to her: even in an institution for the blind, she had always been the one who was different.

Howe only brought her to Perkins because she was an unusual specimen. It was her singular isolation from language and culture that made her valuable to him, first as a scientific experiment and later in his campaigns for education of the disabled. In her heyday, people came to see her exhibited as if to a freak show—and then donated money to Perkins. Some imagined her as an angel, purer than any mortal child; others found her strange, grotesque, a little unnerving. Howe and her female teachers wanted her to be well behaved, helpful, and obedient, but they neither expected nor desired her to seem like everyone else.

FROM THE BEGINNING, the world judged the two women as if they were contestants in a deaf-blind Miss America pageant. Laura was the outdated prototype, inferior in beauty and accomplishments and deficient in congeniality; Keller was the almost normal winner, talented, charming, altruistic, good-looking, even sexy. Laura was quaint and old-fashioned, a relic of the nineteenth century; Keller was the latest improvement, a talking, sociable, active disabled celebrity.

Such comparisons do justice to neither woman. Keller became the success she was because at her side she had Sullivan, the selfless, smart, loving teacher-companion that Laura always thought she wanted. Her teacher's devotion made Keller's life as a beloved public figure possible, but also exacted a price. Even if she rebelled inwardly at Sullivan's "merciless" expectations, Keller had to appear to embrace them. Except in her angry dreams, she suppressed the pain and rage she must at times have felt. "I demand that the world be good," she wrote, "and lo, it obeys. I proclaim the world good, and facts range themselves to prove my proclamation overwhelmingly true."[14]

Compared to Keller, Laura led a dull, dependent existence. She was born too soon to benefit from Braille. Her sharp, inquisitive mind probably did not develop to its full potential. Although she longed for intimacy, she never again found it after Wight left Perkins. Yet Laura achieved a kind of of freedom. Because she felt no compulsion to please, she could choose her own friends and make demands upon them. Malleable only up to a point, she stubbornly asserted her right to make her disconcerting "deaf" noises. She was no more generous, noble, or altru-istic than the rest of us, and she never pretended to suffer fools gladly. Defying Howe, she converted to the religion that suited her. And through all her sorrows and disappointments, Laura managed to remain her unalterable self: witty, irritable, curious, demanding, and, in her way, brilliant.

·◦〗 N O T E S 〖◦·

Abbreviations

AR   *Annual Reports of the Trustees of the Perkins Institution and Massachusetts Asylum for the Blind.* Howe wrote Reports 1–11 and 13–43.

HHL   Harvard Houghton Library

JWH   Julia Ward Howe

LDB   Laura Dewey Bridgman

MHS   Massachusetts Historical Society

PSA   Perkins School Archives

SGH   Samuel Gridley Howe

SW   Sarah Wight (Bond)

WHS   Wayland Historical Society

PROLOGUE: Laura

1. *Boston Evening Transcript,* June 14, 1851.
2. Sir William Blackstone, *Commentaries on the Laws of England* (1765–1769), I:1:8:18.
3. Charles Darwin, *The Expressions of the Emotions in Man and Animals* (1872) (New York: Philosophical Library, 1955), pp. 196, 212, 266, 273, 285, 310.

4. Laura E. Richards, ed., *The Letters and Journals of Samuel Gridley Howe*, II (Boston: Dana Estes, 1909), p. 107.

5. Quoted in Harold Schwartz, *Samuel Gridley Howe, Social Reformer, 1801–1876* (Cambridge, Mass.: Harvard University Press, 1956), p. 41.

CHAPTER ONE: The Chevalier

1. Maud Howe and Florence Howe Hall, *Laura Bridgman: Dr. Howe's Famous Pupil and What He Taught Her* (Boston: Little, Brown, 1903), p. 28.

2. John King Lord, *A History of the Town of Hanover, N.H.* (Hanover: Dartmouth Press, 1928), pp. 16–17.

3. SGH, "Laura Bridgman," *Barnard's American Journal of Education* (December 1857): 383.

4. M. Howe and F. Hall, p. 145.

5. Jonathan Messerli, *Horace Mann* (New York: Knopf, 1972), p. 30.

6. JWH, *Memoir of Dr. Samuel Gridley Howe with Other Memorial Tributes* (Boston: Albert J. Wright, 1876), p. 83.

7. Ibid., p. 5.

8. SGH to Horace Mann, undated ms., PSA.

9. George Combe to SGH, March 15, 1840, typescript, PSA.

10. Harold Schwartz, *Samuel Gridley Howe, Social Reformer, 1801–1876* (Cambridge, Mass.: Harvard University Press, 1956), p. 8. For an overview of Howe's life, I have relied on this readable and accurate biography.

11. *Letters and Journals*, I, pp. 29–30.

12. Schwartz, p. 18.

13. Quoted in Franklin B. Sanborn, *Dr. S. G. Howe, The Philanthropist* (New York: Funk and Wagnalls, 1891), pp. 79–80.

14. SGH to William Sampson, July 24, 1831, *Letters and Journals*, I, p. 385.

15. John Jay Chapman, "Dr. Howe," in *"Learning" and Other Essays* (New York: Moffat, Yard, 1910), p. 109.

16. Lewis P. Simpson, *The Man of Letters in New England and the South* (Baton Rouge: Louisiana State University Press, 1973), p. 30.

17. John L. Thomas, "Romantic Reform in America, 1815–1865," *American Quarterly* 17 (Winter 1965): 656–68.

18. Josiah Quincy, "Address to the Citizens of Boston, on the 17th of September, 1830, the Close of the Second Century from the First Settlement of the City," in *A Municipal History of the Town and City of Boston, During Two Centuries, from September 17, 1630, to September 17, 1830*, ed. Josiah Quincy (Boston: Charles C. Little and James Brown, 1852), p. 350.

19. Ronald Story, *The Forging of an Aristocracy: Harvard and the Boston Upper Class, 1800–1870* (Middletown, Conn.: Wesleyan University Press, 1980), p. 3.

20. Frederic Cople Jaher, *The Urban Establishment: Upper Strata in Boston, New York, Charleston, Chicago, and Los Angeles* (Chicago: University of Illinois Press, 1982), pp. 32–55.

21. Horace Mann, "Means and Objects of Common School Education" (1837), in *Lectures on Education* (New York: Arno Press, 1969), p. 13.

22. Jaher, pp. 56–58.

23. Story, pp. 7–10.

24. Jaher, p. 58.

25. See David J. Rothman, *The Discovery of the Asylum: Social Order and Disorder in the New Republic* (Boston: Little, Brown, 1971), for an introduction to the asylum movement in the United States.

26. William Ellery Channing, *Works* (Boston: American Unitarian Association, 1897), p. 164.

27. Harriet Martineau, *Society in America* (New York: AMS Press, 1966), III, p. 191.

28. Charles Dickens, *American Notes for General Circulation*, eds. John Whitley and Arnold Goldman (New York: Penguin, 1972), ch. 3.

29. *Letters and Journals*, I, p. 387.

30. Quoted in Laura Richards, *Samuel Gridley Howe* (New York: Appleton-Century, 1935), p. 71.

31. Ibid.

32. John Greenleaf Whittier, *Works*, 7 vols. (Boston: Houghton Mifflin, 1892), IV, p. 80.

CHAPTER TWO: Institutions

1. William Paulson, *Enlightenment, Romanticism, and the Blind in France* (Princeton, N.J.: Princeton University Press, 1987), pp. 95–105.

2. Ibid., p. 96.

3. Nicholas Mirzoeff, *Silent Poetry: Deafness, Sign, and Visual Culture in Modern France* (Princeton, N.J.: Princeton University Press, 1995), p. 67; Rosemarie Garland Thomson, *Extraordinary Bodies: Figuring Physical Disability in American Culture and Literature* (New York: Columbia University Press, 1997), p. 35.

4. Quoted in Richard S. French, *From Homer to Helen Keller: A Social and Educational Study of the Blind* (New York: American Foundation for the Blind, 1932), p. 111.

5. William H. Prescott, "Asylum for the Blind," *Biographical and Critical Miscellanies* (Philadelphia: Lippincott, 1890), pp. 68–69. People younger than thirty were presumed to be educable at a school for the blind.

6. SGH, "Education of the Blind," *North American Review* 37 (1833): 55.

7. Ibid., p. 53.

8. For a complete biography of Gallaudet and a history of the Hartford school, see Harlan Lane, *When the Mind Hears: A History of the Deaf* (New York: Random House, 1984).

9. SGH to T. C. Cary, May 12, 1850, *Letters and Journals,* II, p. 46.

10. Versions of this story are repeated by M. Howe and F. Hall, p. 7, and by Richards in *Samuel Gridley Howe,* p. 58, and *Letters and Journals,* I, p. 389.

11. Richard M. Bernard and Maris Vinovskis, "The Female School Teacher in Ante-Bellum Massachusetts," *Journal of Social History* 10 (March 1977): 332.

12. For more details of the careers of Beecher, Dix, and Peabody, see Thomas J. Brown, *Dorothea Dix, New England Reformer* (Cambridge, Mass.: Harvard University Press, 1998); Bruce A. Ronda, *Elizabeth Palmer Peabody, A Reformer on Her Own Terms* (Cambridge, Mass.: Harvard University Press, 1999); and Kathryn Kish Sklar, *Catharine Beecher: A Study in American Domesticity* (New Haven: Yale University Press, 1973).

13. John Greenleaf Whittier, "The Hero," in *Letters and Journals,* I, pp. vii–x; Horace Mann, "Dr. Samuel Gridley Howe" (a sermon preached to the students of Antioch College), *Monthly Journal* 2 (August 1861): 364–75; and Sanborn, p. v.

14. *Letters and Journals,* I, p. 391.

15. Schwartz, pp. 43–44.

16. *Letters and Journals,* I, pp. 409–10.

17. Ibid., p. 410.

18. Gabriel Farrell, *The Story of the Blind* (Cambridge, Mass.: Harvard University Press, 1956), pp. 27–28.

19. *Letters and Journals,* I, pp. 403–407.

20. Quoted in Deborah Pickman Clifford, *Mine Eyes Have Seen the Glory: A Biography of Julia Ward Howe* (Boston: Little, Brown, 1979), p. 206.

21. Sanborn, p. 106.

22. SGH, "Education of the Blind," *North American Review,* pp. 47–48.

23. Ibid., pp. 34–38.

24. Ibid., pp. 40–43.

25. Ibid., p. 21.

26. SGH, "Education of the Blind," *Literary and Theological Review* 3 (1836): 280.

27. SGH, "Education of the Blind," *North American Review,* p. 43.

28. Second AR, p. 11.

29. Third AR, pp. 12–13.

30. SGH, "Address of the Trustees of the New England Institution for the Education of the Blind to the Public" (Boston: Carter, Hendie, and Co., 1833), p. 11. [First AR]

31. Second AR, p. 11.

32. "Education of the Blind," *North American Review,* p. 56; First AR, p. 5.

33. Quoted in Lane, p. 229.

34. Douglas C. Baynton, *Forbidden Signs: American Culture and the Campaign Against Sign*

Language (Chicago: University of Chicago Press, 1996), pp. 17–21; Lois Banner, "Religious Benevolence as Social Control: A Critique of an Interpretation," *Journal of American History* 60 (June 1973): 34.

35. French institutions began with the goal of inclusion, but, as Howe observed, quickly became invested in separating the blind from the rest of the population. Paulson, p. 95.

36. Sixteenth AR, pp. 64–65.

37. SGH, "Education of the Blind," *Lectures Delivered Before the American Institution of Instruction, 1836; Journal of the Proceedings*, p. 5.

38. Ibid., p. 25.

39. Pride in Perkins's embossed printing led Howe and his loyal successors initially to oppose the introduction of the dot printing used in Braille. Officially adopted in France in 1863, the Braille method did not win acceptance at Perkins until 1879, three years after Howe's death.

40. Michael Monbeck, *The Meaning of Blindness* (Bloomington: Indiana University Press, 1973), pp. 110, 143.

41. Martin Jay, *Downcast Eyes: The Denigration of Vision in Twentieth-Century French Thought* (Berkeley: University of California Press, 1993), p. 11; John Hull, *Touching the Rock: An Experience of Blindness* (New York: Pantheon, 1990), pp. 55–66.

42. Charles Baudelaire, *Les Fleurs du Mal* (New York: Doubleday, 1961), p. 88. My translation.

43. "Seeking Laws for Disabilities of the Attitude," *New York Times*, July 26, 2000; "Reaching Out to Disabled Employees, With Mixed Results," *New York Times*, July 26, 2000.

44. SGH, "Education of the Blind," *North American Review*, p. 49.

45. Oliver Sacks, *Seeing Voices* (Berkeley: University of California Press, 1989), p. 27; Lane, p. 286.

46. Second AR, pp. 9–10.

47. *Letters and Journals*, II, p. 16.

48. Nineteenth AR, pp. 18–19.

49. Second AR, pp. 5–6.

50. Horace Mann, "Dr. Samuel G. Howe," *The Monthly Journal* 2 (August 1861): 373; Chapman, pp. 115–16.

CHAPTER THREE: Mind

1. E. C. Sanford, *The Writings of Laura Bridgman* (San Francisco: Overland Monthly Publishing, 1887), pp. 8–9. Laura wrote at least three versions of her memoirs. Excerpts from two of them are reprinted in Mary Swift Lamson, *Life and Education of Laura Dewey Bridgman* (Boston: Houghton, 1878), pp. 345–46, and M. Howe and F. Hall, pp. 273–76. Fragmentary memoirs in Laura's hand also survive in the PSA.

2. Ibid., p. 9.

3. Harmony Bridgman to SGH, June 28, 1841, PSA.

4. Harmony Bridgman to SGH, March 15, 1838; Harmony Bridgman to SGH, undated, beginning "Reverend Sir," PSA.

5. Ibid.; Harmony Bridgman to SGH, January 28, 1841, PSA.

6. Harmony Bridgman to SGH, undated, beginning "Reverend Sir," PSA.

7. Sanford, pp. 9–13.

8. Outbreaks of scarlet fever (a form of streptococcal infection characterized by a bright red rash) were not as devastating as diphtheria epidemics, but dangerous nonetheless. For a history of scarlet fever in North America, see John Duffy, *Epidemics in Colonial America* (Baton Rouge: Louisiana State University Press, 1953), and Laurel Thatcher Ulrich, *A Midwife's Tale: The Life of Martha Ballard Based on Her Diary, 1785–1812* (New York: Vintage, 1990), pp. 40, 44–45. As a complication of scarlet fever, deaf-blindness was very unusual. Most deaf-blind people were born that way, as the result of congenital anomalies (hydrocephaly, fetal alcohol syndrome, microcephaly), or of prenatal exposure to diseases such as rubella, herpes, syphilis, or toxoplasmosis. The more usual postnatal causes are asphyxia, encephalitis, meningitis, stroke, and head injury. See the website for deaf-blindness: www.tr.wou.edu/dblink. The fever that caused Helen Keller's deaf-blindness has never been identified; possibly, she and Laura were in fact the victims of meningitis.

9. LDB, autobiographical ms. dated 1885, PSA.

10. David Downer, *The Downers of America, with Genealogical Record* (Newark, N.J.: n.p., 1900), pp. 55–58.

11. Sanford, p. 14.

12. Ibid., p. 12.

13. Ibid., p. 10.

14. SGH, "Laura Bridgman," *Barnard's American Journal of Education* (December 1857): 389.

15. Sanford, pp. 9–10.

16. Ibid., p. 16.

17. Ibid., p. 15.

18. Quoted in Lamson, p. 347.

19. Sanford, pp. 14–16.

20. Ibid., p. 14.

21. Ibid., p. 16.

22. SGH, "Laura Bridgman," p. 387.

23. LDB, autobiographical ms. dated 1885, PSA.

24. M. Howe and F. Hall, p. 35.

25. Sanford, p. 15.

26. SGH, "Laura Bridgman," p. 387.

27. David Goode, *A World Without Words: The Social Construction of Children Born Deaf and Blind* (Philadelphia: Temple University Press, 1994), pp. 24–25.

28. Asa Tenney to SGH and Daniel and John Bridgman, September 17, 1839, PSA.

29. Ibid.

30. Martineau, III, pp. 197–99.

31. Forty-third AR, p. 82.

32. SGH, "Laura Bridgman," p. 386.

33. Fifty-eighth AR, p. 359.

34. Jean-Jacques Rousseau, *Discourse on the Origin of Inequality,* trans. Donald A. Cress (Indianapolis: Hackett, 1992), p. 10.

35. Ibid., p. 11.

36. René Descartes, "Meditation VI," in *Philosophical Works,* trans. Elizabeth Haldane and G.R.T. Ross (New York: Dover, 1931), I, p. 192.

37. Quoted in Ernst Cassirer, *The Philosophy of the Enlightenment,* trans. Fritz Koelln and James Pettegrove (Princeton, N.J.: Princeton University Press, 1932), p. 95.

38. John Locke, *An Essay Concerning Human Understanding,* II:1:2.

39. See Paulson, pp. 21–71, for a complete history and analysis of the Molyneux problem.

40. Roger Shattuck, *The Forbidden Experiment: The Story of the Wild Boy of Aveyron* (New York: Farrar, Straus and Giroux, 1980), pp. 43–45.

41. Étienne Bonnot de Condillac, *Treatise on the Sensations,* trans. Geraldine Carr (Los Angeles: University of California Press, 1930), p. 239.

42. Ibid., pp. 171–80.

43. Denis Diderot, *Letter on the Blind for the Use of Those Who See,* in *Selected Writings,* ed. Lester Crocker, trans. Derek Coltman (New York: Macmillan, 1966), p. 17.

44. Ibid.; Diderot, *Letter on the Deaf and Dumb for the Use of Those Who Hear and Speak,* in *Selected Writings,* p. 34.

45. Joseph-Marie Degérando, *The Observation of Savage Peoples* (1800), trans. F.C.T. Moore (Berkeley: University of California Press, 1969), pp. 61, 63.

46. Ibid., p. 72.

47. Shattuck, p. 75. Excellent accounts of the Wild Boy of Aveyron are provided both by Shattuck and by Harlan Lane, *The Wild Boy of Aveyron* (Cambridge, Mass.: Harvard University Press, 1979). Jean-Marc Itard's own narrative is translated and appended to Lucien Malson's *Wolf Children and the Problem of Human Nature,* trans. Edmund Fawcett, Peter Ayrton, and Joan White (New York: Monthly Review Press, 1972).

CHAPTER FOUR: Found

1. Reuben Mussey to Lewis Weld, April 14, 1837, reprinted in *Twenty-first Report of the Directors of the American Asylum at Hartford for the Education and Instruction of the Deaf and Dumb* (Hartford, Conn.: Hudson and Skinner, 1837), pp. 41–42.

2. SGH to R. D. Mussey [n.d.], 1837, PSA.

3. R. D. Mussey to SGH, July 10, 1837, PSA.

4. James Barrett to SGH, July 10, 1837, attached to Mussey's letter of the same date, PSA.

5. Diderot, *Letter on the Blind*, p. 19.

6. Miss Dudley, former matron of the American Asylum, to Lewis Weld, March 27, 1837, reprinted in the *Twenty-first Report of the Directors of the American Asylum at Hartford*, p. 30.

7. Lydia Sigourney, "The Deaf and Blind Girl," in *The Deaf and Dumb: or, a Collection of Articles Relating to the Condition of Deaf Mutes; their Education, and the Principal Asylums*, ed. Edwin Mann (Boston: D. K. Hitchcock, 1836), pp. 241–42.

8. Quoted in Gary E. Wait, "Julia Brace," *Dartmouth College Library Bulletin* 33 (November 1992): 9.

9. Sigourney, "The Deaf, Dumb, and Blind Girl," in *The Deaf and Dumb*, p. 101.

10. George Combe, *Notes on the United States of North America During a Phrenological Visit in 1838–9–40* (Philadelphia: Carey and Hart, 1841), II, p. 166; William Ingalls, *Phrenology not Opposed to the Principles of Religion; Nor the Precepts of Christianity* (Boston: Dutton and Wentworth, 1839), p. 11.

11. See, for example, the Tenth AR, p. 36, and the Thirteenth AR, p. 68.

12. Eleventh AR, p. 37.

13. Charlotte Brontë, *Jane Eyre* (1847), ed. Q. D. Leavis (New York: Penguin, 1966), pp. 96–97. Visitors to nineteenth-century asylums frequently observed that blind girls and women took an interest in jewelry, fabrics, and the latest fashions. See, for example, Michael Anagnos, *Fourth Annual Report of the Kindergarten for the Blind* (Boston: George Ellis, 1890), p. 77; and Lewis Weld, "Letter to the President and Directors of the Asylum," in *Twenty-first Report of the Directors of the American Asylum at Hartford*, p. 25.

14. SGH, "Laura Bridgman," p. 338. Harlan Lane provides a complete history of nineteenth-century criticisms of Sign. See also Douglas Baynton, *Forbidden Signs: American Culture and the Campaign Against Sign Language* (Chicago: University of Chicago Press, 1996); Carol Padden and Tom Humphries, *Deaf in America: Voices from a Culture* (Cambridge, Mass.: Harvard University Press, 1988); Sacks, *Seeing Voices*; and Jonathan Rée, *I See a Voice: Deafness, Language and the Senses—A Philosophical History* (New York: Metropolitan Books, 1999).

15. SGH, "Laura Bridgman," p. 338.

16. Messerli, pp. 30, 41.

17. D. H. Meyer, *The Instructed Conscience: The Shaping of the American National Ethic* (Philadephia: University of Pennsylvania Press, 1972), pp. 4–6. For descriptions of the moral philosophy course, see also Stow Persons, *American Mind* (New York: Holt, 1958), pp. 191–93; George P. Schmidt, *The Old Time College President* (New York: Columbia University Press, 1930), pp. 108–45; and Daniel Walker Howe, *The Unitarian Conscience: Harvard Moral Philosophy, 1805–1861* (Middletown, Conn.: Wesleyan University Press, 1988), pp. 1–4.

18. Henry F. May, *The Enlightenment in America* (New York: Oxford University Press, 1976), pp. 344–48; Herbert W. Schneider, *A History of American Philosophy*, 2nd ed. (New York: Columbia University Press, 1963), pp. 216–18; Douglas Sloan, *The Scottish Enlightenment and the American College Ideal* (New York: Columbia Teachers College Press, 1971), pp. 214, 238–43.

19. Thomas Reid, *Essays on the Active Powers of the Human Mind* (Cambridge, Mass.: M.I.T. Press, 1969), p. 315.

20. Thomas Reid, "Essays on the Intellectual Powers of Man," in *Inquiry and Essays*, eds. Ronald Beanblossom and Keith Lehrer (Indianapolis: Hackett Publishing, 1983), p. 259.

21. Frederick Copleston, *A History of Philosophy* (New York: Doubleday, 1959), V, p. 377.

22. Henry Adams, *The Education of Henry Adams* (New York: Modern Library, 1931), p. 35.

23. Ralph Waldo Emerson, "Historic Notes of Life and Letters in New England," in *The Portable Emerson*, ed. Carl Bode (New York: Penguin, 1981), p. 604.

24. Degérando, pp. 63–64.

25. Ninth AR, p. 25.

26. Samuel Eliot to F. Hall, July 5, 1889, PSA.

27. Sanford, p. 18.

28. M. Howe and F. Hall, p. 40.

CHAPTER FIVE: Awakening

1. Sanford, p. 19.

2. SGH to Margaret Teague, October 21, 1837, PSA.

3. SGH to Daniel Bridgman, November 8, 1837, PSA.

4. SGH, "Laura Bridgman," p. 390.

5. Sixth AR, p. 10.

6. Ibid., p. 9.

7. Eleventh AR, p. 7.

8. SGH to M. Ramon de la Tagua, June 2, 1838, PSA.

9. Helen Keller, *The Story of My Life* (Garden City, N.Y.: Doubleday, 1955), p. 36.

10. SGH, "Laura Bridgman," p. 392.

11. Ninth AR, p. 25.

12. Quoted in Lamson, p. 6.

13. Keller, *Story of My Life*, p. 36.

14. Ninth AR, p. 26.

15. SGH, "Laura Bridgman," p. 393.

16. Ibid.

17. John Kitto, *The Lost Senses* (Edinburgh: William Oliphant, 1848), p. 99. For a complete history of finger spelling, see Jonathan Rée.

18. Lamson, pp. 7–8.

19. Eighth AR, p. 14.

20. Lamson, p. 21.

21. Ninth AR, p. 37.

22. Seventh AR, pp. 14–16.

23. Eighth AR, p. 16.

24. Ibid.

25. I am indebted to Benjamin Smith for this interpretation.

26. Ninth AR, p. 31.

27. Jill de Villiers and Peter de Villiers, *Language Acquisition* (Cambridge, Mass.: Harvard University Press, 1978), p. 237; Carol Chomsky, "Analytic Study of the Tadoma Method: Language Abilities of Three Deaf-Blind Subjects," *Journal of Speech and Hearing Research* 29 (1986): 336–39.

28. Eighth AR, p. 16.

29. Ibid.

30. Reprinted in facsimile in Lamson, p. 19.

31. Ninth AR, p. 31.

32. Tenth AR, p. 26.

33. Ibid., p. 19.

34. Thirteenth AR, p. 17.

35. Sixth AR, p. 13.

36. Tenth AR, p. 25.

37. SGH to Margaret Teague, October 21, 1837, PSA.

38. Locke, *Essay Concerning Human Understanding*, III:9:9.

39. SGH, *Thoughts on Language: A Lecture Delivered Before the American Institute of Instruction* (Boston: Ticknor, 1842), p. 3.

40. Ninth AR, pp. 40–41; SGH, *Thoughts on Language*, pp. 2–3, 9, 12, 46.

41. Combe, *Notes on the United States of North America*, II, p. 204.

42. John R. Davies, *Phrenology, Fad and Science: A 19th-Century American Crusade* (New Haven: Yale University Press, 1955), pp. 17–18, 25. See also: Madeleine Stern, "Introduction," in *A Phrenological Dictionary of Nineteenth-Century Americans* (Westport, Conn.: Greenwood, 1982), pp. ix–xix; David De Giustino, *Conquest of Mind: Phrenology and Victorian Social Thought* (Totowa, N.J.: Rowan and Littlefield, 1975).

43. Messerli, p. 351; Julia Ward Howe, *Reminiscences, 1819–1899* (Boston: Houghton Mifflin, 1900), p. 133.

44. SGH, *Discourse on the Social Relations of Man, Delivered Before the Boston Phrenological Society* (Boston: March, Capen, and Lyon, 1837), p. 11.

45. Ibid., pp. 7, 27–30.

46. SGH, *Oration at Ceremonies on Laying the Corner-stone of the New York State Institution for*

the Blind at Batavia, New York, Thursday, Sept. 6, 1866 (Batavia, N.Y.: Henry Todd, 1866), p. 31.

47. Combe, II, p. 204.

48. Steven Pinker, *The Language Instinct: How the Mind Creates Language* (New York: HarperCollins, 1994), pp. 18, 124–25.

49. SGH, "Laura Bridgman," p. 384.

50. Eric Lenneberg, *Biological Foundations of Language* (New York: Wiley, 1967), p. 155.

51. Pinker, pp. 37–38, 291–95; Russ Rymer, *Genie: A Scientific Tragedy* (New York: Harper-Collins, 1993), pp. 87–88.

52. Professor Neil Smith of University College, London, has helped me understand the distinction between using language and knowing it. My summary of critical-period theory is based on the famous fourth chapter of Lenneberg's *Biological Foundations of Language*, pp. 125–87.

53. Granville Stanley Hall, "Laura Bridgman," in *Aspects of German Culture* (Boston: Osgood, 1881), p. 243.

54. Lila R. Gleitman, "Biological Dispositions to Learn Language," in *Child Language*, eds. Margery B. Franklin and Sybil S. Barten (New York: Oxford University Press, 1988), p. 175; Chomsky, p. 344.

55. Lamson, p. 69; Tenth AR, p. 25.

56. Eleventh AR, pp. 32–33.

57. Tenth AR, pp. 25, 27.

58. Eleventh AR, pp. 23–24.

59. G. S. Hall, "Laura Bridgman," p. 251.

60. In the spirit of pure speculation, Professor Neil Smith suggested this possibility to me.

61. Dr. Katherine Dalsimer told me about PANDAS, and Dr. Kathy Berkman provided me with information.

62. Tenth AR, p. 26; Eleventh AR, p. 24.

CHAPTER SIX: The Angel

1. Thomas Carlyle to SGH, October 23, 1842, PSA.

2. Ibid.

3. Ninth AR, p. 23.

4. Charles Summer to William Ellery Channing, May 26, 1842, in *Memoir and Letters of Charles Summer*, ed. Edward L. Pierce (New York: Arno, 1969), II, p. 210.

5. M. Howe and F. Hall, p. 81.

6. *Evening Transcript*, June 14, 1851.

7. Justin Winsor, *The Memorial History of Boston* (Boston: James Osgood Co., 1881), IV,

p. 273; Hugh Chisolm, "Laura Dewey Bridgman," *Encyclopædia Britannica*, 11th ed. (New York: Cambridge University Press, 1910), IV, p. 559; "Laura Bridgman," *New York Times*, May 14, 1883; Julia Ward Howe, *Reminiscences*, p. 87; *Proceedings of the Public Meeting on Behalf of the Printing Fund for the Blind Held at Tremont Temple, Friday, April 1, 1881* (Boston: Wright and Potter, 1881), p. 24; *Boston Post*, December 21, 1887.

8. "Laura Bridgman," *The Mother's Monthly Journal* 7 (January 1841): 27.

9. "Visit to the Blind Asylum at South Boston," *The Youth's Magazine or Evangelical Miscellany* (June 1841): 207.

10. "Interesting Interview," reprinted in *The Emancipator and Free American*, December 9, 1841.

11. George Moore, *The Power of the Soul over the Body, Considered in Relation to Health and Morals* (New York: Harper and Brothers, 1845), pp. 47–48.

12. W. Holmes, "To Laura Bridgman," undated, unidentified newspaper clipping, PSA.

13. Anonymous, in *Echoes of Nature* (Philadelphia: Biddle, 1845), p. 23.

14. Lydia Sigourney, "Laura Bridgman: The Deaf, Dumb, and Blind Girl of the Boston Institution for the Blind," *Godey's Lady's Book* 16 (June 1838): 252.

15. Mary Klages, *Woeful Afflictions: Disability and Sentimentality in Victorian America* (Philadelphia: University of Pennsylvania Press, 1999), pp. 102–103, argues that Howe's reports were written in two rhetorical modes, one "professional" and addressed to reformers and educators, the other "sentimental" and addressed to laypeople.

16. Eighth AR, p. 6.

17. SGH to Sigourney, April 20, 1838, PSA.

18. Ninth AR, pp. 28–29.

19. Ibid., p. 23.

20. John Angell James, *The Young Man's Friend and Guide Through Life to Immortality* (London: Hamilton, Adams, 1842), p. 13. See Karen Halttunen, *Confidence Men and Painted Women: A Study of Middle-Class Culture in America, 1830–1870* (New Haven: Yale University Press, 1982), p. 26.

21. SGH, "Notes on Laura Bridgman," in Fifty-eighth AR, p. 349; Eighteenth AR, p. 48.

22. Halttunen, p. 26, remarks on the popularity of navigational metaphors in conduct-book writing. Eleventh AR, pp. 34–36; Tenth AR, pp. 29–30.

23. Ninth AR, p. 39.

24. Ibid.; Tenth AR, p. 30.

25. Eleventh AR, p. 24.

26. Ingalls, p. 11.

27. M. Howe and F. Hall, p. 84; Lamson, p. 134.

28. Lamson, p. 114.

29. Ibid., pp. 46, 102.

30. Ibid., pp. 65–66.

31. Ibid., pp. 74, 77, 106.

32. Ibid., p. 72.

33. M. Howe and F. Hall, p. 92.

34. Ibid., p. 79.

35. Lamson, p. 101.

36. Sumner to Francis Lieber, January 5, 1842, in *Memoir and Letters of Charles Sumner*, II, p. 199.

37. Sanford, p. 20.

38. Lamson, pp. 80–81, 103, 135; Francis Lieber, "The Vocal Sounds of Laura Bridgman," in *Miscellaneous Writings* (Philadelphia: Lippincott, 1880), pp. 452, 460–64.

39. Thirteenth AR, p. 27; Lamson, p. 47.

40. Quoted in Jacques Derrida, *Memoirs of the Blind: The Self-Portrait and Other Ruins*, trans. Pascale-Anne Brault and Michael Naas (Chicago: University of Chicago Press, 1993), p. 106.

41. Dorothy Burlingham, *Psychoanalytic Studies of the Sighted and the Blind* (New York: International Universities Press, 1972), p. 338.

42. SGH, "Notes on Laura Bridgman," in Fifty-eighth AR, p. 355.

43. Ninth AR, p. 37.

44. Tenth AR, p. 29; Eleventh AR, p. 34.

45. Edward Bulwer-Lytton, *The Last Days of Pompeii* (New York: Dutton, 1906), p. 179.

46. D. H. Lawrence, "The Blind Man," in *The Complete Short Stories* (New York: Penguin, 1961), II, pp. 350, 355; Raymond Carver, "Cathedral," in *Cathedral: Stories* (New York: Vintage, 1984), pp. 209–28.

47. Eighteenth AR, pp. 20–21.

48. Ninth AR, pp. 37–38.

49. SGH to Mary Howitt, July 31, 1847, transcription, PSA. Presumably with Howe's permission, Howitt reprinted his letter in her own article on Laura in *Howitt's Journal* 2 (October 9, 1847): 225–26.

50. See Richard Brodhead, *Cultures of Letters: Scenes of Reading and Writing in Nineteenth-Century America* (Chicago: University of Chicago Press, 1993), pp. 51–65; and Leo Braudy, *The Frenzy of Renown* (New York: Oxford University Press, 1986), pp. 465–66.

51. Brodhead, p. 53; Halttunen, pp. 102–12; Ronald J. Zboray, *A Fictive People: Antebellum Economic Development and the American Reading Public* (New York: Oxford University Press, 1993), pp. 5–36.

52. Joan D. Hedrick, *Harriet Beecher Stowe: A Life* (New York: Oxford University Press, 1994), p. 224; Braudy, pp. 499, 578.

53. Julia Burnham, "Reminiscences of Laura Bridgman," typescript, PSA.

54. Quoted in Daniel Poole, *Dickens' Fur Coat and Charlotte's Unanswered Letters: The Rows and Romances of England's Great Victorian Novelists* (New York: HarperCollins, 1997), p. 146.

55. Peter Ackroyd, *Dickens* (New York: HarperCollins, 1990), pp. 342, 344.

56. See Edward F. Payne, *Dickens Days in Boston: A Record of Daily Events* (Boston: Houghton Mifflin, 1927).

57. M. Howe and F. Hall, pp. 105–106.

58. Dickens, *American Notes*, p. 103.

59. Dickens to SGH, April 4, 1842, PSA.

60. Elisabeth Gitter, "Laura Bridgman and Little Nell," *Dickens Quarterly* 8 (June 1991): 76.

61. Dickens, *American Notes*, pp. 81–82, 94.

62. "Bearing One Another's Burdens," *Youth's Penny Gazette* 7 (September 26, 1849): 1.

CHAPTER SEVEN: Second Acts

1. Dickens to C. C. Felton, December 31, 1842, in appendix to *American Notes*, p. 328.

2. Edgar Johnson, *Charles Dickens: His Tragedy and Triumph* (New York: Penguin, 1977), p. 224.

3. Mrs. E. W. Farnham, "Laura Bridgman," *The Prisoner's Friend* 1 (1848): 105.

4. Rowland Gibson Hazard, *Essays on Language and Other Papers* (Boston: Phillips, Sampson, 1857), p. 801.

5. Farnham, "Laura Bridgman," p. 105.

6. Moore, *The Power of the Soul*, p. 47; Mary Howitt, "Laura Bridgman," *Howitt's Journal* 2 (October 9, 1847): 225.

7. Howitt, "Laura Bridgman," p. 228.

8. Horace Mann, "Laura Bridgman," *The Common School Journal* 3 (February 1, 1841): 35.

9. W. Holmes, "To Laura Bridgman," undated, unidentified newspaper clipping, PSA. I have not succeeded in identifying this poet.

10. Charles Sumner to George Sumner, September 4, 1842, in *Memoir and Letters of Charles Sumner*, II, p. 222.

11. *Letters and Journals*, II, pp. 106–107.

12. Ibid., p. 115.

13. George Ticknor to Maria Edgeworth, July 10, 1840, in *Life, Letters, and Journals of George Ticknor*, ed. George S. Hillard (Boston: Houghton Mifflin, 1909), II, p. 194.

14. M. Howe and F. Hall, pp. 59–60; Ninth AR, p. 43.

15. SGH to Timothy Reed, November 18, 1840, PSA. In some documents, Lucy's last name is spelled "Read."

16. Tenth AR, pp. 35–36.

17. SGH to Timothy Reed, November 18, 1840, PSA.

18. Tenth AR, p. 36.

19. SGH to J. Shaw, March 6, 1841, PSA.

20. M. Howe and F. Hall, p. 81.

21. Tenth AR, pp. 36, 38.

22. Brodhead, p. 22.

23. Tenth AR, pp. 36–37.

24. Helen Keller, *Teacher: Anne Sullivan Macy* (Garden City, N.Y.: Doubleday, 1955), p. 24.

25. Dorothy Herrmann, *Helen Keller: A Life* (New York: Knopf, 1998), pp. 44–46.

26. Tenth AR, p. 37.

27. Ibid., p. 38.

28. Mary Swift, Journal, June 11, 1841, PSA.

29. SGH to Mann, July [1841], HHL b44M-314 (863).

30. Tenth AR, pp. 36–39.

31. Ibid., p. 41.

32. Although Reed's letters to Howe have not survived, the family's complaints are clear from Howe's detailed, point-by-point replies of September 10, 1841, and June 12, 1842, PSA.

33. SGH to Timothy Reed, September 10, 1841, PSA.

34. The objectionable letter was probably the one Howe wrote on July 5, 1841, to Colonel Stone of the *Commercial Advertiser*. In that long and by no means private letter, Howe describes Lucy Reed as "sullen and unsocial," and "so intractable . . . that I feared she might be insane," PSA and reprinted in Sanborn, pp. 163–65.

35. SGH to Timothy Reed, June 12, 1842, PSA.

36. Tenth AR, p. 32.

37. Ibid., pp. 32–35; Eleventh AR, p. 41.

38. Swift, Journal, February 21, 1845.

39. M. Howe and F. Hall, p. 255.

40. Eleventh AR, p. 41.

41. Ibid., p. 44.

42. Charles Dickens, *The Old Curiosity Shop*, ed. Angus Easson (New York: Penguin, 1972), p. 72.

43. Tenth AR, pp. 32–33.

44. Lamson, p. 106.

45. M. Howe and F. Hall, p. 200.

46. Gary E. Wait, "Julia Brace," p. 9.

47. SGH, "Laura Bridgman and Julia Brace," *Commercial Advertiser*, November 1841, reprinted in Sanborn, pp. 161–62, and in various newspapers, including *The Emancipator and Free American*, December 9, 1841.

48. Ibid.

49. Tenth AR, p. 43. For another explanation of Brace's "failure" at Perkins, see Lane, pp. 292–93.

50. Wait, "Julia Brace," pp. 9–10.

51. Philip Caswell to Howe, April 13, 1850, and April 30, 1850, PSA.

52. Ishbel Ross, *Journey Into Light: The Story of the Education of the Blind* (New York: Appleton-Century-Crofts, 1951), p. 237.

53. John Epps, *Internal Evidence of Christianity Deduced from Phrenology* (Edinburgh: John Anderson, 1827), p. 60.

54. Tenth AR, p. 31.

55. Daniel Walker Howe, p. 96.

56. Ninth AR, pp. 40–42; Tenth AR, p. 31.

57. For explanations of Unitarian doctrine, see Sidney Ahlstrom, *A Religious History of the American People* (New Haven: Yale University Press, 1972), pp. 388–402; Daniel Walker Howe, pp. 151–66; and Henry May, pp. 329–53.

58. The Dedham ruling effectively allowed the members of each parish to choose their own minister. As a result, orthodox members in more than eighty parishes seceded, abandoning their meetinghouses, parsonages, endowments, and records to the Unitarians, and struggling, like the Methodists and Baptists, to survive as dissenters. But the Liberals did not enjoy their tax-supported comfort for long. The "exiled" orthodox soon made common cause with other dissenters in amending the state constitution. For histories of the Congregational schism, see Ahlstrom, pp. 388–402; Daniel Walker Howe, pp. 219–20; Winthrop S. Hudson, *Religion in America* (New York: Scribner's, 1965), pp. 159–62; William R. Hutchison, *The Transcendentalist Ministers: Church Reform in the New England Renaissance* (New Haven: Yale University Press, 1959), pp. 1–21; and Ann C. Rose, *Transcendentalism as a Social Movement, 1830–1850* (New Haven: Yale University Press, 1981), pp. 1–8.

59. See Messerli, pp. 221–50; B. A. Hinsdale, *Horace Mann and the Common School Revival in the United States* (New York: Scribner's, 1937), pp. 210–32; and Raymond B. Culver, *Horace Mann and Religion in the Massachusetts Public Schools* (New York: Arno, 1969), for histories of the Massachusetts common-school controversy.

60. Mann to Combe, December 1, 1844, in Mary Peabody Mann, *Life of Horace Mann* (Boston: Walker, Fuller, and Co., 1865), p. 230–32.

61. SGH to Mann, March 27, 1841, in *Letters and Journals*, II, p. 105.

62. Mann to Combe, October 13, 1841, in *Life of Horace Mann*, p. 156; Schwartz, p. 129.

63. Mann to Combe, December 1, 1844, in *Life of Horace Mann*, p. 232.

64. Walt Whitman, "Leaves of Grass" (1855), in *Complete Poetry and Prose* (New York: Library of America, 1982), p. 85.

65. Eleventh AR, pp. 37–38; SGH to David Ely Bartlett, September 3, 1841, PSA.

66. Eleventh AR, pp. 37–38.

67. Ibid., p. 38.

68. M. Howe and F. Hall, p. 289.

CHAPTER EIGHT: Sea Changes

1. Combe to SGH, March 15, 1840, typescript copy, PSA.
2. Henry Wadsworth Longfellow to John Forster, February 28, 1843, in Andrew Hilen, ed., *The Letters of Henry Wadsworth Longfellow* (Cambridge, Mass.: Harvard University Press, 1982), II, p. 510.
3. *Letters and Journals*, I, pp. 330–31.
4. Clifford, p. 203.
5. Carlos Baker, *Emerson Among the Eccentrics: A Group Portrait* (New York: Viking, 1996), pp. 7, 82.
6. Mary H. Grant, *Private Woman, Public Person: An Account of the Life of Julia Ward Howe from 1819 to 1868* (Brooklyn, N.Y.: Carlson, 1994), p. 2.
7. JWH, *Reminiscences*, p. 82.
8. Ibid.
9. SGH to Sumner, February 18, 1844, in *Letters and Journals*, II, p. 152.
10. Lamson, p. 169.
11. Ibid., p. 213.
12. Ibid., pp. 167–68.
13. Tenth AR, p. 24.
14. Lamson, pp. 169–70.
15. Lydia Drew to SGH, February 18, 1840
16. Campbell Waterhouse of the Duxbury historical Society put me in touch with Susan Basile. She told me about Lloyd Morton, who kindly shared his recollections.
17. Sanford, p. 20.
18. Jeannette Howe to Harmony Bridgman, August 7, 1843, PSA.
19. LDB to Elizabeth Everett, May 1, 1843, quoted in Lamson, p. 171.
20. Lamson, p. 222.
21. Ibid., p. 227.
22. LDB to SGH, March 24, 1844, quoted in Lamson, p. 245.
23. Ibid., pp. 245–46.
24. LDB to JWH, April 2, 1844, quoted in Lamson, p. 247.
25. LB to JWH, June 25, 1844, quoted in Lamson, pp. 258–59.
26. Laura Richards and Maud Howe Elliott, with Florence Howe Hall, *Julia Ward Howe, 1819–1910* (Boston: Houghton Mifflin, 1915), I, p. 105.
27. Fifteenth AR, pp. 24–25.
28. Richards, *Samuel Gridley Howe*, pp. 8–9, 123–24; Maud Howe Elliott, *Three Generations* (Boston: Little, Brown, 1923), p. 35.
29. Lamson, p. 136.
30. M. Howe and F. Hall, p. 169.
31. G. Stanley Hall, "Laura Bridgman," p. 274.

32. Thirteenth AR, p. 22.

33. Eighteenth AR, p. 79.

34. Ibid., p. 83.

35. Forty-third AR, p. 95.

36. Thirteenth AR, p. 50.

37. Ibid., pp. 32–33.

38. Ibid.; Eighteenth AR, p. 64.

39. Thirteenth AR, p. 29.

40. Eighteenth AR, p. 64.

41. Laura E. Richards, *Laura Bridgman: The Story of an Opened Door* (New York: Appleton, 1928), p. 84.

42. Thirteenth AR, p. 28.

43. M. Howe and F. Hall, pp. 149–50.

44. For a philosophical history of the problem of teaching religion to the deaf, see Jonathan Rée, pp. 141–60.

45. Lamson, p. 162.

46. Specimens of these extraordinary transcriptions are preserved in *The First State Normal School in America: The Journals of Cyrus Peirce and Mary Swift*, ed. Arthur O. Norton (Cambridge, Mass.: Harvard University Press, 1926).

47. Lamson, pp. 276–77.

48. Ibid., p. 276.

49. Ibid., pp. 228–29.

50. Rev. A. Stevens, "Sketch of Laura Bridgman, The Blind and Deaf Mute," *The Ladies' Repository* 7 (September 1847): 278–89.

51. Thirteenth AR, pp. 12–13.

52. Fifteenth AR, p. 6.

53. Sixteenth AR, p. 34.

54. Thirteenth AR, pp. 15–17.

55. Clifford, p. 88.

56. Grant, p. 65; Clifford, p. 78. Dread of the dangers of pregnancy and childbirth is a common theme in nineteenth-century biography and memoir. See Hedrick, *Harriet Beecher Stowe*, for a fascinating account of the physical toll of frequent pregnancy and of the ensuing emotional strain on even the most loving couples.

57. Messerli, p. 411.

58. Mann to SGH, October 8, 1844, quoted in Richards, *Samuel Gridley Howe*, p. 160.

59. SGH to Mann, October 9, 1844, quoted in Messerli, p. 418.

60. Ninth AR, p. 23.

61. Tenth AR, p. 29.

62. Ibid., pp. 28–29.

63. In *Extraordinary Bodies*, p. 25, Rosemarie Garland Thomson argues that disabled women

are usually viewed as asexual. However, a tradition of erotically charged representations of blind women in painting, literature, and film suggests that blindness is, to some extent, different from other disabilities in its sexual implications. See Elisabeth G. Gitter, "The Blind Daughter in Dickens's *Cricket on the Hearth*," *Studies in English Literature 1500–1900*, 39 (Autumn 1999): 675–89.

64. Denise Levertov, "A Solitude," in *Poems, 1960–1967* (New York: New Directions, 1983), p. 70. For an explanation of the concept of psychic talion, see Sigmund Freud, "Psychogenic Visual Disturbance According to Psycho-analytical Conceptions" (1910), in *Collected Papers*, ed. Ernest Jones, trans. Joan Rivière (New York: Basic Books, 1959), II, pp. 110–11.

65. Schwartz, p. 114.

66. Fifteenth AR, pp. 24–25.

67. Lamson, p. 361.

CHAPTER NINE: Teachers and Teaching

1. Francis Lieber to his wife, July 13, 1843, in *The Life and Letters of Francis Lieber*, ed. Thomas Perry Sergeant (Boston: Osgood, 1882), p. 176; JWH to Louisa Ward, June 17, 1843, quoted in Richards and Elliott, *Julia Ward Howe*, I, p. 82.

2. Ninth AR, p. 42.

3. Thirteenth AR, pp. 23–24, 27.

4. Ibid., pp. 39–41.

5. Ibid., p. 41.

6. Maria Edgeworth to SGH, May 24, 1845, Chapin Library of Rare Books, Williams College.

7. Peter Gregg Slater, *Children in the New England Mind in Death and Life* (Hamden, Conn.: Archon Books, 1977), pp. 140–50.

8. Brodhead, pp. 18–19; Daniel Calhoun, *The Intelligence of a People* (Princeton, N.J.: Princeton University Press, 1973), pp. 176–79.

9. Brodhead, pp. 20–22.

10. Thirteenth AR, p. 41.

11. LDB, memoir beginning "I should be glad," copied in SW's hand [1848?], p. 9, PSA.

12. Lamson, p. 342.

13. SW, Journal I, February 9, 1846; September [n.d.], 1846, PSA.

14. Lamson, p. 277. As Cyrus Peirce's favorite student and the daughter of a successful doctor, Swift had influential allies. Although at the time she did not reply directly to Howe's published 1844 attack, some pressure was evidently exerted on him to apologize. He included what amounted to a retraction in his AR of the next year. To a description of Swift as an "able and excellent teacher," he added a conciliatory footnote: "It is possible that

some remarks in my last Report may have been construed into censure of Miss Swift; but they were not intended for that effect. She fulfilled her duty with ability and conscientiousness": Fourteenth AR, p. 30.

15. Mary Swift Lamson, *Records of the First Class of the First State Normal School in America, Established at Lexington, Massachusetts, 1839* (Boston: Printed for the Class, 1903), p. 196.

16. For a history of the establishment of the early normal schools, see Messerli, pp. 298–301, 319–24.

17. Lydia Drew to SGH, February 18, 1840, PSA.

18. Arthur O. Norton, "Introduction," in Peirce and Swift, *The First State Normal School*, p. xlix.

19. Peirce, who was plagued by exhaustion and ill health, kept only sketchy notes; Swift's journal, running to 143 printed pages, provides a detailed record of every day between August 1, 1839, and April 4, 1840. See Peirce and Swift.

20. Lamson, *Records of the First Class*, pp. 193–94.

21. See the Lamson family papers, MHS.

22. Paul Swift to SGH, April 10, 1840, PSA.

23. Paul Swift to SGH, November 7, 1841, PSA.

24. Ninth AR, p. 42; Lamson, p. 136.

25. Eleventh AR, p. 37.

26. Horace Mann, "Lecture II, 1838: Special Preparation, A Pre-Requisite to Teaching," in *Lectures on Education* (New York: Arno Press, 1969), p. 72.

27. Nancy F. Cott, *The Bonds of Womanhood: "Woman's Sphere" in New England, 1780–1835* (New Haven: Yale University Press, 1977), p. 34.

28. Milton Rugoff, *The Beechers: An American Family in the Nineteenth Century* (New York: Harper and Row, 1981), p. 61.

29. Combe, *Notes on the United States of America*, I, p. 57.

30. Mann, "Lecture II," pp. 73–75.

31. Ibid., p. 73.

32. Hedrick, pp. 44–45; Rugoff, p. 61.

33. For records of Mary Swift Lamson's activities, see the Lamson family papers, MHS, and the clipping files at the Alumni House, Framingham State College.

34. "A Christian Pioneer: Mrs. Mary Swift Lamson," *The Congregationalist and Christian*, March 13, 1909.

35. SGH, *An Essay on Separate and Congregate Systems of Prison Discipline, Being a Report Made to the Boston Prison Discipline Society* (New York: Arno, 1974), pp. 16, 19.

36. Ibid., p. 29.

37. Ibid., p. 26.

38. Lamson, p. 278.

39. Eliza Rogers to SGH, May 26, 1845, PSA.

40. See David Donald, *Charles Sumner and the Coming of the Civil War* (New York: Knopf, 1965), pp. 122–25.

41. Carroll Smith-Rosenberg, *Disorderly Conduct: Visions of Gender in Victorian America* (New York: Knopf, 1985), p. 69.

42. Donald, pp. 86–87.

43. SGH, *A Letter to J. H. Wilkins, H. B. Rogers, and F. B. Fay, Commissioners of Massachusetts for the State Reform School for Girls* (Boston: Ticknor and Fields, 1854), p. 20.

44. Ibid., pp. 20, 30–31.

45. John Burt Wight, "Reminiscences," 1866, WHS.

46. "Request for dismissal from the Church of Christ," March 13, 1828, typescript copy, WHS.

47. William Lee Raymond, *The First Parish, Wayland Massachusetts, 1640–1940* (privately printed, 1940), p. 15. See also Philemon Russell to Jacob Reeves, June 12, 1834, typescript copy, WHS. Implying that Wight was not an effective minister, Russell recommended a replacement who would be likely "to build up and enliven your Church and Society."

48. John Burt Wight, "Reminiscences."

49. I am indebted to Helen Fitch Emery and Jo Goeselt of the WHS for this information.

50. SW, ms. with the heading "Record of the girls School—February 1844," entries dated March 5, March 16, March 24, and March 30, WHS.

51. SGH, *Essay on Separate and Congregate Systems of Prison Discipline*, p. 54.

52. SW, "Record of the girls School," August 7 and August 9, 1844.

53. Ibid., July 16, 1844.

54. Ibid., August 6, 1844.

55. Fourteenth AR, pp. 30–31.

56. Ibid., p. 31.

57. Ibid.

CHAPTER TEN: Attachments

1. LDB, 1849 ms. memoir in Wight's hand, p. 10, PSA.

2. LDB, Journal, April 30–May 3, 1844, PSA.

3. Ibid., August 29, 1845.

4. LDB to Sarah Grout Wight (Mrs. John Burt Wight), September 14, 1845, PSA.

5. SW, Journal I (1845–1848), PSA.

6. Ibid., October 20, 1845.

7. Ibid., December 10, 1845.

8. Ibid., September 22, October 6, October 23, December 12, December 21, 1845.

9. Ibid., February 16, 1847.

10. Ibid., September 14, 1846.

11. Ibid.

12. Horace Mann, "On School Punishments," in *Lectures on Education*, pp. 311, 314, 316.

13. Mary Mann, *Moral Culture of Infancy*, 2nd ed. (New York: Schermerhorn, 1869), pp. 119–20, 147, 166, 170–72.

14. SW, Journal I, December 13, 1844.

15. Ibid., October 6, 1845.

16. Ibid., March 10, 1846.

17. Ibid., October 3, 1845.

18. Ibid., September 18, 1847.

19. Ibid., December 12, 1845.

20. SW, Journal II (1848–1849), November 16, 1848, and January 25, 1849.

21. SW, Journal I, October 24, 1845.

22. Ibid., May 10, 1847; July 11, 1847. It is clear from Wight's journal that Laura often went for scheduled lessons with Howe, only to find that he was absent or otherwise occupied.

23. Ibid., May 1, 1847.

24. Ibid., July 11, 1847.

25. Ibid., October [n.d.], 1846.

26. Ibid., November 3, 1845.

27. Ibid., October 23, 1845.

28. Ibid., February 9, 1846.

29. Fifteenth AR, pp. 23–27.

30. Ibid., p. 26.

31. Fourteenth AR, p. 29.

32. Fifteenth AR, p. 27.

33. SGH to H. Scott, July 15, 1847, PSA.

34. Joan Jacobs Brumberg, *Fasting Girls: The History of Anorexia Nervosa* (Cambridge, Mass.: Harvard University Press, 1988), pp. 137–38.

35. Ibid., pp. 140, 177.

36. Lois W. Banner, *American Beauty* (Chicago: University of Chicago Press, 1983), p. 45.

37. SW, Journal I, September 14, 1846.

38. Ibid., December 24, 1845.

39. Ibid., September 1, 1846.

40. Fifteenth AR, p. 24.

41. SW, Journal I, June [n.d.], 1846.

42. LDB to Harmony Bridgman, August 23, 1846, PSA.

43. SW, Journal I, June [n.d.], 1846.

44. LDB, 1849 memoir, transcribed in SW's hand, PSA.

45. LDB to Harmony Bridgman, July 16, 1846, PSA.

46. SW, Journal I, October 18, 1847.

47. SW, Journal II, November 4, 1848.

48. Ibid., April 10, 1849.

49. SW, Journal I, September 18, 1847.

50. SW, Journal II, November 16, 1848.

51. Swift, Journal, August 19, 1844.

52. SW, Journal II, January 25, 1849.

53. SW, Journal I, September 14, 1846.

54. SW, Journal II, December 13, 1848.

55. Eighteenth AR, pp. 59–60.

56. LDB, Journal, January 4, 1847; September 13, 1847; January 3, 1850; March 18, 1850.

57. Eighteenth AR, p. 60.

58. SW, Journal II, November 10, 1848.

59. LDB, Journal, September 7, 1848.

60. Ibid., December 13, 1849.

61. Ibid., December 4, 1849.

62. Ibid., February 8, 1850.

63. Ibid.

64. Ibid., June 1, 1848.

65. Ibid., March 13, 1850.

66. Ibid.

67. Ibid., March 14, 1850.

68. SW, Journal II, January 27, 1849.

69. LDB, Journal, August 22, 1848.

70. SW's written protest to Howe has not survived. However, his point-by-point reply makes her objections clear. SGH to SW, May 27, 1850, HHL b44M-314 (1030).

71. Eighteenth AR, p. 53.

72. Ibid., p. 51.

73. SW, Journal I, October 6, 1845.

74. SGH to SW, May 27, 1850, HHL b44M-314 (1030).

75. Longfellow, *Letters*, III, p. 209.

76. JWH to SW, April 3 [no year], HHL 52M-301. There are three affectionate letters from JWH to SW in HHL.

77. Eighteenth AR, pp. 88–89.

78. LDB to Harmony Bridgman, August 11, 1850, PSA.

79. SW to SGH, August 18, 1850, PSA.

80. Mary Paddock to SGH, August 20, 1850; SW to SGH, August 18, 1850, PSA.

81. SW to SGH, November 14, 1850, PSA.

82. SW, Journal II, April 10, 1849.

83. SW to SGH, November 14, 1850, PSA.

84. LDB to Harmony Bridgman, January 2, 1851, PSA.

CHAPTER ELEVEN: Lamentations

1. LDB to SW, November 16, 1850, PSA.

2. LDB to SW, December 15, 1850, PSA.

3. LDB to Mary Rogers, February 8, 1847, reprinted in M. Howe and F. Hall, p. 212. Martha Jane Tenney, *The Tenney Family or the Descendants of Tomas Tenney of Rowley, Massachusetts, 1638–1904* (Concord, N.H.: Rumford Press, 1904), p. 115, incorrectly records the date of Asa Tenney's death as December 29, 1847. In fact, he died a year earlier.

4. SW, Journal I, June 1, 1847.

5. Ibid., February 1, 1847.

6. LDB to Mary Rogers, February 8, 1847.

7. SW, Journal I, June 1, 1847. Apparently Howe was not happy with Wight's teachings on the afterlife. In late June, when they returned to Boston, he told her he would take over Laura's religious instruction. By July 12, he had changed his mind and gave Wight permission to answer Laura's questions on all subjects: SW, Journal I, July 12, 1847.

8. LDB to Harmony Bridgman, January 2, 1851, PSA.

9. Harmony Bridgman to SW, February 1, 1851, PSA.

10. Ibid.

11. Harmony Bridgman to SGH, March 22, 1851, PSA.

12. Schwartz, pp. 144–45.

13. SGH to Dr. H. I. Bowditch, February 3, 1846, in *Letters and Journals*, II, p. 242.

14. Quoted in Stephen B. Oates, *To Purge This Land With Blood: A Biography of John Brown*, 2nd ed. (Amherst: University of Massachusetts Press, 1984), p. 351.

15. SGH to Harmony Bridgman, March 25, 1851, PSA.

16. LDB to SW, May 13, 1851, PSA.

17. Ibid.

18. LDB to SW, August 8, 1851, PSA.

19. LDB to Edward Bond, July 13, 1851, PSA.

20. LDB to Edward Bond, September 21, 1851, PSA.

21. Ibid.

22. LDB to Harmony Bridgman, November 30, 1851, PSA.

23. E. J. Miller and G. V. Gwyne, *A Life Apart: A Pilot Study of Residential Institutions for the Physically Handicapped and the Young Chronic Sick* (Philadelphia: Lippincott, 1972), p. 50.

24. SW, Journal I, September 15, 1845.

25. Richards, *Laura Bridgman*, p. 128.

26. SW, Journal I, September 15, 1845.

27. SW, Journal II, January 27, 1849.

28. M. Howe and F. Hall, pp. 199–200.

29. Harmony Bridgman to SGH, May 8, 1852, PSA.

30. SGH to Daniel and Harmony Bridgman ["My Friends,"], October 23, 1852, PSA.

31. SGH to LDB, October 23, 1852, PSA.

32. LDB to SGH, November 13 [or 17?], 1852, PSA.

33. SGH to Daniel and Harmony Bridgman, December 6, 1852, PSA.

34. SGH to LDB, December 6, 1852, PSA.

35. LDB to Mary Swift Lamson, December 12, 1852, Lamson papers, MHS.

36. Ibid.

37. Harmony Bridgman to SGH, December 27, 1852, PSA.

38. Harmony Bridgman to SGH, February 10, 1853, PSA.

39. LDB to SGH, January 16, 1853, PSA.

40. Harmony Bridgman to SGH, December 27, 1852, PSA.

41. SGH to LDB, January 8, 1853, PSA.

42. LDB to SGH, January 16, 1853, PSA.

43. M. Howe and F. Hall, pp. 263–64.

44. LDB to Harmony Bridgman, March 13, 1853, PSA.

45. LDB to SW (Bond), December 11, 1853, PSA.

46. LDB to Harmony Bridgman, May 29, 1853, PSA.

47. Three letters from Dorothea Dix to SW dated August 28, September 6, and September 12, 1850, survive in the PSA. Unfortunately, there are no letters from SW to Dix in the Dix papers at HHL.

48. LDB, Journal, January 12, 1853, typescript, PSA.

49. Dix's letter to SGH has not survived, but he quotes it in his reply of November 5, 1853, PSA.

50. SGH to Dorothea Dix, November 5, 1853, PSA.

51. Donald, p. 269.

52. Brown, *Dorothea Dix*, pp. 219, 241.

53. SGH to Dorothea Dix, November 5, 1853, PSA.

54. Harmony Bridgman to SGH, September 10, 1857, PSA.

55. LDB to Harmony Bridgman, February 26, 1854, PSA.

56. LDB to Mary Swift Lamson, December 12, 1852, Lamson papers, MHS.

57. SW to SGH, November 14, 1850, PSA.

58. SGH to Addison Bridgman, August 22, 1853, PSA.

59. LDB, Journal, December 13, 1849.

60. LDB to Addison Bridgman, August 26, 1849, quoted in Lamson, pp. 327–28.

61. LDB, Journal, December 26, 1849.

62. Ibid., February 13, 1853[5?].

63. LDB, undated ms. page, beginning "Sunday night I had some pleasant dreams." It is surprising that this document survived. The pages missing here and there from LDB's journal suggest that Howe's daughters or the Bridgman family may have destroyed embarrassing material.

64. LDB to Addison Bridgman, June 24, 1860, Manuscripts Division, Brown University Library.

65. Burt Nichols Bridgman and Joseph Clark Bridgman, *Genealogy of the Bridgman Family, Descendents of James Bridgman* (Hyde Park, Mass.: n.p., 1894), p. 63.

66. LDB to Mary Bridgman, May 6, October 23, and October 29, 1859, PSA.

67. John Downer Bridgman to SGH, November 17, 1859, PSA.

68. For details of Howe's involvement with Brown, see Oates, pp. 187–88, 233–38, 248–51, 313–14; and Schwartz, ch. 13 and ch. 14.

69. *Letters and Journals,* II, p. 442.

70. See Donald, pp. 282–97, for a full account of Sumner's speech and the ensuing attack.

71. *Letters and Journals,* II, pp. 417–28.

72. JWH, *Reminiscences,* p. 254.

73. Quoted in *Letters and Journals,* II, p. 436.

74. Oates, pp. 318, 313.

75. *Letters and Journals,* II, p. 438.

76. LDB to Rev. Jonathan Herrick, July 23, 1862, transcription, possibly by Mrs. Herrick, PSA.

77. Ibid.

CHAPTER TWELVE: Legacies

1. LDB to Eliza Rogers, January 8, 1864, quoted in Lamson, p. 356.

2. LDB to Rev. Jonathan Herrick, July 13, 1862, typescript copy, PSA.

3. M. Howe and F. Hall, pp. 285–86.

4. SW, Journal II, November 10, 1848. Wight remarked that Laura's "very strong feeling" about the injustice of slavery did not affect her equally strong "prejudice against persons colored." Wight tried to "remove" this puzzling prejudice which, she said, "can hardly be natural."

5. SGH to Governor John A. Andrew, May 25, 1861, in *Letters and Journals,* II, pp. 483–93.

6. Schwartz, pp. 247–67.

7. Grant, p. 140.

8. Ibid., pp. 109, 140–41.

9. Clifford, p. 157.

10. Longfellow to Sumner, May 21, 1863, in *Letters of Longfellow,* IV, p. 327.

11. Fifteenth AR, pp. 28–29.

12. Sarah Herrick to Miss Wood, June 26, 1878, PSA. This letter was obviously written in response to a request from Wood, a matron at the Perkins Institution in the 1870s and '80s, for the details of Laura's religious conversion. It is hard to imagine why Wood was interested, unless she was inquiring on behalf of Howe's daughters, who may already have been gathering information for their biography of Laura.

13. John King Lord, *A History of the Town of Hanover, N.H.* (Hanover: Dartmouth Press, 1928), pp. 108–11.

14. Sarah Herrick to Miss Wood, June 26, 1878, PSA.

15. LDB to Jonathan Herrick, July 23, 1862, PSA.

16. Sarah Herrick to Miss Wood, June 26, 1878, PSA.

17. LDB to Jonathan Herrick, July 23, 1862, PSA.

18. Sarah Herrick to Miss Wood, June 26, 1878, PSA.

19. Ibid.

20. M. Howe and F. Hall, p. 286.

21. E. J. Miller and G. V. Gwynne, *A Life Apart,* p. 80.

22. Ibid., p. 80.

23. "Holy Home," in M. Howe and F. Hall, pp. 289–90. Laura made copies of several versions of this poem. Several of these ms. copies are in the PSA; one is in the Lamson papers, MHS.

24. LDB to Jonathan Herrick, July 13, 1862, PSA.

25. Reprinted in Lamson, p. 367.

26. Sarah Herrick to Miss Wood, July 26, 1878, PSA.

27. Ibid.

28. LDB to SGH, October 16, 1864, PSA.

29. Emma Coolidge Weston to Edward E. Allen [1924], typescript, PSA.

30. Ibid.

31. LDB to SW (Bond), December 11, 1874, PSA.

32. LDB to Eliza Rogers, March 10, 1861, quoted in Lamson, p. 351.

33. LDB to Lamson, May 30, 1868, MHS.

34. LDB to Lamson, September 7, 1884, MHS.

35. LDB to Lamson, July 30, 1876, MHS.

36. LDB to Lamson, May 30, 1875, MHS.

37. LDB to Lamson, January 30 and May 11, 1876, MHS.

38. *Massachusetts Vital Records* 302 (1878), pp. 147, 164. Wight's brother Henry died at the McLean Asylum in 1886 at the age of sixty-six of "chronic melancholia" and "softening of the brain": *Massachusetts Vital Records* 374 (1886), pp. 193, 229. The latter diagnosis raises the possibility that he might have suffered from Alzheimer's disease.

39. LDB to Lamson, January 26, 1879, MHS.

40. Typescript letters to Edward Allen by Julia Burnham, Sarah Lane, Grace Walker, and Mary C. Moore, PSA.

41. Cora Davis Gleason, "Recollections of Laura Bridgman," September 1924, typescript, PSA.

42. Lillian R. Garside to Edward Allen [1924], typescript, PSA.

43. Estella Blackmur Hurd to Edward Allen, May 15, 1924, typescript, PSA.

44. Ibid.

45. Weston to Allen, PSA.

46. G. Stanley Hall, pp. 239, 245, 251.

47. Sigmund Freud, "The Uncanny" (1919), in *The Collected Papers*, trans. Joan Rivière (New York: Basic Books, 1959), IV, pp. 375–77.

48. G. Stanley Hall, p. 241.

49. Ibid., p. 256.

50. Ibid., pp. 264, 270.

51. Ibid., p. 259.

52. Ibid., p. 243.

53. Elaine Showalter, *The Female Malady: Women, Madness, and English Culture, 1830–1980* (New York: Penguin, 1985), pp. 52, 55.

54. SGH, *Oration at Ceremonies on Laying the Corner-stone of the New York State Institution for the Blind at Batavia*, p. 40.

55. *Letters and Journals*, II, p. 48.

56. SGH, "Letter in Regard to Certain Changes to be Made in the Perkins Institution for the Blind," April 12, 1868, p. 6.

57. Third AR, pp. 10–11.

58. Daniel Walker Howe, pp. 128–29.

59. Paulson, p. 96.

60. SGH, "Letter in Regard to Certain Changes," pp. 14–15.

61. Ibid., p. 15.

62. SGH, *Oration at Ceremonies*, p. 39.

63. LDB to Collina (Lina) Bridgman, December 23, 1860, PSA.

64. Sarah A. Stover, "Written to read when Bridgman Cottage was dedicated, 1913," typescript, PSA. Sarah Stover was a retired Perkins sewing teacher.

65. LDB to SGH, March 11, 1872, PSA.

66. M. Howe and F. Hall, p. 298.

67. Ibid., pp. 300–301.

68. Lane, p. 225.

69. Lamson, p. 7.

70. Harmony Bridgman to SGH, November 16, 1858; December 1, 1858, PSA.

71. For photographs of both Bridgman houses, see Frank Barrett, Jr., *Hanover, New Hampshire* (Dover: Arcadia, 1998), II, pp. 58, 90.

72. I am grateful to Marilyn Christie for helping me sort out Bridgman's complicated land transactions.

73. Deed signed by Daniel and Harmony Bridgman on December 16, 1867, and registered on December 20, 1867, *Grafton County Records*, Woodsville, N.H.

74. Will, signed on November 28, 1868, by Daniel Bridgman; probate records filed in Grafton County December 15 and December 16, 1868.

75. M. Howe and F. Hall, p. 292; SGH, *Latest Particulars of the History of Laura Bridgman* (Edinburgh: Neill & Co., 1877), p. 8.

76. Ulrich, p. 281.

77. LDB to SW (Bond), June 28 [1868], PSA.

78. SGH to Harmony Bridgman [summer? 1868], PSA.

79. M. Howe and F. Hall, p. 291.

80. Quoted in ibid.

81. LDB to Lamson, October 1, 1872, MHS.

82. LDB to Lamson, May 10, 187[4?], MHS.

83. LDB to Eliza Rogers, July 17, 1870, PSA.

84. Ibid.

85. LDB to Lamson, November 26, 1871, MHS.

86. LDB to Lamson, September 7, 1884, MHS.

87. Ibid.

88. M. Howe and F. Hall, p. 292.

89. LDB to Lamson, November 26, 1871, MHS.

90. SGH to Isaac Bridgman, January 30, 1872, PSA.

91. SGH to Harmony Bridgman, November 28, 1873, PSA.

92. Forty-third AR, p. 89.

93. SGH to Harmony Bridgman, November 28, 1873, PSA.

94. Ibid. SGH had already written to Mrs. Bridgman in 1871 promising to provide for Laura at Perkins; that letter, alluded to in Laura's correspondence, has not survived.

95. SGH, will of May 24, 1873, *Massachusetts Probate Record Book* 484; Suffolk County.

96. Ibid.

97. Forty-third AR, p. 96.

98. For sexual conflict in the Howes' marriage, see Grant.

99. Quoted in M. Howe and F. Hall, pp. 309–10.

100. LDB to SW (Bond), February 6, 1876, PSA.

101. LDB to Lamson, January 30, 1876, MHS.

102. LDB to SW (Bond), February 6, 1876, PSA.

CHAPTER THIRTEEN: Revisions

1. Michael Anagnos, Sixtieth AR, p. 301.

2. John Bridgman to SGH, November 17, 1854; SGH to Harmony Bridgman, November 18, 1854, PSA.

3. Harmony Bridgman to SGH, May 25, 1868; SGH to Harmony Bridgman, undated reply, PSA.

4. SGH, "Notes on Laura Bridgman," in Fifty-eighth AR, pp. 34–75.

5. Chapman, p. 129.

6. Eleventh AR, p. 27.

7. Kitto, p. 43.

8. Lamson, p. xxxi.

9. Edwards A. Park, "Introduction," in Lamson, pp. xxii, xxv.

10. Harmony Bridgman to David Hall, June 28, 1878, PSA.

11. Fifty-sixth AR, pp. 96–97.

12. Grant, p. 187.

13. Farrell, p. 63; Ross, p. 218.

14. Quoted in *Proceedings of the Public Meeting on Behalf of the Printing Fund*, p. 31.

15. Ross, p. 215.

16. "Here in Boston," *Boston Post*, December 21, 1887.

17. Fifty-seventh AR, p. 64.

18. M. Howe and F. Hall, p. 320.

19. Fifty-seventh AR, pp. 62–65.

20. Ibid., p. 59.

21. Ibid., p. 66.

22. Anagnos, *Fourth Annual Report of the Kindergarten*, p. 56.

23. Keller, *Story of My Life*, p. 125.

24. Fifty-sixth AR, p. 94.

25. Ibid., pp. 72–75.

26. Ibid., pp. 79, 96.

27. Nella Braddy, *Anne Sullivan Macy: The Story Behind Helen Keller* (Garden City, N.Y.: Doubleday, Doran, 1933), p. 62.

28. Quoted in Herrmann, p. 34.

29. Joseph P. Lash, *Helen and Teacher: The Story of Helen Keller and Anne Sullivan Macy* (New York: Delacorte, 1980), p. 56.

30. Helen Keller, *Midstream: My Later Life* (Garden City, N.Y.: Doubleday, Doran, 1929), p. 247.

31. Lash, p. 95.

32. Keller, *Midstream*, pp. 245–46.

33. Ibid., p. 246.

34. M. A. Knowlton, ms. memoir, headed "Copied July 1893." Knowlton was the matron of Laura's cottage.

35. According to M. Howe and F. Hall, p. 329, only Collina, Nelly, and an unnamed cousin attended the funeral; a fragmentary clipping from an unidentified newspaper in the files of the New Hampshire Historical Society suggests that Laura's brothers were there, too.

36. Unidentified newspaper, May 27, 1889, New Hampshire Historical Society.

37. M. Howe and F. Hall, p. 330.

38. Ibid., pp. 331–32.

39. Collina (Lina) Bridgman Simmons to Michael Anagnos, May 28, 1889, PSA.

40. Henry H. Donaldson, "Anatomical Observations On the Brain and Several Sense-Organs of the Blind Deaf-Mute, Laura Dewey Bridgman," *American Journal of Psychology* 3.3 (September 1890): 293, 300–301.

41. Ibid., pp. 310, 314.

42. "The Life of Laura Bridgman," *New York Times*, November 17, 1889, p. 16.

43. Eighteenth AR, p. 82.

44. SGH, "Laura Bridgman," p. 383.

45. Donaldson, p. 294.

46. Collina Simmons to Florence Howe Hall, September 13, 1889, PSA.

47. Collina Simmons to Florence Howe Hall and Maud Howe Elliott, October 14, 1889, PSA.

48. For the complete list, see the JWH papers, Schlesinger Library, Harvard University.

49. Sixtieth AR, p. 301.

50. Lash, p. 289.

51. Herrmann, p. 135.

EPILOGUE: Passing

1. Quoted in Lash, p. 315.

2. According to Keller, Sullivan said, "Helen, you will be glad when you recall the merciless prodding to which I sometimes subjected you." See *Teacher*, p. 155.

3. "Helen Keller," Arts and Entertainment Network "Biography" documentary, produced by David Wolper.

4. D. F. Moore, *Educating the Deaf: Psychology, Principles, and Practices*, 2nd ed. (Boston: Houghton Mifflin, 1978), p. 225.

5. Donald Davie, "To Helen Keller," in *Collected Poems, 1950–1970* (New York: Oxford University Press, 1972), p. 217.

6. Lash, p. 113; Keller, "Address at Mt. Airy," in *Story of My Life*, pp. 334–35.

7. Kitto, p. 18.

8. Maud Howe Elliott, *Three Generations* (Boston: Little, Brown, 1923), p. 228; Richard Harrity and Ralph G. Martin, *The Three Lives of Helen Keller* (Garden City, N.Y.: Doubleday, 1962), p. 107.

9. Keller, "Address at Mt. Airy," p. 335.

10. Helen Keller, *Optimism* (New York: Crowell, 1903), p. 20.

11. Bruno Bettelheim, "Miracles," *The New Yorker* 56 (August 4, 1980): 89–90.

12. Georgina Kleege, "Blind Rage: An Open Letter to Helen Keller," *Southwest Review* 83.1 (1998): 56.

13. Ibid., p. 59.

14. Keller, *Optimism*, p. 18.

·⸱◌[ACKNOWLEDGMENTS]◌·⸱

MY ACKNOWLEDGMENTS MUST begin with the librarians whose patience and skill made my research possible: Kenneth Stuckey and his successor, June Tulikangas, of the Perkins School for the Blind; Danielle Kovacs, Special Collections Librarian at Framingham State College; and the librarians and curators of the Harvard Houghton Library, the Massachusetts Historical Society, the Brown University Manuscripts Library, and the Chapin Library of Rare Books at Williams College. I thank these institutions for permission to quote from material in their collections. As always, I am indebted to the John Jay College librarians for their dedication and resourcefulness.

At the Wayland Historical Society, I was fortunate to enlist the help of Helen Emery and Jo Goeselt, both expert historical sleuths. Campbell Waterhouse of the Duxbury Historical Society not only provided me with information on the Drew and Morton families, but also put me in touch with Susan Basile and Lydia Drew's great-grandson, Lloyd Morton, who were willing to share handed-down stories about Laura. Frank J. Barrett, Jr., the author of a pictorial history of Hanover, New Hampshire, kindly filled me in on town geography. I thank Rian Keating, Hanoverian, thespian, and former student, for finding Laura's grave. Virginia Licklider and Ragnhild Bairnsfather provided me with able research assistance in Boston. I am grateful also to Marilyn Christie, a gifted and enthusiastic genealogist who tracked down information in New Hampshire that I might otherwise never have discovered.

Many colleagues, friends, and generous scholars responded to my questions, read and commented on chapters, and offered ideas. Among those who will recognize their contributions are Michael Blitz, Paul Brenner, Richard Brodhead, Sheila Colon, J. Roderick Davis, Janice Dunham, Eli Faber, John Glavin, Jay and Judy Greenfield, Susan Hartung, Betsy Hegeman, Jacqueline Jaffe, Karen Kaplowitz, Sondra Leftoff, Patricia Licklider, Gerald Markowitz, Adrienne Munich, Jane Mushabac, Eric Nelson, Jill Norgren, Barbara Odabashian, Juana Ponce de Leon, David Rosner, Frederik and Judith Rusch, Shirley Sarna, Susan Schlechter, Linda Schrank, Dennis Sherman, Gillian Silverman, Anthony Simpson, Benjamin Smith, Dian Smith, Neil Smith, Garrett Stewart, and Mark Taylor.

My thanks to Suzanne Cohn for wise counsel; to Marc Dolan for always understanding my questions (and knowing the answers); to John Pittman for keeping me on course philosophically; to Catherine Kudlick for teaching me about the history of the blind; and to Robert Crozier for making work fun. For their psychological insights into Laura, I am indebted to Dr. John McDevitt, Dr. Katherine Dalsimer, and Dr. Kathy Berkman.

I thank Terry Pristin for introducing me to Eric Wensberg, who gave me the confidence to tell Laura's story. Through Terry, I also met my agent, the irrepressible Molly Friedrich. Rebecca Saletan, my editor at Farrar, Straus and Giroux, knew just where my manuscript needed strengthening; I was fortunate to have her and Katrin Wilde guiding me.

Without Carol Groneman's example and warm encouragement, I never would have embarked on this project. As I wrote, Anya Taylor's voice, curious and exacting, was always in my head. She read each chapter, sometimes in several drafts, and her questions, objections, and proddings shaped my thinking. Infelicitous phrases seldom escape Karen Wunsch's eye, and I thank her for her careful reading of my manuscript.

Authors are often grateful to their families simply for leaving them alone to write, but in my case the debts are more substantial. My parents, Joseph and Anna Gesmer, not only provided me with all the comforts of home while I did my Boston research, but also heartened me by their interest in Laura. I am lucky to have two children, Emily and Michael Gitter, who are accomplished writers. Emily showed me the way out of several blind alleys and advised me on troublesome passages; Michael, from a greater distance, patiently talked me through attacks of computer panic. Above all, I thank Max Gitter, whose clear, lively prose is the mark I always shoot for. He commented incisively on every chapter, helping me to untangle my thoughts. In writing this book, as in many endeavors, I counted on him.

abolitionists, 167–68, 225, 243, 247

Adams, Henry, 74

affectional discipline, 180–81, 195–98, 202–3

Africans, 63

Alcott, Bronson, 202

Alden, Lizzie, 231

Allen, Edward, 256–57

alphabet: manual, *see* finger spelling; metal-type, 82

American Asylum for the Deaf and Dumb (Hartford), 26–27, 54, 69, 84, 139–41, 263

American Board of Foreign Missions, 20

American Freedmen's Inquiry Commission, 248

American Indians, 63

American Notes (Dickens), 5, 8, 123, 125, 279

American Polish Committee, 30, 31

American Revolution, 32, 48, 52, 204

American Sign Language, *see* sign language

American Sunday School Union, 124

Anagnos, Michael, 275–81, 284, 287–88

Andover Theological Seminary, 275

anesthetics, pioneering use of, 24

anorexia nervosa, 207–10

anthropology, 63, 74

Antioch College, 248

asylum movement, nineteenth-century, 23–24, 33–34, 175; *see also specific institutions*

Auburn (New York) State Prison, 190, 191

"Aveugles, Les" ("The Blind") (Baudelaire), 40

Bacon, Francis, 93

Bancroft, George, 17, 93

Baptists, 13, 50, 72–73, 147, 246, 249–54, 283, 310*n58*

Barnard's American Journal of Education, 286

Barnum, P. T., 106, 120, 121

Barrett, James, 66–68

"Battle Hymn of the Republic, The" (Howe), 150, 248, 270

Baudelaire, Charles, 40

Beecher, Catharine, 28, 180, 188

Beecher, Lyman, 18

Bell, Alexander Graham, 41, 279, 292

Berkeley, George, 56, 59, 73

Bettelheim, Bruno, 291

Bible, 34–35, 38, 29, 144, 147, 205, 214, 222, 245

"Birth-Mark, The" (Hawthorne), 124

Blackmur, Estella, 257

Blackstone, William, 4

"Blind, The" ("Les Aveugles") (Baudelaire), 40

"blindisms," 36

"Blind Man, The" (Lawrence), 119

"Blind Rage: An Open Letter to Helen Keller" (Kleege), 292

Blind Terror (movie), 7

Blind Witness (movie), 7

Blink (movie), 7

Boland, E. S., 285

Bond, Edward, 215, 219–20, 227, 228, 255

Bond, Sarah Wight, 176, 193–224, 226–30, 239, 245, 247, 249, 252, 320n4; and Addison's relationship to Laura, 239; attachment of Laura to, 199–201, 212–14; boarding of Laura at Wayland with, 226–27; chosen by Howe as Laura's teacher, 193, 194; courtship of, 215, 219–20; death of, 255, 256; departure from Perkins of, 220, 223, 293; disciplining of Laura by, 197–98, 201–4; family background of, 193–94; and Howe's 1849 annual report, 217–20; Lamson and, 274; and Laura's anorexia nervosa, 207–10; letters from Laura to, 221–23, 226, 227, 231, 233, 236, 255, 266, 270; marriage of, 227–29; pedagogical approach of, 195–97; physical and mental illnesses of, 216, 220, 256; religious instruction of Laura by, 203–6, 208, 318n7; replacement for, 232, 234, 235, 237; Sullivan compared to, 275; teaching journals of, 194–95, 274; on visit to Bridgman family, 210–11, 213

Boston House of Industry, 122

Boston House of Reformation for Juvenile Offenders, 122

Boston Latin School, 13, 22

Boston Post, 104

Boston Prison Discipline Society, 190, 191

Boylston School for Neglected and Indigent Boys, 122

Brace, Julia, 69–72, 81, 84, 139, 140–41

Bradford, Thomas, 137

Braille system, 23, 281, 293, 299n39

Bridgman, Abel (Laura's great-uncle), 250

Bridgman, Addison Daniel (Laura's brother), 47, 50, 210–11, 214, 215, 223, 232, 233, 239–42, 245, 264

Bridgman, Asa (Laura's grandfather), 250

Bridgman, Augusta (Laura's aunt), 242

Bridgman, Collina (Laura's sister), *see* Simmons, Collina Bridgman

Bridgman, Daniel (Laura's father), 8, 11, 12, 45, 47, 88, 100, 115, 130, 154, 169, 287; autobiography project proposed to, 272; death of, 264–68, 270; disciplining of Laura by, 48, 49; financial support of Laura by, 263; as Hanover town selectman, 66; Howe's letters to, 79; Howe's offer to educate Laura accepted by, 68, 75; ill health of, 223; lack of interest in Laura of, 114, 154; Laura brought to Perkins by, 78; and Laura's return to Hanover, 233–35; marriage of, 48; religion of, 147, 246, 249–50

Bridgman, Ellen (Nelly; Laura's sister), *see* Simmons, Ellen Bridgman

Bridgman, Frances Collina (Laura's sister), 46, 47

Bridgman, Harmony Downer (Laura's mother), 8, 11–12, 47–50, 100, 113, 130, 169, 215, 264, 287; autobiography project proposed to, 272; background of, 48; correspondence of Laura and, 88, 114, 154,

211–12, 222, 236, 238; after Daniel's death,
265–67; emotional volatility of, 159, 213;
financial support of Laura by, 263; Howe's
letters to, 79, 268, 269; Howe's offer to educate Laura accepted by, 68, 75; Laura
brought to Perkins by, 78; and Laura's
death, 283; Laura's illness described by, 45–
47; and Laura's return to Hanover, 233–34;
marriage of, 48; and Mary's death, 242,
245; religion of, 147, 246, 249–52, 254; reunions of Laura and, 100, 107–8, 114, 154,
211; and Wight's departure from Perkins,
223–26, 231

Bridgman, Harriet (Hattie) Taylor (Laura's
sister-in-law), 264–67

Bridgman, Isaac (Laura's great-uncle), 250

Bridgman, John Downer (Laura's brother),
47, 50, 210, 223, 232, 239, 240, 242, 264–
68, 284

Bridgman, Laura: Addison and, 239–42;
adult life at Perkins of, 141, 229–31, 236–
38, 245, 253–57, 259, 261–63, 293–94;
Anagnos and, 276–77; annual reports on,
90–92, 100–104, 106–7, 110–12, 119–20,
158, 177–80, 217–19, 267–70; anorexia of,
207–10, 234–36; arrival at Perkins of, 78–
80, 129, 130; attachment to Howe of, 114–
15; attachment to Wight of, 212–17, 220–
22, 226–29; baptism of, 147, 246–47, 249–
54; biographies of, 272–75, 286–88, 290;
birth of, 25; Carlyle on, 102–3, 124; childhood discipline of, 48–49, 112, 190–92,
197–98, 201–4; and cultural theme of victimization, 109–10; death of, 282–84, 286;
devotional verse by, 253; Dickens on, 5, 8,
121–25; dissection of brain of, 284–86;
dreams of, 158, 210, 240–41; early childhood in New Hampshire of, 3–4, 11, 18,
47–50; fame of, 4–6, 70, 100–101, 104–7,
120–21, 174–75, 189; family background

of, 11–12; fever causing blindness and
deafness of, 3, 26, 45–47; financial support
for, 263–68; first encounter of Howe and,
75–77; gifts given by admirers to, 71; during Howe's absences, 152–58, 169; and
Howe's death, 256, 268–71; Howe's discovery of, 66–68; Howe's disenchantment
with, 158–60, 166–69, 175; and Howe's
marriage, 150–52, 155–56; Howe's
renown as educator of, 44; imagination of,
214–15; infancy of, 96–97; inquisitiveness
of, 97–100; jubilee celebration for, 277–
78; Keller and, 282, 289, 292–93; language
acquired by, 80–91, 95–97, 100, 101;
mother's concern for, 223–24; mother's
reunion with, at Perkins, 107–8; noises
made by, 115–18, 177, 178, 294; and other
deaf-blind students, 128, 132–35, 137–40;
parents' lack of interest in, 114, 154;
phrenology applied to, 94–95; physical affection craved by, 181, 182, 206; poems
about, 105–6, 126; psychological evaluation of, 257–59; and relationships with
other Perkins students, 112, 157, 190–91,
200–201; religious instruction of, 141–42,
144–46, 160–66, 183, 204–6; return to
New Hampshire in adulthood of, 231–35,
238–39; self-punishment of, 207; sense of
smell of, 71; sexual innocence of, 119,
169–74, 269; significance of life of, 6–8;
and sign language, 41, 54; suicidal fantasies of, 209–10; Sullivan and, 280–81;
teachers of, 176–98 (*see also* Bond, Sarah
Wight; Lamson, Mary Swift; Morton, Lydia Drew); Tenney and, 50–54, 222–23;
vacations from Perkins of, 154, 191, 199,
200, 217, 226, 227, 255; visits home of, 112,
154, 210–12; willfulness and aggression of,
112–13; and younger sister Mary's death,
242, 245

Bridgman, Mary (1826-1832; Laura's sister), 45–47

Bridgman, Mary (1842-1859; Laura's sister) 210, 224, 232, 233, 238, 242, 244, 245, 249, 251, 252

Bridgman, Phoebe (Laura's aunt), 46, 47

Brontë, Charlotte, 71

Brooks, Phillips, 278

Brooks, Preston, 243

Brown, John, 175, 226, 243–45

Brown University, 13–14, 22, 72–73, 193

Brumberg, Joan, 209

Bulwer-Lytton, Edward, 118

Bunker Hill Monument, 20

Burlingham, Dorothy, 117

Byron, George Gordon, Lord, 15, 17

Calvinism, 18, 101, 109, 110, 142–43, 169, 177, 180, 193, 275

Carlyle, Thomas, 102–3, 113, 124, 174

Carter, Abby, 127

Carter, Sophia, 127

Cartesian dualism, 57–58

Carver, Raymond, 119

Caswell, Alexis, 14

Caswell, Oliver, 136–39, 141, 152–53, 160, 269

"Cathedral" (Carver), 119

Catholics, 143, 237

Channing, William Ellery, 18, 38, 74, 93

Chapman, John Jay, 17, 44, 273

Chapman, Jonathan, 122

Charcot, Jean, 258

charitable institutions, 18–20, 22; see also specific institutions

Cheselden, William, 61

Child, Lydia Maria, 180

Choate, Rufus, 43, 75, 126

Chomsky, Carol, 97

citizenship, 37

City Lights (movie), 7

Civil War, 241, 247–48, 252

Clark University, 257, 284

cognitive psychology, 60–61; on language acquisition, 95–97

Cogswell, Alice, 26

Combe, George, 14, 71, 93, 95, 103–4, 144, 148, 149, 187

common schools, 187; controversy over religious instruction in, 168–69, 175; training of teachers for, 184

Common Sense philosophy, 73–74, 91, 92, 146

Commonwealth, 225

Compromise of 1850, 225

Condillac, Étienne Bonnot de, 56, 60, 62, 64, 65, 73

Congregationalists, 50, 52, 143, 163, 189, 193, 250, 310n58

Congress, U.S., 39, 243

"Conscience Whigs," 225

Constitution of Man considered in Relation to External Objects, The (Combe), 93

Cooper, James Fenimore, 30, 31

craniology, see phrenology

critical-period hypothesis, 96

Cummins, Maria, 109

Dark Victory (movie), 7

Dartmouth College, 66, 75, 239, 250, 267, 272

Darwin, Charles, 5

Davie, Donald, 290

Dedham decision (1820), 143, 310n58

Degérando, Joseph-Marie, 28, 63, 66, 69, 74

Democratic Republicans, 13

Descartes, René, 57–59, 73, 91, 92

Dickens, Charles, 5, 8, 20–21, 52, 108, 120–25, 127, 138, 172, 279

Diderot, Denis, 56, 61–62, 66, 68–69, 117

discipline, affectional, 180–81, 195–98, 202–3

Discourse on the Origin of Human Inequality (Rousseau), 56

Dix, Dorothea, 28, 75, 236–38

Donaldson, Henry H., 284–87

Drew, Lydia, *see* Morton, Lydia Drew

Eastern State Penitentiary (Philadelphia), 190

Edgeworth, Maria, 109, 174, 180

Edison, Thomas, 291

educational reform, 180, 202–3

Elements of Mental and Moral Philosophy, Founded Upon Experience, The (Beecher), 28

Eliot, Samuel, 43, 75–76

Elliotson, John, 121

Elliott, Maud Howe (Samuel's daughter), 11, 114, 137, 162, 235, 247, 272, 274, 286–87, 291

Elssler, Fanny, 120

Emancipation League, 248

embossed-letter reading method, 23, 25, 34–35, 39, 82

Emerson, Ralph Waldo, 17–18, 149

Encyclopaedia Britannica, 104

Enlightenment, 18, 23, 56–62, 73

Eskimos, 63

Everett, Edward, 15, 93, 103

exhibitions of disabled, 42–43; at Perkins, 5, 70, 106, 174, 186, 293

facial signals, affiliative, 39–40

Fasting Girls: The History of Anorexia Nervosa (Brumberg), 209

Federalists, 13

Felton, Cornelius Conway, 44, 122

female victimization, as cultural theme, 70, 108

feral children, 63–65

Fiji Mermaid, 106

finger spelling, 6, 81, 83–86, 112, 181, 211, 232, 251

Finney, Charles, 18

First Lessons in Grammar on the Plan of Pestalozzi (Peabody), 28

Fisher, John Dix, 23–28, 31, 34

Foucault, Michel, 24

Free Soil movement, 175, 219, 225, 247, 248

French writing board, 87

Freud, Sigmund, 173, 258

Friends, Religious Society of, *see* Quakers

Fugitive Slave Act (1850), 225

Gall, Franz Josef, 92

Gallaudet, Thomas Hopkins, 26–28, 37, 38, 40, 42, 54, 84, 140, 263

General Tom Thumb (Charles Stratton), 106

Gleason, Cora Davis, 257

Goode, David, 53

Gordon-Lennox, Charles Henry, 6th duke of Richmond, 174

Greek mythology, 176

Greek revolution, 15–17, 28–30, 42, 175

Hale, Edward Everett, 278, 284

Hall, Florence Howe (Samuel's daughter), 11, 75, 76, 114, 137, 162, 235, 247, 272, 274, 275, 286–87

Hall, Granville Stanley, 99, 100, 257–59, 284–85, 288

Harpers Ferry, Brown's raid on, 175, 243

Hartford Female Seminary, 28, 188

Harvard University, 13, 15, 18–20, 44, 74, 75, 143, 185; Divinity School, 193; Medical School, 14, 23, 285

Harvard University press, 185

Haüy, Abbé Valentin, 34, 42

Haverford College, 186

Hawthorne, Julian, 287

Hawthorne, Nathaniel, 18, 109, 124, 287

Herrick, Jonathan, 246, 249, 251–52, 254, 275

Herrick, Sarah, 246, 251, 254, 275

Herrmann, Dorothy, 131

Higginson, Thomas Wentworth, 243, 287

Hillard, George, 75, 192

Historical Sketch of the Greek Revolution (Howe), 16, 21

Hoare, Louisa, 180

"Holy Home" (Bridgman), 253

Holmes, Oliver Wendell, 18

Holmes, W., 126

Homans, John, 283

Hottentots, 63

Houghton, Lord, *see* Milnes, Richard Monckton

Howard, George William Frederick, 7th earl of Carlisle (Viscount Morpeth), 174

Howe, Jeannette (Samuel's sister), 78, 113, 114, 134, 135, 151, 152, 154, 156, 157, 169, 278

Howe, Joseph, 13

Howe, Julia Romana (Samuel's daughter), 151, 276

Howe, Julia Ward (Samuel's wife), 8, 32, 154–56, 244, 267, 270; Anagnos and, 276; aversion to blind of, 156; Lamson's biography of Laura criticized by, 274; at Laura's jubilee celebration, 277, 278; marriage of, 148–51; public lecture tours of, 162, 268–69; *Reminiscences* of, 104

Howe, Sammy (Samuel's son), 248

Howe, Samuel Gridley: abolitionism of, 225–26, 242–45; absences from Perkins of, 126–27, 152–58, 169, 181; adulation of, by progressives, 125–26; affectional discipline advocated by, 180–81; annual reports of, 5–6, 90–91, 100–104, 106–7, 110–12, 119–20, 125, 132, 158, 181, 189, 217–19, 267–70, 273, 281, 286; appointed director of New England Asylum, 22, 27–

29; and arrival of Laura at Perkins, 78–80; attachment of Laura to, 114–15; biography of Laura attempted by, 272–74; and Boston elite, 43; Carlyle and, 102–3, 124; during Civil War, 247–49; concerned for Laura after Wight's departure, 221, 223–24, 226–27; cottage system instituted by, 259–61; death of, 256, 268–71; and Dickens's visit, 121–25; disenchantment with Laura of, 158–60, 166–69, 175; educational philosophy of, 35–41; education of, 13, 72–74; European fact-finding tour of, 29–30, 33–36, 41; family background of, 13; and financial support for Laura, 263–69; first encounter of Laura and, 75–77; in Greek revolution, 15–17, 21–22; heroic image of, 28–29, 33; inspirational prose of, 37; language-instruction methods of, 81–85, 87–89; Laura brought to Boston by, 3; and Laura's adult life at Perkins, 229–31, 236–38; and Laura's anorexia, 208, 210, 234–36; and Laura's baptism, 147, 247, 249, 252; and Laura's fame, 104–7, 120–21, 174–75, 189; and Laura's return to New Hampshire, 231–35; and Laura's sexuality, 119, 169–74, 269; marriage of, 148–52, 168, 269; moral quarantine of Laura by, 190–92; mother's reunion with Laura staged by, 107–8; New England Asylum opened by, 41–43; and New England Renaissance, 17; other deaf-blind students of, 128–41; personality of, 12–13; phrenology practiced by, 92–96; pious rhetoric of, 109–10; in Polish independence campaign, 30–32; promotion of Laura by, 5–6; and reactions of "normal" people to disabled, 116–18; recruitment of Laura by, 66–68; religious instruction policy of, 141–42, 144–46, 160–66, 183, 204–6; search for deaf-blind student by, 54–56, 68–72; sign language opposed by, 41, 72, 81; as surrogate father, 12; teachers employed by, 176 (*see also* Bond, Sarah Wight; Lamson, Mary Swift; Morton, Lydia Drew); Unitarianism of, 13, 110, 141–43, 146

Howells, William Dean, 287

Howitt, Mary, 119

humanitarianism, progressive, 24–25, 40, 75

Hume, David, 56, 73

Industrial School for Girls, 189

Ingalls, William, 71, 112

Institution des Jeunes Aveugles (Paris), 23, 24

Irish immigrants, 238

Itard, Jean-Marc Gaspard, 64, 72, 81

Jackson, Andrew, 19, 21, 93

Jackson, Helen Hunt, 180

James, William, 287

Jane Eyre (Brontë), 71

Jeffersonians, 13, 38

Jennifer 8 (movie), 7

Jewett, J. P., 120

Johnston, General Joe, 241

Jutten, D. B., 283–84

Kansas-Nebraska Act (1854), 243, 244

Keller, Helen, 4, 6, 8, 77, 81, 140, 278–80, 289–93, 300n8, 325n2; attempts at speech of, 290–91; attractiveness of, 229; awareness of language awakened in, 83; corporal punishment of, 131; at Perkins, 281–82; positive outlook of, 262, 292; public fascination with, 7; publication of autobiography of, 288; Sullivan's approach in teaching language to, 281; writing ability of, 290

Kentucky Institution of the Blind, 127

Kimball Union Academy, 223, 239

Kitto, John, 84, 273–74, 290

Klages, Mary, 306n15

Kleege, Georgina, 292

Lafayette, Marquis de, 15, 30, 32

Lamson, Edwin, 189

Lamson, Mary Swift, 151–53, 155–57, 169, 176, 181–89, 191, 197, 200, 314n19; and Laura's religious instruction, 161, 163, 164, 166, 183; biography of Laura by, 183, 272, 274–75, 287; correspondence of Laura and, 189, 255–56, 266; departure from Perkins of, 183, 189; during Dickens's visit, 122; hired by Howe, 185–87; Howe's criticism of, 177–81, 190, 192, 217, 313n14; incompatibility of Laura and, 182–83; Keller and, 290; Laura's visits to, 189, 210; Lucy Reed and, 132; marriage of, 189; at Massachusetts Normal School, 184–85; Oliver Caswell and, 137, 139; playthings purchased for Ellen Bridgman by, 233–34; visits to Laura by, 189; Wight hired as replacement for, 193, 199

Lancaster, Joseph, 16

Lane, Harlan, 41

language acquisition, 80–91, 95–98, 281

Language Instinct, The (Pinker), 95

Lansdowne, marquess of, *see* Petty-Fitzmaurice, Henry Charles Keith

Laplanders, 63

Last Days of Pompeii, The (Bulwer–Lytton), 118

Laura Bridgman: Dr. Howe's Famous Pupil and What He Taught Her (Howe and Hall), 76, 286–88, 290

Laura Bridgman: The Story of an Opened Door (Richards), 230

Lawrence, Abbot, 126

Lawrence, D. H., 119

Letter on the Blind for the Use of Those Who See (Diderot), 61, 62, 68

Letter on the Deaf and Dumb for the Use of Those Who Hear and Speak (Diderot), 61

Levertov, Denise, 173

Lieber, Francis, 103

Life and Education of Laura Dewey Bridgman, The (Lamson), 183, 272

Lind, Jenny, 120, 121

literature, disabled children in, 108–9

Locke, John, 4, 58–59, 64, 92, 180, 273

Longfellow, Henry Wadsworth, 18, 44, 75, 122, 149, 150, 192, 219, 249

Loring, George, 84, 263

Loring Fund, 263, 268, 269

Lowell Institute, 20

Luther, Martin, 117

Magnificent Obsession (movie), 7

Mann, Horace, 8, 75, 126, 127, 132, 184; at Brown, 14; death of, 248; disciplinary approach of, 130, 180, 202; and Howe's annual reports, 6, 103; marriage of, 150–51; nonsectarian common schools advocated by, 143–44, 168; phrenology embraced by, 93; prison-reform views of, 190; sign language opposed by, 41, 292; on women as teachers, 187–89

Mann, Mary Peabody, 20, 151, 180, 202, 203

manual alphabet, *see* finger spelling

Martineau, Harriet, 20, 54–56, 69, 75, 81

Massachusetts General Hospital, 20

Massachusetts House of Corrections, 122

Massachusetts legislature, 25, 43, 225

Massachusetts Normal School, 184, 185, 189

Massachusetts School for Idiotic and Feeble-Minded Youth, 225

Massachusetts State Board of Education, 143

Massachusetts State Hospital for the Insane, 122

Massachusetts State Supreme Judicial Court, 143

mathematics, techniques for teaching to blind, 34

McLean Asylum, 194, 256, 321*n38*

Melville, Herman, 109

Memorial History of Boston, 104

meningitis, 300*n8*

Merriam, Franklin, 254

Messer, Asa, 72–73

Messerli, Jonathan, 168–69

metal-type alphabet, 82

Methodists, 310*n58*

Mexican War, 225

Midwife's Tale, A (Ulrich), 265

Milnes, Richard Monckton, 1st Baron Houghton, 174

mind-body dualism, 57–58

Miner, A. A., 278

Mitchell, Edward, 250

Molyneux, William, 58–61, 91

Moore, George, 105

moral education, 195–97

moral philosophy, 72–73

More, Hannah, 109

Morpeth, Lord, *see* Howard, George William Frederick

Morton, Cyrus, 153

Morton, Lloyd, 153

Morton, Lucy Drew, 153

Morton, Lydia Drew, 79–80, 98, 113, 151, 153–54, 176–77, 189, 222; correspondence of Laura and, 153; departure from Perkins of, 151, 153, 154, 169, 186; disciplining of Laura by, 112; and Howe's 1844 annual report, 177; Lamson and, 274; and Laura's acquisition of language, 83–86, 88–89; Laura's visits to, 115, 153, 235–36, 255; Loring and, 263; Lucy Reed and, 132; marriage of, 153; at Massachusetts Normal

School, 184–85; on visit to Bridgmans, 114

Mother's Monthly Journal, 104

Moulton, Mary, 245, 261, 277

Mussey, Reuben, 66, 67, 76

nativism, 237–38

New England Asylum for the Education of the Blind, 22, 25, 27, 28, 41–43; *see also* Perkins Institution for the Blind

New England Renaissance, 17–18

New Jersey, College of, 73

New York Commercial Advertiser, 104–5

New York Public Library, 288

New York Times, 104, 286; *Book Review*, 288

Nightingale, Florence, 174

North American Review, 15, 33, 43

Notes on the United States of America (Combe), 187

Observation of Savage Peoples, The (Degérando), 63

Old Curiosity Shop, The (Dickens), 123, 138

Oliver Twist (Dickens), 22

On the Education of Deaf-Mutes (Degérando), 69

oralism, 26, 41, 175, 292

Paddock, Mary, 220, 235

Paley, William, 73

Paris Institute for Deaf-Mutes, 55, 64, 84

Park, Edwards A., 275

Parker, Theodore, 17, 243, 248

Patch of Blue, A (movie), 7

Paulson, William, 24

Peabody, Elizabeth Palmer, 20, 42, 202

Peabody, Mary, *see* Mann, Mary Peabody

Pediatric Autoimmune Neuropsychiatric Disorders Associated with Streptococci (PANDAS), 100

Peirce, Cyrus, 184, 185, 313*n14*, 314*n19*

penal reform, 175, 190, 191

Perkins, Col. Thomas H., 43

Perkins Institution for the Blind, 3, 7, 11, 51, 86, 89, 150, 194, 211, 234–36, 239, 292; admission of black students to, 167–68; Anagnos as director of, 276; annual reports on, 5–6, 90–92, 100–104, 125, 132, 158, 181, 217, 267–69, 273, 286; benefactors of, 215; board of trustees of, 20, 90; cottages established at, 259–61; daily routine at, 79–80; decision to enroll Laura at, 54, 67; departures of teachers from, 151, 153, 183, 213, 219–20, 223, 226–27; Dickens's visit to, 121–23; director's apartments at, 149, 151–52, 157, 192; Dix's visits to, 236–37; exhibition days at, 5, 70, 106, 174, 186, 293; growth of, under Howe's leadership, 43; Harmony Bridgman's visit to, 107–8; Howe's absences from, 127, 151–58; jubilee celebration for Laura at, 277–78; Julia Brace at, 139–41; Keller and, 279–82; language instruction techniques at, 80–90; Laura's adulthood at, 253–55, 263; Laura's arrival at, 78–79; Laura's death at, 283–84; Laura's relationships with other students at, 112, 190–91, 201; Laura's summer vacations away from, 114, 115, 154, 266; library of, 8, 285; Lucy Reed at, 128–35; Oliver Caswell at, 136–39, 141; origins of, *see* New England Asylum for the Education of the Blind; phrenology and, 92, 95; progressive educators' visits to, 202; progressive humanitarianism of supporters of, 25; recollections of Laura by former teachers and graduates of, 256–57; religious education at, 144–47; teachers at, 163, 176, 194, 215, 230 (*see also* Bond, Sarah Wight; Lamson, Mary Swift; Morton, Lydia Drew);

Perkins Institution for the Blind (*cont.*)
   timeliness of Laura's education at, 96, 97;
   workshop at, 40, 166, 231
personal demeanor, training of blind in, 36–
   37
Peter of Hanover (feral child), 63
Petty-Fitzmaurice, Henry Charles Keith, 5th
   marquess of Lansdowne, 174
Philadelphia Institution for the Blind, 259
philhellenism, 15, 21
phrenology, 14, 92–96, 99, 103, 112, 121, 142,
   148, 195–97, 206
physical education of blind, 36
Pinker, Steven, 95
Polish nationalism, 30–32, 42, 175
*Power of the Soul over the Body, Considered in
   Relation to Health and Morals* (Moore), 105
Prescott, William H., 17, 43, 126
Princeton University, 73
Principles of Moral and Political Philosophy
   (Paley), 73
prison reform, 175, 190, 191
Protestants, 143, 281; *see also specific denomi-
   nations*
psycholinguistics, 96, 99–100

Quakers, 50, 52, 53
Quincy, Josiah, 18

Radcliffe College, 289
reading, techniques for teaching, *see* Braille
   system; embossed-letter reading method
Reed, Lucy, 128–35, 138, 141, 150, 196, 309n34
Reed, Timothy, 130, 132–35
Reid, Thomas, 73, 74, 92
religion: instruction of Laura in, 141–42,
   144–46, 160–66, 183, 204–6; Gallaudet's
   emphasis on, 37; *see also specific denominations*
Revolutionary War, *see* American Revolution

Richards, Laura Howe (Samuel's daughter),
   11, 21, 27, 76, 114, 162, 230, 272, 274
Richmond, duke of, *see* Gordon-Lennox,
   Charles Henry
Rogers, Eliza, 122, 136, 137, 163, 191, 255,
   267, 274
Rousseau, Jean-Jacques, 56, 57, 59, 273
rubella syndrome, 53
Russell, Philemon, 315n47

Sacks, Oliver, 41
Salpêtrière, 258
Sanborn, Franklin B., 33, 243
scarlet fever, 300n8
Second Great Awakening, 163, 193
"Secret Six," 243
Sedgwick, Catherine, 109, 180
Self-Education (Degérando), 29
Senate, U.S., 44, 225, 243, 245
Sicard, Abbé, 55, 67
sign language, 27, 41, 69, 72, 81, 83, 84, 96,
   140, 292
Sigourney, Lydia Huntley, 5, 69–71, 105–6,
   109, 139, 180
Sill, Edward Rowland, 5
Simmons, Carlos, 266
Simmons, Collina Bridgman, 210–12, 224,
   232, 265, 266, 283, 284, 287, 325n35
Simmons, Ellen (Nelly) Bridgman, 224, 233–
   34, 251, 265–67, 283, 284, 325n35
Simmons, Timothy Dwight, 266
slavery, opposition to, 225, 238, 243–45, 320n4
Smith, Gerrit, 243
Smith, Joseph, 185
Smith, Mrs. (school matron), 79, 108, 278, 283
Smith, Sydney, 174, 176
Society for the Diffusion of Useful Knowl-
   edge, 273
Society of the Observers of Man, 63, 64,
   68

Some Thoughts Concerning Education (Locke), 180

South Sea Islanders, 63

speech, deaf, 26, 41, 290–91; *see also* oralism

Spurzheim, Johann, 93

Stearns, George L., 243

Story of My Life, The (Keller), 83, 288, 290

Stowe, Harriet Beecher, 109, 120

Sullivan, Anne, 6, 83, 131, 275, 279–82, 289, 290, 293, 325*n*2

Sumner, Charles, 8, 44, 75, 126–27, 192, 244, 249; during Dickens's visit, 122; Howe's annual reports circulated by, 103; and Howe's marriage, 150, 151; Laura's dislike of, 112; prison-reform views of, 190, 191; in U.S. Senate, 44, 225, 243, 248

Sutherland, Harriet, 2nd duchess, 174

Swift, Mary, *see* Lamson, Mary Swift

Swift, Paul, 186

tabula rasa theory, 4, 58, 59

Taylor, Zachary, 247

teaching profession: feminization of, 28, 187–88; training for, 184

Tenney, Asa, 50–54, 100, 129, 211, 215, 222, 245

Tenney, Major Silas, 52

Thomas, Edith, 278, 279

Thomson, Rosemarie Garland, 312*n*63

Ticknor, George, 17, 93, 103, 126

Trappist monks, 84

Troy Female Seminary, 28

Ulrich, Laurel Thatcher, 265

Uncle Tom's Cabin (Stowe), 120

Unitarians, 6, 38, 110, 141–43, 146, 184, 193–94, 215, 217, 236, 310*n*58; anthropological interests of, 74–75; among Boston elite, 13, 19; liberal humanitarianism of, 18; missionary work of, 227; and phrenology, 92, 142; sentimental popular fiction of, 109; among teachers at Perkins, 163

United States Sanitary Commission, 247

vanity, female, 71

victimization, cultural theme of, 70, 108–110

Victor, the Wild Boy of Aveyron, 63–65, 72, 75, 81

Victoria, Queen of England, 4, 287

Vigilance Committee, 225

Voltaire, 56, 73

Wait Until Dark (movie), 7

War of 1812, 48

Ward, Annie, 150

Ward, Sam, 150

Ware, Henry, 93

Warner, Susan, 109

Washingtonia, 16–17

Webster, Daniel, 126

Weston, Emma Coolidge, 257

Whigs, 225

Whipple, Thomas, 250

Whitman, Walt, 144

Whittier, John Greenleaf, 18, 21–22

"whole child" philosophy of education, 195

Wight, Henry, 194, 321*n*48

Wight, John Burt, 193–94, 315*n*47

Wight, Sarah, *see* Bond, Sarah Wight

Willard, Emma, 28

Witherspoon, John, 73

Wordsworth, William, 174

World Without Words, A (Goode), 53

writing, technique for teaching to blind, 87–88

Wundt, Wilhelm, 257

Young Women's Christian Association (YWCA), 189

Youth's Magazine, 104

Youth's Penny Gazette, 124